In the same era that humanity reaches into space, countless people are being shot, gassed and hanged by their own governments. Judicial killing lingers on as a state-sanctioned practice, violating the most fundamental human rights.

Some people may find this report disturbing. It is, for it is about a world with executions. But it also points the way to a world where basic human rights are respected, where the death penalty is progressively abolished, and where a report on killing by the state will one day be obsolete.

Amnesty International is a worldwide movement independent of any government, political persuasion or religious creed. It plays a specific role in the international protection of human rights:

– it seeks the *release of prisoners of conscience.* These are people detained for their beliefs, colour, sex, ethnic origin, language or religion who have not used or advocated violence;
– it works for *fair and prompt trials* for all *political prisoners;*
– it opposes the *death penalty* and *torture* or other cruel, inhuman or degrading treatment or punishment of *all prisoners* without reservation.

Amnesty International is impartial. It does not support or oppose any government or political system, nor does it support or oppose the views of the prisoners whose rights it seeks to protect. It is concerned solely with the protection of the human rights involved in each case, regardless of the ideology of the government or the beliefs of the victim.

Amnesty International, as a matter of principle, condemns the torture and execution of prisoners by anyone, including opposition groups. Governments have the responsibility for dealing with such abuses, acting in conformity with international standards for the protection of human rights.

Amnesty International does not grade governments according to their record on human rights: instead of attempting comparisons, it concentrates on trying to end the specific violations of human rights in each case.

Amnesty International acts on the basis of the United Nations Universal Declaration of Human Rights and other international instruments. Through practical work for prisoners within its mandate, Amnesty International participates in the wider promotion and protection of human rights in the civil, political, economic, social and cultural spheres.

Amnesty International has more than 700,000 members, subscribers and supporters in over 150 countries and territories, with over 3,800 local groups in more than 60 countries in Africa, the Americas, Asia, Europe and the Middle East. Each group works on behalf of prisoners of conscience in countries other than its own. These countries are balanced geographically and politically to ensure impartiality. Information about prisoners and human rights violations emanates from Amnesty International's Research Department in London. No section, group or member is expected to provide information on their own country, and no section, group or member has any responsibility for action taken or statements issued by the international organization concerning their own country.

Amnesty International has formal relations with the United Nations (ECOSOC), UNESCO, the Council of Europe, the Organization of American States and the Organization of African Unity.

Amnesty International is financed by subscriptions and donations from its worldwide membership. To safeguard the independence of the organization, all contributions are strictly controlled by guidelines laid down by the International Council. Details of income and expenditure are available on request from the International Secretariat.

WHEN THE STATE KILLS...

*The death penalty:
a human rights issue*

Amnesty International

WHEN THE STATE KILLS...

The death penalty: a human rights issue

1989

Amnesty International USA

322 Eighth Avenue, New York, NY 10001

First published 1989
by Amnesty International Publications
1 Easton Street, London WC1X 8DJ, United Kingdom

© Copyright Amnesty International Publications 1989

ISBN 0-939994-45-3
AI Index: ACT 51/07/89
Original Language: English

Printed in the United States of America
Production by Artworkers, London

Contents

Appendices 241

1. Why abolish the death penalty?

The time has come to abolish the death penalty worldwide. The case for abolition becomes more compelling with each passing year. Everywhere experience shows that executions brutalize those involved in the process. Nowhere has it been shown that the death penalty has any special power to reduce crime or political violence. In country after country, it is used disproportionately against the poor or against racial or ethnic minorities. It is often used as a tool of political repression. It is imposed and inflicted arbitrarily. It is an irrevocable punishment, resulting inevitably in the execution of people innocent of any crime. It is a violation of fundamental human rights.

Over the past decade an average of at least one country a year has abolished the death penalty, affirming respect for human life and dignity. Yet too many governments still believe that they can solve urgent social or political problems by executing a few or even hundreds of their prisoners. Too many citizens in too many countries are still unaware that the death penalty offers society not further protection but further brutalization. Abolition is gaining ground, but not fast enough.

The death penalty, carried out in the name of a nation's entire population, involves everyone. Everyone should be aware of what the death penalty is, how it is used, how it affects them, how it violates fundamental rights.

The death penalty is the premeditated and cold-blooded killing of a human being by the state. The state can exercise no greater power over a person than that of deliberately depriving him or her of life. At the heart of the case for abolition, therefore, is the question of whether it has the right to do so.

When the world's nations came together four decades ago to found the United Nations (UN), few reminders were needed of what could happen when a state believed that there was no limit to what it might do to a human being. The staggering extent of state brutality and terror during World War II and the consequences for people throughout the world were still unfolding in December 1948, when the UN General Assembly adopted without dissent the Universal Declaration of Human Rights.

The Universal Declaration is a pledge among nations to promote fundamental rights as the foundation of freedom, justice and peace. The rights it proclaims are inherent in every human being. They are not privileges that may be granted by governments for good behaviour and they may not be withdrawn for bad behaviour. Fundamental human rights limit what a state may do to a man, woman or child.

No matter what reason a government gives for executing prisoners and what method of execution is used, the death penalty cannot be separated from the issue of human rights. The movement for abolition cannot be separated from the movement for human rights.

The Universal Declaration recognizes each person's right to life and categorically states further that "No one shall be subjected to torture or to cruel, inhuman or degrading treatment or punishment." In Amnesty International's view the death penalty violates these rights.

Self-defence may be held to justify, in some cases, the taking of life by state officials: for example, when a country is locked in warfare (international or civil) or when law-enforcement officials must act immediately to save their own lives or those of others. Even in such situations the use of lethal force is surrounded by internationally accepted legal safeguards to inhibit abuse. This use of force is aimed at countering the immediate damage resulting from force used by others.

The death penalty, however, is not an act of self-defence against an immediate threat to life. It is the premeditated killing of a prisoner who could be dealt with equally well by less harsh means.

There can never be a justification for torture or for cruel, inhuman or degrading treatment or punishment. The cruelty of the death penalty is evident. Like torture, an execution constitutes an extreme physical and mental assault on a person already rendered helpless by government authorities.

If hanging a woman by her arms until she experiences excruciating pain is rightly condemned as torture, how does one describe hanging her by the neck until she is dead? If administering 100 volts of electricity to the most sensitive parts of a man's body evokes disgust, what is the appropriate reaction to the administration of 2,000 volts to his body in order to kill him? If a pistol held to the head or a chemical substance injected to cause protracted suffering are clearly instruments of torture, how should they be identified when used to kill by shooting or lethal injection? Does the interpolation of legal process in these cruelties make their inhumanity justifiable?

The physical pain caused by the action of killing a human being cannot be quantified. Nor can the psychological suffering caused by fore-knowledge of death at the hands of the state. Whether a death sentence is carried out six minutes after a summary trial, six weeks after a mass trial or 16 years after lengthy legal proceedings, the person executed is subjected to uniquely cruel, inhuman and degrading treatment and punishment.

The death penalty may also encompass other human rights violations. When a state jails people solely because of their beliefs, it violates the right to freedom of belief and expression. The death penalty is sometimes used to silence forever political opponents or to eliminate "troublesome" individuals. Whenever and wherever used, it finally and unalterably severs a person's right to hold opinions and to speak freely because it takes that person's life.

When a state convicts prisoners without affording them a fair trial, it denies the right to due process and equality before the law. The irrevocable punishment of death removes not only the victim's right to seek legal redress for wrongful conviction, but also the judicial system's capacity to correct its errors.

Like killings which take place outside the law, the death penalty denies the value of human life. By violating the right to life, it removes the foundation for the realization of all rights enshrined in the Universal

... I have no doubt that a humane treatment even of a murderer will enhance man's dignity and make society more human.
Jaya Prakash Narayan, former leader of the Janata party, India

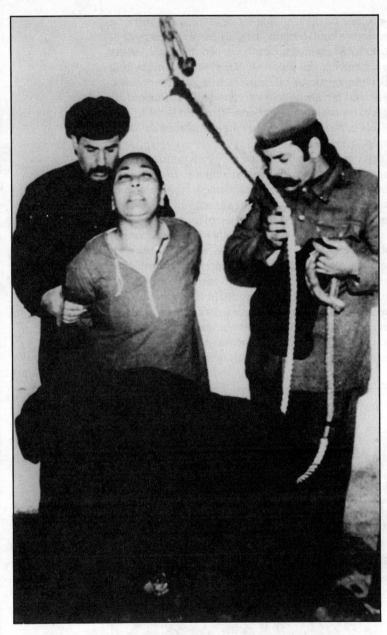

In Cairo, prison officials prepare to execute Samiha Abdul Hamid, convicted of murdering her husband. Murder is an atrocious crime – but this does not justify execution, which is a violation of human rights. Human rights are accorded *every* human being, the best and the worst; they are not favours to be granted by governments for good behaviour or withdrawn for bad. © *Associated Press*

Declaration of Human Rights.

As the Human Rights Committee set up under the International Covenant on Civil and Political Rights has recognized, "The right to life ... is the supreme right from which no derogation is permitted even in time of public emergency which threatens the life of the nation..." In a general comment on Article 6 of the Covenant issued in 1982, the Committee concluded that "all measures of abolition [of the death penalty] should be considered as progress in the enjoyment of the right to life within the meaning of Article 40" (see Appendix 3).

Many governments have recognized that the death penalty cannot be reconciled with respect for human rights. The UN has declared itself in favour of abolition. Today 35 countries have abolished the death penalty for all crimes, as documented in this report. Another 18 have abolished the punishment for all but exceptional offences such as wartime crimes. Another 27 countries and territories may be considered abolitionist *de facto* – they no longer carry out executions. Some 80 countries, therefore – over 40 per cent of all countries in the world – have abolished the death penalty in law or in practice.

However, some 100 countries retain and use the death penalty. Unlike torture, "disappearances" and extrajudicial executions, most judicial executions are not carried out in secret or denied by government authorities. Executions are often announced in advance. In some countries they are carried out in public or before a group of invited observers.

No government publicly admits to torture or other grave violations of human rights, although privately some officials may seek to justify such abuses in the name of the "greater good". But retentionist governments, those that keep the death penalty, for the most part openly admit to using it: they do not so much deny its cruelty as attempt to justify its use; and the arguments they use publicly to justify the death penalty resemble those that are used in private to justify other, secret abuses.

The most common justification offered is that, terrible as it is, the death penalty is necessary: it may be necessary only temporarily, but, it is

Use of the death penalty violates the very values that make society worth protecting. In Liberia, members of the public, including young children, look on as the bodies of 28 people are buried by an earth-shifter after their execution. © *Camera Press*

4

argued, only the death penalty can meet a particular need of society. And whatever that need may be, it is claimed to be so great that it justifies the cruel punishment of death.

The particular needs claimed to be served by the death penalty differ from time to time and from society to society. In some countries the penalty is considered legitimate as a means of preventing or punishing the crime of murder. Elsewhere it may be deemed indispensable to stop drug-trafficking, acts of political terror, economic corruption or adultery. In yet other countries, it is used to eliminate those seen as posing a political threat to the authorities.

Once one state uses the death penalty for any reason, it becomes easier for other states to use it with an appearance of legitimacy for whatever reasons they may choose. If the death penalty can be justified for one offence, justifications that accord with the prevailing views of a society or its rulers will be found for it to be used for other offences.

Whatever purpose is cited, the idea that a government can justify a punishment as cruel as death conflicts with the very concept of human rights. The significance of human rights is precisely that some means may never be used to protect society because their use violates the very values which make society worth protecting. When this essential distinction between appropriate and inappropriate means is set aside in the name of some "greater good", all rights are vulnerable and all individuals are threatened.

The death penalty, as a violation of fundamental human rights, would be wrong even if it could be shown that it uniquely met a vital social need. What makes the use of the penalty even more indefensible and the case for its abolition even more compelling is that it has never been shown to have any special power to meet any genuine social need.

Countless men and women have been executed for the stated purpose of preventing crime, especially the crime of murder. Yet, as documented in Chapter 2 of this report, study after study in diverse countries has failed to find convincing evidence that the death penalty has any unique capacity to deter others from committing particular crimes. The most recent survey of research findings on the relation between the death penalty and homicide rates, conducted for the UN in 1988, has concluded that "This research has failed to provide scientific proof that executions have a greater deterrent effect than life imprisonment. Such proof is unlikely to be forthcoming. The evidence as a whole still gives no positive support to the deterrent hypothesis."[1]

Undeniably the death penalty, by permanently "incapacitating" a prisoner, prevents that person from repeating the crime. But there is no way to be sure that the prisoner would indeed have repeated the crime if allowed to live, nor is there any need to violate the prisoner's right to life for the purpose of incapacitation: dangerous offenders can be kept safely away from the public without resorting to execution, as shown by the experience of many abolitionist countries.

Nor is there evidence that the threat of the death penalty will prevent politically motivated crimes or acts of terror. If anything, the possibility of political martyrdom through execution may encourage people to commit such crimes.

The gallows is not only a machine of death but a symbol. It is the symbol of terror, cruelty and irreverance for life; the common denominator of primitive savagery, medieval fanaticism and modern totalitarianism.
Arthur Koestler, writer

A defendant in Budapest, Hungary is convicted in 1982 of burglary and the murder of a nine-year-old child. The most recent executions in Hungary were carried out in 1985. The death penalty is often justified as a sign of how seriously society condemns crimes such as murder. But the execution of a convicted murderer can never be a condemnation of killing: it *is* killing.
© *Popperfoto*

Every society seeks protection from crime. Far from being a solution, the death penalty gives the erroneous impression that "firm measures" are being taken against crime. It diverts attention from the more complex measures which are really needed. In the words of a former British Prime Minister, "... the constant emphasis on capital punishment is preventing us from giving real attention and real resources to the problems of crime in a modern democracy ... We must recognize that if we really are to tackle the penal problems of the country we must turn our attention to that, instead of automatically saying that the answer is hanging and flogging."[2]

When the arguments of deterrence and incapacitation fall away, one is left with a more deep-seated justification for the death penalty: that of just retribution for the particular crime committed. According to this argument, certain people deserve to be killed as repayment for the evil done: there are crimes so offensive that killing the offender is the only just response.

It is an emotionally powerful argument. It is also one which, if valid, would invalidate the basis for human rights. If a person who commits a terrible act can "deserve" the cruelty of death, why cannot others, for similar reasons, "deserve" to be tortured or imprisoned without trial or simply shot on sight? Central to fundamental human rights is that they are inalienable. They may not be taken away even if a person has committed

I am 200 times a murderer but I won't kill another man.
John P Radclive
former executioner,
Canada

the most atrocious of crimes. Human rights apply to the worst of us as well as to the best of us, which is why they protect all of us.

What the argument for retribution boils down to is often no more than a desire for vengeance masked as a principle of justice. The desire for vengeance can be understood and acknowledged but the exercise of vengeance must be resisted. The history of the endeavour to establish the rule of law is a history of the progressive restriction of personal vengeance in public policy and legal codes.

If today's penal systems do not sanction the burning of an arsonist's home, the rape of a rapist or the torture of a torturer, it is not because they tolerate the crimes. Instead, it is because societies understand that they must be built on a different set of values from those they condemn.

An execution cannot be used to condemn killing; it *is* killing. Such an act by the state is the mirror image of the criminal's willingness to use physical violence against a victim.

Related to the argument that some people "deserve" to die is the proposition that the state is capable of determining exactly who they are. Whatever one's view of the retribution argument may be, the practice of the death penalty reveals that no criminal justice system is, or conceivably could be, capable of deciding fairly, consistently and infallibly who should live and who should die.

All criminal justice systems are vulnerable to discrimination and error. Expediency, discretionary decisions and prevailing public opinion may influence the proceedings at every stage from the initial arrest to the last-minute decision on clemency. The reality of the death penalty is that what determines who shall be executed and who shall be spared is often not only the nature of the crime but also the ethnic and social background, the financial means or the political opinions of the defendant. The death penalty is used disproportionately against the poor, the powerless, the marginalized or those whom repressive governments deem it expedient to eliminate.

Human uncertainty and arbitrary judgments are factors which affect all judicial decisions. But only one decision – the decision to execute – results in something that cannot be remedied or undone. Whether executions take place within hours of a summary trial or after years of protracted legal proceedings, states will continue to execute people who are later found to be innocent. Those executed cannot be compensated for loss of life and the whole society must share responsibility for what has been done.

It is the irrevocable nature of the death penalty, the fact that the prisoner is eliminated forever, that makes the penalty so tempting to some states as a tool of repression. Thousands have been put to death under one government only to be recognized as innocent victims when another set of authorities comes to power. Only abolition can ensure that such political abuse of the death penalty will never occur.

When used to crush political dissent, the death penalty is abhorrent. When invoked as a way to protect society from crime, it is illusory. Wherever used, it brutalizes those involved in the process and conveys to the public a sense that killing a defenceless prisoner is somehow acceptable. It may be used to try to bolster the authority of the state – or of

... the important point is that every person can improve himself and should be given the opportunity to do so, however serious his mistakes have been. The reason for this ... is that deep down inside each human being there exists the potentiality of development towards the highest good. A death penalty would totally destroy that potentiality. Such punishment is not a correction. It can only be an act of revenge.
Professor Emeritus Rawi Bhavilai, Thailand

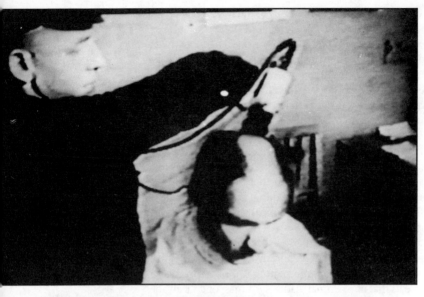

Prisoners sentenced to death are treated as men and women without a future. The unique horror of the death penalty is that from the moment the sentence is pronounced, the prisoner is forced to contemplate the prospect of being taken away to be put to death at an appointed time. The process is a dehumanizing one. Here, 27-year-old Valery Dolgov, sentenced to death for murder in 1986, is prepared for his cell in Latvia by having his head and moustache shaved. After, he will put on the uniform of a condemned prisoner.
© *Riga films*

those who govern in its name. But any such authority it confers is spurious. The penalty is a symbol of terror and, to that extent, a confession of weakness. It is always a violation of the most fundamental human rights.

This report describes how the death penalty is used throughout the world. The report also defines the choice before each society and each of its citizens. It is a choice about the sort of world people want and will work to achieve: a world in which the state is permitted to kill as a legal punishment or a world based on respect for human life and human rights – a world without executions.

1 United Nations, *The question of the death penalty and the new contributions of the criminal sciences to the matter,* a report to the United Nations Committee on Crime Prevention and Control, United Nations Social Affairs Division, Crime Prevention and Criminal Justice Branch, Vienna, 1988, page 110.

2 Edward Heath, former Prime Minister of the United Kingdom, speaking in a debate on the death penalty in the House of Commons (lower house of parliament) on 13 July 1983. *House of Commons, Official Report, Parliamentary Debates (Hansard),* vol. 45, No. 20, 13 July 1983, column 911.

2. The test of logic and experience

The case for the death penalty rests on a claim that executions fulfil important needs of society that cannot be met in other ways. Whether executions are carried out in public or shielded from view behind prison walls, the argument used is that the death penalty is necessary, at least temporarily, for the good of society.

The argument has two major flaws.

First, it can never justify the violation of fundamental human rights. Torture cannot be justified by arguing that in some situations it might be useful. International law clearly states that a cruel, inhuman or degrading punishment is always prohibited, even in time of the gravest public emergency.

Second, despite centuries of experience with the death penalty and many scientific studies of the relationship between that penalty and crime rates, there is no convincing evidence that it is uniquely able to protect society from crime or to meet the demands of justice. In many ways it does the opposite.

Governments perform no more serious act than taking human life. If a state executes individuals claiming that such killings are necessary and beneficial, the evidence supporting its case should be beyond doubt, not merely speculative. In the words of a leading member of the United Kingdom parliament during a debate on the death penalty in 1983: "If the deterrent case is to be accepted, if we are to vote for capital punishment as a deterrent, we at least ought to be sure that it deters. If we are to hang men and women by the necks until they are dead, we ought to do it on more than a hunch, a superstition, a vague impression..."[1]

The death penalty is presented as a uniquely effective and appropriate way to prevent and punish crime, but numerous studies conducted in different countries and using different methodologies have failed to establish that it deters it more effectively than other punishments. Even though executing people does prevent them from committing further crimes, it is impossible to determine whether those executed would actually have repeated the crimes of which they were convicted. Unlike imprisonment, which also incapacitates, the death penalty entails the inherent risk of judicial errors which can never be corrected.

When retribution is used to justify the death penalty, the criminal justice system becomes an instrument of vengeance. Even if such a goal were acceptable, use of the death penalty would not achieve just results. No criminal justice system has shown itself capable of consistently and fairly selecting who should live and who should die in all cases. Experience demonstrates that whenever the death penalty is used some people will be killed while others who have committed similar or even worse crimes will be allowed to live. Some offenders benefit from the services of more skilled lawyers; some from having more sympathetic judges or juries; some from their political connections or higher social

In executing someone, we rule out irrevocably any possibility, however remote, of subsequent repentance, conversion, or reconciliation; we exclude finally the possibility of moral development and of the growth of conscience.
Irish Commission for Justice and Peace

status. Although these factors occur in any criminal justice system, they become intolerable when the result for the unlucky is death by execution.

Some 80 countries have now abolished the death penalty either in law or in practice. These countries have different cultures, traditions and socio-political systems. They have different levels of economic development and many of them confront difficult social problems. Yet none is known to have experienced social or political ill-effects which could clearly be linked to abolition of the death penalty. It is rare for a society to bring back the death penalty once it has been abolished, despite calls from some quarters to restore it.

A serious examination of the arguments propounded in favour of the death penalty reveals that it is not only wrong but unnecessary.

Sayyid Hassan Sayyid 'Abd al-Hadi al-Hakim is one of the 16 members of the Hakim family whose execution the Iraqi government has acknowledged. Accused of sabotage, all were relatives of Ayatollah Muhammad Baqer al-Hakim, leader of the Iraqi Shi'i opposition living in exile in Iran. It is reported that some had been tortured before execution and that none had been tried.

Deterrence

The argument most frequently used for the death penalty is deterrence: it is necessary to kill an offender to dissuade other people from committing the same kind of crime.

At first glance, this appears to be a plausible argument. What could more effectively stop those willing to kill or commit other serious crimes than the threat of the most terrible of punishments, death? What more forceful way could be found to respond to the strong desire of ordinary people to be protected against crime?

Empirical evidence, however, does not support the argument. Moreover, its common sense logic rests on questionable assumptions.

It is incorrect to assume that all or most of those who commit such serious crimes as murder do so after rationally calculating the consequences. Murders are most often committed in moments of passion, when extreme emotion overcomes reason. They may also be committed under the influence of alcohol or drugs, or in moments of panic, for example when the perpetrator is caught in the act of stealing. Some people who commit violent crime are highly unstable or mentally ill. In none of these cases can fear of the death penalty be expected to deter.

A Japanese prison psychiatrist studied 145 convicted murderers between 1955 and 1957. He could find none who remembered thinking they might be sentenced to death before committing the crime. "Despite their knowledge of the existence of the death penalty" the prisoners had been "incapable because of their impulsiveness and their inability to live except in the present, of being inhibited by the thought of capital punishment."[2]

After 35 years in the Prison Medical Service, a British doctor found that "Deterrence is by no means the simple affair that some people think ... A high proportion of murderers are so tensed up at the time of their crime as to be impervious to the consequences to themselves; others manage to persuade themselves that they can get away with it."[3]

This last point underlines another weakness in the deterrence argument. Those offenders who plan serious crimes in a calculated manner may decide to proceed despite the risks in the belief that they will not be caught. The key to deterrence in such cases is to increase the likelihood of detection, arrest and conviction. The death penalty may even be counter-productive in that it diverts official and public attention from efforts needed to bring about real improvements in combating crime.

The deterrence argument is not borne out by the facts. If the death penalty did deter potential offenders more effectively than other punishments, one would expect to find that in analyses of comparable jurisdictions, those which have the death penalty for a particular crime would have a lower rate of that crime than those which do not. Similarly, a rise in the rate of crimes hitherto punishable by death would be expected in states which abolish the penalty and a decline in crime rates would be expected among states which introduce it for those crimes. Yet study after study has failed to establish any such link between the death penalty and crime rates.

The first major report on capital punishment prepared for the UN and published in 1962 considered the possible effects of removing various offences from the list of capital crimes. The report concluded that "All the information available appears to confirm that such a removal has, in fact, never been followed by a notable rise in the incidence of the crime no longer punishable with death."[4]

The United Kingdom Royal Commission on Capital Punishment (1949-1953) examined the available statistics on jurisdictions which had abolished or ceased using the death penalty for murder. From its survey of seven European countries, New Zealand and individual states within Australia and the USA, the Commission concluded that "there is no clear evidence in any of the figures we have examined that the abolition of capital punishment has led to an increase in the homicide rate, or that its reintroduction has led to a fall".[5]

Recent crime figures from abolitionist countries similarly fail to show that abolition has harmful effects. Although there were more murder and manslaughter convictions in South Australia in the five years after abolition than in the five years before, a longer-term study showed "that abolition of the death penalty had no effect on homicide trends in that state". The death penalty was abolished there in 1976. In Jamaica, there was

> The way we have carried out executions historically in the United States appears to have contributed slightly but significantly to the increase in homicides.
> William J Bowers and Glenn L Pierce, criminologists, USA

11

little change in the homicide rate during a moratorium on executions between 1976 and 1980, despite a rash of political shootings during the 1980 general election. In Canada, the homicide rate per 100,000 population fell from a peak of 3.09 in 1975, the year before the abolition of the death penalty for murder, to 2.74 in 1983, and in 1986 it reached its lowest level in 15 years. In the United Kingdom, the number of homicides has risen since the abolition of the death penalty for murder, but the increase has been far smaller than for other serious violent offences.[6]

Reviewing the evidence on the relation between changes in the use of the death penalty and crime, the report on the death penalty prepared for the UN Committee on Crime Prevention and Control in 1988 stated that, although no definite conclusions could be drawn about the impact of changes in the death penalty alone (as these could have been associated with other social and penal changes affecting crime), nevertheless "the fact that all the evidence continues to point in the same direction is persuasive *a priori* evidence that countries need not fear sudden and serious changes in the curve of crime if they reduce their reliance upon the death penalty".[7]

Most empirical studies on the deterrent effect of the death penalty have been conducted in countries with developed traditions of statistical

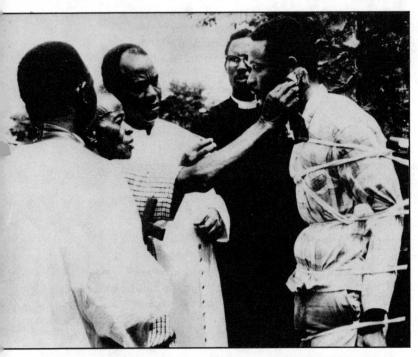

In Nigeria, a father takes final leave of his son, convicted of armed robbery. Usually, however, relatives stay away from the prisoner out of a deep sense of shame, so the authorities often require executions to be carried out in the prisoner's family compound or home town where its impact on the family and the local community will be greatest. A study published in 1988 that reviewed crime figures in Nigeria between 1967 and 1985 concluded that the death penalty had not reduced the number of armed robberies. © *Camera Press*

research and the resources to conduct such research.[8] However, evidence from other countries – and relating to other crimes as well as murder – has also failed to establish that the death penalty deters crime more effectively than do other punishments.

In Nigeria, a professor of law and criminology compared statistics on murders and executions between 1967 and 1985 and found that "murder incidents have consistently increased during most of this period" even though murder had been punishable by death and almost everyone knew this. Armed robbery, too, had increased since the period before it became a capital offence throughout Nigeria in 1970. The professor found that between 1967 and 1970 an average of 994 armed robberies were committed each year but that the annual average rose to 1,500 between 1971 and 1985. He concluded that the studies in Nigeria "have demonstrated clearly that no efficacy can be shown for the operation of the death penalty" for murder and armed robbery in Nigeria.[9]

One of the few studies purporting to show that the death penalty does have a clear deterrent effect (and therefore often cited by those favouring the death penalty) was that of Isaac Ehrlich, a United States (US) economist . He used a statistical method known as "regression analysis" to examine the possible effect of executions and other variables on homicides in the USA as a whole between 1932 and 1970. During that period, and especially in the 1960s, homicides increased while executions declined. In an article published in 1975, Isaac Ehrlich concluded that his investigation had indicated "the existence of a pure deterrent effect of capital punishment" and suggested that "an additional execution per year over the period in question may have resulted, on average, in 7 or 8 fewer murders".[10]

This study has been extensively criticized on methodological grounds. Although Isaac Ehrlich's research included a number of variables likely to affect the homicide rate, he had omitted others which might also have done so, such as the increasing availability of guns. Crime in general had increased during the 1960s, but the rate of growth in homicides was less than that of other crimes against the person. The decline in executions could not have affected homicide rates in places where the death penalty had already been abolished or fallen into disuse, yet the growth in homicides during the 1960s was as great in states that previously did not carry out executions as in those that previously did.

A panel comprising criminologists, statisticians, political scientists, psychologists, economists and other experts, established by the US National Academy of Sciences in 1975 to provide "an objective technical assessment" of studies of the effects of sanctions on crime rates, reported in 1978 that Isaac Ehrlich's analyses provided "no useful evidence on the deterrent effect of capital punishment". More broadly, the panel also found that "the current evidence on the deterrent effect of capital punishment is inadequate for drawing any substantive conclusions".[11]

Some research has even suggested that executions may temporarily result in more homicides. Two US researchers analysed monthly homicide rates in New York State between 1907 and 1963, incorporating a wide range of controls. They concluded that there had been, on average, two additional homicides in the month immediately after an execution. They

> The death penalty is no more effective a deterrent than life imprisonment ... While police and law enforcement officials are the strongest advocates of capital punishment, the evidence is overwhelming that police are no safer in communities that retain the sanction than in those that have abolished it.
> Supreme Court Justice Thurgood Marshall, USA

suggested that this momentary rise in homicides might be due to a "brutalizing" effect of executions, similar to the effect of other violent events such as publicized suicides, mass murders and assassinations.[12] A month-by-month analysis of executions and first-degree murders in Chicago from 1915 to 1921 produced similar findings.[13]

The fact that no clear evidence that the death penalty has a unique deterrent effect has emerged from the many studies made, and the methodological difficulties inherent in all such studies, point to the futility of relying on the deterrence hypothesis as a basis for public policy on the death penalty. This suggests that further studies of the deterrent effect of the death penalty are unlikely to contribute to the debate. This point was made by the US National Academy of Sciences panel in its report cited above. Because the non-experimental methods necessarily used in such studies could not meet the rigorous standards of proof required if public policy were to be based on the results, the panel concluded that "research on this topic is not likely to produce findings that will or should have much influence on policy makers".[14]

Two US criminologists have recently made the further point that if the death penalty does indeed deter homicide more effectively than does imprisonment, that effect can at most be slight, since any major effect would have been detected by the studies already made. In their view there is now room for debate "only about whether the marginal deterrent effect is nil or very small in relation to total homicide volume".[15]

Preventing prisoners from repeating their offences

According to the incapacitation argument, a prisoner must be killed (and thus "incapacitated") in order to ensure that he or she never repeats the crime.

Clearly, once killed, a person is incapacitated forever. A policy of execution in order to incapacitate cannot, however, be based solely on the undeniable fact that dead people cannot commit crimes. Such a policy must rely on the assumption that the state can accurately determine at the time of sentencing which prisoners will repeat their crimes: if not, the state must be willing to include among those executed a considerable number of people who would not do so. The incapacitation-by-death argument also assumes that it is impossible to find any other effective means of preventing recidivism (offences committed after release).

Neither of these assumptions is borne out by the facts.

Sufficient experience has accumulated to enable parole institutions in various countries to administer the conditional release of selected prisoners. Their judgments are based on the most up-to-date information available from a variety of sources on a prisoner's history, character and monitored behaviour in prison. But the argument of incapacitation requires that accurate assessments of potential future dangerousness be made at the time of sentencing, when much less is known about a prisoner. In a brief submitted to the US Supreme Court in 1982 in a case involving the use of psychiatric testimony in the decision to impose a death sentence, the American Psychiatric Association said that "the large body of research indicates that even under the best of conditions,

Details of several people sentenced to death in China displayed on the wall of a public building; a large red tick on each poster indicates that the sentence has been carried out.

psychiatric predictions of long-term future dangerousness are wrong in at least two out of every three cases".[16]

The evidence available indicates that the rate of recidivism among prisoners convicted of murder tends to be quite low. The United Kingdom Royal Commission on Capital Punishment (1949-1953) obtained information on 129 male prisoners in England and Wales sentenced to death for murder but reprieved and later released between 1934 and 1948. Of these prisoners, 112 were "doing well when last heard of". Only one prisoner was reconvicted of murder. At the time of the Royal Commission his was the only such case since the beginning of the century, and it was a special case, according to Viscount Templewood, the former British Home Secretary (the cabinet minister responsible for criminal policy and decisions on clemency). The prisoner's release was unusual – it might not have been granted at all but for wartime conditions – and he received no supervision after release.[17]

The Royal Commission found similarly low recidivism rates among prisoners convicted of murder in other European and English-speaking countries studied. In the six other European countries from which information was obtained, only three cases of recidivism emerged. "The evidence seems conclusive that the release of life-sentence prisoners involves little risk at present," the Royal Commission stated. "... any convicted murderers whom it would be unsafe ever to release are likely to be in the category of the mentally abnormal..." As for the risk of fresh killings being committed while the person concerned was still in prison, this too was found to be low: "... the evidence given to us in the countries we visited, and the information we received from others, were uniformly to the effect that murderers are no more likely than any other prisoners to commit acts of violence against officers or fellow prisoners or to attempt escape; on the contrary it would appear that in all countries murderers are, on the whole, better behaved than most prisoners".[18]

Figures analysed by the US criminologist Thorsten Sellin corroborate these findings. He found, for example, that the incidence of killings in prison by inmates convicted of murder was low or nil. None of the 16 prisoners who had killed someone during 1964 and 1965 while in Californian prisons was serving a sentence for capital murder. Similarly, out of 342 male prisoners paroled in California between 1945 and 1954 while serving sentences for first-degree murder, one had been re-convicted of second-degree murder (not punishable by death) as of mid-1956. In Michigan, 268 prisoners convicted of first-degree murder were paroled between 1959 and 1972; only one was reconvicted (and not for a violent crime). In Pennsylvania, out of 607 prisoners released on parole while serving life sentences (most of them probably for first-degree murder, which was punishable by death) in the previous 37 years, only one had repeated the crime of first-degree murder as of 1969. As Thorsten Sellin observed, "paroled murderers do sometimes repeat their crime, but … among parolees who commit homicides, they rank very low".[19]

Prevention of possible future murders can be achieved by incarcerating people in prison or other institutions. This method is already employed in the case of some individuals who might commit future crimes – that is, of compulsively anti-social people or of the violently insane. Humanitarian principles enshrined in both domestic and international laws prohibit the execution of the insane. If states have found incarceration to be an effective means of incapacitating insane killers, why is it not possible to use it to incapacitate the "normal" ones?

Proponents of the incapacitation argument have pointed to cases in which inadequate parole procedures have resulted in the release of convicted killers who should not have been set free. But the response should not be to execute more prisoners but rather to improve the parole procedures.

A recent study of 239 men released on parole at various times in the 1960s and 1970s after serving some part of a sentence of life imprison-ment in Great Britain, found that out of the 192 men who had been convicted of murder, two had murdered again after release. Investigation of both cases revealed possible errors of judgment, either in the decision to release the men or in their subsequent supervision. Both men were back in prison, where they were likely to remain for the rest of their lives. In contrast, most of the men released "settled back into the community quite well".[20]

Incarceration in prisons and other institutions which isolate offenders from society has one great advantage over the death penalty as a means of incapacitation: the mistakes which result from fallible judicial systems can be corrected, at least partially. The death penalty, on the other hand, takes the lives of offenders who might well have been rehabilitated as well as the lives of people wrongly convicted.

Retribution

Unlike the arguments of deterrence and incapacitation, the retribution argument maintains that certain offenders must be killed not to prevent crime but because of the demands of justice. Execution is deemed to be a

Murderer is man plus murder. Real justice is done when the judge punishes the murder and restores the man.
Former Justice
V R Krishna Iyer,
Supreme Court
of India

repayment for an evil deed: by killing the offender society shows its condemnation of the latter's crime.

The persuasiveness of the argument that certain offenders deserve to die is rooted in the deep aversion felt by law-abiding citizens to terrible crimes. But close examination of how the death penalty actually works shows that the retribution argument is fundamentally flawed.

Because of the unique nature of the death penalty, retribution as a basis for it makes impossible demands on the criminal justice system. Demand for the death penalty as a matter of justice runs up against the injustice and arbitrariness of the penalty in practice. A society's restraints on using the death penalty in certain cases, along with the biases inherent in all legal systems and the sheer fallibility of human judgment, preclude the possibility of creating a system which can ever mete out death in a fair way.

In the USA, Thorsten Sellin examined statistics on prosecutions, convictions and executions for murder and concluded that "retributive capital justice is tainted by bias and by the influence of factors beyond the control of courts of justice, such as the poverty of the defendant, which prevents him from engaging competent counsel skilled in the art of criminal defence".

He noted that relatively few killers were executed. In California, for example, of 7,053 people imprisoned between 1950 and 1973 following conviction for felonious homicide, 61 per cent were sentenced to death and only 1.5 per cent were executed. More recent figures show a similarly stark contrast: while 25 prisoners were executed in the USA in 1987, the Federal Bureau of Investigation (FBI) reported 20,100 murders and non-negligent manslaughters during the same year. The wide gap between the number of executions and murders in the USA indicated to Thorsten Sellin an "actual, if not philosophical, repudiation of retribution by death ... we seem to be torn between a desire to see murderers suffer the ultimate penalty and a reluctance to exact it. Even those who ardently advocate retribution by death often paradoxically stress that it should be used sparingly, for fear that otherwise it would dull our moral sensitivity and lose its terrifying force."[21]

Such analyses suggest a sacrificial element in the use of the death penalty. Since it is impossible to follow through fully the logic of the retribution argument, a token number of prisoners are executed – in effect, sacrificed – to satisfy popular demand.

Once it is acknowledged that not everyone who commits murder should die (and the facts show that all societies acknowledge this) then doubts about the fairness of selecting those who are to be executed must arise.[22]

Even a decision to execute everyone convicted of a particular crime would fail to meet the fundamental requirements of fairness. Especially in legal systems that rule out consideration of mitigating factors as grounds for imposing a less harsh sentence, mandatory death penalties may create an arbitrary threshold for deciding who is to live and who will die. In Singapore, for example, the death penalty is mandatory for possession of more than 15 grams of heroin: only a tiny difference in the amount found on a person can mean the difference between life and death.

In the USA, the inherent unfairness of mandatory death sentences

Sadamichi Hirasawa, divorced by his wife and disowned by his sons, lived his last 37 years confined under sentence of death. He died in a Japanese prison hospital in 1987 at the age of 95. Sadamichi Hirasawa had confessed to the murder of 12 bank clerks but retracted his confession at the trial saying that it had been coerced. He had appealed unsuccessfully for a retrial 17 times. © *Asahi Shimbun*

resulted in a ruling by the US Supreme Court in 1976 that mandatory death penalties defeat the "constitutionally indispensable" requirement in capital cases of "consideration of the character and record of the individual offender and the circumstances of the particular offence".[23]

On the other hand, attempts to achieve fairness in the USA by using an optional death penalty have resulted in a system that functions in many ways like a judicial lottery. The prisoners executed are not necessarily only those who have committed the most heinous crimes, but also those who had less skilled lawyers to defend them, or harsher prosecutors or judges, or where some factor other than their guilt or the heinousness of the crime, such as race or social class, determined their sentences.[24]

There is no convincing argument that society cannot find ways other than killing to express its condemnation of crime. Indeed, the publicity surrounding an execution may divert attention from the crime to the person who committed it. Far from being condemned for his or her deeds, the criminal may actually become a focus of sympathy. As has been found in countries where the death penalty has been abolished, a sufficiently severe punishment which is compatible with international human rights standards can adequately demonstrate society's condemnation of the crime in question. Unlike the death penalty, non-lethal punishments can reflect the values of society rather than the values of the killer.

The death penalty and political violence

Bombings, kidnappings, assassinations of public officials, aircraft hijackings and other politically motivated acts of violence often kill or maim not only the intended targets of attack but bystanders as well. These acts understandably provoke strong public outcry and may result in demands for the death penalty to be used. Yet as public officials responsible for fighting such crimes have repeatedly pointed out, executions are as likely to increase acts of terror as to stop them.

As a professor of criminology in Canada has observed: "Those who really think that the reinstitution of capital punishment will put an end to, or will produce a reduction in the number of terrorist incidents are either extremely naive or under an illusion. Standard punishments, including the death penalty, do not impress terrorists or other political criminals who are ideologically motivated and dedicated to make sacrifices for the sake of their cause ... Moreover, terrorist activities are fraught with danger and the terrorist runs all kinds of deadly risks without being intimidated by the prospect of immediate death. Is it conceivable that he will be deterred by the remote and low risk of the death penalty?"[25]

Those responsible for drafting laws have pointed out how hard it is to define acts of terror in legal statutes. It is difficult, if not impossible, to isolate politically motivated crimes warranting the death penalty without, in effect, punishing the perpetrators for their political views as well as for their crimes. Furthermore, such isolation may well confer special recognition on the deeds of violent groups – something governments usually seek to avoid.[26]

Executions for politically motivated crimes may result in greater publicity for acts of terror, thus drawing increased public attention to the perpetrators' political agenda. Such executions may also create martyrs whose memory becomes a rallying point for their organizations. For some men and women convinced of the legitimacy of their acts, the prospect of suffering the death penalty may even serve as an incentive. Far from stopping violence, executions have been used as the justification for more violence as opposition groups have seized the opportunity to bolster their legitimacy by using in reprisal the same "death penalty" that governments claim the right to impose.

British authorities ruling Palestine hanged several members of the underground Zionist Irgun organization in the 1940s following their conviction on charges of bombings and other violent attacks. Menachem Begin, former Irgun leader and later Prime Minister of Israel, reportedly told a former British Government minister that the executions had "galvanized" his group, which subsequently hanged several British soldiers in retaliation. Menachem Begin said the hangings "got us the recruits that we wanted, and made us more efficient and dedicated to the cause ... you were not sentencing our terrorists to death, you were sentencing a lot of your own people, and we decided how many".[27]

On 17 September 1975 a firing-squad in Spain executed five members of opposition groups who had been convicted after summary trials of killing members of the government's security forces. Four days later three police officers were shot dead and a fourth fatally wounded,

My personal view is that there should not be any death penalty. This is too final. It has not worked in Nigeria where hanging and execution was carried out in public.

High Court Judge, Justice Anthony Lawrence, Zambia

reportedly in reprisal.

In August 1980 the Government of Angola convicted nine members of the opposition group *União Nacional para a Independência Total de Angola* (UNITA), National Union for the Total Independence of Angola, on charges of organizing a bombing campaign. The nine prisoners were executed on 22 August, the day after sentencing. On 23 August UNITA "sentenced" to death 15 people described as government soldiers and immediately executed them.

As France's then Minister of Justice, Robert Badinter, said in 1985: "... history and contemporary world events refute the simplistic notion that the death penalty can deter terrorists. Never in history has the threat of execution halted terrorism or political crime. Indeed, if there is one kind of man or woman who is not deterred by the threat of the death penalty, it is the terrorist, who frequently risks his life in action. Death has an ambiguous fascination for the terrorist, be it the death of others by one's own hand, or the risk of death for oneself. Regardless of his proclaimed ideology, his rallying cry is the fascist *'viva la muerte'* [Long live death]".[28]

Drug-trafficking

Drug abuse and trafficking pose major problems for the world community. In the words of the UN Secretary-General: "Illicit drugs wherever they are produced or used contaminate and corrupt, weakening the very fabric of society. Increasing worldwide abuse is destroying uncounted useful lives ... The suffering of individuals is not the only cost. Illicit drugs and crime go hand in hand. The allure of tremendous profits constitutes a

Over 20 countries now provide for the death penalty for drugs offences, but there is no clear evidence that it has a unique deterrent effect. In Malaysia, the number of registered drug addicts has increased since the death penalty became mandatory for drugs offences in 1983. © *Abbas/Magnum*

potent attraction to criminals, and drug-trafficking frequently entails other criminal acts, including bribery, larceny, the corruption of public officials and even murder."[29]

Responding to the drug menace, over 20 countries now have laws making drug-related offences punishable by death. As shown in this report, at least 10 introduced laws providing for the death penalty for drugs offences during the past decade (1979 to 1988).[30] Hundreds of prisoners convicted of drugs offences have been executed.

The rationale for using the death penalty is that it will deter drug-traffickers more effectively than other punishments. But despite the hundreds of executions there is no clear evidence of a decline in drug-trafficking which could clearly be attributed to the threat or use of that penalty.[31]

In Iran, for example, executions in drug-related cases began years before the 1979 revolution and since the revolution more than 1,000 prisoners are reported to have been executed after conviction of drugs offences – yet drug abuse and trafficking continue to be serious problems.

In Malaysia, where the death penalty has been mandatory for drugs offences since 1983, officials have, on occasion, publicly recognized the penalty's ineffectiveness. For example, the then acting Inspector General of Police of Malaysia was reported as saying in January 1985 that death sentences did not seem to have deterred traffickers.[32] Although Amnesty International has no detailed statistics on drug-trafficking in Malaysia, government figures as reported in the national press record an increase in the number of registered drug addicts from 79,000 in 1979 to 102,807 in January 1985, 111,688 in April 1986 and 128,741 in June 1988.

The lack of deterrent effect was cited at the December 1985 meeting of the UN Expert Group on Countermeasures to Drug Smuggling by Air and Sea: "... in the experience of several experts, the fact that capital punishment appeared on the statute books as the maximum penalty did not necessarily deter trafficking; indeed in some cases it might make prosecution more difficult because courts of law were naturally inclined to require a much higher standard of proof when capital punishment was possible or even mandatory ... The most effective deterrent was assuredly the certainty of detection and arrest."[33]

Even as the death penalty is introduced in the fight against drug-trafficking in certain countries, its use is being rejected elsewhere. On 10 April 1985 three men were publicly executed by firing-squad in Nigeria following conviction for drugs offences. At least one case involved offences committed before the introduction of a decree which set up military tribunals empowered, with retroactive effect, to impose death sentences for drugs offences. The executions provoked considerable public protest. Among the objections made were that death was too harsh a punishment for the offences involved; that killing would brutalize rather than reform; that the death penalty was unfair and not a deterrent. A number of other prisoners were sentenced to death, but there were no further executions in drugs cases. In 1986 the decree was amended, removing provision for the death penalty for drugs offences. Death sentences imposed for such offences but not carried out were commuted to terms of imprisonment.

I remember the one who was executed, Lim Seng, and I hoped by his death there [would] be less narcotic addiction in our country, but today we have more. There is now a Narcotics Command, the whole Command to deal with narcotics addiction. So therefore the life of that man that was snuffed out to discourage drug addiction has been lost in vain ...
Teodulo Natividad, author of the 1972 Dangerous Drugs Act, Philippines

In response to the drugs threat, a world conference at ministerial level was organized by the UN. The International Conference on Drug Abuse and Illicit Trafficking, held in Vienna from 17 to 26 June 1987, adopted a "Comprehensive Multidisciplinary Outline of Future Activities in Drug Abuse Control". This outline included such measures as the prevention and reduction of demand through education and control of drug abuse in the workplace; improved programs for the treatment of addicts; control of supply through crop elimination and redevelopment of areas formerly used to cultivate illicit drug crops; disruption of major trafficking networks through controls over ships and aircraft and surveillance of borders; facilitation of the extradition of alleged traffickers; and forfeiture of the proceeds of trafficking. There was no recommendation of the death penalty either in the outline or in the declaration adopted by the conference.

Public opinion

One reason sometimes given for retaining the death penalty – and put forward even by officials who say that they personally oppose the punishment – is that public opinion demands it. They cite polls apparently showing strong support for the death penalty, then argue that the time is not ripe for abolition, and even that it would be undemocratic in the face of such support for the punishment.

The first response to this argument is that respect for human rights must never be dependent on public opinion. Torture would never be permissible even if there were public support for its use in certain cases.

Second, public opinion on the death penalty is often based on an incomplete understanding of the relevant facts, and the results of polls can vary according to the way questions are asked. It is incumbent on officials responsible for policy on this matter not only to listen to the public but also to ensure that the public is fully informed. Many more people might well support abolition if they were properly informed of the facts surrounding the use of the death penalty and the reasons for abolition.

In Japan, where officials have cited public support for the death penalty as a reason for its retention, opinion polls conducted by the government have been criticized by the Japan Federation of Bar Associations as imprecise and not fairly interpreted. In a 1967 poll conducted by the Prime Minister's office, 71 per cent of respondents thought the death penalty should be retained. But 61 per cent of these respondents based their support for the death penalty on its unproved deterrent effect, and 74 per cent incorrectly believed that the number of heinous crimes was increasing in Japan. Furthermore, 49 per cent of those polled agreed that the punishment should be suspended pending a future decision on the issue. Only 26 per cent disagreed with an experimental suspension of the death penalty.

Some research suggests that attitudes towards the death penalty can change with more knowledge of the facts. A 1975 study of a random sample of adults in a US university town found that most knew little about the effects of the death penalty, and that support for it declined when people were exposed to information. Some of the 181 subjects of the

... capital punishment can neither prevent crime nor can it reform criminals. It is an entirely negative punishment. It can only satisfy the desire for revenge of the victim's family and the public. It can by no means promote social justice or a sense of humanity.

Wu Shu-chen, Democratic Progressive Party member of the Legislative Assembly, Taiwan

An execution room in Japan (Osaka detention centre) where public opinion polls in favour of retaining the death penalty there have been criticized by the Japanese Bar Association as unfair and imprecise. In one poll in 1967, 61 per cent of respondents based their support on its unproved deterrent effect, while only 26 per cent were against an experimental suspension of the death penalty.

experiment were asked to read an essay giving facts and arguments on the effects of the death penalty. Before reading it, 51 per cent of the subjects said they favoured the death penalty, while 29 per cent were against it and 20 per cent were undecided. After the reading, support for the penalty had dropped to 38 per cent and opposition had grown to 42 per cent, with 20 per cent undecided. Among the control group, who were asked to read an essay on an unrelated topic, opinions on the death penalty remained substantially unchanged.[34]

Some polls repeated over a period of years have indicated that while the decision to abolish the death penalty may at first appear to be contrary to majority opinion, abolition may come to be accepted in time. In the Federal Republic of Germany, for example, public support for the death penalty has declined steadily since abolition, apart from temporary increases in support following politically motivated killings. In 1950, a year after the death penalty was abolished, 55 per cent of those asked "Are you in principle for or against the death penalty?" said they were for it, and only 30 per cent were opposed. When the same question was asked in 1973, only 30 per cent said they favoured the death penalty. The percentage favouring the death penalty dropped to 26 in 1980, 24 in 1983 and 22 in 1986, by which time 55 per cent of respondents said they were opposed to the penalty – a reversal of the 1950 figure.[35]

The financial cost

One justification sometimes offered for the death penalty is simply that it is cheaper to kill certain prisoners than keep them in prison. But financial considerations cannot justify the violation of the most basic human rights.

In fact, some studies made in Canada and the USA show that in those countries, use of the death penalty is more expensive than life imprisonment. A 1982 study in the US state of New York found that the average capital trial and first stage of appeals alone would cost the taxpayer about $1.8 million, more than twice as much as it would cost to keep a person in prison for life. A number of judges, prosecutors and other officials oppose the death penalty precisely because they believe that the enormous concentration of judicial services on a relative handful of cases diverts valuable resources away from other, more effective areas of law enforcement.[36]

Alternative punishments

Alternatives to the death penalty already exist, both in abolitionist countries and in those which retain the death penalty but have abolished it for certain offences. Even for crimes punishable by death, an alternative penalty will be provided if the court decides not to impose a death sentence or if the sentence is commuted. There is no indication that methods used in these societies are less effective than those used by societies which execute certain offenders in order to deal with crime.

Without doubt there is much still to be done to prevent people becoming victims of crimes, including crimes of violence. As discussed in the United Nations and elsewhere, the measures needed to tackle crime include: addressing the relevant socio-economic factors such as poverty, inequality and unemployment; strengthening social standards on and attitudes towards crime; education through the mass media on what the public can do to protect itself and reduce the opportunities for crime; helping to improve crime detection and the arrest of offenders; programs for the rehabilitation of offenders enabling them to lead productive social lives; programs to address the needs of victims of crime, including compensation for damages sustained; and research into patterns of crime and better ways of preventing and detecting it.

Amnesty International has not adopted any specific proposal for what punishment should replace the death penalty. Its position is that any alternative should not constitute cruel, inhuman or degrading treatment or punishment, nor should it contravene the UN Standard Minimum Rules for the Treatment of Prisoners.

The death penalty does not stamp out crime. It is a pseudo-solution which diverts attention from the measures needed to prevent crime, by creating the false impression that decisive measures are being taken. The death penalty does not protect society, but rather distracts attention from the urgent need for methods of effective protection which at the same time uphold and enhance respect for human rights and life.

Like torture, the death penalty is cruel, inhuman and degrading. It destroys human lives and violates human rights. The alternative to the death penalty, like the alternative to torture, is abolition.

1 Roy Hattersley, speaking in a debate on the death penalty in the United Kingdom House of Commons (lower house of parliament) on 13 July 1983, *op. cit.* column 905.

2 Sadataka Kogi, "Etude criminologique et psycho-pathologique de condamnés a mort ou aux travaux forcés à perpétuité au Japon", *Annales Medico-psychologiques,* 117th year, No. 2, part 3, October 1959.

3 W. F. Roper, "Murderers in custody" in *The hanging question,* ed. Louis Blom-Cooper, Duckworth, London, 1969, page 103.

4 United Nations, *Capital punishment,* UN Department of Economic and Social Affairs, New York, 1962. UN publication, sales No. 62.IV.2, page 54.

5 United Kingdom Royal Commission on Capital Punishment 1949-1953, *A report presented to Parliament by command of Her Majesty,* Her Majesty's Stationery Office, London, 1953 pages 23, 358-359.

6 United Nations, *The question of the death penalty and the new contributions of the criminal sciences to the matter, op. cit.* page 81.

7 *Ibid.* page 80.

8 *Ibid.* chapter six.

9 A. A. Adeyemi, "Death penalty: criminological perspectives; the Nigerian situation", in *The Death Penalty. Travaux de la Conférence Internationale tenue à l'Institut Supérieur International de Sciences Criminelles, Syracuse-Italie, 17 au 22 mai 1987, Revue Internationale de Droit Pénal,* vol. 58, Nos. 3 and 4 (1987), Erès, Paris, 1988, pages 489-494.

10 Isaac Ehrlich, "The deterrent effect of capital punishment: a question of life and death", *American Economic Review,* vol. 65, No. 3 (June 1975), pages 398-414.

11 Alfred Blumstein, Jacqueline Cohen and Daniel Nagin, eds. *Deterrence and incapacitation: estimating the effects of criminal sanctions on crime rates,* National Academy of Sciences, Washington, 1978, page 62.

12 William J. Bowers and Glenn L. Pierce, "Deterrence or brutalization: what is the effect of executions?" *Crime and Delinquency,* October 1980, pages 453-484.

13 William C. Bailey, "Disaggregation in deterrence and death penalty research: the case of murder in Chicago", *Journal of Criminal Law and Criminology,* vol. 74, No. 3, 1983, pages 827-859.

14 Alfred Blumstein, Jacqueline Cohen and Daniel Nagin, *op. cit.* page 63.

15 Franklin E. Zimring and Gordon Hawkins, *Capital punishment and the American agenda,* Cambridge University Press, Cambridge, London , New York 1986, pages 180-181.

16 *Amicus curiae* brief submitted to the US Supreme Court in 1982 in the case of *Barefoot v. Estelle.*

17 Viscount Templewood, *The shadow of the gallows,* Gollancz, London, 1951, pages 95-96.

18 United Kingdom Royal Commission on Capital Punishment 1949-1953, *op. cit.* pages 216-217, 229, 486-491.

19 Thorsten Sellin, *The penalty of death,* Sage Library of Social Research, vol. 102, Sage Publications, Beverly Hills, London, 1980, pages 110-118.

20 J. B. Coker and J. P. Martin, *Licensed to Live,* Blackwell, Oxford and New York, 1985, pages 155-159, 230.

21 Thorsten Sellin, *op. cit.* pages 55, 71-73.

22 Richard O. Lempert, "Desert and deterrence: an assessment of the moral bases of the case for capital punishment", *Michigan Law Review,* vol. 79, No. 6 (May 1981), page 1182.

23 *Woodson v. North Carolina,* 428 US 280, page 304. In a later ruling, in the case of *Sumner v. Shuman* (1987), the Supreme Court held that the prohibition of "cruel and unusual punishments" under the US Constitution guaranteed to all defendants facing possible death sentences the right "to present any relevant mitigating evidence that could justify a lesser sentence".

24 Amnesty International, *United States of America: the death penalty,* Amnesty International Publications, London, 1987.

25 Ezzat A. Fattah, "Current debates on the death penalty as a deterrent" (paper delivered at the seminar on "The death penalty in the world", Bologna, Italy, 28-30 October 1982). Amnesty International London, 1982, AI Index: ACT 05/19/82, page 13.

26 Douwe Korff, "The death penalty and terrorism" (paper delivered at the seminar on "The death penalty in the world"), *op. cit.*

27 Former Minister of State J. D. Concannon, speaking in a debate on the death penalty in the House of Commons of the United Kingdom on 19 July 1979, *House of Commons, Official Report, Parliamentary Debates (Hansard),* vol. 970, No. 42, 19 July 1979, column 2101.

28 Robert Badinter, statement at a seminar on the abolition of the death penalty and arbitrary, summary and extrajudicial executions, organized by Amnesty International at the Seventh United Nations Congress on the Prevention of Crime and the Treatment of Offenders, Milan, Italy, 27 August 1985. Amnesty International, London, 1985, AI Index: ACT 05/27/85.

29 Statement of the UN Secretary-General to the UN Economic and Social Council, 24 May 1985.

30 Bahrain, Bangladesh, Brunei Darussalam, China, Kuwait, Mauritius, Qatar, Saudi Arabia, Sri Lanka, United Arab Emirates. Nigeria introduced the death penalty for drugs offences in 1984 but abolished it in 1985. The USA introduced the penalty for drug-related killings in 1988 under federal law; it had previously existed under some state laws. Some other countries expanded the scope of the death penalty for drugs offences or made it mandatory. But most countries which introduced the death penalty for drugs offences during the past decade had not executed anyone for these offences as of mid-1988.

31 Amnesty International, *The death penalty: no solution to illicit drugs,* 1986, AI Index: ACT 05/39/86.

32 *New Straits Times,* 5 January 1985.

33 *Report of the Expert Group on Countermeasures to Drug Smuggling by Air and Sea,* Vienna, 9-13 December 1985, document prepared for the ninth special session of the Commission on Narcotic Drugs, UN document E/CN.7/1986/11/Add.3.

34 Austin Sarat and Neil Vidmar, "Public opinion, the death penalty, and the Eighth Amendment: testing the Marshall hypothesis", in *Capital Punishment in the United States,* Hugo Adam Bedau and Chester M. Pierce, eds. AMS Press, New York, 1976, pages 190-223.

35 Manfred Möhrenschlager, "The abolition of capital punishment in the Federal Republic of Germany; German experiences", in *The death penalty. Travaux de la Conférence Internationale tenue à l'Institut Supérieur International de Sciences Criminelles, Syracuse-Italie, 17 au 22 mai 1987, Revue Internationale de Droit Pénal,* vol. 58, Nos. 3 and 4 (1987), Erès, Paris, 1988, page 513.

36 *Capital losses: the price of the death penalty for New York State,* a report from the New York State Defense Association to the Senate Finance Committee and other sections of the legislature, April 1982.

3. The death penalty in practice

The death penalty is not an abstract issue. The decision to apply it means that living men and women must be singled out and put to death. It is the realities of its use around the world and not just theories about the death penalty that underline the urgent need to abolish it.

The death penalty does not provide unique protection or benefit to society but it is a unique punishment – cruel in the extreme and irrevocable. When such a punishment is applied by systems which must be subject to human error and prejudice the result is that justice will not be served but perverted.

The death penalty and discrimination

It would be surprising if such a terrible and final punishment did not tend to be inflicted mostly on the vulnerable members of a society – the poor, the mentally disturbed and members of racial, religious or ethnic minorities. Throughout the world it is applied disproportionately to the disadvantaged, and death sentences are imposed on people at the lower end of the social scale who would not have faced the death penalty if they

In Saudi Arabia the corpses of those executed by beheading are reportedly displayed publicly for 45 minutes. Public executions are often thought to be a deterrent against serious violent crimes, but research carried out in the USA suggests that executions there may have a "brutalizing" effect on society, resulting ultimately in more violence. © *Sipa Press*

had come from a more favoured sector of society. This can happen because they are less able to function effectively within the criminal justice system (through lack of knowledge, confidence or funds), or because that system in some way reflects the predominantly negative attitude towards them held by society at large and by those in power. There is also evidence that some offenders are more likely to face the death penalty if their victims come from the more favoured sectors of society.

In the USA, a detailed study tried to discover why killers of white victims in the state of Georgia during the 1970s had received the death penalty approximately 11 times more often than killers of blacks. The researchers found racial disparities in the treatment of similar offenders at every stage of the judicial process from indictment to sentencing. The most significant points at which racial disparities could affect the likelihood of an eventual death sentence were the prosecutor's decisions on a) whether or not to permit a defendant to plead to the lesser charge of voluntary man-slaughter which was not punishable by death; and b) whether or not to seek a penalty hearing at which a death sentence could be imposed once a defendant had been convicted of murder.[1] Although there was no significant racial impact in cases of killings with highly aggravated features or with low levels of aggravation, the researchers found that there was an intermediate range of cases where offenders whose victims were white were 20 per cent more likely to be sentenced to death than those whose victims were black.

In April 1987 the US Supreme Court upheld, by a five to four majority, a death sentence against which the prisoner had appealed on grounds of racial discrimination. Although the court accepted the validity of the study just cited for the purpose of argument, it ruled that Warren McCleskey, a black prisoner in Georgia, had provided insufficient evidence of "intentional discrimination" against him. The majority opinion acknowledged, however, that "disparities in sentencing are an inevitable part" of the criminal justice process and that any system of determining guilt or punishment "has its weaknesses and potential for misuse". The four dissenting judges said that the study showed a risk of racially biased discrimination that clearly violated the US Constitution. One of the four, Justice Brennan, called the risk "intolerable by any standards". Several executions which had been stayed pending the outcome of the case were carried out shortly after the Supreme Court decision.[2]

In South Africa, death sentences are imposed disproportionately on black defendants (including those officially described as "coloureds") by an almost entirely white judiciary. All South African judges are white, except for one black judge in the Bophuthatswana "homeland". Similarly, assessors appointed by the judge to sit with him or her on capital cases are almost always white. Execution is most likely if the victim is white and the defendant black. For example, between June 1982 and June 1983, 81 blacks were convicted of murdering whites and nearly half (38) were hanged. By contrast, out of 52 white defendants who were convicted of murdering whites, one was hanged. None of the 21 whites convicted of murdering blacks was executed, but 55 of the 2,208 blacks convicted of murdering blacks were hanged.

Now, what a state of society is that, which knows of no better instrument for its own defence than the hangman and which proclaims ... its own brutality as external law?
Karl Marx

28

Relatives stand by the graves of three South Africans, the first to be executed for treason in 70 years (June 1983). South Africa has one of the highest rates of judicial executions in the world, and death sentences are imposed disproportionately on the black population by a largely white judiciary.
© *Afrapix*

Most black defendants in South Africa are too poor to hire their own lawyers. In capital cases the court will appoint a defence lawyer, although this is not required by law. However, court-appointed advocates are usually the most junior members of the bar and are paid much less than privately retained advocates. The reduced fees allow for only a minimum amount of time for pre-trial consultation and do not permit the appointment of an attorney who, in the South African legal system, is crucial for the proper preparation of a capital defendant's case.

The poverty of a large number of black capital trial defendants thus jeopardizes their cases and may result in harsher penalties for them. What makes the situation still worse is that in murder trials the onus is on the accused to prove any extenuating circumstances: it is plain that inexperienced court-appointed counsel are likely to be less successful in preparing this aspect of the accused's defence. Moreover, trials are conducted in either of the two official languages, English or Afrikaans. Since neither is the first language of the vast majority of black people, black defendants must rely on interpreters, which often puts them at a disadvantage.

In Jamaica, the research team of the official Committee on Capital Punishment and Penal Reform appointed in 1979 interviewed 40 of the 81 prisoners then under sentence of death. They found that the large majority were from the lower socio-economic strata of society. They had grown up in violent neighbourhoods and many had received little or no education: four were illiterate and 21 were semi-literate. Most were first offenders

Death row in Louisiana State Penitentiary in the USA. Of the more than 2,000 prisoners on death row in the USA, the vast majority are too poor to hire their own defence counsel and almost half are from racial or ethnic minorities. Furthermore, a system of "plea bargaining" can result in US offenders whose crimes and circumstances were similar receiving very different sentences. © *Gamma*

and many appeared not to have had the benefit of adequate counsel.[3] Amnesty International's own investigations have found that most prisoners facing capital charges in Jamaica are too poor to pay for private counsel and are represented by court-appointed legal aid lawyers at their trial and local appeal. Legal aid fees are extremely low, a fraction of the minimum fee charged by a privately retained lawyer, and such cases tend to be assigned to newly-qualified, inexperienced counsel.

Is the death penalty used arbitrarily?

Even if the effects of racial discrimination or economic inequality could be eliminated, other possible sources of error and inconsistency would remain in any criminal justice system devised and administered by fallible human beings. Arbitrary decisions which deprive people of their liberty are unacceptable and should be corrected. Arbitrary decisions which deprive people of life are intolerable and without remedy.

Who lives and who dies may ultimately be determined by factors not directly related to guilt or innocence: errors, misunderstandings, different interpretations of the law, or the different orientations of prosecutors, judges or jury members. The discovery of a technical error on the part of the police, prosecuting authorities or a judge may result in a sentence being quashed. A defence lawyer's lack of skill or delayed access to evidence may lead to execution. Human fallibility makes it impossible for the death penalty to be fairly and consistently applied. As the French statesman Lafayette said in a parliamentary debate in 1830, "I shall ask for the abolition of the death penalty until I have the infallibility of human judgment demonstrated to me."

Despite elaborate legal safeguards designed to eliminate capricious and unfair sentences in the USA, whether a death sentence is ultimately imposed or not is largely determined by decisions taken by prosecutors at an early stage of the judicial process. They have wide discretion over whether or not to seek the death penalty in a given case, and in practice only a minority of crimes for which death is a possible penalty are tried as capital offences. Decisions leading to an eventual death sentence may be based on factors beyond the circumstances of the crime itself, including financial and community pressures, the race and social status of the offender and victim, and where the crime was committed.

In any retentionist country, a prisoner's fate may depend on which judge hears the case. In India, three men convicted in a murder case were sentenced to death in 1975. Although all three filed appeals to the Supreme Court, their cases were dealt with in different ways, apparently because the appeals were heard by different judges. In 1977 Kashmira Singh's death sentence was commuted at his first appeal. Jeeta Singh's appeal, however, was dismissed and he was executed in October 1981 after his petition for clemency was rejected. (A subsequent judgment implied that the court may have been unaware of the previous commutation of Kashmira Singh's sentence.) Harbans Singh's appeal was also rejected. Scheduled to be executed the same day as Jeeta Singh, he filed a review petition. At this second appeal the Supreme Court recommended commutation, noting that as Kashmira Singh's death sentence had been commuted, it would be a "sheer travesty of justice" to allow him to be executed. "It is unfortunate that Jeeta Singh could not get the benefit of the commutation of Kashmira Singh's sentence," the court observed.[4]

Risks to the innocent

The fallibility which leads to the discriminatory or arbitrary imposition of the death penalty also makes inevitable the execution of some prisoners who have been wrongly convicted. A poorly prepared defence, missing evidence, or even a decision of the investigating authorities to pin the guilt falsely on the accused can all result in wrongful conviction. Such convictions are difficult to reverse, as appellate courts will often not consider new evidence, confining themselves only to points of law.

Prisoners have been executed during the past decade despite strong doubts over their guilt. Others have been freed after a re-examination of their cases showed they had been wrongly convicted. It is impossible to determine how many innocent people have been put to death (a study published in 1987 concluded that 23 innocent people have been executed in the USA alone this century – see below). Judicial reviews or investigations into possible error rarely occur once a prisoner has died. What is certain is that abolition is the only way to ensure that such mistakes do not occur.

Howsoever careful may be the procedural safeguards erected by the law before death penalty can be imposed, it is impossible to eliminate the chance of judicial error.
Former Chief Justice P N Bhagwati, Supreme Court of India

During a debate on the death penalty in the House of Commons in the United Kingdom in April 1987, Roy Jenkins, a former Home Secretary (the cabinet minister responsible for decisions on the commutation of death sentences), said that during two terms in office, "I had to deal with 10 capital cases in which there were varying degrees of doubt, some quite simply amounting to wrongful conviction." Not all of the prisoners were hanged, "... but two were, and more would have been had the death penalty not been abolished in 1965." He said, "It is my view that the frailty of human judgment ... is too great to support the finality of capital punishment."[5]

During the past decade prisoners under sentence of death in several countries have been freed after the courts found that they had been wrongly convicted. Often such wrongful convictions are reversed only after persistent efforts and there are probably many cases the true facts of which have never come to light.

In Japan, Sakae Menda was sentenced to death in March 1950 for a murder committed in 1948. Thirty-three years after that sentence, in 1983, he was found not guilty and released. For over three decades he had lived with the prospect of execution. He had applied unsuccessfully for a retrial five times before his sixth request was granted in 1979, after the Japanese Supreme Court in 1975 eased the standards for granting retrials. He had originally confessed to the crime, but later retracted his confession and said that he was innocent. Other evidence presented at the original trial was questioned and an alibi was produced for the time of the murder. He was acquitted after the retrial court accepted his alibi and decided that his original confession was not credible.

In Taiwan, Chang Kuo-chieh, aged 74, who had been convicted of a murder committed in 1973, was acquitted by the Taiwan High Court in February 1982. He had confessed to the crime, but parts of his statement contradicted the facts of the case or did not match the results of investigations into the crime. After his original conviction, the courts reconsidered the case 11 times before eventually declaring him innocent.[6]

Cases in which incompetence and corruption led to innocent people being sentenced to death have recently been exposed by news media in the USSR, as part of an emerging debate on the merits of abolishing the death penalty. One case involved Vladimir Toisev, a villager from the Belorussian republic, sentenced to death in 1970 for murder. He spent 18 months awaiting execution before having his sentence commuted (but was released only in 1987, after 14 years and eight months' imprisonment). In October 1987, *Znamya yunosti*, Banner of Youth, said investigators had extracted a confession from Vladimir Toisev during night-time interrogations, and had beaten his 15-year-old brother in order to obtain corroborative evidence. When the real culprit emerged they suppressed the information to conceal what they had done.

A 1987 study presented evidence that 350 people convicted of capital crimes in the USA between 1900 and 1985 were innocent of the crimes charged. In most cases the discovery of new evidence resulted in acquittal, pardon, commutation of sentence or dismissal of the charges, often years after the original conviction. Some prisoners escaped execution by minutes, but 23 were actually executed.[7]

It is curious, but till that moment I had never realized what it means to destroy a healthy, conscious man. When I saw the prisoner step aside to avoid the puddle I saw the mystery, the unspeakable wrongness, of cutting a life short when it is in full tide. This man was not dying, he was alive just as we are alive ... His eyes saw the yellow gravel and the grey walls, and his brain still remembered, foresaw, reasoned – even about puddles. He and we were a party of men walking together, seeing, hearing, feeling, understanding the same world; and in two minutes, with a sudden snap, one of us would be gone – one mind less, one world less.

George Orwell, writer, UK

Clemency as a safeguard

When all judicial appeals have been exhausted, a death sentence may still be postponed or set aside through the exercise of clemency. This usually takes the form of a decision to commute the death sentence to a lesser punishment such as life imprisonment. Deriving from an ancient prerogative of monarchs who had life and death powers over their subjects, clemency is usually exercised by the chief executive of the country or other jurisdiction in which the death penalty is used. (The related terms "mercy", "pardon" and "reprieve" are sometimes used to refer to clemency, although these can also sometimes have other meanings: reprieve, for example, often refers to a temporary suspension in the carrying out of a punishment.)

The last hope for a prisoner sentenced to death, clemency can be used to correct possible errors, to mitigate the harshness of punishment and to compensate for the rigidity of the criminal law by taking into account factors relevant to an individual case for which the law makes no allowance.

The right of anyone sentenced to death to seek clemency is well established in international human rights instruments.[8] As shown in this report, virtually all countries make legal provision for the exercise of clemency in death penalty cases. Yet the exercise of clemency, even if done generously, remains essentially arbitrary – and in some cases hardly seems to be considered at all.

In deciding whether or not to grant clemency one authority may seek the advice of an appointed commission, review medical and prison reports and judicial records, and interview or receive submissions from people connected with the case, including the prisoner's relatives and friends. Another authority may consider that only the most perfunctory examination of the case is sufficient. Some authorities may try to give the prisoner every benefit of the doubt; others may consistently uphold death sentences imposed by the courts.

Some authorities may apply a more generous standard than the courts are allowed to use in sentencing, making extra allowances for provocation or mental abnormality, or taking account of such factors as a public feeling that the execution would be unjust. The authority may decide to commute a sentence because he or she "feels that despite the verdict of the jury there is a scintilla of doubt as to the prisoner's guilt... [because] the death sentence differs from any other sentence because of its irrevocable character..."[9] Another authority may hold that such matters are for the courts and that the law should generally be allowed to take its course.

Although some authorities may be generous in exercising clemency, others do so on very limited grounds only, grounds which are sometimes not publicly known. An Amnesty International mission which visited four US states in June 1985 found that none of those states gave reasons for granting or denying clemency. In practice, the authorities took a very narrow view of the role of executive clemency, apparently considering that the current system of judicial review ensured that death sentences were fairly imposed and had largely dispensed with the need to exercise the prerogative of mercy.[10]

Even an official who wishes to give the prisoner every benefit of the doubt may lack the time and facilities to go into the matter thoroughly. Viscount Templewood, who during two years as Home Secretary in the United Kingdom had to decide the fate of 47 prisoners sentenced to death, later wrote, "More than once, I had two capital cases to decide at the same time. Capital cases were brought to me in the midst of a mass of cabinet and departmental work. There were dozens of other urgent questions that were claiming my attention, yet I had to say the fatal yes or no within a few hours, or at most a few days. My information ... inevitably came to me at second hand. My decision was bound to be based on the advice of others... Each case that came before me impressed me more strongly with the inevitable danger of making a mistake."[11]

A prisoner's fate may be determined by the personal decision of an official, by the policy of a political party or by other factors which have nothing to do with the circumstances of the individual case.

After New Zealand's Labour Party took office in 1935, for example, all death sentences were regularly commuted, and in 1941 the death penalty was abolished for murder. After the Nationalist Party regained power in 1950, the death penalty was reinstated and executions were resumed. Arguing successfully for abolition of the death penalty in a 1961 parliamentary debate, Minister of Justice J. R. Hanan said: "In the last 25 years the penalty has been changing with every change of government. The first result is that the punishment the murderer receives is not necessarily governed by the gravity of his crime. On the contrary, what may determine whether he is to live or die is which party is in power." [12]

Despite its defects, clemency is still seen as a last (and, sometimes, only) means of correcting judicial anomalies. But it is an illusion to suppose that the inherent arbitrariness and fallibility of human justice can somehow be made right by a process which itself is arbitrary. As the Indian Supreme Court Justice Krishna Iyer observed in a judgment in the case of *Rajendra Prasad v. State of Uttar Pradesh* (1979), the courts must not be "complacent in the thought that even if they err the clemency power will and does operate to save many a life condemned by the highest court to death ... Executive commutation is no substitute for judicial justice; at best it is administrative policy, and at worst pressure-based partiality".

Violations of international restrictions and safeguards

The foundation for international human rights protection was laid in the Universal Declaration of Human Rights, adopted by the UN General Assembly in 1948. Since then many further texts have been adopted at both international and regional levels to strengthen the legal protection of human rights and create mechanisms to ensure their enforcement. Although an outright prohibition of the death penalty has not yet been agreed internationally, the nations of the world have nonetheless agreed on minimum standards which should be observed in countries which retain the punishment. But even these minimum standards continue to be violated, as shown in this report.

The sources of these standards are varied.

Foremost is the International Covenant on Civil and Political Rights

(ICCPR), adopted by the UN General Assembly in 1966 and binding on all states which become parties to it. Other countries are also expected to observe its provisions: thus in resolution 35/172 of 15 December 1980, the UN General Assembly urged member states "to respect as a minimum standard" the relevant articles.

The Geneva Conventions of 12 August 1949 and the Additional Protocols to those conventions contain safeguards on the use of the death penalty in armed conflict.

The "Safeguards guaranteeing Protection of the Rights of Those Facing the Death Penalty" (the "ECOSOC safeguards"), adopted by the UN Economic and Social Council (ECOSOC) in 1984 and endorsed by the UN General Assembly the same year, list the most important restrictions and safeguards on the death penalty, drawn largely from the ICCPR.

At the regional level, the American Convention on Human Rights is binding on all members of the Organization of American States which become parties to it. Its provisions on the death penalty are similar to those in the ICCPR.[13]

These international texts restrict the offences for which the death penalty may be used. They exclude the use of the penalty for certain categories of offenders and provide for procedures to be followed in all death penalty cases, including procedures for fair trial, appeal to a higher court and consideration of clemency. (The main texts are given in the appendices to this report, along with information on procedures for ensuring their observance and a chart showing which restrictions and safeguards appear in which texts.)

Restriction to the 'most serious crimes': the death penalty as an exceptional punishment

The concept of proportionality has long been used in establishing penalties: the severity of a punishment should not be disproportionate to the gravity of the offence. The concept of proportionality between the severest of punishments and the gravest of crimes is embodied in Article 6 of the ICCPR: "In countries which have not abolished the death penalty, sentence of death may be imposed only for the most serious crimes". Language to the same effect appears in Article 4 of the American Convention on Human Rights.

The 1984 ECOSOC safeguards on the death penalty state that the scope of the "most serious crimes" punishable by death "should not go beyond intentional crimes, with lethal or other extremely grave consequences." Here the proportionality is between the loss of the offender's life and the "lethal or other extremely grave consequences" of the crimes of which the offender has been convicted.

In a general comment on Article 6 of the ICCPR issued in 1982, the Human Rights Committee set up under the Covenant declared that states parties to the Covenant which have not abolished the death penalty "are obliged to limit its use and, in particular, to abolish it for other than the 'most serious crimes'" (see Appendix 3). The long lists of crimes punishable by death in the country entries in this report show how far this stricture is from being observed.

My primary concern here is not compassion for the murderer. My concern is for the society which adopts vengeance as an acceptable motive for its collective behaviour. If we make that choice, we will snuff out some of that boundless hope and confidence in ourselves and other people, which has marked our maturing as a free people.
Pierre Elliott Trudeau, former Prime Minister of Canada

In its general comment on Article 6 of the ICCPR, the Human Rights Committee stated that the death penalty should be "a quite exceptional measure". This notion has been expressed in court judgments. In the case of *Bachan Singh v. State of Punjab*, for example, the Indian Supreme Court ruled in 1980 that the death penalty for murder should not be used "save in the rarest of rare cases". The notion is embodied in the laws of a number of countries. In the USSR, for example, the death penalty is described in the current criminal code as "an exceptional measure of punishment until its complete abolition".

Many countries, while retaining the death penalty in law, carry out executions not at all or only rarely. In some countries, however, the death penalty is far from exceptional. Each year a very few countries account for the majority of all executions recorded by Amnesty International, and a handful of countries regularly carry out 100 executions or more a year.[14] Of the 3,399 executions recorded by Amnesty International worldwide between 1985 and mid-1988, 2,219 – 65 per cent – were carried out in just four countries (see Appendix 17, table 1).

The notion of restricting the scope of the death penalty and making it, at most, an exceptional punishment, should be seen within the framework of the goal of total abolition. In its general comment the Human Rights Committee said that Article 6 of the ICCPR "refers generally to abolition in terms which strongly suggest ... that abolition is desirable". In 1971 the UN General Assembly affirmed that "in order fully to guarantee the right to life, provided for in Article 3 of the Universal Declaration of Human Rights, the main objective to be pursued is that of progressively restricting the number of offences for which the death penalty may be imposed,

Salah Shawki (second from left) receiving a death sentence for rape, which until 1980 was not a capital offence in Egypt. Countries which extend the scope of the death penalty are acting contrary to the United Nations General Assembly call for progressive restriction of offences punishable by death. Moreover, all possibilities of rehabilitating an offender are abruptly terminated when sentence is passed. © *Popperfoto*

Murder is the single crime most commonly punishable by death today. Many countries which use the death penalty execute only prisoners convicted of murder: as shown in this report, of the 63 countries known to have carried out executions between 1985 and mid-1988, 25 did so only for murder. Elsewhere, however, there have been executions for a wide range of crimes, including some offences not resulting in loss of life or even involving the use of violence.

Between 1985 and mid-1988 prisoners were executed for adultery (Iran, Saudi Arabia), prostitution (Iran), running a brothel and showing pornographic films (China), taking bribes (USSR), embezzlement (China, Ghana, Somalia) and economic corruption (Iraq), as well as other crimes not resulting in loss of life such as kidnapping (China, Malaysia), rape (China, Egypt, South Africa, Syria, Thailand, Tunisia, United Arab Emirates), robbery or armed robbery (China, Ghana, Iran, Kenya, Republic of Korea, Nigeria, Saudi Arabia, Syria, Taiwan, Tunisia, Uganda, United Arab Emirates, Zaire, Zambia) and drug-trafficking (China, Iran, Malaysia, Saudi Arabia, Singapore, Syria, Thailand).

with a view to the desirability of abolishing this punishment in all countries".[15]

The objective was reaffirmed by the General Assembly in resolution 32/61 of 8 December 1977 (see Appendix 8). In line with this objective is the principle that the scope of the death penalty should not be expanded. This principle is enunciated in Article 4 of the American Convention on Human Rights, which states that application of the penalty "shall not be extended to crimes to which it does not presently apply" and that "The death penalty shall not be re-established in states that have abolished it."

Sixteen countries have abolished the death penalty during the past decade (see Appendix 16), and several others have restricted its scope. But 38 countries have enacted laws extending the death penalty to new crimes, although not all of them have carried out executions for those crimes. As shown in this report the death penalty has been introduced for a variety of offences, including rape, armed robbery, infanticide, drug-trafficking, black marketeering, illegal currency dealing, military offences, use of explosives, conspiracy against the government, membership of specified banned organizations, abetment of *sati* (self-immolation of a widow), and sorcery, magic and similar practices which might seriously harm the victim or cause disturbances.

Non-retroactive use

A basic principle of judicial fairness, spelled out in international instruments (see appendices), is that a person should not be judged guilty for something which was not a crime at the time, or punished more severely than was then provided by law. The death penalty has, nonetheless, been used retroactively in several cases during the past decade. As mentioned in Chapter 2, three men were publicly executed in Nigeria in 1985 after being convicted of drugs offences under a decree introduced by the military government in 1984 with retroactive effect. At least one of the three had committed the offence before the decree was introduced. After widespread protests and a change of military government, the decree was amended the next year to remove the death penalty for drugs offences.

In Nepal, bomb explosions in June 1985 led to the introduction of a Destructive Crimes (Special Control and Punishment) Act providing for the death penalty with retroactive effect. In 1987 a special court sentenced four men to death *in absentia*. They were convicted under the act of involvement in the bombings, which had been carried out before the law came into force.

Other cases where the death penalty was used retroactively are included later in this chapter.

Exclusion of young people

The notion that young people should not suffer the death penalty stems from the recognition that they are not fully mature – hence, not fully responsible – and that they are more likely to be capable of reform. This notion has been incorporated into international human rights texts dealing with the death penalty. A minimum age of 18 years at the time of the offence was established in the death penalty provisions of the Fourth Geneva Convention of 12 August 1949 Relative to the Protection of Civilian Persons in Time of War. The same minimum is set by Article 6 of the ICCPR, the American Convention on Human Rights and the ECOSOC safeguards.

As shown in Appendix 17, table 2, at least 72 countries have laws specifically setting a minimum age of 18 years or more below which the death penalty may not be used. A further 12 countries may be presumed to exclude the use of the death penalty against offenders under 18 by virtue of their accession to the ICCPR or the American Convention on Human Rights without reservation to the relevant provisions of those treaties.

The fact that these provisions are so widespread, the fact that leading international instruments set a minimum age of 18 and the fact that the death penalty is so rarely used against offenders under 18, even in countries where the law sets a minimum age lower than 18 or none at all, imply that the minimum age limit of 18 may be taken as the currently accepted standard under customary international law. However, at least eight people who were under 18 at the time of the offence have been executed in four countries during the past decade: one in Bangladesh, one in Barbados, three in Pakistan and three in the USA. An unknown number of young people under 18 have also been executed in Iran and Iraq.

Responding to pressure, several US states have raised their minimum age for the death penalty during the past few years. But as of August 1988,

Retribution or legal vengeance seems difficult enough for a government to justify where adult offenders are involved and vengeance against children for their misdeeds seems quite beyond justification... The spectacle of our society seeking legal vengeance through the execution of children should not be countenanced by the ABA [American Bar Association].

American Bar Association, Criminal Justice Section, USA

International human rights standards prohibit the use of the death penalty on those aged under 18 at the time of the crime. However, at least six countries have carried out executions on such citizens in the last ten years. Shown here is Mohammed Selim, executed in Bangladesh reportedly at the age of 17 (although his age was disputed by the authorities).

no fewer than 28 prisoners in 12 US states were under sentence of death for crimes committed when they were below 18 years of age.[16]

Exclusion of the elderly

The American Convention on Human Rights states that death sentences may not be imposed on people who were over 70 years old at the time of the offence. Neither the ICCPR nor the ECOSOC safeguards exclude the elderly from the death penalty, but in August 1988 the UN Committee on Crime Prevention and Control decided to recommend to the UN Economic and Social Council that UN member states retaining the death penalty should be advised to establish "a maximum age beyond which a person may not be sentenced to death or executed". (Such maximum age limits are already provided by law in several countries.) The Economic and Social Council was due to consider the recommendation in 1989.

Several people over 70 either at the time of the offence or of sentencing are known to have been executed or sentenced to death in the past decade. In Sudan, Mahmoud Mohamed Taha, the 76-year-old leader of the Republican Brothers, an Islamic organization, was sentenced to death and hanged in Khartoum in 1985 for the non-violent expression of his beliefs. He was executed despite a provision in Sudan's laws which excludes anyone over 70 from the death penalty (his case is described later in this chapter). Fyodor Fedorenko, a 78-year-old prisoner deported from the USA, was executed in the USSR in 1987 after being convicted of war crimes committed during World War II. Another elderly man, Andrija Artukovic, aged 86, extradited from the USA, was convicted of war crimes

39

Several people aged over 70 have been executed in the past decade. The execution of 76-year-old Mahmoud Mohamed Taha in Sudan (seen here with his wife and daughters) caused an international outcry: it contravened Sudanese law and Mahmoud Mohamed Taha himself was a prisoner of conscience detained on account of his non-violent political activities.

in Yugoslavia and sentenced to death in May 1986. Despite public pressure for the execution to be carried out Zagreb district court ruled in April 1987 that his health had deteriorated to the point that he could not legally be executed. He died in a prison hospital in 1988.

Occasionally a prisoner is kept under sentence of death even though he or she is very old. Sadamichi Hirasawa, an artist, died of pneumonia in a Japanese prison hospital on 10 May 1987 at the age of 95. He had been under sentence of death for 37 years, longer than any other prisoner in the world known to Amnesty International. He had been sentenced to death in May 1950 after being convicted of killing 12 bank staff during a 1948 bank robbery. Initially he had confessed to the murders, but he retracted the confession at his trial, saying it had been coerced. After that he had consistently maintained his innocence and had applied for a retrial 17 times; every application was rejected by the courts.

Exclusion of pregnant women and new mothers

Under Article 6 of the ICCPR: "Sentence of death ... shall not be carried out on pregnant women." The same exclusion appears in the American Convention on Human Rights. New mothers are not to be executed under the Additional Protocols to the Geneva Conventions of 1949. The 1984 ECOSOC safeguards preclude the execution both of pregnant women and new mothers. The reason for these provisions is to avoid harm to the unborn or newly-born child.

As documented in this report, at least 84 countries which retain the death penalty in law specifically preclude its use against pregnant women. The exact restriction varies: commonly, pregnant women are not to be executed, and in some laws there is a specified period after childbirth during which they must be allowed to live before being executed. In some countries pregnant women are exempted from being sentenced to death.

Amnesty International has not recorded any case of a pregnant woman being sentenced to death or executed during the past decade.

In at least two countries, Mongolia and Guatemala, women are exempted from the penalty. A Mongolian representative told the Human Rights Committee in 1980 that one of the reasons for this was that "exemption of women from the death penalty was a significant step towards its complete abolition".[17]

Exclusion on grounds of mental incapacity

It is generally accepted that people who are not of sound mind should not be held criminally responsible for their acts and, by extension, that such offenders would not be sentenced to death under the normal workings of a national criminal justice system. A related principle is that a prisoner under sentence of death who is of unsound mind should not be executed, on the grounds that such a prisoner is incapable of understanding the nature of the punishment.

In the past decade, several prisoners who were either mentally ill or mentally retarded have been executed in the USA, despite restrictions guarding against this. In January 1986 James Terry Roach was executed in South Carolina even though the trial judge had found him to be mentally retarded, to be suffering from a personality disorder (later identified as the hereditary illness Huntington's chorea) and to have acted under the domination of an older man, a co-defendant in the case. Furthermore, at 17, James Roach was a minor at the time of the crime.
© Jeff Amberg

These principles are not enunciated in the ICCPR or the American Convention on Human Rights, but the ECOSOC safeguards on the death penalty state that death sentences shall not be carried out "on persons who have become insane". In August 1988 the UN Committee on Crime Prevention and Control took a step further by recommending to the Economic and Social Council that UN member states retaining the death penalty be advised to eliminate the death penalty "for persons suffering from mental retardation or extremely limited mental competence whether at the stage of sentence or execution". The Economic and Social Council was to consider this recommendation in 1989.

Several factors suggest that a substantial number of mentally incapacitated people may be sentenced to death and executed: the lack of agreement on the criteria and diagnosis of insanity, and the extent to which "diminished responsibility" should apply to lesser forms of mental illness or other abnormalities such as very low intelligence; and the scarcity of facilities for diagnosing mental illness in many parts of the world. In the USA, the evidence suggests that many prisoners under sentence of death may be mentally handicapped or suffer from mental illness. Since 1984 at least six people diagnosed as mentally handicapped or as borderline cases have been executed there, and at least five prisoners suffering from mental illness have been executed in the country during the same period.

Unfair trials

Defendants on trial for their lives must obviously be afforded scrupulously fair trials. When accepted standards for a fair trial are ignored or set aside the death penalty becomes open to political abuse and the risk of executing the innocent is increased.

Many prisoners during the past decade have been executed in cases where procedural safeguards were deficient or absent. As shown in this report, cases continue to be heard in special courts, often in secret, without adequate legal representation for the defendant and before judges who are not always competent or independent. Proceedings have been speeded up, leaving insufficient time to prepare an adequate defence. Access to counsel has been limited; sometimes there is no legal representation at all. Special courts have been empowered to pass death sentences, often with no right of appeal; the authority of such courts has been extended into the realm of the ordinary criminal law, supplanting the regular courts and removing safeguards previously afforded by the latter. In some countries executions have been carried out within hours of sentencing, leaving no time for appeals or petitions for clemency.

Article 14 of the ICCPR enumerates standards for a fair trial. These include the right of anyone facing a criminal charge to a fair and public hearing by a competent, independent and impartial tribunal; the right to be presumed innocent until proved guilty; the right to be informed promptly of the nature and cause of the crimes with which the defendant is charged; the right to have adequate time and facilities for the preparation of a defence; the right to communicate with counsel of the defendant's choosing; the right to free legal assistance for defendants

To repay brutality with brutality, in my opinion, does not serve any useful purpose.
President Sir Dawda Jawara, Gambia

unable to pay for it; the right to examine witnesses for the prosecution and to present witnesses for the defence; the right of everyone convicted of a crime to have the conviction and sentence reviewed by a higher tribunal. The American Convention on Human Rights and other regional instruments also include standards for fair trial.

The norms for fair trial have been incorporated explicitly into international human rights standards on the death penalty, including the ICCPR.[18] Although this Covenant is binding under international law only on states which become parties to it, the UN General Assembly has especially made clear its wish that fair trial standards should be respected in death penalty cases in all countries.[19]

In 1984 the Economic and Social Council adopted its set of safeguards on the death penalty, incorporating the ICCPR's fair trial provisions. The ECOSOC safeguards provide, in particular, that a person may be sentenced to death only on the basis of "clear and convincing evidence leaving no room for an alternative explanation of the facts". Anyone sentenced to death must have the right to appeal to a higher court, "and steps should be taken to ensure that such appeals shall become mandatory". Also, a death sentence must not be carried out "pending any appeal or other recourse procedure or other proceeding relating to pardon or commutation of the sentence". Later in 1984, and in subsequent years, the General Assembly made clear its wish that the ECOSOC safeguards be observed.[20]

Many people, including political prisoners, have been sentenced to death after unfair trials. In Turkey, for example (above), death sentences have been imposed after mass trials (with sometimes more than 1,000 defendants) which have not met international standards of fairness. In one such trial in 1986 the judge ruled that confessions extracted under torture could be used in evidence. © *Sipa Press*

Despite the undisputed acceptance at the international level of safe-guards for fair trials in all death penalty cases, many countries have empowered special or military courts to pass death sentences without affording full fair trial safeguards or right of appeal. Often such courts are set up in periods of political tension, during periods of civil unrest or after coup attempts, and they frequently operate in a highly charged political atmosphere which militates against a defendant receiving a fair trial. Although some special courts have been abolished during the decade, such courts still retain jurisdiction over death penalty cases in at least 37 countries at the time of writing. At least three other countries have laws which do not provide for the right of appeal in some death penalty cases.[21] Although lack of such provisions do not necessarily result in the death penalty being used, executions have been carried out after procedurally deficient trials in at least 20 countries during the past 10 years, and in some countries there have been a great many such executions. Thousands of prisoners have been executed during the past decade after procedures which did not conform to international norms for a fair trial.

After the creation of the Islamic Republic of Iran in 1979, Islamic Revolutionary Courts were set up to try a series of offences, including crimes against internal and external security and the Islamic offence of "corruption on earth" and being "at enmity with God", a broad term which could be applied to political opponents of the government. Of the many people executed, Amnesty International knows of no case in which a defendant before an Islamic Revolutionary Court on a political charge was permitted to be represented by a lawyer or to exercise the right of appeal. Often executions were carried out so soon after sentencing as to leave no time to appeal or petition for clemency. In some cases a presumption of the guilt of the accused meant that the trial lasted a matter of minutes and consisted only of the reading out of the charge and the passing of sentence. There have been reports of convictions in political cases being based on confessions which may have been extracted under torture. Of the thousands of people who have been executed in Iran since 1979, many were tried and executed in secret for their non-violent political opposition to the government and some are reported to have been executed for their religious beliefs.

In Iraq, where hundreds of executions are reported to be carried out each year, most death sentences are imposed by permanent or temporary special courts. The majority of these trials are held *in camera*; access to a lawyer (government-appointed) is severely restricted (in some instances confined to the day of the trial), and confessions extracted under torture are frequently used as a basis for conviction. Defendants charged with capital offences are frequently denied the right to call witnesses on their behalf or to submit evidence refuting the charges. The role of defence counsel is said to be often restricted to pleading for clemency or reduction of sentence. The government only rarely makes public the fact of an execution. Many executions, particularly of political prisoners and army deserters, are reported to be carried out secretly in prisons. Among those executed have been members of banned political parties, suspected government opponents, students and civilians arrested as hostages, including children. The bodies of some executed prisoners have been

The fruit of my experience has this bitter after-taste: that I do not now believe that any one of the hundreds of executions I carried out has in any way acted as a deterrent against future murder. Capital punishment, in my view, achieved nothing except revenge.
Albert Pierrepoint, former executioner, UK

After the overthrow of the Liberian Government in 1980, 13 members of the former administration were executed after unfair trials. Shown on trial before a military tribunal is the former Chairperson of the True Whig Party, Reginald Townsend. He was allowed no defence counsel and when he attempted to speak in his own defence he was ordered by the tribunal chair to "keep it short". He was executed shortly afterwards. © *Camera Press*

returned to their families bearing marks of torture.

In China, defendants have no right to be presumed innocent; access to a lawyer is limited and few people are able to exercise effectively the right to defence. Safeguards for a fair trial were further curtailed in 1983 with the introduction of legislation aimed at speeding up the procedures for prosecution, trial, appeal and review, in connection with a nationwide campaign against crime. Defendants were denied the right to receive a copy of the indictment before trial, and the time limit for appeal was reduced from 10 to three days. During the first three months of the campaign, Amnesty International recorded over 600 executions in only a few places in China; the total number of executions is believed to have been in the thousands.

After a military government took power in Nigeria, a decree was issued in 1984 setting up Robbery and Firearms Tribunals empowered to impose death sentences for armed robbery. A serving or retired High Court judge may preside alone or with a senior military officer and a senior police officer who are not required to have legal training. There is no right of appeal to a higher court and the proceedings have been extremely swift in some cases. For example, Dafaru Oluwole and seven other people were convicted of armed robbery and sentenced to death by a Robbery and Firearms Tribunal in Kwara State on 17 July 1984. All eight prisoners reportedly claimed they were innocent. The sentences were confirmed by the State Military Governor on 18 July and the eight

45

prisoners were publicly shot by firing-squad the next day. Between 1985 and mid-1988, 439 people are known to have been executed for armed robbery in Nigeria, but the true figure is undoubtedly higher.

In Guatemala, the military government that seized power in 1982 issued a decree establishing secret military tribunals empowered to pass death sentences for a wide range of political offences. Four prisoners convicted under the decree were executed by firing-squad in a cemetery at dawn on 17 September. The impending executions had been announced only 12 hours previously, when the men's families first learned of their relatives' whereabouts (they had "disappeared" some time earlier). Another 11 prisoners were executed the following year. There were inconsistencies in the evidence against those executed, and strong indications that they had "confessed" under torture. Most of them had no access to defence counsel, and an appeals mechanism was instituted only after international protests following the first executions. The decree was rescinded after a military overthrow of the government in August 1983.

An instrument of political repression

Over the years, efforts have been made to prevent the death penalty being used in blatantly political ways. Since the mid-19th century a number of countries have included provisions in their laws or constitutions to prohibit or limit the use of the death penalty in political cases; the latest to do so was Côte d'Ivoire, whose National Assembly in 1981 modified the Penal Code to exclude the death penalty for political offences. The American Convention on Human Rights includes a provision that "In no case shall capital punishment be inflicted for political offences or related common crimes", and in 1981 the UN Sub-Commission on Prevention of Discrimination and Protection of Minorities adopted a resolution recommending abolition of the death penalty for political offences.[22] Yet during the past decade the death penalty has continued to be used as an instrument of political repression. Rulers have executed their political rivals, or have tried to use the threat of the death penalty to silence their opponents. The death penalty has been used to consolidate power after coups and coup attempts. Members of opposition political groups have been eliminated as a matter of political expediency.

Even when executions have not taken place, the threat of execution has been present through laws providing for the death penalty for non-violent political acts such as forming or being involved in political parties or groups "opposed to the principles of the al-Fateh Revolution of September" 1969 (Libya); organizing a "counter-revolutionary" secret society (China); "flight from the state and refusal to return to the fatherland on the part of a person sent on service or allowed temporarily to leave the state" (Albania); "committing treason against the country and the people by illegally leaving or attempting to leave the country" (Ethiopia); carrying out activities to illegally overthrow the government (Taiwan); publishing or distributing "anti-state propaganda" (Somalia); collusion in any verbal or physical act hostile to the revolution (Syria); any deed, speech or writing incompatible with the socialist order (Syria); publicly and flagrantly insulting the President of the Republic or his deputy (Iraq).

The death penalty is sometimes used by governments to rid themselves of political opposition. In Iran 1) the corpses of opposition activists are displayed in Kerman (© *Absalon/ Sipa Press*) 2) condemned Kurdish rebels are shot by firing-squad (© *Associated Press*) and 3) a member of the People's Mojahedine Organization of Iran is hanged. His body was left on display for other prisoners to see. Thousands of political prisoners were executed in the early 1980s in Iran and at least hundreds more were put to death in mass executions after July 1988.

In some cases the death penalty has been directed at prominent individual political opponents. Zulfikar Ali Bhutto, founder of the Pakistan People's Party (PPP) and Prime Minister of Pakistan since 1973, was overthrown in a military coup by General Zia ul-Haq in July 1977, arrested in September 1977 and charged with complicity in the murder of a political opponent (in 1974). In a published interview, General Zia referred to Zulfikar Ali Bhutto as "a murderer" who would "not be able to escape severe punishment".

Three months after the trial began in October 1977, Zulfikar Ali Bhutto said that the presiding judge was biased and had acted in an insulting and humiliating way towards him. The most direct evidence against him, to the effect that he had personally ordered the elimination of the man murdered, was given by the former Director General of the Federal Security Force. Amnesty International noted in 1978 that this man "was himself indicted upon these charges; however, he had been granted a pardon at an earlier stage and therefore his evidence, which is that of an informer, should be regarded with considerable suspicion".

During the trial the government conducted a huge propaganda campaign to discredit the deposed Prime Minister; lengthy white papers were issued and there were regular television and radio programs accusing him of being corrupt, cruel and unpatriotic. During widespread agitation in support of Zulfikar Ali Bhutto, hundreds of his supporters

47

were imprisoned, flogged and allegedly tortured under martial law regulations. His party newspaper was banned and all political activities were outlawed.

In March 1978 Zulfikar Ali Bhutto was convicted and sentenced to death. His appeal to the Supreme Court was rejected in February 1979 by a vote of four to three, and a review petition was rejected by the Supreme Court in March 1979. Appeals to President Zia from the UN Secretary-General, Pope John Paul II, US President Jimmy Carter, King Khaled of Saudi Arabia and the leaders of most European and Arab countries were rejected. Zulfikar Ali Bhutto was hanged in secret in the early hours of 4 April 1979; his execution was announced nine hours later, after he had already been buried.

Mahmoud Mohamed Taha, 76-year-old leader of the Republican Brothers movement and a persistent critic of the Sudanese Government, was arrested with four other members of the movement on 5 January 1985. The movement advocated a new approach to Islam and had engaged in non-violent political activities. On 7 January the five men went on trial, charged with "undermining or subverting the constitution", a capital offence. They admitted distributing leaflets calling for the repeal of Islamic laws introduced in 1983, appealing for a peaceful political solution to the conflict in southern Sudan and advocating an Islamic revival based on the *Sunna* (the teachings of the Prophet).

The five prisoners were found guilty of subversion the next day and sentenced to death. On 16 January the Court of Appeal confirmed the sentences, ruling that the five men were also guilty of "heresy" in advocating an unacceptable form of Islam, an offence they had not been charged with. The court gave the defendants one month in which to "repent or die". On 17 January President Jaafar Mohamed Nimeiri, exercising his presidential review of the sentences, confirmed them and reduced the repentance deadline to three days.

Mahmoud Mohamed Taha was hanged before a large crowd in Kober Prison in Khartoum North on 18 January. The day after they had been forced to watch their leader being hanged, the other four men appeared on television, publicly "repenting" their opposition to the Islamic laws and declaring Mahmoud Mohamed Taha a heretic. They were then freed.

In other cases, governments have sentenced their political opponents to death in the hope of silencing them or winning them over to their side.

Kim Dae-jung, who had been narrowly defeated in a presidential election in the Republic of Korea (South Korea) in 1971, spent much of the next eight years in prison, exile or under house arrest before his rearrest on 17 May 1980. His arrest followed a wave of strikes and student demonstrations and he was accused of instigating unrest in an attempt to overthrow the government. He was accused of being a communist and of organizing an insurrection in the city of Kwangju between 18 and 27 May 1980. His trial before a military tribunal opened in the capital, Seoul, on 14 August. Access was restricted and Amnesty International delegates were denied entry to observe the trial. The prosecution based its case on confessions made by Kim Dae-jung and his co-defendants during interrogation. Kim Dae-jung categorically denied the charges. He told the court he had been kept in an underground cell for 60 days, questioned 15

Here it is like a little factory where they just process hangings.
Brian Currin, Director of Lawyers for Human Rights, South Africa

48

hours a day and threatened with torture until he signed some documents. His co-defendants stated that they had been beaten, intimidated and deprived of sleep to force them to sign confessions. Severe limitations were placed on the defence: several civil rights lawyers had been taken into custody beforehand and others were intimidated into not taking up the case; no witnesses for the defence were allowed to appear.

During the trial, the Korean press were ordered to print in full the 156-page indictment but were not allowed to report the denials made by the defendants.

Kim Dae-jung was sentenced to death on 17 September 1980. On 3 November the sentence was upheld by a military court of appeal and finalized by the Supreme Court. On 23 January 1981 President Chun Doo-hwan commuted the sentence to life imprisonment after appeals from the governments of the USA, Japan and European countries. Kim Dae-jung was released from prison in December 1982. He spent two years in the USA before returning to South Korea in 1985. He was one of the main candidates in the presidential election of 1987 and now heads the leading opposition party in the National Assembly.

In an interview after his release, Kim Dae-jung said that while he was in prison awaiting trial, "A high-ranking military junta officer came to see me and he proposed two choices... He told me: 'If you are cooperative with us we can save your life and we can guarantee everything except becoming president.' That is, they would allow me to become prime minister ... anything except president. He also told me: 'Otherwise you would be surely killed. I am very frank with you. You should decide here, to save your life or to abandon your life.' But I refused to cooperate with him. I told him, 'You know I can never betray my people. Democracy is my fundamental belief. I can never abandon my belief, so I cannot be cooperative with you.' He came to see me three times, but every time I refused. He told me, 'You will be killed; don't put any hope in the trial.' That was his final remark. And after that I was put on trial."

Orton Chirwa, a former Minister of Justice of Malawi who helped draft the constitution when his country became independent in 1964, went into exile after a dispute with Life-President Dr Hastings Kamuzu Banda in 1964. He and his wife were arrested in December 1981 (they later stated in court that they had been abducted and brought back to Malawi by security agents). In July 1982 they were brought to trial on charges of having "prepared, endeavoured or conspired to overthrow the Malawi Government by force or other unlawful means".

The trial was held before a Traditional Court consisting of five chiefs who were not required to have any form of legal training. Orton and Vera Chirwa were denied the right to legal representation and were not allowed to call witnesses; normal rules on the admissibility of evidence were disregarded. The Chirwas were convicted and sentenced to death on 5 May 1983. On 7 February 1984 the sentences were confirmed by the National Traditional Court of Appeal where, as in the lower court, proper legal safeguards were lacking. An Amnesty International delegate attempted to observe the appeal proceedings but was refused access to the court. In a commentary on the appeal court judgment, he said that although much of it was well-reasoned and demonstrated that the trial – judged by

It also is evident that the burden of capital punishment falls upon the poor, the ignorant, and the under-privileged members of society.
Supreme Court Justice Thurgood Marshall, USA

Relatives receiving news of executions in South Africa. Most black defendants are too poor to hire their own lawyers and must instead rely on those appointed by the court – usually the most junior members of the bar – whose fees allow for little consultation with their client before the trial and do not permit the hiring of an attorney, crucial to the preparation of the case. Too often, whether a prisoner is to die or live ultimately depends on his or her ability to pay for adequate defence. © *Afrapix*

normal legal standards – was so riddled with irregularities that the convictions could not stand, ultimately "tradition" and "custom" had been invoked to "cure every irregularity and illegality" and justify upholding the convictions.

In late May 1984, in response to reports that the Chirwas faced imminent execution, an international appeal was launched urging President Banda not to execute them. The government announced on 30 June 1984 that the sentences had been commuted to life imprisonment. Earlier in the year, an unprecedented appeal for clemency had been sent by the UN Commission on Human Rights; appeals were also made by the 10 member states of the European Community. Earlier appeals had been made by President Moi of Kenya, President Shagari of Nigeria and other leaders.

Orton and Vera Chirwa remain in prison at the time of writing. Amnesty International has adopted them as prisoners of conscience and is working for their release, believing them to be detained solely on account of the non-violent expression of their political beliefs.

As shown in this report, the death penalty is frequently used after military coups against people connected with the former government, and, after coup attempts, against the alleged plotters. Those accused are usually tried in haste and without proper safeguards for a fair trial.

Sometimes they are sentenced to death under legislation hurriedly introduced with retroactive effect. Death sentences have been imposed in such cases in at least 14 countries during the past decade, and executions have been carried out in at least 12 countries.

In Ghana, the government of General Frederick Akuffo was overthrown in a coup on 4 June 1979 after heavy fighting in the capital, Accra. In the first of several so-called "house-cleaning" exercises, the new military administration ordered the arrest of some 100 wealthy businessmen and former high officials. On 16 June former Head of State General Ignatius Acheampong and a high-ranking officer were executed for "using their position to amass wealth while in office and recklessly dissipating state funds to the detriment of the country". Ten days later General Akuffo was also executed along with former Head of State General Akwasi Afrifa and four senior officers. None of the executed was allowed a fair trial or the right of appeal.

The country returned briefly to civilian rule later in the year, but since another military coup in 1981 a number of people have been executed for alleged involvement in a series of attempts to overthrow the government. All were convicted in summary trials before Public Tribunals, special courts created in 1982. The members of these tribunals were appointed by the military administration, were not required to have legal training and were given no specific protection against dismissal.

In Liberia, many former officials, senior officers and managing directors of publicly-owned corporations were arrested immediately after a military coup on 12 April 1980. A decree was issued defining the crime of high treason, effective retroactively and punishable by death. A Special Military Tribunal was established consisting entirely of soldiers, which, within a week of the coup, began hearings against 14 former senior officials charged with "high treason, rampant corruption, misuse of public office and the abuse of civil and human rights". The defendants were not allowed defence counsel or to present evidence. After hurried proceedings the military tribunal submitted its verdict on 13 of the accused to the military government, which ordered their execution. They were publicly executed by firing-squad on a beach in Monrovia, the capital, on 22 April 1980.

In Suriname, an unofficial moratorium on executions of over 50 years' standing ended in 1982 after Sergeant-Major Wilfred Hawkes was convicted of attempting to overthrow the military government – which itself had come to power in a 1980 coup. His trial and conviction took place under a decree introduced on 11 March 1982, the day of the attempted coup, and thus applied retroactively in his case. The decree empowered military courts to impose death sentences with no right of appeal on any person considered a serious danger to national security during wartime or a state of emergency. Sergeant-Major Hawkes was convicted at a summary one-day trial and was executed by firing-squad on 13 March. The decree was rescinded on 23 March, 10 days after the execution.

By the time I walked into that police station to kill, I wasn't a man. I was an aimed weapon. I was so full of hate I could shoot a man as easily as shoot a wall. Nothing meant anything to me ... At the time capital punishment would have been absolutely no deterrent.

Maurice Cadieux, convicted murderer, Canada

1 These findings are reported in David C. Baldus, George Woodworth and Charles A. Pulaski Jr., *Equal Justice and the Death Penalty* (to be published).

2 *McCleskey v. Kemp* (1987).

3 Jamaica Committee on Capital Punishment and Penal Reform, *Report of the Committee to Consider Death as a Penalty for Murder in Jamaica*, December 1981.

4 *Harbans Singh v. State of Uttar Pradesh*, 1982.

5 *House of Commons, Official Report, Parliamentary Debates (Hansard)*, vol. 113, No. 85, 1 April 1987, column 1150.

6 *China News*, 12 February 1982.

7 Hugo Adam Bedau and Michael L. Radelet, "Miscarriages of justice in potentially capital cases", *Stanford Law Review*, vol. 40, No. 1, November 1987, pages 21-179.

8 Article 6 of the ICCPR states, "Anyone sentenced to death shall have the right to seek pardon or commutation of the sentence. Amnesty, pardon or commutation of the sentence of death may be granted in all cases." Similar provisions appear in the American Convention on Human Rights, the Third and Fourth Geneva Conventions of 12 August 1949, and the 1984 safeguards on the death penalty adopted by ECOSOC (see Appendix 4).

9 United Kingdom Royal Commission on Capital Punishment 1949-1953, *Minutes of evidence*, Her Majesty's Stationery Office, London, 1949-1953, page 4.

10 Amnesty International, *United States of America: the death penalty, op. cit.* pages 100-107.

11 Viscount Templewood, *op. cit.* pages 59-60.

12 Barry Jones ed., *The penalty is death; capital punishment in the twentieth century; retentionist and abolitionist arguments with special reference to Australia*, Sun Books in association with the Anti-Hanging Council of Victoria, Melbourne, 1968, page 279.

13 Other important regional instruments are the European Convention on Human Rights which is now binding on all members of the Council of Europe, and the African Charter on Human and People's Rights binding on members of the Organization of African Unity which ratify it. Both these instruments prohibit torture and inhuman or degrading treatment or punishment. Both spell out standards for fair trial and prohibit a person being found guilty of an act which was not an offence at the time of its commission.

14 In 1987, for example, at least 172 people were executed in South Africa – 164 executions were reported in official statistics and at least eight were carried out in the nominally independent "homelands". Amnesty International recorded 158 executions in Iran and 132 in China during the same year, but the true totals were believed to be higher. These three countries alone accounted for 60 per cent of all executions recorded by Amnesty International in 1987. Hundreds more have been reported from Iraq each year, but Amnesty International does not know the precise figures and is not always able to ascertain whether those executed were tried and convicted of offences punishable by death or were executed extrajudicially.

15 UN General Assembly resolution 2857 (XXVI) of 20 December 1971 on capital punishment.

16 For further information see Victor L. Streib, *Death Penalty for Juveniles*, Indiana University Press, Bloomington, 1987.

17 Summary record of the 202nd meeting of the Human Rights Committee held on 21 March 1980, UN document CCPR/C/SR.202.

18 Article 6 states that a death sentence may not be imposed "contrary to the provisions of the present Covenant". This implies that the fair trial standards in Article 14 and the non-retroactivity set forth in Article 15 are applicable in death

penalty cases. Article 6 also states that the death penalty "can only be carried out pursuant to a final judgment rendered by a competent court" – that is, a death sentence cannot be carried out if an appeal is still being heard such that the sentence has not yet become, in the language of the law, "final".

19 UN General Assembly resolution 2393 (XXIII) of 26 November 1968, resolution 35/172 of 15 December 1980 and numerous later ones; see Appendix 9 for text of the 1980 resolution.

20 In addition to the right of appeal, the right to seek clemency, and the call for automatic appeals as set forth in the ECOSOC safeguards, another possible safeguard is to establish that death sentences may not be carried out until a certain minimum period of time has elapsed. This safeguard is provided in the Third and Fourth Geneva Conventions of 12 August 1949.

21 Bahrain, Bulgaria, United Arab Emirates.

22 Resolution 1 (XXXIV), adopted without a vote by the Sub-Commission at its 34th session on 3 September 1981, recommended the UN Commission on Human Rights "to request the Economic and Social Council to call upon Governments to abolish capital punishment for political offences".

4. The cruelty of the death penalty

The death penalty requires the state to carry out the very act which the law most strongly condemns. In virtually every legal system the severest sanctions are provided for the deliberate and premeditated killing of a human being; but no killing is more premeditated or cold-blooded than an execution; and just as it is not possible to create a death penalty system free of caprice, discrimination or error, so it is not possible to find a way to execute a person which is not cruel, inhuman or degrading.

An execution, like physical forms of torture, involves a deliberate assault on a prisoner. Seven principal methods are used today. As shown in Appendix 17, table 3, hanging and shooting are the most widespread. Hanging is provided for in the laws of 78 countries and shooting in those of 86 – where both methods are specified, shooting is often reserved for wartime crimes or for death sentences passed by military courts. These numbers include countries where the death penalty is retained in law but no longer used.

Death by electrocution, poisonous gas and lethal injection of poison are prescribed and used in the USA alone; the method varies from state to state within the USA. Under Islamic law, beheading by sword is prescribed in five countries, and stoning in seven countries for sexual crimes; not all of these countries have used these methods during the past decade. In addition, the guillotine is prescribed in the People's Republic of the Congo and in Belgium for offences under the penal code but is no longer used.

Occasionally there are reports of other methods being used. Three prisoners were executed by being pushed off a cliff, according to a report in the Iranian press in October 1987; the three were said to have chosen this method in preference to being crushed to death or beheaded.

Methods of execution
Hanging

The prisoner is made to hang from a rope tied around the neck and is killed by the force of the rope exerted against the body pulled down by the force of gravity. Unconsciousness and death are brought about by damage to the spinal cord, or – if that is insufficient – by asphyxiation due to constriction of the trachea.

In 1888 an official British committee appointed to consider how executions could be carried out in a "becoming manner" reported on procedures designed (in the words of the report of the United Kingdom Royal Commission on Capital Punishment of 1949-1953) "to ensure speedy and painless death by dislocation of the vertebrae without decapitation".[1] The modern form of hanging now used in many countries stems from the recommendations of that committee. After the rope is placed around the neck and tightened, a trap-door under the prisoner's feet is opened. The distance that the prisoner will fall depends on the length of the rope, which is calculated according to the prisoner's height and weight so as to sever the spinal cord without detaching the head. A hanging of this sort requires skill and experience: a trained executioner must be able to calculate precisely the length of rope for the "drop" required to obtain a swift result.

The United Kingdom Royal Commission on Capital Punishment evaluated various methods of execution for their "humanity, certainty and

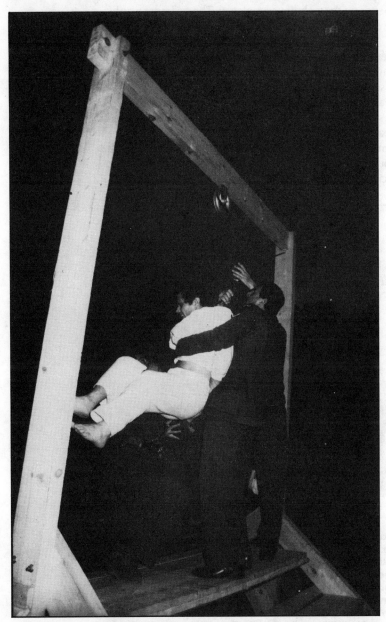

In Beirut, Lebanon 1983, Ibrahim Tarraf screamed his innocence while jerking his head out of the noose and fighting his execution to the end. © *Sipa Press*

decency" and concluded that hanging, then the method in the United Kingdom, should be retained. Autopsies of 58 executed prisoners showed that the effective cause of death was "fracture dislocation of cervical vertebrae with laceration or crushing of the [spinal] cord"; such dislocation, the Commission concluded, "causes immediate unconsciousness and there is no chance of a later recovery of consciousness since breathing is no longer possible".[2] However, whether a prisoner loses consciousness immediately through trauma to the spinal cord, or more slowly through strangulation, depends on the technique employed. The suffering may be prolonged if the executioner has miscalculated and something goes wrong.

Before the modern form of hanging was developed in the 19th century, execution by hanging caused a slow and distressing death by strangulation. The old, slow method of hanging is still used in some countries, where prisoners are hoisted by a rope tied around the neck or are dropped only a short distance. Amnesty International has received reports of such executions during the past decade in Iran and Libya.

Even with the modern method, guards have sometimes had to finish the hanging by pulling down on the legs of the suspended prisoner. Although unconsciousness may have intervened before, the prisoner's

The 1980 public execution in Mauritania of Sidi Ould Matalla, who had been convicted of murder. Shooting by firing-squad does not necessarily result in immediate death – the squad may have been told to aim at the trunk of the body rather than the head (it is an easier target), and may be shooting from a considerable distance. In Taiwan in 1988, for example, a prisoner was found to be breathing over an hour after the first two volleys had been fired. In 1953 a United Kingdom Royal Commission rejected shooting by firing-squad as an execution method as it does "not possess even the first requisite of an efficient method, the certainty of immediate death". © *Popperfoto*

body may jerk in spasms and the heart may continue beating for some minutes.

When a Thai construction worker stood on the gallows facing a crowd as he was about to be executed in Kuwait on 16 November 1981, "For a moment his face expressed all the incomprehension, anguish and desperation," the *Arab Times* reported. "He took more than nine minutes to die because, as the medical report revealed afterwards, his slight weight did not suffice to break his neck. He died of suffocation."[3]

Shooting

Execution is carried out either by a single executioner or by a firing-squad. The prisoner is killed by one or a combination of effects: damage to vital organs such as the heart, damage to the central nervous system or haemorrhage.

Although a point-blank pistol shot to the head should produce immediate unconsciousness, the process is likely to take longer in shootings by firing-squad, where soldiers are firing from further away – and thus with less accuracy – and may be told to aim at the trunk, which is easier to hit than the head. This problem was recognized by the United Kingdom Royal Commission which, when reviewing various methods of execution for possible use in the country, found execution by firing-squad unacceptable both because it would require "a multiplicity of execution-ers" and because "it does not possess even the first requisite of an efficient method, the certainty of causing immediate death".[4]

While some prisoners may remain conscious after the first shot even in normal executions by firing-squad, some executions have been designed to prolong the pain. In July 1986 it was reported that the Military Governor of Niger State, Nigeria, had ordered that prisoners convicted of armed robbery should be executed by successive volleys of bullets fired at intervals, starting with shots aimed at the ankles. A state official was quoted in the *National Concord* newspaper of 25 July 1986 as saying, "By intermittent shooting, the armed robber will not only pay dearly for his crime, but also suffer to the death." Two people were reportedly executed in this way.

Electrocution

Electrocution was introduced in the USA in 1888 on the grounds that it would be more humane than hanging. The procedure is as follows: after securing the prisoner to a specially built chair, the executioners attach moistened copper electrodes to the prisoner's head and leg, which have been shaved to ensure effective contact between the electrodes and the skin. Powerful surges of electric current are applied for brief periods. Death is caused by cardiac arrest and respiratory paralysis.

Electrocution produces visibly destructive effects as the body's internal organs are burned; the condemned prisoner often leaps forward against restraining straps when the switch is thrown; the prisoner may defecate, urinate or vomit blood. Eye-witnesses always report that there is a smell of burned flesh.

What then is capital punishment but the most premeditated of murders, to which no criminal's deed, however calculated it may be, can be compared? For there to be an equivalence, the death penalty would have to punish a criminal, who had warned his victim of the date at which he would inflict a horrible death on him, and who from that moment onward had confined him at his mercy for months. Such a monster is not encountered in private life.
Albert Camus, writer, France

Although unconsciousness should follow the first jolt of electricity, there have been cases where this has not happened. When authorities in the state of Louisiana electrocuted Willie Francis, a 17-year-old black youth, in 1946, he survived the first attempt. An official witness said, "I saw the electrocutioner turn on the switch and I saw the [prisoner's] lips puff out and swell, his body tensed and stretched. I heard the one in charge yell to the man outside for more juice [electricity] when he saw that Willie Francis was not dying, and the one on the outside yelled back he was giving him all he had. Then Willie Francis cried out, "Take it off. Let me breathe." Afterwards Willie Francis reportedly said, "I felt a burning in my head and my left leg, and I jumped against the straps. I saw little blue and pink and green speckles." A new death warrant was signed and he was executed a year later, after the US Supreme Court had ruled that this second execution would not violate the US Constitution.[5]

Whether or not the prisoner loses consciousness after the first jolt of electricity, the vital organs may continue to function, necessitating further jolts to finish the prisoner off. Thus when Alpha Otis Stephens was executed by electrocution in Georgia in December 1984, the *New York Times* newspaper reported on 13 December that the first two-minute charge of electricity, applied at 12.18 am, failed to kill him and that he "struggled for breath for eight minutes" before a second charge was applied. "His body slumped when the current stopped ... but shortly afterward witnesses saw him struggle to breathe. In the six minutes allowed for the body to cool before doctors could examine it, Mr Stephens took about 23 breaths." The second, fatal, charge was applied at 12.28 am after two doctors had examined him and said he was still alive. When John Louis Evans was executed by electrocution in Alabama in April 1983 it required three separate charges of 1,900 volts over 14 minutes before he was officially pronounced dead, according to eye-witness accounts. The execution of William Vandiver by electrocution in Indiana on 16 October 1985 was reported to have taken 17 minutes, requiring five charges of electricity before he was pronounced dead.[6]

Lethal injection

Execution by lethal injection involves the continuous intravenous injection of a lethal quantity of a short-acting barbiturate in combination with a chemical paralytic agent. The procedure is similar to that used in a hospital to administer a general anaesthetic, but the drugs are injected in fatal quantities. In Texas, one of the 19 US states which prescribe lethal injection as a method of execution, three drugs are used together: sodium thiopental, pancuronium bromide and potassium chloride. The first of these is a barbiturate which makes the prisoner unconscious, the second is a muscle relaxant which paralyses the diaphragm and thus arrests the motion of the lungs, and the third causes cardiac arrest.

Although advocates of lethal injection have claimed that it is more humane than other methods of execution, a number of doctors have described problems which may arise. Some prisoners with a record of prolonged intravenous drug abuse may have scarred veins and surgery may be needed to cut into a deeper vein. If the prisoner struggles during

Taking a human life, even with subtle rites and sanction of the law, is retributive barbarity and violent futility ...

Former Justice V R Krishna Iyer, Supreme Court of India

Lethal injection of poison is permitted as a method of execution in 18 states in the USA. Any struggling by the prisoner may cause the poisons to enter a muscle or artery, which would cause pain. Finding a suitable vein in which to insert the needle is not necessarily straightforward, and occasionally requires minor surgery. In a case reported in Texas in 1985 there were 23 attempts to insert the needle before a viable spot was located – the process took 40 minutes. During the execution of Raymond Landry in December 1988 a tube attached to the needle began to leak and the mixture spurted out across the room towards witnesses, because, according to the Texas Attorney General, "there was more pressure in the hose than his veins could absorb". Witnesses reported hearing groans and it was a further 17 minutes before the prisoner was pronounced dead. © *Gamma*

the execution, the poison may enter an artery or muscle tissue and cause pain. If the components of the lethal solution are not balanced or if they combine prematurely, the mixture may thicken, clog the intravenous line and slow the process of death. If the anaesthetizing barbiturate does not take effect quickly, the prisoner may be conscious of suffocating as his or her lungs become paralysed.

James Autry was executed by lethal injection in Texas on 14 March 1984. He had previously been scheduled for execution in November 1983 and at that time had been strapped to a stretcher and was undergoing the first stage of the lethal injection process (a saline solution was being dripped into his veins) when his execution was stayed. The US news magazine *Newsweek* reported on 9 April 1984 that at his execution in March, James Autry "took at least ten minutes to die and throughout much of that time was conscious, moving about and complaining of pain". A prison doctor, who was present at the execution, was later reported to have said that the catheter needle may have become clogged, slowing down the execution.

Lethal injection was first introduced in law as a method of execution in the US states of Oklahoma and Texas in 1977. The first prisoner to die by lethal injection was Charles Brooks, in Texas in December 1982. As of 1 December 1988, 34 prisoners had been executed by lethal injection in four US states.

Gassing

Here the prisoner is secured to a chair in an airtight chamber; a stethoscope strapped to his or her chest is connected to earpieces in the adjacent witness room so that a doctor can monitor the progress of the execution. Cyanide gas is released in the chamber, poisoning the prisoner when he or she inhales. Death is caused by asphyxiation due to inhibition by the cyanide gas of the respiratory enzymes which transfer oxygen from the blood to the body cells.

Although unconsciousness may follow rapidly, the process will take longer if the prisoner tries to prolong his or her life by holding the breath or breathing slowly. As with other methods of execution, the vital organs can continue to function for a short time whether or not the prisoner has become unconscious. For example, when Jimmy Lee Gray was executed on 2 September 1983 in Mississippi, he reportedly had convulsions for eight minutes and gasped 11 times, striking his head repeatedly on a pole behind him. Some of the witnesses said that he did not appear to be dead when prison officials asked them to leave the witness room.

Beheading

Under the method used in Saudi Arabia and Qatar and prescribed by law in the Yemen Arab Republic and the United Arab Emirates, the head is severed from the body with a sword. Although it is intended that the weapon's sharp blade will cut quickly through to the spinal cord, causing unconsciousness from spinal shock, several blows may be needed to do this because the sword is a relatively light tool and the speed of execution depends on the strength and accuracy of the executioner.

Stoning

Execution by stoning is usually carried out after the prisoner has been buried to the neck or otherwise restrained. Death may be caused by damage to the brain, asphyxiation, or a combination of injuries. Because a person may sustain severe blows without losing consciousness, stoning can cause a protracted death.

In Iran, one of the six countries where stoning is prescribed by law, the procedure is designed to ensure that death does not come from a single blow. Article 119 of the Islamic Penal Code of Iran (*Hodoud* and *Qisas*) states: "In the punishment of stoning to death, the stones should not be too large so that the person dies on being hit by one or two of them; they should not be so small either that they could not be defined as stones."

A report allegedly from an eye-witness to a stoning in Iran reads: "The lorry deposited a large number of stones and pebbles beside the waste ground, and then two women were led to the spot wearing white and with sacks over their heads ... [they] were enveloped in a shower of stones and transformed into two red sacks ... The wounded women fell to the ground and Revolutionary Guards smashed their heads in with a shovel to make sure that they were dead."

Waiting for execution

The cruelty of the death penalty is not restricted to the actual moment of execution. Its unique horror – and one which cannot be relieved by developing more "humane" methods of killing – is that, from the moment the sentence is pronounced, the prisoner is forced to contemplate the prospect of being taken away to be put to death at an appointed time. During each stage of the appeals process, the prisoner may suffer an agonizing conflict between the desire to live in hope and the need to prepare for possible imminent death. This conflict can make some prisoners so despondent that they choose to drop their appeals and submit to execution as if it were a form of suicide.

Prisoners sentenced to death are treated as men and women without a future. Often they are separated from the general prison population and held in special places, known in some countries as "death rows". There they may be subjected to prolonged isolation and enforced idleness which must add to the torment of waiting to be executed.

A criminologist who interviewed at length 35 prisoners under sentence of death in Alabama, USA, in 1978, found that many of them were intensely preoccupied with the thought of execution. They speculated about the mechanics of electrocution and its likely effects on the body, which they visualized in great detail. They were anxious about how they would behave during the walk to the death chamber, whether they would break down, whether the execution would be painful, and how the memory or image of the execution would affect their families. For many prisoners these and similar thoughts had become obsessive. Some prisoners had recurring and vivid nightmares in which they went through the execution process step by step.

The researcher noted that the prisoners' contact with family and

We have no way of planning anything because we don't know what's going to happen. We may go to the gas chamber, we may not ... You exist and you wait and you wait and you think about it every day. Not your own death, but the death of the other people.
Prisoner on death row, USA

friends often deteriorated in the face of the prospect of permanent separation and a sense of the futility of pursuing relationships. He found that loss of contact with the outside world and the isolated conditions under which the condemned inmates were confined on death row produced widespread feelings of abandonment, leading to what he termed "death of the personality"; in some instances this happened long before the execution. This condition was characterized by severe depression, apathy, loss of a sense of reality and both physical and mental deterioration.[7]

There have been similar reports from other countries. For example, in Jamaica, where several years usually elapse between the time of conviction and the exhaustion of a prisoner's legal appeals, a number of prisoners are reported to have become severely mentally ill or depressed while on death row, and there have been several suicides. Two men, both of whom had spent more than five years on "death row", were found hanging in their cells within a few days of each other in November 1986. Ronald Holmes, sentenced to death in 1981, apparently committed suicide on 30 April 1988; he was reported to have become particularly depressed after being issued with an execution warrant in February 1987. He had spent nine days in the "death cell" awaiting execution before being granted a reprieve the day before the execution was scheduled.

The conditions in which condemned prisoners are kept can exacerbate the inherently cruel, inhuman and degrading experience of being under sentence of death. A 1987 judgment by the Trinidad and Tobago High Court referred to the conditions of "appalling barbarity" in which the two appellants had been kept under sentence of death for more than 10 years. The "death row" in the Port-of-Spain prison consisted of two rows of small cells facing each other near the gallows. It had apparently been built to house prisoners just before their execution, but with the lengthening of the appeals procedures, prisoners were being kept there for many years. Each prisoner was kept in a cell measuring approximately 9ft by 6ft, and because part of this space was taken up with a bed, table and slop pail, one prisoner said he could only take two paces inside his cell. The prisoners were confined to their cells approximately 23 hours a day, with an hour's exercise in a small yard, conducted with handcuffs on.

A consultant psychiatrist who had treated prisoners on the Trinidad and Tobago death row said in an affidavit cited in the court judgment that in his opinion "prolonged incarceration under such conditions produces psychological changes of a depressed and euphoric type. Prolonged confinement in such a small area invariably results in claustrophobia, and often results in chronic anxiety and depression. Prisoners tend to become compliant and in some cases, eventually lose the will to live. The prolonged confinement in a small cell with a light kept burning by night could be regarded as a form of psychological torture".[8]

Even in the best of "death row" conditions, prolonged waiting for execution must add to the suffering of those sentenced to death. As the United Nations Special Rapporteur on torture observed in his 1988 report to the UN Commission on Human Rights, if "persons who have been sentenced to death have to wait for long periods before they know whether the sentence will be carried out or not" and "if the uncertainty ... lasts

The nearer the day came, the less cheerful Hanada [a fellow prisoner] became. He attended neither exercise or prayers, and kept crying. Looking at him closely, I was dragged into the fear of death more and more, so I could neither eat nor sleep. Even when I did my exercises, I did not feel that my feet stamped on the ground. I felt as if I were a living wax figure.

Sakae Menda, acquitted after spending 32 years under sentence of death, Japan several years ... the psychological effect may be equated with severe mental suffering, often resulting in serious physical complaints ... it may be asked whether such a situation is reconcilable with the required respect for man's dignity and physical and mental integrity."

Some prisoners have been kept under sentence of death for many years before being executed. Mohammad Munir, arrested in July 1968, was a former member of parliament and former head of a trade union federation led by the banned *Partai Komunis Indonesia* (PKI), Indonesian Communist Party, which had been blamed by the authorities for a coup attempt in 1965. Mohammad Munir was charged with rebellion, convicted in 1973 and sentenced to death. The sentence was upheld by the Indonesian High Court in 1981 and by the Supreme Court in 1983; in October 1984 his petition for clemency was rejected by President Suharto. On 15 May 1985, nearly 17 years after his arrest, the 68-year-old prisoner was secretly executed by firing-squad on a deserted island near Jakarta, the capital. He and his family had been notified of the decision to proceed with the execution only four days earlier.

Later in 1985 and in 1986, 13 other prisoners linked to the PKI or to military units which supported a 1965 coup attempt blamed on the PKI

In January 1988 a group of prisoners in St. Catherine Prison, Jamaica, including several on death row, protested over prison conditions. Jamaica has one of the highest per capita death row populations in the world. In a 1982 case two judges said that the long confinements on death row there amount to "... a cruel and dehumanizing experience", and "inhuman and degrading punishment in violation of the Jamaican Constitution". © *The Daily Gleaner*

were executed after being under sentence of death for more than 10 years. In 1987 two men were executed for the murder of a young woman, 25 years after their sentences were imposed.

The cruelty of lengthy confinement under sentence of death has been considered by the courts in a number of countries. Noel Riley and four other Jamaican prisoners were sentenced to death in 1975 and 1976, during a period when executions in the country were suspended. Warrants for execution were issued in 1979, but the five men appealed to the Jamaica Supreme Court and the executions were stayed. In 1982, by a narrow margin of three to two, their appeal was rejected by the Judicial Committee of the Privy Council in England, which serves as the final court of appeal for Jamaica[9] in cases involving points of law of great or exceptional public importance which are likely to have implications for other cases. The two dissenting judges, however, said that the five men had "proved that they had been subjected to a cruel and dehumanising experience" and that their execution, "against the background of the lapse of time since conviction", would violate the Jamaican Constitution. According to the dissenting judges, "Prolonged delay when it arises from factors outside the control of the condemned man can render a decision to carry out the sentence of death an inhuman and degrading punishment."[10] The five men were executed three months after the decision was handed down.

For prisoners who have not given up hope, the period between the announcement and the carrying out of the execution must be a time of agony. The threat of execution is one of the most terrifying forms of torture, as shown in many testimonies of torture victims received by Amnesty International.

In the UN Convention against Torture and Other Cruel, Inhuman or Degrading Treatment or Punishment, adopted by the UN General Assembly in 1984, torture is defined as "severe pain or suffering, whether physical or mental", inflicted by or with the acquiescence of a public official for certain specified purposes. The death penalty has been called a form of torture: as in the UN definition, it involves the infliction of severe pain or suffering, both mental and physical.

For many that mental pain reaches a peak as they grasp the fact of their imminent execution. A prisoner in Jamaica, Nathan Foster, under sentence of death for seven and a half years, went into a state of panic when an official read him the warrant for execution in February 1988. During the ensuing struggle with prison guards his arm was broken. His broken arm was strapped behind his back as prison guards brought him up the gallows steps to be hanged 10 days later.

The abbot of a Buddhist monastery in Thailand, who had given the last sermon to over 200 prisoners before execution between 1967 and 1985, described the agony manifested by many of them: "When the time for their execution came, they would not be able to stand on their feet and had to be helped to the execution stake. This happened similarly to Chinese people convicted on narcotics offences. They usually lost self-control and cried out wildly."[11]

How much warning condemned prisoners receive of the day on which they are to be executed varies from country to country. In Japan, a prisoner is notified one or two days in advance at most, and in some cases not at all; a prisoner who has exhausted all legal appeals against the death sentence may never know whether the next time he or she is called from the condemned cell will be the last one or not.

In several Caribbean countries, the standard practice is to inform a prisoner on a Thursday of an execution to be carried out the next Tuesday. A barrister with experience of Caribbean cases described the practice in Trinidad and Tobago:

"The decision is announced, without forewarning, between one o'clock and four on Thursday afternoon. The inmates of death row spend each Thursday in a state of terror, straining to hear the creak of a door which is only opened when there is a death warrant to be read. The prison official entrusted with this task strides up and down the row of tortured men, stops suddenly at the cage of the victim, clears his throat and reads out the warrant for his execution."[12]

The ritual of execution

As the date of an execution approaches, preparations for putting the prisoner to death begin. The condemned prisoner may be kept under special surveillance to prevent a suicide which would rob the state of its chance for punishment. The prisoner may be placed in solitary confinement, increasing the sense of isolation during the last days of life.

Executions and their preparations follow set procedures, which in some countries are spelled out in great detail in administrative regulations. Through those details, the execution takes on the character of a ritual.

Under official guidelines at Florida State Prison, USA, a "death-watch" procedure begins when the "death warrant" is read to the prisoner, four weeks before the execution date. The prisoner is moved to a special cell near the electrocution room. The second phase of the procedure begins four days before the execution when the prisoner is placed under constant observation by a prison officer positioned in front of the cell. The prisoner's remaining property is removed and the prisoner is measured for clothing to be worn during the execution. A death certificate is prepared giving the cause of death as "legal execution by electrocution". The regulations specify a "last meal" at 4.30am and the shaving of the prisoner's head and right leg between 5 and 6am for an execution to take place at 7am. As a stay of execution may be granted at any moment in the proceedings, some prisoners have gone through the first stages of the process several times.

Other rituals of execution are carried out in public. Although most countries which retain the death penalty in law now provide that executions are to be held behind prison walls, public executions have been carried out in at least 18 countries during the past decade,[13] often before crowds numbering in the thousands. Eye-witness accounts indicate that some prisoners have died slowly, and their sufferings could be seen when something went wrong with the execution or if a slow method of execution was used. Police officers have had to restore order as crowds, excited by the spectacle, became unruly.

One of three prisoners executed publicly in Kuwait on 27 October 1981

To make a person sit, day after day, night after night, waiting for the time when he will be led out of his cell to his death is cruel and barbaric ... To be a mother or father and watch your child going through this living hell is a torment more painful than anyone can imagine.
Petition presented to President Botha from relatives of condemned prisoners in 1988, South Africa

had to be forcibly pushed up the steps to the gallows, "ranting and raving each step of the way" according to an account in a Kuwaiti newspaper. "He did not stop shouting his innocence in between calling in the name of God – even when the noose was slipped around his neck," the newspaper reported. After the executions, the vast crowds outside the execution square "began surging forward each time the gates were opened for a while to let in more onlookers. The police had to use their belts to flail back some of the more unruly sections of the crowd."[14]

In China, condemned prisoners are frequently paraded through the streets in trucks and displayed before "mass sentencing rallies" held to publicize their sentences. At these rallies they are usually made to face the crowd with heads bowed and placards hanging around their necks while their crimes are denounced. After execution, their names and the charges against them are displayed on wall posters with a large red tick to show that they have been executed.

An eye-witness wrote an account of the mass public execution of 45 prisoners on a grassy creek bed outside the city of Zhengzhou, China, on 23 September 1983. The prisoners were led to a row of 45 wooden stakes; "Some had lost the use of their legs from fear" and had to be dragged to the stakes. Forty-five police officers aimed rifles at the prisoners' heads and shot them all at once at close range. Bodies which lay quivering on the ground were shot again. After the executions, the crowd watching from

Made to bow their heads and wearing placards denouncing their crimes, condemned prisoners in China endure public humiliation immediately before their execution as they are paraded through the streets. It is believed that thousands of Chinese were executed in a nationwide crackdown on crime during the last five months of 1983. However, the death penalty has never been shown to protect society from serious crime.

the banks of the creek bed "surged down from the banks and closed in, shouting. The front rows broke through the police line to where the bodies lay, and stopped short in horror as they got near enough to make out details. But the pressure behind them was too great; many were pushed ahead and forced to trample the bodies. Some fell sprawling over them ... to protect the bodies, a policeman pulled out one of the numbered stakes, scooped up some brains on the circular sign, and held the people at bay with it."[15]

After the Chief Minister of Punjab province, Pakistan, pledged to hand out "exemplary punishments" for particularly heinous crimes, public executions were resumed on 18 January 1988 after a gap of about 10 years in the country. An execution carried out in February 1988 was attended by "ten thousand people and hundreds of riot police" according to prison officials quoted in the press.[16] The newspaper *Dawn* commented on 12 March:

"We can be sure of the dehumanising effects of such spectacles on the minds of ordinary people. At the same time, it is extremely doubtful if such executions can serve the purpose of deterrence. It is surprising that the administration should not be mindful of the long-term social consequences of putting cruelty on public display ... such punishments will project the image of the state as ... a perpetrator of violence."

Effects of executions on others

The process of sentencing to death and executing a prisoner makes special demands on people drawn from a variety of professions. Some are employees of the state – police officers, prosecutors, judges, doctors, prison guards. Others include lawyers who represent the defendant, expert witnesses called to testify during trials, or jurors who must decide on the verdict. For many, it is a harrowing experience.

For guards and others who may have come to know a condemned prisoner over a period of years, the prisoner's execution can be deeply disturbing. In Trinidad and Tobago a report by a commission on prison reform, submitted to the parliament in early 1980, stated that when it is announced that a death sentence is to be carried out, "the effect on the whole prison is traumatic. The Prison Officers and inmates are in a state of shock for well over 24 hours after the announcement. The Chaplains and Officers present at the execution deeply desire that such a task be not required of them..."[17]

In the United Kingdom, a few days before a 1983 parliamentary debate at which the reintroduction of the death penalty for murder was being proposed, the chairperson of the Prison Governors Branch of the Society of Civil and Public Servants sent an open letter to the Home Secretary (the cabinet minister responsible) following a series of meetings around the country. The letter predicted that if executions in prison were resumed: "Staff relationships will deteriorate, prisoner reaction will escalate, and force will become more widely used ... We believe such changes would move the prison service back towards the Dark Ages."

Doctors or other health personnel may be called on to participate in executions. The response of the medical profession to the ethical conflicts

I am opposed to the death penalty and so are most of my senior and most experienced colleagues, simply because its continuation prevents the reforms necessary to increase the effectiveness of criminal justice.
Sir Robert Mark, former Commissioner of Metropolitan Police, UK

Schoolgirls in China witness a defendant being sentenced to death. China is one of several countries to have expanded the scope of the death penalty in recent years. © *South China Morning Post*

posed by such participation is described in Chapter 5.

The cruelty of the death penalty extends to the family and friends of the person being punished. If an execution is carried out in secret, the family may be denied a chance to say goodbye or may never even know the fate of their relative. If the execution is known, their grief over the prisoner's death will have added to it the humiliation of the degrading way it occurred. The prisoner's family will carry with them a sense of despair and helplessness at being unable to stop his or her death, which resulted not from an accident or illness but from a series of potentially reversible decisions by other people acting in the name of the state.

An execution also affects the relatives of the victims of the crime for which the prisoner is being executed. For the crime of murder, it has been argued that the death penalty is the only way to compensate for the suffering caused, by demonstrating that justice has been done. But an execution cannot restore life or lessen the loss to the victim's family. Far from relieving the pain, the lengthy trial and appeals procedures in many death penalty cases may instead prolong the anguish of victims' families and hinder the healing process. The publicity surrounding an execution may draw attention away from the victim of the crime and focus it on the prisoner instead, increasing the sense of rejection often experienced by victims' relatives.

The fact that the death penalty is provided for by law for certain serious crimes fosters the belief that it is the appropriate penalty for such crimes. The inevitable fact that lesser penalties are imposed in some cases, and that some death sentences are overturned on appeal, albeit on valid legal grounds, may cause families of victims to feel that they have been cheated of justice, creating frustration and disillusionment with the law.

Although some families of murder victims have said the execution of the convicted killer brought a sense of relief, others have said that, despite their loss, they did not believe the death penalty should be used. One such

> ... when the state punishes with death, it ... transgresses the prohibition against cruel and unusual punishment.
> Justice William J Brennan, USA

Beheading by sword is provided as a method of execution in at least four countries, including the Yemen Arab Republic, where this execution was carried out. Several blows are sometimes needed to sever the head depending on the weight of the sword and the strength and accuracy of the executioner.
© *Camera Press*

is Kenji Oora, whose 20-year-old sister was murdered in 1963 in Japan; the killer was never found. At a meeting of the Japanese Council on Crime and Delinquency in 1982 he said that the sorrow of the victim's family is unimaginable. The family of an executed prisoner would suffer the same sorrow, he said. He did not believe the state had the right to inflict such pain and sorrow; for that reason he opposed the death penalty.[18]

Although a victim's relative may wish for the death penalty at first, this feeling can change over time. In 1985, 10 years after Andy Thomas and Kirkland Paul were sentenced to death in Trinidad and Tobago for the murder of a young police officer, the victim's mother, Ella Juri, said in a newspaper interview that she no longer believed they should be executed (they were then still on "death row"). "I say release them. Give them a chance, because they have suffered enough already," she said.[19] They were released under a presidential amnesty in 1987 to mark the 25th anniversary of the country's independence.

The feelings of relatives of murder victims who appeal for the lives of the perpetrators to be spared out of compassion deserve respect. So do the pain and suffering of distraught relatives who call for vengeance. But ultimately the argument over the death penalty must rest not on emotions but on reason and universal respect for human rights. The cruelty of the death penalty is evident in spite of modern attempts to make the actual killing more "humane", for the cruelty resides in the fact and consequences of the state deciding to take a prisoner's life, not merely in how it takes that life. The imposition and carrying out of a death sentence violates human rights. Since World War II voices calling for an end to that violation – for abolition of the death penalty worldwide – have become part of the international struggle for all human rights.

1 United Kingdom Royal Commission on Capital Punishment 1949-1953, *Report, op. cit.* page 247.

2 *Ibid.* pages 248-256.

3 *Arab Times*, 17 November 1981, public executions ended in Kuwait in 1985.

4 United Kingdom Royal Commission on Capital Punishment, 1949-1953, *Report op. cit.* page 249.

5 Details of the execution were given in the US Supreme Court judgment in *Louisiana ex rel. Francis v. Resweber*, 329 US 459 (1947).

6 These and other recent executions are described in Amnesty International, *United States of America: the death penalty, op. cit.* pages 114-119.

7 Robert Johnson, *Condemned to die; life under sentence of death*, Elsevier, New York and Oxford, 1981.

8 Trinidad and Tobago High Court judgment in *Andy Thomas and Kirkland Paul v. Trinidad and Tobago* (1987).

9 The three-judge majority accepted that "long delay in the execution of a death sentence, especially delay for which the condemned man himself is in no way responsible, must be an important factor to be taken into account in deciding whether to exercise the prerogative of mercy".

10 Judgment by the Judicial Committee of the Privy Council in *Noel Riley and Others v. The Attorney General and Another* (1982).

11 *Bangkok World*, 16 September 1986.

12 *New Statesman*, 11 January 1974.

13 Cameroon, China, Gabon, Iran, Iraq, Kuwait, Liberia, Libya, Mauritania, Nigeria, Pakistan, Saudi Arabia, Somalia, Sudan, Syria, Uganda, United Arab Emirates, Arab Republic of Yemen.

14 *Kuwait Times*, 28 October 1981.

15 Liu Fong Da and John Creger, "Execution day in Zhengzhou", *American Spectator*, December 1986.

16 *Reuter*, 2 February 1988.

17 Trinidad and Tobago Commission of Enquiry appointed to Enquire into the Existing Conditions at the Prisons and to Make Recommendations for Reform in the Light of Modern Concepts of Penal Practice and Rehabilitation Measures, *Final report*, Government Printery, Trinidad, 1980, page 49.

18 Amnesty International, *The death penalty in Japan; report of an Amnesty International mission to Japan; 21 February-3 March 1983*, Amnesty International Publications, London, 1983, page 19.

19 *Trinidad Express*, 8 February 1985.

5. Towards worldwide abolition

ABOLISH DEATH PENALTY

People around the world campaign for an end to executions; clockwise: Sweden, the USA (© *Popperfoto*), the USA and Pakistan.

"It was with some degree of shame I read the following words recently in the 1983 *World Book Encyclopaedia*," a member of Western Australia's Legislative Council said in a debate on the death penalty in August 1984. "Many countries ... have repealed the death penalty since 1900. Canada abolished capital punishment in 1976. In Australia, the Federal Government and all of the six states except Western Australia have repealed the death penalty." The Honourable Lyla Elliott continued, "I think it is rather an indictment of this State that we still have on our statute book the sentence of death of a human being, and that in Western Australia we are still fighting a battle in 1984 that was fought and won decades ago in other enlightened civilised societies."[1]

The battle was soon won. The elected representatives of the state of Western Australia abolished the death penalty in 1984, and the next year Australia became completely abolitionist when the state of New South Wales abolished the penalty for the only remaining exceptional crimes still punishable by death. Australia had now joined the growing list of abolitionist countries which have affirmed fundamental human rights by removing from their laws the ultimate cruel, inhuman and degrading punishment.

The victory in Australia became part of the long history of the movement for abolition. The first recorded parliamentary debate on the death penalty was held in 427 BC when Diodotus, arguing that the penalty was not a deterrent, persuaded the Athenian Assembly in Greece to reverse its decision to execute all adult males of the rebellious city of Mitylene.[2] During the first century AD, Amandagamani, the Buddhist King of Lanka (Sri Lanka), abolished the death penalty during his reign, as did several kings who followed him.[3] In 818 AD Emperor Saga of Japan removed the death penalty from Japanese law, and there was no death penalty in the country for the next three centuries.

The modern abolitionist movement is usually said to have begun in Europe with the publication of Cesare Beccaria's *On Crimes and Punishments* in Italy in 1764. The book contained the first sustained, systematic critique of the death penalty.

In 1786 Grand Duke Leopold of Tuscany promulgated a penal code, based on Beccaria's ideas, which completely eliminated the death penalty. In 1846 the US territory (later state) of Michigan became the first jurisdiction in the world permanently to abolish the death penalty for murder. And in 1863 Venezuela became the first country permanently to abolish the death penalty for all offences. Others followed over the next decades.

Since World War II, as the movement for human rights has grown, so the momentum for abolition has gathered. During the past decade, on average, at least one country a year has eliminated the death penalty for ordinary crimes or for all crimes, and today over 40 per cent – nearly half – of all countries in the world have abolished the death penalty in law or practice.

The political will to abolish the death penalty comes ultimately from within a country. International human rights treaties establish restrictions and safeguards on the use of the death penalty in countries which have not abolished it. International public opinion generates pressure to stop executions. The experience of countries which have abolished the death penalty gives ample evidence that the punishment is neither desirable nor necessary. But it is the people and leaders of each country who must take the decision that a commitment to human rights and to finding genuine solutions to the problems of crime is furthered by an end to the death penalty.

Abolition sometimes comes very quickly – dramatic political changes may create new opportunities for the promotion of human rights.

Former Emperor of the Central African Republic, Jean-Bedel Bokassa, who had been sentenced to death for human rights abuses, had his sentence commuted to life imprisonment by President André Kolingba (left) in 1988.
© *Popperfoto*

Countries such as Argentina, Brazil, Haiti, Nicaragua, Peru and the Philippines have all abolished the death penalty over the last decade after emerging from periods of political repression. Elsewhere, the process may be protracted, requiring extensive consultation and courageous political leadership. Individual citizens, organizations and influential leaders all have an important role to play.

This chapter describes different measures which have been taken towards worldwide abolition of the death penalty. None of the steps automatically leads to abolition, but each can save lives. Each can help to create a climate where abolition is possible, and hasten the day when the death penalty is an evil that belongs to history.

A step forward: commutation of sentences

Every commutation of a sentence of death is an affirmation of the value of life. Many commutations are also a testimony to the importance of international concern and action.

Many prisoners have had their death sentences commuted during the past decade, some despite their notoriety. When former Emperor Jean-Bedel Bokassa returned from exile to the Central African Republic in 1986, he was tried and sentenced to death for crimes committed while he was in power, but in February 1988 President André Kolingba commuted the sentence to life imprisonment.

Some countries, while retaining the death penalty in law, have a long tradition of not carrying out executions. For example Belgium, with one exception, has not executed anyone for a common crime since 1863.

By not carrying out death sentences, a country eventually becomes abolitionist in practice. Bahrain, Bhutan, Bolivia, Côte d'Ivoire, Greece, Ireland, Madagascar and Senegal are among the 27 countries which can be considered abolitionist *de facto*: none of them has carried out an execution during the past 10 years or more.

No legal order can sustain itself unless it reflects a moral order...
Former Justice V R Krishna Iyer, Supreme Court of India

The practice of not carrying out executions is a way of testing this part of a country's penal policy, of establishing that the death penalty is not needed and that public opinion will accept non-lethal punishments. In a number of countries formal abolition has been preceded by a period during which the death penalty was not used.

Sweden carried out its last execution in 1910 and abolished the death penalty for peacetime offences in 1921, but the number of executions had been declining for more than a century before. In Cyprus, the last execution was in 1962 and the death penalty was abolished for all but exceptional crimes in 1983. The last execution reported in the national media of the German Democratic Republic (GDR) was in 1974. (Although outside sources have claimed that unreported executions were carried out, most recently in 1980, Amnesty International has not been able to verify these claims.) The GDR's Council of State abolished the death penalty by decree in July 1987 and the necessary legislative changes were approved in December that year.

Some death sentences have been commuted after worldwide appeals for clemency. The case of Kim Dae-jung, then opposition leader in the Republic of Korea, provides such an example. Sentenced to death in 1980, his sentence was commuted in 1981 after strong protest from several governments, including a telegram from the President of the European Parliament (the parliamentary body of the European Community) and appeals from several international human rights groups. A similar protest resulted when former Minister of Justice Orton Chirwa and his wife Vera were sentenced to death in Malawi in 1983. Their sentences were commuted in 1984 after appeals from, among others, the Presidents of Kenya and Nigeria, the Secretary-General of the United Nations, the General Secretary of the World Council of Churches and the Secretary-General of the Inter-African Union of Lawyers (see Chapter 3). However, international appeals failed to save the lives of South African poet Benjamin Moloise in 1985, of a number of alleged former communist leaders secretly executed in Indonesia since 1985, and of many other prisoners.

During the past decade death sentences have been commuted not only in individual cases but also in groups, often in connection with general amnesties marking some special occasion. In Thailand, for example, 48 death sentences were commuted to mark the 1983 bicentenary of the reigning dynasty, and 65 were commuted on the King's 60th birthday in 1987. In 1984 Gambian President Dawda Jawara commuted 33 death sentences, and in Swaziland all death sentences were commuted in 1986 to mark the coronation of King Mswati III. In 1987 President Juvénal Habyarimana of Rwanda commuted all confirmed death sentences, reportedly benefiting 537 prisoners, while in the Republic of Korea two death sentences were commuted in 1988 on the occasion of the inauguration of President Roh Tae-woo.

In Tunisia, three death sentences were commuted after a change of government in November 1987 and no executions have been carried out since then.

In Pakistan, former Prime Minister Zulfikar Ali Bhutto was executed in 1979 despite worldwide appeals. On taking office as Prime Minister of

Pakistan in December 1988, his daughter Benazir Bhutto requested Acting President Ghulam Ishaq Khan to commute all death sentences to life imprisonment. The Acting President immediately suspended all executions.

In November 1986 Governor Toney Anaya commuted all five outstanding death sentences in the state of New Mexico, USA as a parting gesture before leaving office. In an address on US Thanksgiving Day, Governor Anaya called for the abolition of the death penalty "because it is inhumane, immoral, anti-God and incompatible with an enlightened society". He urged the country to "put an end to this macabre national death march".

In Libya, Colonel Mu'ammar Gaddafi called for the abolition of the death penalty in March 1988. In May the death penalty was debated by the Basic People's Congresses, and on 12 June the General People's Congress adopted a constitutional document setting abolition as an aim of Jamahiri society, affirming the right to commutation and outlawing certain methods of execution. On 13 June Colonel Gaddafi intervened to commute all existing death sentences.

The danger of retaining the death penalty in law while refusing to use it is that executions may suddenly be resumed should policy change. The execution of Sergeant Major Wilfred Hawker in 1982 after a one-day summary trial was the first in Suriname in over 50 years (see Chapter 3). In Mauritius, the first execution in over 23 years was carried out in 1984 following a change of government. In 1981 Gambia carried out what was believed to be its first execution since independence in 1965. Other countries which have resumed executions in the past decade after a gap of 10 years or more are Benin, Dominica, Guyana, Saint Christopher and Nevis, and Saint Lucia.

The only way to prevent prisoners' lives depending on the whims of public policy is to enshrine abolition of the death penalty in a country's laws.

Official commissions on the death penalty

In countries where it is difficult to proceed immediately to a decision on abolition, creating a commission of inquiry may be a useful way of obtaining the facts on which a decision can be based. An official commission can serve to remove the issue of the death penalty from the political and emotional climate which so often surrounds it. The findings of a commission can provide officials, legislators and the public with an objective body of information to guide decisions on the issue.

Since World War II official commissions have succeeded in collecting and publishing new information on the death penalty in a number of countries. Three of the most outstanding have been those in the United Kingdom,[4] Ceylon[5] (now Sri Lanka) and Jamaica.[6] Each of their reports constituted a substantial record of the national experience of the death penalty which could be used in subsequent debate on the issue.

The three commissions used a variety of investigative techniques. All three held public hearings and received oral and written submissions from people such as civil servants, judges, police representatives, prison governors, religious leaders and representatives of organizations con-

I regard the death penalty as a savage and immoral institution which undermines the moral and legal foundations of a society. A state, in the person of its functionaries, who like all people are inclined to making superficial conclusions, who like all people are subject to influences, connections, prejudices and egocentric motivations for their behaviour, takes upon itself the right to the most terrible and irreversible act – the deprivation of life. Such a state cannot expect an improvement of the moral atmosphere in its country. I reject the notion that the death penalty has any essential deterrent effect on potential offenders. I am convinced that the contrary is true – that savagery begets only savagery.
Andrei Sakharov, USSR

cerned with penal policy. The British Commission obtained information from other countries by means of a questionnaire and by visiting several countries to inspect prisons and hear evidence. The Ceylon Commission held sittings in six cities and visited eight penal institutions and a mental hospital. The Jamaican Committee visited prisoners under sentence of death and appointed a research team to study the circumstances of murders in Jamaica and the characteristics of the people on death row.

The three commissions made various recommendations. The British Commission, which had not been empowered to consider abolition as such, did not recommend substantial changes in the operation of the death penalty except to change the test for determining criminal responsibility for people who might be insane or mentally abnormal. On the other hand, the Ceylon Commission, with one dissent, concluded that nothing in the experience of suspending the death penalty three years earlier justified its reintroduction. The Jamaican Committee said it believed that the death penalty for murder should be abolished, but that public opinion would not accept abolition at the time, in view of the level of violent crime in the country. Instead, it said, steps should be taken towards abolition, including limiting the scope of the death penalty and commuting all death sentences imposed before the date when the Committee's report was to have been submitted.

What happened to these recommendations differed from country to country. In the United Kingdom, the House of Commons went against the Royal Commission's recommendation to leave the law of murder substantially unchanged and decided in 1957 to specify that the death penalty would apply only to certain types of murder. When this law was put into

The Parliament buildings in Barbados. A 1979 study initiated by the government there concluded that the death penalty should be abolished. The study led to the government establishing the Committee on Penal Reform which said in its report that the death penalty should be debated in and decided on by Parliament. Amnesty International is not aware of any steps that have been taken to act upon the recommendations of either the study or the report. Barbados is the only country in the English-speaking Caribbean that does not exempt those under 18 from the death penalty. © *Camera Press*

practice it led to such anomalies that Parliament abolished the death penalty for murder in Great Britain provisionally in 1965 and permanently in 1969.

In Ceylon, the Commission's recommendations were overtaken by the assassination of the Prime Minister and the reintroduction of the death penalty in 1959, but during the past decade no death sentences have been carried out in Sri Lanka (as of November 1988).

In Jamaica, the Committee's recommendations were not implemented; one prisoner was executed in 1980 while the Committee was still sitting, and the recommendation of commuting earlier death sentences was ignored. The Committee's observations on the inadequacy of legal representation in death penalty cases were confirmed in a later Amnesty International study (see Chapter 3). The Committee's report was not made public officially until March 1987.

In 1980 Amnesty International submitted to the US authorities a proposal for a Presidential Commission on the Death Penalty in the USA. The Commission, Amnesty International said, should investigate such aspects of the death penalty as its discriminatory imposition, the arbitrariness of indictments and prosecutions, adequacy of legal representation of the poor and the possibility of error in death penalty cases.

The proposal was not taken up. Since then, as executions have been carried out in increasing numbers, the problems which Amnesty International believed should be examined by an official commission in the USA have, if anything, become more pronounced.

The death penalty and medical ethics

Members of various professions are involved in the administration of the death penalty from the initial arrest of a suspect to the carrying out of an execution or the granting of clemency. For many, participation in the death penalty process may not only be personally distressing but may pose conflicts between professional ethical demands and the actions which they are called on to perform. As a result of these disturbing experiences and their "inside" view of the death penalty process, professionals who are directly involved often become the most eloquent opponents of the death penalty.

In recent years ethical issues surrounding the death penalty have most often been raised in the medical profession. Medical ethics emphasize respect for life and enjoin doctors to practise for the good of their patients and never to do harm. Yet doctors have often been called on to participate directly in executions and to take part in the death penalty process in other ways. The introduction of lethal injection in the USA, a technique of execution based on medical science, has heightened the concern. In response, a number of medical organizations have adopted resolutions or statements opposing the involvement of health personnel in executions as a violation of medical ethics. Some have gone further to express opposition to the death penalty as such.

Some of the problems posed by participation in the death penalty process have been vividly described in an account published in the *Journal of Clinical Psychiatry* in 1978. As a young attending doctor in a

... the death sentence is abominable, as abominable as the crime itself. Our state must be based on love, not hatred and victimization. Our penal code must be based on rehabilitation rather than annihilation.

Chenjerai Hove, poet, Zimbabwe

77

prison in Ceylon (now Sri Lanka), Dr Abdul H. Hussain was required to give medical care to condemned prisoners, to assess their physical fitness prior to execution, to assess physical deformities in the neck or elsewhere which could interfere with an execution, to consult executioners on such matters as the optimal length of rope, and finally to witness the execution and certify death.

As described in the article, one 45-year-old prisoner was physically healthy the day before execution but was bathed in sweat, with a rapid pulse and with elevated blood pressure. On the eve of the execution he paced the floor of his cell like a caged animal. When the trap door of the execution platform was opened and the hooded prisoner dropped into the pit below, "For a few minutes the body dangled frantically at the end of the thick rope and then gradually quieted. Dr Hussain walked down the narrow stairway into the side of the pit and listened to the man's heart which now was rapid rate but regular; gradually the heart slowed, became very irregular and after about 13 minutes, ceased beating. Then the body was taken off the rope."

According to the article, "Dr Hussain's role as medical officer, psychiatrist and medical examiner in these proceedings still troubles him greatly today ... He feels a sense of guilt, and of outrage at having been used as a youthful, immature physician ... He now vehemently avers he would go to prison himself if faced with the same situation today rather than so serve. Much as a soldier who has killed for his society in a wrong war might feel, Dr Hussain feels a killer and deplores his own weakness not to have acted otherwise ... As a physician he saw himself as a healer and alleviator of human misery. Here he was called upon to expedite the taking of a life."[7]

In 1977 the US states of Oklahoma and Texas became the first jurisdictions in the world to adopt lethal injection as a method of execution. In a 1980 article, two doctors analysed the procedure of lethal injection in the light of the ethical principles of the medical profession. They wrote that requiring a doctor to prepare, administer or supervise lethal injections would violate medical ethics and would be "a perversion of biomedical knowledge and skill for a nonmedical purpose". In particular, they considered that "it would ... be ethically improper for physicians to monitor the condemned prisoner's condition during the drug administration and to carry on this action to pronounce his death when heartbeat and respirations were found to be absent. To perform such a continuous role would be so intimately a part of the whole action of killing as to deny any consideration as a separate medical service ... It is similar to the physician who examines the prisoner intermittently during torture or prolonged interrogation and pronounces him physically fit to continue his ordeal."[8]

In July 1980 the House of Delegates of the American Medical Association adopted a resolution stating that "A physician, as a member of a profession dedicated to preserving life when there is hope of doing so, should not be a participant in a legally authorized execution," although "A physician may make a determination or certification of death as currently provided by law in any situation."[9]

At the Assembly of the World Medical Association (WMA) held in Lisbon in 1981, the Assembly adopted a resolution "that it is unethical for

As one whose husband and mother-in-law have both died the victims of murder assassination, I stand yet firmly and un-equivocally opposed to the death penalty for those convicted of capital offences. An evil deed is not re-deemed by an evil deed of retaliation. Justice is never advanced in the taking of human life. Morality is never upheld by legalized murder.
Coretta Scott King, widow of murdered Martin Luther King, Jr., USA

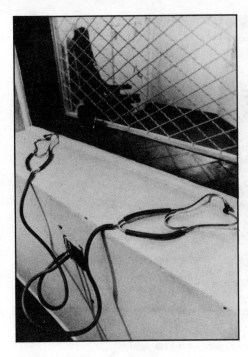

Doctors are members of a profession whose aim is to preserve life. Many consider participation in an execution to be unethical and abhorrent. Although in some countries the role of a doctor is confined to certifying death, elsewhere doctors are called on to monitor the progress of an execution so that it can continue if the prisoner is not yet dead. Medical bodies in over 20 countries are on record as opposing the participation of doctors in executions.
© *Jackson Hill*

physicians to participate in capital punishment, although this does not preclude physicians certifying death".

Resolutions opposing the participation of doctors in the death penalty or supporting the WMA's position have been passed by medical bodies in Australia, Denmark, Finland, Iceland, Ireland, New Zealand, Norway, Portugal and Sweden. Officials of medical associations in France, Japan, the Netherlands, Poland and Singapore have said their organizations oppose the participation of doctors in the death penalty.[10]

In 1985 the Turkish Medical Association (TMA) wrote to the Turkish Government urging the abolition of the death penalty. Basing its position on the 1981 WMA resolution it asked that doctors be excluded from the execution room and for an end to the requirement that a physician certify a condemned prisoner as fit for execution. As a result, six members of the TMA's Central Council were charged with an offence under the Law on Associations which prohibits political statements by all associations. After a prolonged trial they were acquitted in September 1986 by Ankara State Security Court. The TMA has drafted a new code of medical ethics which specifies that a doctor may not be present during an execution. The code is still passing through a number of legal steps necessary before it can be officially promulgated.

To date, national medical associations and congresses of doctors in at least 19 countries are thus formally opposed to the participation of doctors in executions. Some medical organizations have gone further by opposing not only participation in executions but the death penalty itself. They include such bodies in Chile, Peru and Switzerland.[11] Stands on medical ethics on the death penalty have also been taken by organizations of special groups of doctors and by other branches of the medical profession.

In January 1989 at least 75 people were executed in Iran for drugs offences. The executions followed new provisions that further expanded the scope of the death penalty for drugs offences. © *Keyhan*

In 1980 the American Psychiatric Association stated that it "strongly opposes any participation by psychiatrists in capital punishment, that is, in activities leading directly or indirectly to the death of a condemned person as a legitimate medical procedure". The Committee on Ethics of the American Nurses Association declared in 1983 that it is a "breach of the nursing code of ethical conduct to participate either directly or indirectly in a legally authorized execution". The Third World Congress on Prison Health Care held in Bristol, United Kingdom, in August 1988, adopted a resolution that prison health personnel should in no way participate in carrying out executions.

In the USA, several state medical associations have adopted resolutions in line with the American Medical Association resolution of 1980 or have indicated their support for that resolution. In Oklahoma, regulations requiring a doctor to order the toxic drugs and supervise the execution process have been changed to eliminate this role for the Medical Director of the state Corrections Department.

The statements of medical ethics discussed above refer mainly to direct participation in actual executions. Two areas where health professionals may find themselves in ethical dilemmas not covered in existing codes are testifying in court proceedings where their evidence could lead to a defendant's execution, and evaluating the mental or physical health of, or providing health care to, a prisoner under sentence of death where this could hasten the prisoner's execution.

Testimony by health professionals, particularly psychiatrists, is a common occurrence in court proceedings in determining the competence of a defendant to stand trial or to be held responsible for his or her actions. In

The Sharpeville Six in South Africa were sentenced to death in 1985 having been convicted of murder for having "common purpose" with the actual killers of a black town councillor. The case provoked an international campaign to save their lives and in November 1988 the death sentences were commuted to life imprisonment. © *Afrapix*

jurisdictions where the death penalty may be imposed, evidence given by psychiatrists or other mental health professionals can be a significant factor in whether a prisoner lives or dies. Whether testifying about the mental condition of the prisoner at the time of the crime or about his or her mental capacity in general, the medical witness plays a qualitatively different role in death penalty cases from that played while giving evidence in non-capital cases. The giving of testimony which may directly lead to the death of the person examined is a challenge to the basic ethical tenet of *primum non nocere.*

Similar dilemmas are posed for health professionals asked by the state to assess whether a prisoner is competent to be executed. Effectively they are asked to make a life or death decision in which professional judgment may be in conflict with a personal regard for the value of life. Also troublesome is the statutory requirement in some jurisdictions that a prisoner whose execution is postponed for reason of physical or mental illness should be restored to a sufficient level of health to permit execution.

In 1981 a Declaration on the Participation of Doctors in the Death Penalty was formulated by the Medical Advisory Board of Amnesty International and adopted by Amnesty International's International Executive Committee. The Declaration was revised in 1988 to include reference to other members of the medical profession. It lists elements of participation in executions which Amnesty International holds to be in violation of medical ethics and refers to other forms of involvement in the death penalty which may pose ethical dilemmas for the individual health professional (see Appendix 13).

International treaties to abolish the death penalty

Since World War II the death penalty has increasingly come within the ambit of international human rights standards adopted by governments in the UN and regional intergovernmental organizations. As described in Chapter 3, one element in these evolving standards has been the establishment of restrictions and safeguards to be observed in countries where the death penalty has not yet been abolished. During the past decade a second element has emerged: the development of treaties on the actual abolition of the death penalty.

Such a treaty is an agreement to abolish the death penalty, binding under international law among those states which decide to become parties to it. One such treaty in Western Europe has already entered into force; it is in the form of an Optional Protocol to the European Convention on Human Rights, abolishing the death penalty for peacetime offences. Two similar treaties are under development: within the UN, an Optional Protocol to the International Covenant on Civil and Political Rights (ICCPR) and, within the Americas, an Optional Protocol to the American Convention on Human Rights.

The European Convention on Human Rights was concluded in 1950, long before the adoption of the ICCPR, and does not contain the restrictions and safeguards on the death penalty which appear in that Covenant. Instead, Article 2 on the right to life makes provision for the

If ... we are to be sincere in our efforts to reduce violence, there is one type of violence that we can with complete certainty eliminate. That is the killing of criminals by the state. The question is, will people learn to respect life better by threat or by example? And the uniform answer of history, comparative studies and experience is that man is an emulative animal.
Norval Morris and Gordon Hawkins, criminologists, USA

On 28 January 1987 Dr Christian Broda, former Minister of Justice of Austria and the architect of the Sixth Protocol, was awarded the European Human Rights Prize of the Council of Europe. In his acceptance speech to the Parliamentary Assembly of the Council of Europe, given shortly before his death, Dr Broda said that with the signing and ratification of the Sixth Protocol by many member states "the worldwide campaign against capital punishment has taken a major step forward". Explaining his own reasons for opposing the death penalty, he said: "I belong to a generation which witnessed the appalling misuse made of the death penalty by the totalitarian dictatorships of our century in their efforts to track down and wipe out their political opponents. I was a very young man when the champions of democracy in my own country were court-martialled and hanged in 1934. In the years of misrule by the National Socialists, between 1938 and 1945, 1,184 women and men, including hundreds of Austrian patriots and opponents of fascism, as well as resistance fighters from many European countries, were guillotined on the orders of a single court in Vienna – admittedly the main one ... You can understand why I once said that the best day of my life in Parliament was 7 February 1968, when the elected representatives of the Austrian people unanimously voted to abolish the death penalty in all legal proceedings, including special trials and courts-martial."

death penalty, stating, in part: "No one shall be deprived of his life intentionally save in the execution of a sentence of a court following his conviction of a crime for which this penalty is provided by law."

A number of European countries abolished the death penalty after 1950, and in 1973, an attempt was made to initiate a discussion within the Council of Europe (an association of Western European countries, all of which are parties to the European Convention on Human Rights) through a motion for a resolution calling on member states of the Council to abolish the death penalty.

In 1980 the Parliamentary Assembly of the Council of Europe adopted a resolution calling on the parliaments of member states to abolish the death penalty for peacetime offences and with it a recommendation that the European Convention on Human Rights be amended accordingly. Out of this recommendation came the Sixth Protocol to the European Convention on Human Rights, which was opened for signature on 28 April 1983 and entered into force in 1985 after receiving the necessary minimum of five ratifications.

The Sixth Protocol is the first binding international agreement to abolish the death penalty for peacetime offences. Any member state of the Council of Europe may become a party to it. Article 1 of the Protocol states: "The death penalty shall be abolished. No one shall be condemned to such penalty or executed." Article 2 spells out the only exception to Article 1: a state party may provide for the death penalty "in respect of acts committed in time of war or of imminent threat of war". According to the official commentary on the text, the language of Article 1 seems to imply that a state which becomes a party to the Protocol is obliged to remove the death penalty from its laws. (This obligation, however, would not apply to the exception contained in Article 2.)[12]

In Chile, relatives of political prisoners chain themselves to the railings of the Congress building in Santiago in April 1987 to protest against the death penalty.

As of 1 January 1989, 12 of the 22 member states of the Council of Europe had ratified the Sixth Protocol. Three other member states had signed the Protocol, indicating their intention to ratify it at a future date. Cyprus, Ireland, Liechtenstein, Malta, San Marino, Turkey and the United Kingdom had neither signed nor ratified the Protocol.

Two similar treaties are under development but have not yet been adopted. One is an Optional Protocol to the ICCPR, first proposed by the Federal Republic of Germany at the UN General Assembly in 1980.

A draft of this Protocol, under which the death penalty would be abolished in peacetime, has been forwarded to the UN Commission on Human Rights for consideration at its 1989 session. If accepted there, the Protocol will go to the Economic and Social Council and then to the UN General Assembly for final adoption.

A further initiative for a treaty to abolish the death penalty was made within the Organization of American States at its General Assembly in November 1987. This proposed treaty is in the form of an additional protocol to the American Convention on Human Rights.

A preliminary draft prepared by the Inter-American Commission on Human Rights went further than the European Protocol by outlawing the death penalty completely and not merely in time of peace. The proposal was still under consideration at the time of writing this report.

Both the European Protocol and the other two proposed treaties are welcome steps towards worldwide abolition. Although no country which still retains the death penalty would be obliged to ratify them, these treaties can be attractive to abolitionist countries as a means of adding to national abolition the force of international law. While some retentionist countries occasionally extend the scope of application of the death penalty – in defiance of the UN injunction to the contrary – it is extremely rare for a country that has formally abolished the penalty to reintroduce it. There are frequently pressures in such countries to do so, however, and one universal means of facilitating resistance to such pressures would be the existence of an international obligation preventing reintroduction of the penalty. This may well provide one of the most convincing arguments in favour of the idea of the proposed treaties. They would permit those countries that have abolished the death penalty, and wish to resist fluctuating pressures to return to it, to set up an obstacle that would inhibit a precipitate reversion.

Non-extradition from abolitionist countries

A number of countries which have abolished the death penalty make a practice of refusing to extradite people to countries where they could be sentenced to death or executed, or of granting extradition only after receiving satisfactory assurances that a death sentence will not be imposed or, alternatively, will not be carried out. This practice sometimes takes the form of an administrative decision to seek such assurances through diplomatic channels. In a number of countries, however, it has become the object of legally binding provisions of national law or of international law as observed nationally.

Article 11 of the European Convention on Extradition of 1957 states: "If the offence for which extradition is requested is punishable by death under the law of the requesting Party, and if in respect of such offence the death penalty is not provided for by the law of the requested Party or is not normally carried out, extradition may be refused unless the requesting Party gives such assurance as the requested Party considers sufficient that the death penalty will not be carried out."

Provisions imposing restrictions or safeguards on extradition in cases involving possible death penalties are included in the laws of abolitionist countries, including Austria,[13] Denmark,[14] the Netherlands,[15] Switzerland[16] and the United Kingdom.[17] In Italy, although no similar provision has been enacted in law, a 1979 decision by the Constitutional Court stated that extradition to a country providing for the death penalty for the offence upon which the request is based would be in violation of Article 27 of the Italian Constitution, abolishing the death penalty for peacetime offences. Such provisions are also included in various extradition treaties, such as those between Italy and the USA and between the United Kingdom and the USA.

The content of these provisions varies considerably. The authorities may be required to refuse extradition outright or simply to seek satisfactory

I cannot imagine myself signing a death warrant.
President Zine al-Abidine Ben Ali, Tunisia

assurances before granting it; they may be given discretion to take such action or they may be obliged to do so; the provisions may be designed only to prevent execution or to preclude a death sentence as well.

Restrictions on extradition in death penalty cases are an important means whereby countries, consistently with their own abolitionist position, can extend the non-infliction of the death penalty beyond their borders in cases in which they have a direct interest.

The decision not to reintroduce the death penalty

From time to time, in places where the death penalty has been abolished, voices are raised calling for it to be brought back. The ensuing discussion can help to confirm the wisdom of abolition by reminding people of the reasons why the death penalty was originally abolished and by pointing to the lack of negative consequences.

Occasionally the death penalty is reintroduced by decree in a period of military rule or political tension. Even then the authorities may decide not to use it if the country has an abolitionist tradition. Brazil reintroduced the death penalty under military rule in 1969, as did Argentina in 1976; no death sentences were passed, and the death penalty was later abolished again in both countries for ordinary offences. Nepal reintroduced the death penalty for murder and other crimes after several bomb explosions in 1985, but no one has yet been executed under the new laws.

Some calls for the death penalty never reach the stage of a formal vote. Politically motivated killings prompted calls for the death penalty in both Italy and Peru in the early 1980s, but these calls died down and the issue was never brought to a vote. Elsewhere moves to reintroduce the death penalty have been defeated in parliamentary votes, as happened during the past decade in Papua New Guinea in 1980, in Canada in 1987, in Brazil in 1988, and in the United Kingdom in major debates held in 1979, 1983, 1987 and 1988.

The Senate of the US state of Kansas voted in April 1987 not to reintroduce the death penalty, while in New York State, legislative bills to reintroduce the death penalty have been consistently vetoed by the state governor.

Parliamentary debates and public discussions can help make legislators and members of the public more aware of the reality of the death penalty and the strength of the case against it. Analysing the defeat of a move to restore the death penalty in the UK House of Commons in 1983, two journalists wrote that members of parliament "changed their minds, often because they had never had to listen to the arguments against hanging before. Faced with a real choice, they had to answer to the administrative requirements of the state, not the emotive political demands of party members." One newly elected member of parliament told them he had changed his mind: "It is only when you take part in the debate that the case against hanging becomes overwhelmingly obvious," he said. Another member of parliament conceded that most of his constituents favoured the death penalty but said that "they don't seem to have thought deeply about the arguments and are impressed when they hear them".[18]

I learned ... that the man who killed my husband ... has now been sentenced to death ... the views of myself and my husband's family on capital punishment remain unchanged. We are totally against it. Society condemns murder, but is willing to accept the murder of this man in the name of justice ...
Pauline Maitland, widow of murdered Toronto police officer, Canada

Staff at *The Herald* newspaper in Zimbabwe, 1983, receiving copies of letters appealing against the death penalty imposed on Vera and Orton Chirwa in Malawi. The sentences were commuted in 1984.
© *The Herald*

During the debates and discussions the standard arguments for and against the death penalty are likely to be aired. On the question of deterrence, for example, Paul Torato, the Minister of Justice of Papua New Guinea, told the parliament in 1980 that most killings in the country were committed "under the sway of a violent emotion, such as anger, the desire for revenge or fear of a sorcerer"; the death penalty was unlikely to be a deterrent "for those unplanned killings as a result of sudden outburst of emotion".

Along with the moral and criminological considerations, speakers have also pointed to practical problems with the death penalty, such as the difficulty of drafting laws which in application are seen to be fair. In Great Britain, for example, the attempt to distinguish capital from non-capital murders in the Homicide Act of 1957 had created anomalies which were followed by the provisional abolition of the death penalty in 1965 and its permanent abolition in 1969. As Home Secretary Leon Brittan said during the debate in 1983, "… there were two sorts of anomalies – those which are inherent in any such a categorization, and those which the skilful drafting of legislation might hope to overcome. Both are important, but the first anomaly is more important. Although attempts can be made to single out from other crime murders that are especially prevalent, or that are believed to be more deterrable by the death penalty, the problem remains that any such differentiation, when put into practice, is likely to lead fairly quickly to growing feelings of injustice. There will soon be cases outside, whatever criteria are chosen, that are felt to be more grave than those within them."[19]

Attempts to restore the death penalty can provoke expressions of concern by prominent figures, influential organizations, the news media

87

and other opinion leaders. Their statements against the death penalty can create a moral climate in which members of parliament feel they can risk voting in a way which they know may be unpopular with many of their constituents.

Before the most important of the United Kingdom debates, that in 1983, there were statements from many quarters as well as the traditional abolitionist organizations. The former Commissioner of the London Metropolitan Police, Sir Robert Mark, wrote in the *Observer* newspaper of 10 July that "there is no more certain way to undermine effective law enforcement than to include death in the judicial process". James Prior, then Secretary of State for Northern Ireland, wrote in a letter to his constituency party that the reintroduction of the death penalty could create martyrs and would "make it more difficult to bring terrorists to justice".[20] The Prison Governors Branch of the Society of Civil and Public Servants wrote in an open letter to the Home Secretary that they "could anticipate some resignations" from the Prison Service if the death penalty were restored. There were reports that some lawyers might refuse on grounds of conscience to prosecute in cases involving the death penalty, and it was reported that civil servants in the Home Office were "expected to press for conscience clauses to be inserted in their contracts" so that they would not have to take part in carrying out the death penalty or drafting the relevant legislation.[21] In a move reflecting the emerging Western European consensus against the death penalty, Piet Dankert, President of the European Parliament (the elected parliamentary body of the European Community), wrote to the Prime Minister of the United Kingdom saying that a vote to restore the death penalty would be "an

Nador Prison, Tunisia, where prisoners under sentence of death have been held. For countries which retain the death penalty in law, a change of government can result in a resumption of executions – or a moratorium. After a change of government in Tunisia in November 1987, three death sentences were commuted and there have been no executions since then.

extraordinary and terrible decision", with "negative consequences" for the country's stance on human rights.[22]

At the end of the debate on 13 July 1983, a motion favouring the restoration of the death penalty for murder was defeated by 368 votes to 223 – a margin of 145, larger than in 1979 and much larger than expected. An amendment to the motion favouring restoration of the death penalty for "murder resulting from an act of terrorism" was defeated by a margin of 116; four other amendments referring to other categories of murder were also defeated. The outcome in subsequent debates was similar: motions to restore the death penalty for murder were again defeated by large margins in 1987 and 1988.

In Canada, where the death penalty had been abolished for murder in 1976, the Progressive Conservative Party won the 1984 general election with its leader, Brian Mulroney, pledged to allow a vote on the issue.

A Canadian Coalition Against the Return of the Death Penalty was formed; its members included the Canadian Council of Churches, the Canadian Conference of Catholic Bishops, the Canadian Civil Liberties Union and the Criminal Lawyers' Association. Besides meeting Prime Minister Mulroney formally, the Coalition asked its member organizations to have their individual members and branches visit their members of parliament around the country to impress on them the strength of the case against the death penalty. The organizations took their case to the news media: the issue was examined in television and radio programs and in the press, and major newspapers published editorials opposing reintroduction. Details on the past use of the death penalty in Canada and its present use in the neighbouring USA were presented: just as publicity

Death sentences in Swaziland were commuted as part of the celebrations of the coronation of King Mswati III in 1986. © *Popperfoto*

about violent crime in the USA had contributed to fears of crime in Canada, so now details of the cruelty and arbitrary use of the death penalty in the USA helped to bring home the reality of what its reintroduction would mean for Canada.

After the 1984 election it had seemed almost certain that the large Progressive Conservative Party majority in parliament would ensure passage of a bill to restore the death penalty. But when the issue came to a vote on 30 June 1987, after more than two years of public education and discussion, a motion to restore the death penalty was defeated by 148 votes to 127 – a larger majority than in the original vote to abolish it in 1976.

One other factor in the debates has been strong leadership among those opposed to the death penalty. In the 1980 parliamentary debate in Papua New Guinea, Prime Minister Sir Julius Chan said: "... I am strongly of the view that hanging, or for that matter, any form of extinction of human life, is no deterrent to murder ... Execution or taking a man's life is an act which brutalizes both the executioner, and the community at large..." In the United Kingdom, the three Home Secretaries in office during the four debates all spoke against reintroducing the death penalty for murder even though the Prime Minister was known to favour restoration. In Canada, Prime Minister Brian Mulroney said during the debate in 1987 that he believed the death penalty to be "repugnant" and "profoundly unacceptable". The firm convictions of political leaders and cabinet ministers undoubtedly set an example for other members of parliament to follow in deciding not to bring back the death penalty.

The many voices raised in favour of abolition around the world represent many different cultures, religions and countries. They are united in a very basic conviction: respect for human rights and human life must be the basis of state policy. The death penalty – the premeditated killing of a prisoner by the state – cannot be reconciled with such respect.

Those speaking out in favour of abolition and against continued executions have throughout the centuries been in a minority. But their ideals have progressively gained support. The basis for hope is that as the reality of the death penalty becomes widely known, the movement to rid the world of this human rights violation will continue to grow.

The march towards abolition of the death penalty has already gone far in affirming the value of human life and human rights. The progress made and that yet to come is catalogued in the following pages of this report. The goal: a world without executions.

I shall ask for the abolition of the death penalty until I have the infallibility of human judgment demonstrated to me.
Marquis de Lafayette, France

© *Popperfoto*

© *Doug Magee*

1 Lyla Elliott in the official record of the Legislative Council of Western Australia, 22 August 1984, page 1059. By 1984 all six states except Western Australia had abolished the death penalty for murder. In 1985, New South Wales abolished the death penalty for the three exceptional crimes still punishable by death in the country.

2 Thucydides, *The History of the Peloponnesian War*, Book III, paragraphs 25-50.

3 C.H.S. Jayawardene, "The Death Penalty in Ceylon", *Ceylon Journal of Historical and Social Studies*, vol. 3. No. 2 (July-December 1960), pages 166-186.

4 The Royal Commission on Capital Punishment was appointed in 1949 and submitted its report in 1953.

5 The Ceylon Commission of Inquiry on Capital Punishment was appointed in 1958 and submitted its report in 1959.

6 The Committee on Capital Punishment and Penal Reform (the "Fraser Committee") was established by the Minister of Justice in 1979 and reported in 1981.

7 Abdul H. Hussain and Seymour Tozman, "Psychiatry on death row", *Journal of Clinical Psychiatry*, March 1978, pages 183-187.

8 William J. Curran and Ward Casscells, "The ethics of medical participation in capital punishment by intravenous drug injection", *New England Journal of Medicine*, vol. 302, No. 4 (24 January 1980), pages 226-230.

9 The report of the American Medical Association's Judicial Committee which was before the House of Delegates spelled out the difference between the taking of life through participation in an execution and the certification of death. The report said that whereas medical standards rested on the concept *primum non nocere*, above all do no harm, "It *is* harmful to take a life ..." and that "the active participation by physicians in executions is not required" (emphasis in original). Certification of death, on the other hand, was a function legally required so that public records could certify to the fact of death; in the Judicial Committee's view such certification "is not a part of the act of execution and is not, therefore, improper".

10 Resolutions opposing the participation of doctors in the death penalty have been adopted by the Irish Medical Association in 1981 and by the Nordic Medical Associations, comprising the medical associations of the five Nordic countries (Denmark, Finland, Iceland, Norway and Sweden), in 1986. The Federal Council of the Australian Medical Association in 1981 resolved to support the statement opposing the participation of doctors in the death penalty which was subsequently adopted by the World Medical Association, and the Portuguese Medical Association took a similar position. In 1983 the Council of the New Zealand Medical Association resolved to support the WMA resolution. Officials of the Royal Dutch Medical Association, the Japan Medical Association, the Polish Medical Association, the Singapore Medical Association and the French *Ordre National des Médecins* (National Medical Order) have indicated that their organizations either support the WMA resolution or are opposed to the participation of doctors in the death penalty.

11 In 1980 the *Segundo Congreso Médico Nacional* (Second Medical Congress) of Peru issued a declaration of principles which opposed the death penalty and stated that "Doctors may refuse, and cannot be obliged, to attend, examine, verify or certify the death of a person who has suffered the death penalty, whatever the reason for that punishment." Along similar lines the Central Committee of *Federatio Medicorum Helveticorum* (Federation of Swiss Physicians) in 1982 expressed its opposition to the death penalty and decided to support Amnesty International's Declaration on the Participation of Doctors in the Death Penalty which states that the participation of doctors in executions is a violation of medical ethics.

The *Consejo General* (General Council) of the *Colegio Médico de Chile* (Chilean Medical Association) issued a public statement in December 1987 opposing the death penalty and the involvement of medical professionals in executions. It called for a change in the law requiring a doctor to order a *coup de grâce* in cases where a prisoner survives attempted execution. The association said that "it is not the function of a doctor to officiate or collaborate with the executioner, nor is it morally permissible to determine whether an executed person is still alive so that they can be shot again".

12 Nigel S. Rodley, *The treatment of prisoners under international law*, UNESCO, Paris, Clarendon Press, Oxford, 1987, pages 170-173.

13 Auslieferungs- und Rechtshilfegesetz of 1979, paragraph 20.

14 Extradition Act of 1967, Article 10.

15 Extradition Act of 1967, Article 8.

16 Loi fédérale sur l'entraide internationale en matière pénale of 1981, Article 37.

17 Criminal Justice Act, 1988, Part I, section 9 (11) (b).

18 Christopher Hird and Peter Kellner, *New Statesman*, vol. 106, No. 2731, 22 July 1983, page 6.

19 *House of Commons, Official Report, Parliamentary Debates (Hansard)*, vol. 45, No. 20, 13 July 1983, column 898.

20 *Observer*, 10 July 1983.

21 *The Guardian*, 27 June 1983; *Sunday Times*, 10 July 1983.

22 *The Guardian*, 13 July 1983.

The death penalty worldwide

The death penalty worldwide

This part of the report describes country by country the death penalty in law and practice. One hundred and eighty countries and territories are covered and the entries are arranged alphabetically.

Many governments do not publish information on the use of the death penalty, and in some countries the death penalty is surrounded by secrecy. The length of an entry, therefore, is not an indication of the extent of its use: freely available information may have facilitated a detailed analysis of capital punishment in a particular country, while lack of it in another country may have resulted in a less comprehensive entry. Wherever possible, each entry lists the principle offences punishable by death, indicating whether the death penalty is optional (a court has discretion to impose a death sentence or a less severe one) or mandatory (the court is required to impose a death sentence). Categories of offenders who are excluded from the death penalty under the country's laws (such as those aged under 18 the time of the offence) are also noted.

The entries name the courts empowered to pass death sentences and those which have jurisdiction to hear appeals or review sentences imposed by lower courts. If the judicial procedures provided for by law are known not to conform to internationally agreed standards for a fair trial, this is indicated. If a country has more than one judicial system empowered to pass death sentences – if, for example, military or special courts have jurisdiction over certain cases while the ordinary courts have jurisdiction over others – this too is indicated. The entries describe the country's procedures for the granting of clemency and the method(s) of execution provided for by law.

The entries describe the death penalty both in law and in practice. An account is given of the extent of the use of the death penalty. For example, if there are known to be large numbers of prisoners under sentence of death, if there have been sudden surges of executions or other fluctuations in the pattern of executions, if death sentences are known to have been imposed on prisoners who did not receive a fair trial, or if the death penalty has been used retroactively, this is mentioned. Where condemned prisoners are known to be subjected to special humiliations, executed in public or given little or no time to appeal, this is also stated.

The report is not only about the death penalty today but about progress towards worldwide abolition. If a country has abolished the death penalty, the entry describes, where possible, how abolition was achieved and when the last execution was carried out.

Each country entry begins with four sub-headings intended to give the reader a quick grasp of the country or territory's laws and practice on the death penalty. These are as follows.

Status: This indicates whether, as of mid-1988, the country was abolitionist (the death penalty is abolished for all crimes); abolitionist for all but exceptional crimes, such as wartime crimes; abolitionist in practice, as suggested by the fact that no one has been executed for the past 10 years or more; or retentionist (the death penalty is retained in law and used for ordinary crimes). On a few countries Amnesty International has no record of executions during the past 10 years but is unable to ascertain whether or not executions have in fact been carried out.

Executions 1985 - mid-1988: This indicates the number of executions recorded by Amnesty International between the beginning of 1985 and mid-1988, and the crimes for which the executions were reportedly carried out. In some countries this number is based on official figures; where these are not available, Amnesty International has relied on reports of executions in the national press and other sources. A plus sign (+) indicates that Amnesty International believes the true figure to be higher but is unable to give an exact number.

Other factors: This lists special features of the death penalty during the past decade, such as legislation empowering courts to impose death sentences using procedures which do not conform to international norms for a fair trial; prisoners executed who were under 18 at the time of the offence; secret executions; and executions carried out in public.

Methods of execution: This lists the method(s) provided for by law (although they have not necessarily been used during the past decade).

The country descriptions cover only the death penalty and do not contain information on other human rights violations of concern to Amnesty International unless these are connected to the death penalty – if, for example, condemned prisoners have reportedly been tortured or if people adopted by Amnesty International as prisoners of conscience have faced the death penalty, this is mentioned. The report does not deal with the practice of some governments of executing their real or perceived opponents without invoking the death penalty as provided by law. Hundreds if not thousands of people each year are victims of extrajudicial executions – unlawful and deliberate killings carried out by order of a government or with its acquiescence, outside the judicial process and in violation of international standards which prohibit the arbitrary deprivation of life. Amnesty International regularly appeals to the authorities concerned to stop these abuses and to ensure that all complaints and reports of extrajudicial executions are impartially and effectively investigated. Information on these and other human rights violations of concern to the organization may be found in the annual *Amnesty International Report* and in Amnesty International publications on the countries concerned.

This report is intended to update the information in Amnesty International's earlier report, *The Death Penalty* (published in 1979), and covers the past decade, 1979 to 1988. In some entries information from before 1979 is given as background to the current situation. Where Amnesty International has information on significant developments since mid-1988 this is given at the end of an entry and is indicated by the symbol ▶.

Afghanistan

Status: Retentionist

Executions 1985 - mid-88: Not known

Other factors: Unfair trials

Method of execution: Shooting by firing-squad

The full-scale war in Afghanistan since 1978 has blurred the distinction between judicial executions and extrajudicial executions, and the number of officially announced death sentences bears little resemblance to the total number of those executed by the government. According to former prisoners interviewed by Amnesty International, many executions have been carried out secretly and summarily. The official Afghan media stopped announcing executions in 1985 and the imposition of death sentences in 1987 (though, exceptionally, three sentences were announced in mid-1988), but there have been unofficial reports that executions have continued to take place, particularly at Pul-é-Charkhi Central Prison in Kabul.

The Penal Code provides for the death penalty for a large variety of offences, including murder, armed robbery, looting, plundering public property, armed resistance against security forces, importing weapons or explosives, transporting weapons or explosives, anti-state activities, counter-revolutionary activities, subversive activities, evading military service (in conjunction with other grave offences), and membership of an illegal political organization.

In November 1979 lists of the 12,000 prisoners who had died during detention in the jails of Kabul since the Marxist revolution of April 1978 were posted outside the Ministry of the Interior in Kabul. According to prisoners who survived that period, many of those listed had been executed. Riots followed the posting of the lists and no comprehensive death lists have been issued by the authorities since then.

Between 1980 and 1984 there were 159 death sentences reported by the official media but Amnesty International believes the true figure of death sentences imposed to be higher. Between 1985 and mid-1988 executions were not announced and figures for death sentences imposed were given only for 1985, 1986 and 1988 – these were 40, eight and three respectively. The most detailed data available are those for 1984. In that year, of the 92 death sentences imposed, 36 were for crimes against the person, 37 for crimes against the state and 19 for a multiple offence. Of the 60 executions carried out in 1984, 26 were for crimes against the person, 33 were for crimes against the state and one was for a multiple offence. Of the 40 death sentences imposed in 1985, six were for crimes against the person, 31 were for crimes against the state and three were for multiple offences. In 1986, three death sentences were imposed for crimes against the person and five for crimes against the state.

Charges such as "anti-state activities" and "counter-revolutionary activities" allow the death penalty to be used against political opponents of the government. Former prisoners have testified that in the majority of cases the Special Revolutionary Courts, which deal with all crimes, arrive at decisions quickly, whether or not the crime is punishable by death. There is no defence counsel but defendants are given between 15 and 30 minutes to speak in their own defence. The prosecutor's word is readily accepted and witnesses for or against the accused are rarely produced in court. Under Article 58 of the Republic of Afghanistan's Basic Principles of Governance, death sentences could be carried out only after the approval of the Presidium of the Revolutionary Council. Prisoners under sentence of death could appeal for clemency (commutation) to the Presidium of the Revolutionary Council. This was the procedure until the end of 1987. The new parliament elected in April 1988, which superseded the Revolutionary Council, has yet to decide on the approvals and appeals procedure on the death penalty.

Functionaries of the Special Revolutionary Prosecution Department and of the Special Revolutionary Courts were given the following advice in November 1984 by Babrak Karmal, who was then the President of Afghanistan and General Secretary of the ruling People's Democratic Party of Afghanistan: "Any kind of artificial and false humanity, pity and kindness for the counter-revolutionaries, for the killers and robbers ... would itself be hard-heartedness, cruelty and unkindness to those sacrificed by the counter-revolutionaries." On the same occasion, Babrak Karmal separately advised judges of the Special Revolutionary Courts. He told them, "Acquittal decisions must only be rendered in the event of total and clear innocence of the accused. Instances of determining light punishments for grave crimes must be completely eliminated…" Unofficial reports since then indicate that death sentences continue to be imposed and carried out readily in Afghanistan.

Albania

Status: Retentionist

Executions 1985 - mid-88: Not known

Other factors: Not known

Methods of execution: Shooting by firing-squad; hanging

The Criminal Code of 1977 states, "The death penalty is an exceptional punishment imposed solely for especially dangerous crimes." Although the death penalty is always optional, it is provided for a considerable number of offences, including a number of economic and political offences which do not necessarily result in loss of human life or involve the use of violence.

The death penalty is provided for aggravated homicide, sexual relations under duress (rape) or with minors aged under 14 which have resulted in the death or suicide of the victim, and for assault with intent to rob. Certain economic crimes are punishable by death, including the large-scale appropriation of socialist property and the falsification of currency.

Various military crimes carry the death penalty if committed in wartime or during a state of emergency; for example, avoidance of military service, and the wilful destruction or damaging of military property.

All crimes against the state (except for "inciting to racial or national hostility or dissension") are punishable by death. These crimes include not only "terrorist acts" and "sabotage" but also those which do not necessarily involve the use or advocacy of violence

such as "flight from the state and refusal to return to the fatherland on the part of a person sent on service or allowed temporarily to leave the state", and the crime of "agitation and propaganda against the state" when this is committed in wartime or has resulted in grave consequences.

A death sentence may not be imposed on anyone who was aged under 18 at the time of the offence, nor on a woman who was pregnant at the time of the offence or the trial. A death sentence is commuted to 25 years' imprisonment if a woman offender is found to be pregnant at the time scheduled for execution.

Civilians accused of capital offences are generally tried by ordinary district courts; military benches of these courts try cases involving members of the armed forces. By law, the Supreme Court hears appeals against death sentences within 10 days of receipt of the case, and reviews all death sentences even if no appeal is made. If the death sentence is confirmed by the Supreme Court the defendant may petition for clemency to the Presidium of the People's Assembly; this body must in any case examine and approve all death sentences before they can be carried out. Execution is by shooting unless the court orders hanging.

Three political prisoners, Vangjel Lezha, Fadil Kokomani and Xhelal Koprencka, serving sentences in Spac Labour Camp, were reported by several fellow-prisoners to have been summarily tried and executed in 1978.

Death sentences are not reported in the press and no official figures have been published. A judge from the Federal Republic of Germany was reportedly told by the authorities during a visit to Albania that all death sentences passed in 1982 had been commuted to a term of imprisonment.

In 1983 unofficial sources outside Albania claimed that Fecor Shehu and Kadri Hazbiu, former Ministers of Internal Affairs and Defence respectively, had been executed with two other senior officials (their arrest had been officially announced in 1982). Amnesty International has been unable to confirm these reports.

Algeria

Status: Retentionist

Executions 1985 - mid-88: 12; murder

Other factors: Special courts with deficient procedures

Method of execution: Shooting by firing-squad

Under the Penal Code the death penalty is provided for over 30 offences. These include a number of offences against state security such as treason and spying; embezzlement seriously affecting the higher interest of the nation; and certain crimes against individuals or property such as premeditated murder, use of violence to commit another crime, armed robbery and arson. The death penalty is also provided for under the Algerian Code of Military Justice for a variety of military offences and wartime crimes committed by military personnel.

The death penalty is mandatory unless mitigating circumstances can be proved. Those aged under 18 at the time of the crime may not be sentenced to death and the mentally ill may not be executed. Executions of pregnant women or breast-feeding mothers of children under two are deferred.

Criminal courts, the State Security Court and the military courts all have jurisdiction in trials involving capital offences. The right of defence in cases heard before the State Security Court may be restricted; that is, if the case "has a particular character", the President of the Court may not approve the candidacy of a defence lawyer. However, the wording of the "restriction" is general and vague and its use appears to be open to interpretation.

In recent years there have been at least three trials before the State Security Court of people charged with political offences, each of which fell short of international standards for fair trial. In 1987 four people were sentenced to death (one *in absentia*) after a trial which did not conform to international standards: some defendants were subjected to prolonged incommunicado detention in police custody and allegedly tortured or ill-treated to extract confessions which were later admitted as evidence in court, and after they were transferred to prison, access to families and lawyers was reportedly severely hampered. Most of the defence lawyers were appointed by the court only a few days before the trial began, and they appeared to have access to only a part of the case dossier. The court did not appear to have carried out any investigations into these irregularities and allegations.

Cases heard by criminal and military courts and the State Security Court are not heard by a court of appeal, but the accused may, within a given period specified by law, apply to the Supreme Court for cassation which is competent to review alleged misapplication of the law. The President of the Republic has the right to grant pardon or commute a sentence. Once the Supreme Court has upheld a decision, execution may not be carried out until a plea for clemency has been presented to the President and refused.

Executions are carried out by firing-squad in the municipality where the prisoner is held, in the presence of a doctor. Executions are not permitted on national and religious days.

According to figures available to Amnesty International, between 1985 and mid-1988 there were 12 executions and 15 death sentences passed. Two of these death sentences have been commuted to a term of imprisonment.

Andorra

Status: Abolitionist in practice

Executions 1985 - mid-88: None

Other factors: None

Method of execution: Not applicable

Andorra has no written penal code, but traditionally justice is administered by a court using the law of custom. This unwritten system of justice for penal matters is based on Roman, Justinian, Catalan, Canon, Spanish and Napoleonic law. The system is currently being codified, but it is unlikely to contain any reference to the death penalty. The death penalty has been used only once this century, when in 1943 a citizen convicted of the murder of his two brothers was shot by firing-squad.

Angola

Status: Retentionist

Executions 1985 - mid-88: 15; crimes against the security of the state; homicide

Other factors: Unfair trials

Method of execution: Shooting by firing-squad

Since Angola gained independence from Portugal in November 1975 more than 180 people are known to have been sentenced to death. Most of them are believed to have been executed, although executions are not always announced or reported. Over 100 of these death sentences – most of them for treason and armed rebellion – were imposed between 1980 and 1984, in response to the increasing activities of the armed opposition *União para a Independência Total de Angola* (UNITA), National Union for the Total Independence of Angola. Since 1985, 47 death sentences, most of them passed by military courts, and 15 executions have been recorded.

After independence the legal basis for the application of the death penalty seemed to be the Military Disciplinary Code of 1966 promulgated during the war for independence by the *Movimento Popular da Libertação de Angola* (MPLA), People's Movement for the Liberation of Angola, now the ruling party. Portuguese law, on which Angolan law is based, retained the death penalty for certain war crimes only, but Angola introduced it in February 1978 for offences concerning national security, such as treason, espionage and armed rebellion, and also for aggravated murder (Law No. 3/78 of 25 February 1978). The law implied that the death penalty had previously been imposed in a context of "revolutionary legality" but was now to become a part of the ordinary legal system. A subsequent law (Law No. 16/78 of 24 November 1978) defined 10 crimes for which military personnel could be sentenced to death, including insubordination and desertion in time of war or during military operations. Both these laws provide for a 24-year prison sentence as an alternative to the death penalty and all death sentences are to be referred to a court of appeal. Pregnant women and anyone aged under 18 at the time of the offence cannot be sentenced to death. The power to grant pardon or commute sentences is vested in the President.

The legal basis for death sentences imposed before 1978 was unclear. Four foreigners were executed in 1976 after being convicted of mercenarism, which had not been defined as a crime in Angolan law, and another three people after being convicted of murder, which was not punishable by death under ordinary law. After an unsuccessful coup attempt in May 1977 a special military commission sat secretly the following August and sentenced the suspected leaders to death. Hundreds of people suspected of complicity in the coup were subsequently summarily executed by the security forces.

In July 1979 a series of trials began of suspected armed government opponents, charged under laws promulgated in 1978. Between 1976 and 1984 all the death sentences reported in the (government-controlled) press were imposed by the People's Revolutionary Tribunal, a special court established in May 1976 with jurisdiction over all crimes against the security of the state as well as certain other crimes. Although a right of appeal was mentioned in the 1978 laws, it was not until 1980 that a special Appeals Court was actually established and at least 34 people sentenced to death before then had therefore been unable to lodge appeals.

In its first hearings in July 1980 the Appeals Court confirmed all of the 16 death sentences imposed earlier the same day by the People's Revolutionary Tribunal. On other occasions the Appeals Court has commuted at least two death sentences to prison terms of two and six years. In March 1981, however, it imposed a death sentence on a prisoner originally sentenced to 24 years' imprisonment. In August 1986 the President pardoned three people whose death sentences had been upheld by the Appeals Court in October 1985.

In July 1983, in response to the increasing activities of UNITA guerrillas, Regional Military Tribunals were given jurisdiction over political cases in provinces particularly affected by UNITA activity, and were empowered to impose the death penalty. At least 60 alleged UNITA members were sentenced to death by these courts between 1984 and 1987. By law these death sentences are automatically referred for review to the Armed Forces Military Tribunal. However, it is unclear whether those sentenced to death were able to lodge appeals or to petition for clemency.

Prisoners have been sentenced to death after unfair trials. In particular, defendants are reported to have had little or no access to legal counsel. In one case a defendant who had no legal assistance reportedly asked a fellow prisoner to help him prepare a written statement in his defence; he was subsequently sentenced to death. Defendants are also reported to have been sentenced to death on the basis of statements made under torture, or in the face of inadequate prosecution evidence. On several occasions prisoners have been publicly paraded after being sentenced to death. In April 1985 seven people were paraded before a crowd at a factory in Lubango before being led to the firing-squad.

Death sentences and executions for non-political offences are not often reported. In January 1988 four former soldiers were sentenced to death by the Revolutionary Military Tribunal in Luanda for murdering a family during the course of a robbery. It is not known whether they were executed.

In May 1988 the *Tribunal de Relação*, the court which hears appeals from district courts, commuted a death sentence passed in August 1987 on a man convicted of murder. It was the first time a death sentence had been imposed by an ordinary district court. In its judgment the Appeals Court noted that international opposition to the use of the death penalty to punish ordinary crime was increasing and asserted that states had a duty to protect the right to life.

▶ On 12 December President José Eduardo dos Santos announced that, in commemoration of the 40th anniversary of the Universal Declaration of Human Rights, a law had been drafted to commute the sentences of all prisoners currently under sentence of death. The law, which would be submitted to the national assembly for approval in early 1989 would benefit at least the eight people sentenced to death in 1987 and 1988.

Anguilla

Status: Abolitionist in practice

Executions 1985 - mid-88: None

Other factors: None

Method of execution: Hanging

A mandatory death penalty is provided for murder (Offences against the Person Act), treason and piracy (both under the Piracy Act 1837 [UK]). A death sentence cannot be imposed on anyone who was under 18 at the time of the crime, nor on pregnant women.

Following the trial, appeals may be made to the local court of appeal. If rejected there, prisoners can lodge a final appeal with the Judicial Committee of the Privy Council in England. However, the Privy Council will consider only cases involving constitutional matters or "matters of great public importance".

Since Anguilla seceded from St Christopher-Nevis in 1975, at least one sentence of death has been passed, but this was subsequently commuted to a term of imprisonment. At the time of going to press there were no prisoners under sentence of death. The last execution in Anguilla took place in the 1820s.

Antigua and Barbuda

Status: Retentionist

Executions 1985 - mid-88: 1; murder

Other factors: None

Method of execution: Hanging

The death penalty is mandatory for murder (Offences Against the Person Act, Chapter 58, Part I). Those aged under 18 at the time of the crime and pregnant women cannot be sentenced to death.

Together with six other countries, Antigua and Barbuda is a member of the Organization of Eastern Caribbean States (pending Grenada rejoining). All seven countries share a common judicial system known as the Eastern Caribbean Supreme Court, which consists of a High

Court of Justice and a Court of Appeal. Final appeal is to the Judicial Committee of the Privy Council in England which will consider only cases involving constitutional matters or "matters of great public importance".

Appeals for clemency are considered by the Cabinet which makes a recommendation to the Governor General, who must then act on this recommendation. Death sentences may be commuted to a minimum term of two years' imprisonment.

On 5 May 1988 a man who had been convicted of murder in 1986 was executed. At the time of the execution, the first in nearly nine years, there were reports that the prisoner's appeal to the Eastern Caribbean Court of Appeal had been withdrawn by his lawyer. In cases involving a death sentence, appeals are usually submitted as a matter of course. It is alleged that in this case the prisoner was a victim of poor legal representation. The two other prisoners under sentence of death had their sentences commuted: one to 15 years, and the other to life imprisonment. At the time of going to press there were no prisoners under sentence of death.

Argentina

Status: Abolitionist for all but exceptional crimes

Executions 1985 - mid-88: None

Other factors: None

Method of execution: Shooting by firing-squad

When Argentina returned to civilian rule in December 1983, one of the first acts of the government was to propose the repeal of certain decree laws which had provided for the death penalty for a number of offences. This was approved by the Argentine Congress in August 1984 and the death penalty is no longer included in the ordinary Criminal Code of Argentina.

The Code of Military Justice provides for the death penalty for offences such as treason, espionage, rebellion and mutiny. Article 759 states that any soldier in battle who runs away from the enemy or who panics "may be put to

death instantly, to punish his cowardice and to set an example to the others". The death penalty is optional for all other offences under the Code of Military Justice, and defendants are tried by a military court. In 1984 new legislation was passed which curtailed the scope of military justice, and provided for civilian Federal Appeals Courts to review all military court decisions. The judiciary has traditionally been opposed to the death penalty.

Under military rule (1976-1983) the death penalty was established in law for a number of offences but no judicial death sentences were imposed.

Some jurists remain concerned at the power of the military in wartime to subject both military personnel and civilians to summary executions through the proclamation of emergency regulations (Articles 131 and 132 of the Code of Military Justice). All but one of the officially admitted executions which have taken place since 1900 have been carried out on the basis of such emergency regulations.

Although the prohibition of the death penalty for political offences contained in the 1853 Constitution has often been flouted by military authorities, there has always been an abolitionist tendency, and legislation on the death penalty has frequently been modified. In 1921 the death penalty was abolished for ordinary criminal offences. Although in 1950 the death penalty was reintroduced into the ordinary Penal Code for certain wartime offences, Congress has never reinstated it for peacetime.

Australia

Status: Abolitionist

Executions 1985 - mid-88: None

Other factors: Not applicable

Method of execution: Not applicable

With the passage of the Crimes Amendment Act in New South Wales in May 1985, the death penalty was fully abolished in Australia. The Act removed the death penalty in that state for treason, piracy and arson of military establishments; other states had already abolished it. Queensland was the first to do so in 1922;

followed by Tasmania (1968); Victoria (1975); South Australia (1976); and Western Australia (1984). In 1973 the Australian Commonwealth Government abolished the death penalty for all offences in the Death Penalty Abolition Act. The Act applies to the territories under the direct jurisdiction of the national government, including the Australian Capital Territory (the area around Canberra) and the Northern Territory.

The last hanging in Australia was in Victoria in February 1967, when Ronald Joseph Ryan was executed for the murder of a prison warder. This was a controversial case: two other prisoners testified that the shots which killed the warder may have come from other prison guards, and seven jurors reportedly stated that if they had been aware the death penalty could be imposed, they would have returned a different verdict. Appeals for clemency were made by the churches, politicians, trade unionists and newspapers.

Austria

Status: Abolitionist

Executions 1985 - mid-88: None

Other factors: Not applicable

Method of execution: Not applicable

The death penalty was abolished for ordinary offences in 1919 and this was enshrined in the 1920 Federal Constitution. It was reintroduced in 1933 under military law for ordinary offences, including murder, arson and wilful damage to property, and was extended the following year to include other offences, such as possession of explosives.

In 1950, despite the government wishing to extend the period during which the death penalty could be enforced, the National Assembly voted to abolish it for ordinary offences by 86 to 64 votes. In 1968, the death penalty was abolished for all offences by a unanimous vote.

Article 85 of the Constitution, as amended by Law Paper No. 73/1968, states, "The death penalty is abolished."

The last execution (of a prisoner convicted of murder) was on 24 March 1950.

The Bahamas

Status: Retentionist

Executions 1985 - mid-88: None

Other factors: None

Method of execution: Hanging

The Penal Code provides for a mandatory death penalty for murder (Chapter 48, Title XX), treason (Section 430) and piracy (Section 444). Pregnant women and anyone aged under 18 at the time of the crime may not be sentenced to death.

Following the trial, and if the local court has dismissed the appeal, the prisoner can lodge a final appeal with the Judicial Committee of the Privy Council in England. However, the Privy Council will only consider cases involving constitutional matters or "matters of great public importance".

The Governor General is empowered to grant clemency. A special committee considers the prisoner's trial and appeal records, as well as reports from a doctor, the police and a probation officer and any clemency petition submitted, and will then advise a minister (who is specified in the Constitution). After studying the information and considering the committee's advice, the minister advises the Governor General on whether to grant or deny clemency.

At the time of going to press there were 12 prisoners under sentence of death.

Bahrain

Status: Abolitionist in practice

Executions 1985 - mid-88: None

Other factors: Deficient trial procedures; no right of appeal against sentences imposed for crimes against internal and external security

Method of execution: Shooting by firing-squad

The last executions took place on 9 March 1977 when three men were executed for the murder of a prominent publisher. Since then there have been no known executions, nor any death sentences passed.

The amended 1976 Penal Code provides for the death penalty for a number of offences including crimes against external security, such as undermining the sovereignty of the state, taking up arms against the state and espionage; crimes against internal security, including assaulting the head of state (the Amir) or the Crown Prince so as to threaten their lives, forming or leading an armed group aimed at changing the Constitution or overthrowing the government, and leading other forms of armed rebellion; and for the most serious crimes against the person, including premeditated murder, murder in connection with another crime, murder of a public servant killed in the course of duty, murder carried out by explosives, and armed robbery resulting in death. A new law introduced in July 1984 provides for the death penalty for drug-trafficking.

In time of war a judge may impose the death penalty for any crime against internal security which intended to and succeeded in assisting the enemy, and for any crime which threatened external security.

The death penalty may not be imposed on those aged under 18 at the time of the offence, and the judge may show clemency when there are extenuating circumstances. Mental illness may exempt a person from execution, and execution is delayed if a condemned woman is found to be pregnant.

Defendants may appeal against the verdict and sentence to a higher court within a period of 30 days and sentences may be commuted or annulled by the Amir. However, for offences against internal or external security, which are tried before the Civil Supreme Court of Appeal, there is no right of appeal. Other aspects of trials before the Civil Supreme Court of Appeal, including insufficient access for defendants to their lawyers before the beginning of the trial, and the reliance solely on confessions which in some cases have allegedly been extracted by force to bring a conviction, fail to comply with international standards for a fair trial.

Bangladesh

Status: Retentionist

Executions 1985 - mid-88: 36+; murder

Other factors: Children executed; no right of appeal (March 1982 to March 1986 when under martial law)

Methods of execution: Hanging; shooting by firing-squad

The Penal Code provides for the death penalty for various offences including murder, for which it is most regularly imposed. It is mandatory only when murder is committed by a prisoner already serving a life sentence. Kidnapping a child under 10 years old with intent to murder or cause grievous harm carries an optional death penalty. The Penal Code also provides for the death penalty for certain anti-state acts, such as waging war, attempting to wage war or abetting the waging of war against the state. Abetment of mutiny may be punished by death only when mutiny is committed.

In amendments to the Special Powers Act, 1974 a number of other offences were made punishable by death, including sabotage and certain economic crimes such as counterfeiting currency notes, smuggling, hoarding and dealing on the black market. Similar offences are also punishable by death under the Emergency Powers Act, 1975 which may be applied only at times of a declared state of emergency. It is not known, however, whether the death penalty has been imposed under either of these acts.

The Army Act, 1952 provides for the death

penalty for certain wartime offences as well as for mutiny and desertion when on active service. During the martial law administrations (1975 to 1979 and 1982 to 1986) provision for the death penalty was extended under martial law regulations for both anti-state and economic offences, and the number of executions rose, particularly during the second half of the 1970s.

More recently the death penalty has been provided for a number of other offences. In 1983 a presidential ordinance was issued entitled Cruelty to Women (Deterrent Punishment) Ordinance, which included provision for the death penalty for "causing or attempting to cause death or grievous hurt to any woman for dowry". In 1985, following a number of physical assaults on women, often involving the use of acid, the Penal Code was amended to make the offences of rape, abduction and acid-throwing punishable by death also. Under amendments made early in 1987 to legislation relating to explosives dating from the pre-independence period, the death penalty may also be imposed for causing an explosion likely to endanger life. These amendments were introduced after an increase in the number of such incidents, particularly in the capital of Dhaka. In October 1986 it was announced that a high-level committee had been formed to look into the possibility of making drug-smuggling offences punishable by death.

Apart from during periods of martial law, most capital trials have taken place before a District and Sessions Judge. A death sentence passed by this lower court must always be confirmed by the High Court Division of the Supreme Court, regardless of whether the prisoner submits an appeal. On confirmation by the High Court Division, a prisoner under sentence of death may appeal to the Appellate Division of the Supreme Court within 30 days. Although the Special Powers Act provides for the death penalty, there have been no reports of death sentences being imposed under this law following trials by special courts using summary procedures.

The annual number of executions varies considerably and official statistics are not regularly issued. On 27 May 1980 the then Minister of Home Affairs stated that 424 people had been executed during the previous five years. Many of the executions in that period are believed to have been of members of the armed forces tried in connection with coup attempts in 1977, by martial law tribunals in closed session with no right of judicial appeal. During the martial law administration between March 1982 and November 1986, civilians were regularly tried by martial law courts and in some instances sentenced to death. Again there was no provision for judicial appeal, only for review and confirmation of the proceedings by an administrative body. Twice during this review procedure, sentences of life imprisonment were reported to have been increased to death sentences by the martial law authorities. One of the cases involved three bank employees convicted under martial law of misappropriating funds, the first known instance of the death penalty being imposed for such an offence. The court reportedly sentenced them initially to 30 years' imprisonment and the administrative review body recommended that these sentences should "not be disturbed". In his capacity as Chief Martial Law Administrator, President Hussain Mohammad Ershad increased the sentences to the death penalty in July 1986.

Thirty-five people were reported to have been sentenced to death in 1985, and at least 11 in the years 1986 and 1987. In the first five months of 1988, 26 people were sentenced to death. The majority of the sentences were for murder, although a few people received death sentences for acid-throwing.

According to more recent official figures, the number of executions has again increased. Eleven people were executed in 1985 and 25 in 1986. The figures for 1987 and the first five months of 1988 are not known. One of those executed in 1986 who had been convicted by a martial law court was reportedly only 17 years old when hanged. There was considerable public outcry at this execution (although the government later said he was older). The total number of people executed since the end of 1986 after trial by martial law courts is not known. At the time of going to press some prisoners tried by these courts before their abolition in 1986 were still under sentence of death and unable to appeal against their conviction. Constitutional amendments enacted under martial law validated all sentences passed by martial law courts, which may "not be called into question before any court or tribunal".

Under the Criminal Procedure Code of 1898, both the government and President may commute death sentences – a power granted to the President alone under Article 49 of the Constitution. The Criminal Procedure Code also permits the High Court Division of the Supreme Court to postpone the execution of a pregnant woman or, "if it thinks fit", to commute her sentence to life imprisonment.

Executions are carried out inside prisons by hanging, although the Special Powers Act and military law both provide for execution by shooting.

▶ At the end of June 1988 the death penalty was imposed by a special tribunal on five Pakistanis, convicted under anti-smuggling laws – the first time Bangladesh has imposed the death penalty for drug offences. On 7 July 1988 the Dangerous Drugs (Amendment) Bill was passed, providing for the death penalty for the unauthorized manufacture, trafficking and possession of dangerous drugs. On 8 July 1988 the Cruelty to Women (Deterrent Punishment) (Amendment) Bill was passed, providing for the death penalty for trafficking in women.

Barbados

Status: Retentionist

Executions 1985 - mid-88: None

Other factors: Children under 18 at the time of the offence executed

Method of execution: Hanging

The death penalty is mandatory for convictions of murder (Offences against the Person Act, as amended in 1967, Chapter 141) and high treason (Treason Act, 1980, Chapter 155A). Certain military offences, such as aiding the enemy and mutiny, carry an optional death sentence. Pregnant women are exempt from the death penalty.

Capital cases are tried in the High Court by a judge and 12-member jury which determines the defendant's guilt or innocence. If a defendant is found guilty the judge must impose the death sentence. The court's decision can be overturned only on a point of law when

appealed to the Court of Appeal. Final appeal is to the Judicial Committee of the Privy Council in England which will consider only cases involving constitutional matters or "matters of great public importance". The power to grant clemency lies with the Governor General who acts on the advice of the Barbados Privy Council. This is a 12-member body appointed by the Governor General in consultation with the Prime Minister.

At least six death sentences were imposed in 1985, three in 1986 and one in the first 10 months of 1987 (with the court session still in progress). There were no executions between 1975 and 1980 but there have been several since then: one in 1980; one (of a boy aged 17 at the time of the crime) in 1982; and three, on the same day, in 1984.

Barbados is the only country in the English-speaking Caribbean that does not exempt offenders aged under 18 years from the death penalty: the minimum age limit for both sentencing and execution is 16. According to a letter to Amnesty International from the Attorney General's office in 1981, the operative age is the date of sentencing; thus the death penalty may be imposed on children who were under 16 at the time of the offence, as long as they are 16 or over when sentenced. The Juvenile Offenders Act states, "Sentence of death shall not be pronounced or recorded against a child or young person" (Chapter 138, Section 14). A young person is defined under the law as "someone aged 14 and over and under the age of 16". In 1982, Martin Marsh, convicted of murder committed when he was 17, was executed at the age of 20. In May 1988 there were two people under sentence of death convicted of murder committed at the age of 17: Patrick Greaves and Michael Taylor; their appeals were rejected in November 1986 by the Barbados Court of Appeals.

In ratifying the American Convention of Human Rights, Barbados entered a reservation in respect of Article 4(5) (which specifies as 18 the minimum age for imposition of the death penalty) as it conflicted with its national law; however, it has entered no such reservation in respect of the International Covenant on Civil and Political Rights, to which it is also a party.

Two official studies carried out in Barbados in the last 10 years have examined the death penalty. In 1979 the Government of Barbados invited Professor Howard Jones (University of Cardiff, Wales) to investigate ways in which the penal system could be modernized. With regard to the death penalty he concluded that, "The death penalty should be abolished, unless it is felt that moral feeling in Barbados is so strong that it justified ignoring both the rational case against it and the abolitionist trends in most countries of the world."

Following the submission of his report, the government established the Committee on Penal Reform, one of whose purposes was "to consider the future role of the corporal and capital punishment in the Barbados Penal System". The committee's report stated that because of the controversial nature of the subject, it should be debated in and decided by Parliament. As far as Amnesty International is aware, however, no further steps have been taken to act upon the recommendations of either report.

At the time of going to press there were 14 prisoners under sentence of death, all of them convicted of murder.

Belgium

Status: Abolitionist in practice

Executions 1985 - mid-88: None

Other factors: Public executions permitted

Methods of execution: Beheading by guillotine; shooting by firing-squad

Under the Penal Code of 1867 the death penalty is provided for serious crimes against the person, and specified crimes against state security. In addition, mandatory death sentences were introduced in June 1975 for kidnapping and in June 1976 for hijacking an aircraft, in both cases when aggravating circumstances can be proved. The death penalty is also provided for certain crimes in the Military Penal Code for members of the armed forces. The composition and procedure of the military courts and councils are determined by the rank of the accused. Merchant marine personnel are judged as civilians.

Crimes for which a death sentence may be imposed are heard by a Court of Assize consisting of three magistrates, one of whom acts as the president, and 12 jurors. The whole court votes twice to determine the verdict. The death penalty is mandatory if the jury votes both that the facts of the crime for which the death penalty may be imposed have been proved, and that there are no extenuating circumstances. If only the first condition is satisfied, the death penalty is optional. The death penalty is also mandatory when aggravating circumstances are proved for certain specific crimes such as kidnapping or aircraft hijacking.

There is no right of appeal against the decision, except on procedural grounds to the Court of Cassation which may annul the decision and refer the case back to another Court of Assize. Constitutionally, the King has the power of clemency and may grant pardon or commute a death sentence. In practice, this royal prerogative is passed to the Minister of Justice. By custom, the crown exercises its prerogative by commuting the death penalty to a life sentence.

Since 1863 death sentences for common criminal offences have, with one exception, always been commuted. In March 1918 a front-line military officer was executed after being convicted of the murder of a pregnant civilian. Some 15 people were, however, executed in the course of World War I for crimes against external state security, and about 242 people were executed by firing-squad between November 1944 and August 1950 after being convicted of war-related crimes against the external security of the state. No execution has been carried out since August 1950.

Execution of pregnant women is deferred until after childbirth. Children aged under 16 are judged for all crimes by the youth section of the first degree courts, which cannot impose the death penalty. Those aged over 16 but under 18 may be referred to a Court of Assize at the discretion of the judge in the youth section. However, no sentence of death could be considered legal by this court because it considers itself bound by the International Covenant on Civil and Political Rights which prohibits the imposition of the death penalty for crimes committed by anyone aged under 18.

Execution for crimes under the Penal Code is by public beheading, but by firing-squad for crimes against state security and crimes under the Military Penal Code.

In 1985 a Royal Commission submitted a discussion text to parliament which would reform the 1867 Penal Code. The text, which contains no provision for the death penalty, is still awaiting parliamentary examination. Another commission, established by the Minister of Defence to study "delinquency within the armed forces", proposed in its July 1986 report abolition of the death penalty for all military offences except desertion to the enemy. A legislative initiative to that effect has been announced but there have been no further developments.

Belize

Status: Retentionist

Executions 1985 - mid-88: 1; murder

Other factors: None

Method of execution: Hanging

According to the Criminal Code of 1958 the death penalty is mandatory for murder and may also be imposed for certain offences against the defence ordinance and the "power of the commanding officer". Execution is by hanging. Pregnant women, minors and the insane may not be sentenced to death.

Death sentences may be passed by the Supreme Court. Both the Court of Appeal and the Judicial Committee of the Privy Council in England are empowered to review death sentences and hear appeals. According to the Constitution, the Governor General has the prerogative of mercy acting under the advice of the Belize Advisory Council. Clemency consists of commutation to a term of imprisonment.

The government of Belize informed the UN Secretary-General for his 1985 report on capital punishment that 28 people had been sentenced to death and one execution had been carried out during the period covered. Amnesty International learned of at least three further death sentences imposed between 1985 and 1988, two of them on refugees from the Central American region. Since 1969, four people have been executed for murder, the last being Kent Bowers in June 1985, despite a petition for clemency reportedly signed by 2,500 people.

Benin

Status: Retentionist

Executions 1985 - mid-88: 8; murder

Other factors: Executions resumed in 1986 after a 12-year unofficial moratorium; special courts with no rights of appeal

Method of execution: Shooting by firing-squad

Under the terms of the Penal Code and other laws, offences punishable by death include murder and treason. In August 1987, sorcery, magic and other similar practices which might cause public order disturbances or lead to the death or permanent injury of the victim were also made punishable by death.

In February 1986, a Special Criminal Court was set up to try especially serious cases. The court is empowered to impose the death sentence and there is no right of appeal against its decisions. When a death sentence is imposed by this court, the accused has 24 hours in which to appeal for clemency to the head of state. However, it is not known to have imposed any death sentences yet. In other cases, death sentences may be imposed by ordinary Assize Courts and those sentenced to death may lodge appeals to the Central People's Court. In all cases, death sentences confirmed on appeal must also be reviewed by the head of state. Executions are by firing-squad.

In 1986 the first executions for 12 years were carried out when six people who had been sentenced to death in 1985 on charges of murder and armed robbery, had their appeal rejected by the Central People's Court and then by the head of state. The six men were executed at dawn on 26 May 1986 in the town of Cotonou. It is not believed that the executions were public, but the event was given considerable publicity in the government-controlled press.

Two other people convicted of murder in 1986 were executed by firing-squad in September 1987. As both cases involved murders which were ritual killings, it appeared that the decision to execute them was related to the change in legislation in August 1987 concerning offences involving sorcery and magic. Again, these executions were given wide coverage in the press.

In 1987 the Assize Court in Cotonou passed three death sentences, all *in absentia*. Two of those sentenced were convicted of trying to sell two children, while the other was convicted on charges of trying to poison his father. Benin's Code of Penal Procedure gives those tried in their absence the right to a retrial if they are subsequently arrested.

▶ In June 1988, the Special Criminal Court passed what is believed to be its first death sentences on two men convicted of murder.

In July 1988, four more death sentences were passed *in absentia* by the Cotonou Court of Assize on charges of murder.

Bermuda

Status: Abolitionist in practice

Executions 1985 - mid-88: None

Other factors: None

Method of execution: Hanging

The death penalty is mandatory for premeditated murder (Criminal Law Amendment Act 1980, 286A); treason; being an "accessory after the fact of treason"; and piracy or attempted piracy if accompanied by violence.

The jury's verdict need not be unanimous for a death sentence to be imposed. In July 1987, for example, one death sentence was imposed by a verdict of 11 to one. Final appeal is to the Judicial Committee of the Privy Council in England.

Bermuda's position as a British colony has created some controversy over who is empowered to grant clemency. In 1977, two men convicted of murder who had had their appeals rejected by the Governor General were due to be executed. A petition on their behalf signed by many Bermudan citizens was presented to the Secretary of State for Foreign and Commonwealth Affairs of the United Kingdom, urging him to advise the Queen to exercise the royal prerogative of mercy, and to grant clemency to the two men.

The British authorities argued that power to grant a reprieve lay with the Bermudan authorities and that they could intervene only if there had been a miscarriage of justice. The Bermudan authorities maintained, however, that responsibility rested with the Secretary of State, who said that he could not intervene once the Governor General had denied clemency. For his part, the Governor General claimed that he himself had no legal power to stay the executions but that the Secretary of State was in a position to grant a reprieve on behalf of the Queen at any time, and that the Bermudan authorities "would have been obliged to take cognizance of that".

The issue remained unresolved and the executions were carried out, prompting riots around the country in which people were injured and property was damaged. The government consequently established a commission of inquiry into the causes and prevention of crime. The commission carried out a survey which showed that the incidence of violent crime had fallen between 1970 and 1977 (a period when no executions were carried out). The commission nevertheless recommended that the death penalty be retained.

In June 1980 the House of Assembly voted in favour of retaining the death penalty for cases of premeditated murder, and abolishing it for all other murder offences.

The last executions were carried out in 1977. At the time of going to press there was one person under sentence of death.

Bhutan

Status: Abolitionist in practice

Executions 1985 - mid-88: None

Other factors: None

Method of execution: Not known

According to information provided by official sources in 1972 to the United Nations, only the offences of treason and premeditated murder are punishable by death.

The last death sentences recorded by Amnesty International were imposed in 1974 on six people who were among 52 Tibetans and Bhutanese tried on charges of having plotted to assassinate the King. The King subsequently commuted the six death sentences.

Bolivia

Status: Abolitionist in practice

Executions 1985 - mid-88: None

Other factors: None

Method of execution: Shooting by firing-squad

In 1985 the Bolivian Government informed the UN Secretary-General that Bolivia was totally abolitionist. Although it is certainly true that the country has had a long abolitionist tradition, the present position is far from clear.

In 1973 the Penal Code – which had previously forbidden use of the death penalty – was revised and the penalty restored for four offences: treason, parricide, homicide and "submitting the nation totally or partially to foreign dominion" (not necessarily during wartime and applicable to foreign nationals). However, this seems to contradict Article 17 of the State Political Constitution which prescribes 30 years' imprisonment for all but the last of these offences. Indeed, both this article and the Penal Code state that the purpose of punishment is the correction and social rehabilitation of the criminal.

Appeals against death sentences can be made to the Superior District Court. If upheld by this court, they must be confirmed by the Supreme Court of Justice. According to Article 320 of the Code of Penal Procedure no death sentence may be carried out unless the President of the republic is officially notified by the judge in charge of the case. The President then has 10 days in which to decide whether to commute the sentence to 30 years' imprisonment without parole. If no decision is reached within this period the execution should take place without delay. The same article states that executions are to be carried out by firing-squad in prisons.

In 1986 Gonzalo Peñaranda Fernández was found guilty of the kidnap, rape and subsequent murder of a child, and sentenced to death under Article 252 of the Penal Code which states that murder with malice aforethought is to be punished by death. An appeal on constitutional grounds against the sentence was presented to the La Paz District Court, which commuted it to 30 years' imprisonment on 27 February 1987. This was the first death sentence to be imposed for several years and the case prompted national controversy over the correct interpretation of Article 17.

According to the 1975 Code of Military Justice, military offences are tried by the Permanent Tribunal of Military Justice. The code provides for the death penalty for treason and rebellion (Articles 54, 55 and 70); in time of war, espionage, sabotage and terrorism are to be similarly punished (Articles 56-60 and 63). Appeals against death sentences are made to the Supreme Tribunal of Military Justice and sentences may be commuted to 30 years' imprisonment without parole.

The last execution was in 1974 when a man was executed by firing-squad for the murder and rape of a minor nine years before.

Botswana

Status: Retentionist

Executions 1985 - mid-88: Not known

Other factors: None

Method of execution: Hanging

Botswana's Code of Criminal Law retains the death penalty for murder, treason, an attempt on the life of the head of state and for various military offences such as mutiny and desertion in the face of the enemy. The death penalty is mandatory for murder, except in extenuating circumstances. In cases known to Amnesty International in recent years, the death penalty has been imposed only for murder. Pregnant women, anyone under 18 at the time of the offence and the insane cannot be sentenced to death.

Trials for offences carrying the death penalty are held in the High Court and are public except in matters of national security, in which case they are held *in camera*. Defendants have access to lawyers of their own choosing and a right of appeal to the Botswana Court of Appeal. If the sentence is confirmed on appeal, the case is then considered by the Advisory Committee on the Prerogative of Mercy, consisting of the President, Vice-President, Attorney General and a medical doctor. The President considers the committee's advice and then decides whether to grant clemency. An execution may not take place without a warrant signed by the President.

The Botswana Government informed the United Nations Secretariat that seven death sentences were passed and six executions carried out during the period 1979 to 1983.

In 1984 three people were hanged for murder: Lovemore Sibanda, convicted of murdering his employer; Clement Gofhamodimo, who was deported from the United States as a prohibited immigrant in May 1983 and found guilty of the 1978 murder of a Swiss tourist (although the body of the man said to have been murdered was never found and there were no witnesses to the killing); and Lesenyo Kgeresi.

In May 1986 two Zimbabwean refugees were sentenced to death by the Francistown High Court after being found guilty of murder. Amnesty International has received no further information to indicate whether the sentences have been carried out.

Amnesty International received only unconfirmed reports of one execution each year in 1985 and 1986.

Brazil

Status: Abolitionist for all but exceptional crimes

Executions 1985 - mid-88: None

Other factors: None

Method of execution: Shooting by firing-squad

The last judicial execution was carried out in 1855 on a man convicted of murder, later discovered to have been innocent of the crime. Following public disquiet about this case, death sentences were systematically commuted to life imprisonment, and from 1890 the death penalty was excluded from the Penal Code. In the first republican Constitution of 1891 the death penalty was abolished for common crimes but retained under military legislation for application in wartime, as it is in the 1988 Constitution.

The death penalty has been reintroduced twice in the 20th century – in the periods 1937 to 1945 and 1969 to 1979 for politically motivated crimes of violence. However, no death sentences were imposed during these periods. An attempt to reintroduce the death penalty for murder in the course of robbery, rape or kidnapping in the Constitution of 1988 was defeated in the Constituent Assembly by a vote of 392 to 90. The Assembly also rejected a proposal to hold a plebiscite on the death penalty, but a move for total abolition was defeated.

British Virgin Islands

Status: Abolitionist in practice

Executions 1985 - mid-88: None

Other factors: None

Method of execution: Hanging

Under the Offences Against the Person Act (Cap. 54, Part I), the death penalty is mandatory for murder and for assaulting a person with intent to murder or performing any act which endangers someone's life while committing or attempting to commit the crime of piracy (Piracy Act, Cap. 56). The death penalty cannot be imposed on pregnant women nor anyone who was under 18 years old at the time of the crime.

Following the trial, appeals may be made to the local court of appeal. If rejected there, prisoners may lodge a final appeal with the Judicial Committee of the Privy Council (JCPC) in England. However, the JCPC will consider only cases involving constitutional matters or "matters of great public importance".

There have been no executions in the last 10 years and death sentences have been commuted to life imprisonment.

Brunei Darussalam

Status: Abolitionist in practice

Executions 1985 - mid-88: None

Other factors: None

Method of execution: Hanging

In June 1987 a man was sentenced to death for murder and firearms possession. This was the first death sentence to be imposed since 1967. At the time of going to press he was awaiting the outcome of his appeal to the Judicial Committee of the Privy Council in England. According to information provided to the United Nations by the government in 1985 no executions have been carried out since 1957.

The Sultanate of Brunei became a British protectorate in 1888 but took control of internal matters in 1959. Since an abortive rebellion in December 1962 the Sultanate has been ruled by emergency legislation which has been extended every two years. The Sultanate became fully independent in January 1984 under the new name of Brunei Darussalam, but emergency legislation remains in force.

The number of offences punishable by death has increased since 1979 with the introduction of new legislation or amendments to existing laws. The death penalty is provided for by the Penal Code; the Misuse of Drugs Enactment 1978 as amended by the Emergency (Misuse of Drugs) Amendments Order 1984; the Internal Security Enactment 1982; and the Public Order Enactment 1982. Capital offences include murder; murder in the course of other, specified, crimes; unlawful possession of firearms and explosives; and drug-trafficking. The death penalty is mandatory for these offences.

With no senior judiciary of its own, Brunei's judiciary was for a long time administered by the Chief Justice of Hong Kong. However since Sir Denys Roberts retired as Chief Justice of Hong Kong in March 1988 he has remained as Chief Justice of Brunei. Following an amendment to the Criminal Procedure Code which took effect in January 1988, offences carrying the death penalty are no longer tried by a judge sitting with assessors, but by two judges of the High Court from the Hong Kong judiciary.

Appeals are heard by the President of the Court of Appeal (who is also the current Chief Justice of Hong Kong), accompanied by judges of the Supreme Court of Hong Kong. The Sultan of Brunei is empowered to commute death sentences to terms of imprisonment.

▶ In September 1988 a further two men were sentenced to death for murder.

Bulgaria

Status: Retentionist

Executions 1985 - mid-88: 32+; murder; terrorism; manslaughter

Other factors: No right of appeal against sentences imposed by the Supreme Court

Method of execution: Shooting by firing-squad

The Penal Code of 1968 reduced the number of crimes punishable by death from 50 to 31. Article 38 states that the death penalty is imposed only if the crime has been carried out in an exceptionally serious manner and if the objectives of the punishment "cannot be achieved by a less severe punishment".

An optional death penalty is provided for several crimes against the state including treason, espionage and sabotage. Article 116 lists 11 different types of homicide punishable by an optional death penalty. They include premeditated murder; the killing of a Bulgarian official or an official of an ally; and killing for personal gain. Other offences which carry an optional death penalty include robbery with violence; war crimes; genocide; and preparing epidemic bacteria with the intention of causing infection in other people. In addition, the Penal Code lists five military crimes which carry an optional death sentence.

In May 1985 the National Assembly approved amendments to the Penal Code which provided for an optional death penalty for acts of terrorism by means of explosives or other methods. In October 1986 it approved amendments which provided for an optional death penalty for armed robbery.

The death penalty cannot be imposed on anyone aged under 20 at the time of the crime

(18 for soldiers or in wartime), or on women pregnant at the time of the crime or the sentencing. Pregnant women cannot be executed, the sentence being commuted to a minimum of 15 years' imprisonment. The death penalty cannot be imposed on people extradited from a foreign country for that purpose; in such cases the sentence is commuted to 20 years' imprisonment.

People sentenced to death have the right of appeal to the Supreme Court. However, in serious cases involving political or economic offences, the trial proceedings may take place in the Supreme Court and then there is no right of appeal. After the final decision has been taken and the death sentence confirmed by the Supreme Court, the defendant has the right to petition for clemency. This may be granted by the State Council. A death sentence can be commuted to up to 20 years' imprisonment.

According to official press reports the figures for executions and death sentences imposed (in every case for offences involving loss of life) were 10 executions and one sentence in 1985, 17 executions and one sentence in 1986, three executions and one sentence in 1987, and two executions and three sentences up to 31 May 1988.

Amnesty International is not aware of any significant debate on the death penalty within Bulgaria before early 1988, when a discussion was initiated in the official press and articles appeared in favour of abolition.

Between May 1987 and April 1988, to Amnesty International's knowledge, no death sentences were reported in the Bulgarian press. (Previously, death sentences and executions had been reported.) However, on 25 April 1988 three men were sentenced to death by the Supreme Court for terrorist acts involving loss of life committed in 1984-85. Two executions, both for crimes involving murder, were reported by Radio Sofia on 3 May and 10 May 1988.

Burkina Faso

Status: Retentionist

Executions 1985 - mid-88: None

Other factors: No right of appeal against sentences imposed by the Revolutionary People's Tribunals

Method of execution: Shooting by firing-squad

Although the Penal Code provides for a range of offences to be punishable by death, in practice few death sentences appear to have been imposed between independence in 1960 and June 1984. However in June 1984, nearly a year after President Thomas Sankara took power, seven people were executed after having been found guilty by a military court of plotting to overthrow the government.

According to the Penal Code a number of offences are punishable by a mandatory death sentence, including premeditated murder and treason, unless extenuating circumstances are proved.

After President Sankara came to power in August 1983 a new judicial system, known as the *Justice populaire*, popular justice, was introduced. New courts, the *Tribunaux populaires de la révolution* (TPR), Revolutionary People's Tribunals, were set up to hear cases involving political offences, crimes endangering the internal and external security of the state, embezzlement of public funds and all crimes committed by civil servants in the course of their duties. The ordinary courts retained jurisdiction over other capital cases.

In January 1984 the composition of the TPRs was reduced from 16 to 11 members: two judges, two members of the armed forces and seven members of local political groups known as *Comités de défense de la révolution* (CDR), Committees for the Defence of the Revolution. These committees were, however, disbanded in March 1988 following the coup in October 1987 which overthrew President Sankara. It is not clear whether representatives of the *Comités révolutionnaires*, Revolutionary Committees, which replaced the CDRs, will participate in the TPRs.

Defendants appearing before the TPRs do not have the right to defence counsel, and if convicted have no right of appeal to any higher court. However, the head of state is empowered to commute any death sentence imposed, although in practice no death sentences are known to have been passed by these courts.

In late May 1984 the authorities announced that a number of people had been arrested in connection with an attempt to overthrow the government by force. The alleged ringleader, Colonel Didier Tiendrebéogo, and 25 other people, some of whom were civilians, were charged with plotting to overthrow the government. They were tried before a military court from which there was no right of appeal. Colonel Tiendrebéogo, four other soldiers and two civilians were sentenced to death on 11 June 1984 and were executed the following day. They were not assisted by defence counsel at their trial. No other people are known to have been sentenced to death since 1984.

Burma

Status: Retentionist

Executions 1985 - mid-88: Not known

Other factors: Unfair trials

Method of execution: Hanging

The death penalty is mandatory for high treason and premeditated murder. An optional death penalty is provided for the manufacturing of drugs and drug-trafficking. Execution is by hanging.

Official statistics on the use of the death penalty are difficult to obtain, but it is believed that, although death sentences are apparently often imposed by courts, few executions are carried out. In October 1984 an official report revealed that 112 Burmese had been sentenced to death during the first six months of that year. Amnesty International has recorded reports of five death sentences in 1983, eight in 1985, four in 1986 and three in 1987, but this information is certainly incomplete. Four people were officially reported to have been executed between 1978 and 1984. Those executed included student leader Tin Maung Win, convicted of high treason; Captain Ohn Kyaw Nyunt, con-

victed of attempting to assassinate government leaders; and North Korean Colonel Zin Mo, convicted of premeditated murder of South Korean Government leaders.

Children under 12 of "immature understanding" and those under seven may not be sentenced to death. The law provides for a stay of execution or commutation of death sentences imposed on pregnant women.

Burmese law guarantees the right of appeal. Trials for criminal or political offences punishable by death may apparently be held by courts at the township (district), state, or divisional (provincial) level. It is said that these courts do not always function independently of the security forces. All court judges are lay-people assisted by professional legal advisers. Appeals against death sentences may be filed to the Central Court, which may confirm the sentence, order a retrial or acquit the defendant. If it confirms a death sentence, the defendant may petition the head of state for clemency. Many petitions for clemency reportedly result in commutation of the sentence or an indefinite stay of execution. General amnesties have also resulted in the release of prisoners sentenced to death, such as those of Thakin Soe, Lo Hsing Han and Mahn Ngwe Aung, sentenced to death for treason, who were released during the 1980 general amnesty.

▶ In August 1988, 63 prisoners were reportedly under sentence of death and at least three were executed earlier in the year.

Burundi

Status: Retentionist

Executions 1985 - mid-88: None

Other factors: Special courts; no right of appeal against sentences imposed by the State Security Court

Methods of execution: Hanging; shooting by firing-squad

A range of offences are punishable by death under the terms of the 1981 Penal Code (Decree-Law No. 1/6 of 4 April 1981), but death sentences appear to have been imposed by the courts mainly in cases of murder. Relatively few death sentences are reported and the last executions known to have been carried out occurred in 1980.

Offences punishable by a mandatory sentence of death include premeditated murder and murder in the course of another offence, such as robbery, kidnapping, sorcery or cannibalism. Robbery is punishable by death in cases involving a series of aggravating circumstances. Other capital offences include treason, espionage, desertion from the armed forces in time of war, and leadership of armed bands, groups of mercenaries or insurgent movements. Attempts on the head of state's life are also punishable by a mandatory death sentence. No executions for politically related offences have been reported since the early 1970s.

In all cases reported during the 1980s those sentenced to death have been convicted by ordinary courts and allowed to lodge appeals. A special State Security Court has been established to try offences concerning the security of the state, from which there is no right of appeal, but it is not known to have tried any cases. Death sentences are reviewed by the head of state, who may commute them. Pregnant women who are sentenced to death may not be executed until after their delivery and those who are 18 years of age or less at the time a capital offence is committed are to be sentenced instead to between five and 10 years' imprisonment. Methods of execution provided by law are hanging and firing-squad.

Under legislation maintained from the time when Burundi was administered by Belgium, it is an offence to photograph an execution or to be in possession of a camera in the vicinity.

At least seven people were sentenced to death in 1985. Most of the convictions were for murder, but in October 1985 two people were sentenced to death after being found guilty of carrying out the most serious robbery ever known in the country. In 1986 at least one death sentence was imposed and in 1987 at least two, in all cases for murder. However, no official figures are available to indicate the total number of death sentences, and it is possible that the total is higher.

Few details are known about the number or frequency of executions. In July 1980, six people are reported to have been executed: four had been convicted of violent crimes and two

of practising ritual cannibalism in the course of their activities in the illegal Abananga Yivuza religious sect. All six had evidently been allowed to lodge appeals and to petition for clemency. No executions have been announced since 1980.

Following a military coup in September 1987, the new head of state, Major Pierre Buyoya, ordered all death sentences which had already been confirmed upon appeal to be commuted to life imprisonment. The number of sentences commuted was not reported.

▶ The first executions since 1984 were carried out on seven soldiers in December 1988.

Cameroon

Status: Retentionist

Executions 1985 - mid-88: 2; murder and aggravated theft

Other factors: Executions after unfair trials by military courts; public executions

Methods of execution: Shooting by firing-squad; hanging

Under the Penal Code of 1967 the death penalty is mandatory for premeditated murder, aggravated theft, treason and related offences, such as "participation in a secession" in time of war or during a state of emergency. Pregnant women cannot be executed until after the birth of their child, and those found guilty of committing a capital offence while under the age of 18 receive prison sentences instead of the death penalty.

Those sentenced to death by ordinary courts have a right of appeal to the Appeal Court. However those sentenced by military courts (which have jurisdiction over both civilians and military personnel accused of a wide range of offences, such as subversion and crimes involving the use of firearms), have no right of appeal against sentence nor is the Cassation Court empowered to review the legality of their convictions.

Death sentences are submitted to the President of the Republic for his decision on commutation. Under the Penal Code executions may be by firing-squad or hanging and should be carried out in public unless otherwise ordered by the President. Public executions were reported in the early 1970s and again in 1987 (two), but most executions have not been in public.

In an important amendment to the Penal Code in 1972, the death penalty was introduced for "aggravated theft", a broadly defined crime which includes "theft with force, bearing weapons or by breaking in, by climbing in, or by the use of a false key …" The offence had previously been punishable by a maximum of 20 years' imprisonment. In the years following the amendment, a significant number of people were condemned and executed on this charge. However, executions for aggravated theft are believed to have stopped in 1975. In one case in December 1986, two men were convicted on charges of aggravated theft by the High Court in Mamfe and sentenced to death by firing-squad. They had previous convictions for stealing a clock and a musical set, and on that occasion had been sentenced to 10 years' imprisonment. It is not known if they have been executed. However, in 1987 what are believed to have been the first public executions for more than 10 years were carried out in Douala when two men, both sentenced to death in about 1979 on charges of aggravated theft and murder, were shot by firing-squad.

Executions were carried out in 1984 after trials before military courts which did not conform to international standards of fairness. More than 1,000 people were arrested after an unsuccessful attempt to overthrow the government in April 1984. By the end of that month military courts began trying the cases of both civilians and military personnel accused of offences arising from the attempted coup. The hearings took place in secret at a military camp near the capital, Yaoundé.

In November 1984 President Paul Biya announced that 51 prisoners had been sentenced to death, but the authorities did not reveal the names of those tried or any other information concerning the trials, nor indicate whether the executions had been carried out. This was particularly significant as there had been persistent reports from unofficial sources that 35 or more people were executed on just one occasion at Mbalmayo on 1 May 1984, after being sentenced to death by military courts.

According to unofficial sources the total number executed may have been as high as 120. It was also reported that many of those tried either had no legal counsel or were represented by state counsel appointed only a few hours before their trials began. There were also reports that some defendants were convicted and sentenced to death on the basis of statements made in custody as a result of torture. None of those convicted had a right of appeal.

Military courts have also sentenced civilians to death on other occasions. In March 1988, six civilians were sentenced to death after being convicted by a military court in Yaoundé of aggravated theft and illegal possession of firearms and ammunition.

Canada

Status: Abolitionist for all but exceptional crimes

Executions 1985 - mid-88: None

Other factors: None

Method of execution: Shooting by firing-squad

The death penalty was abolished for capital murder by a vote of Parliament in July 1976 and replaced with a mandatory 25-year prison sentence without parole. It is retained for a number of military offences under the National Defence Act of 1950 (mainly mutiny and offences committed in the presence of an enemy), some of which carry a mandatory death sentence.

The death penalty may be imposed only if the verdict is unanimous. The National Defence Act contains provisions for review and appeal and the execution may be carried out only if approved by the Governor General in Council. Execution is by firing-squad, but no executions have been carried out under this act.

On 30 June 1987, in a free vote, the Canadian House of Commons voted against a motion presented by the government to restore the death penalty for murder by 148 votes to 127, and thus upheld the 1976 abolition decision. During the debate, Prime Minister Brian Mulroney addressed the House of Commons stating his personal reasons for opposing the reintroduction of the death penalty on the grounds of morality and logic.

The last execution was carried out on 11 December 1962.

Cape Verde

Status: Abolitionist

Executions 1985 - mid-88: None

Other factors: Not applicable

Method of execution: Not applicable

The use of the death penalty is forbidden by Cape Verde's Constitution. Article 31 states, "Every citizen has the right to life ... In no case will there be the death penalty..."

The last executions were carried out in 1835 when two leaders of a peasant revolt were hanged. Portugal had abolished the death penalty in 1869, for both itself and its colonies, for all offences except certain war crimes. The *Partido Africano da Independência da Guiné e Cabo Verde* (PAIGC), African Party for the Independence of Guinea and Cape Verde, which came into power in both countries, had promulgated a law in 1966 providing for the death penalty for treason and espionage during its war for independence which was fought in Guinea-Bissau. After Cape Verde's independence in 1975 it temporarily retained Portuguese laws and, presumably, the 1966 law. However, the death penalty was never used. It was finally abolished for all offences by Cape Verde's first Constitution which was promulgated in 1981.

Cayman Islands

Status: Abolitionist in practice

Executions 1985 - mid-88: None

Other factors: None

Method of execution: Hanging

Although there have been no executions since the 1930s, according to the Penal Code the death penalty is still provided for as a mandatory sentence for murder and as an optional sentence for treason (Law 12, 1975). A death sentence may not be imposed on anyone under the age of 18 at the time of the crime nor on pregnant women.

Following trial, and if the local court has dismissed the appeal, the prisoner can lodge a final appeal with the Judicial Committee of the Privy Council (JCPC) in England. However, the JCPC will consider only cases involving constitutional matters or "matters of great public importance".

In 1985 there were reports that a motion to abolish the death penalty would be presented to the Legislative Assembly but Amnesty International has no further information about this.

At the time of going to press there were four prisoners under sentence of death, all convicted of murder.

Central African Republic

Status: Retentionist

Executions 1985 - mid-88: None

Other factors: No right of appeal against sentences imposed by the Special Tribunal; public executions permitted

Method of execution: Shooting by firing-squad

The Penal Code of 1961 provides for the death penalty for a number of offences but in the 1980s, as far as is known, relatively few death sentences have been imposed by the courts. Since President André Kolingba came to power in September 1981 there have been no executions.

Offences punishable by a mandatory death sentence include premeditated murder, parricide, killing in the course of other crimes, such as kidnapping, and armed robbery. Certain acts which might cause loss of life, such as planting a bomb, are punishable by death as are a number of political offences including treason, espionage, attempts to kill government officials, mutiny, and actions likely to cause civil war. The code stipulates that those sentenced to death should be executed in public by firing-squad. The execution of a pregnant woman is deferred until after she has given birth.

Both ordinary courts and the Special Tribunal (a court set up in July 1981 to try political offences) may impose death sentences. There is no right of appeal for those convicted by the Special Tribunal. In practice, capital cases are tried by the main criminal court in Bangui. Those sentenced to death can appeal to the Supreme Court only on points of law; if the appeal is granted they are retried. All death sentences must be confirmed by the head of state.

During the 1970s many suspected opponents of the government of Jean-Bedel Bokassa were executed, the majority of them without trial. Those who had been tried were sentenced to death by a special military court which did not conform to international standards for fair trial.

Jean-Bedel Bokassa was overthrown while out of the country in 1979. He was tried in his absence and sentenced to death in December 1980. A number of his associates, particularly those responsible for killing political prisoners, were also tried and sentenced to death. One group of six was sentenced to death in February 1980, but in August 1980 the Supreme Court ruled that they should be retried. They were sentenced to death again, their pleas for clemency were rejected, and all six were executed by firing-squad in April 1981. Another former official, Jean-Pierre Inga, was also sentenced to death at a retrial in 1981 after being convicted of killing two children. It is not known if his second appeal has ever been heard or whether he is still alive in prison.

Following a bomb explosion in a Bangui cinema in July 1981, a Special Tribunal was set up with jurisdiction over all political cases. In May 1982 it sentenced five people to death, two of them *in absentia*, for their alleged involvement in planting explosives at a French military base. They had no right of appeal; however, the sentences have not been carried out and they are still in prison.

Only one death sentence has been reported in the last five years: in June 1987 a second death sentence was imposed on Jean-Bedel Bokassa, who returned voluntarily to the country in October 1986. He was retried by Bangui's Criminal Court and, after a seven-month trial, was convicted on four charges including conspiracy to murder, embezzlement of public funds and the illegal arrest and detention of

children. His appeal was rejected by the Supreme Court in November 1987 but his sentence was commuted to life imprisonment by President Kolingba in February 1988.

Chad

Status: Retentionist

Executions 1985 - mid-88: None

Other factors: None

Method of execution: Shooting by firing-squad

The Penal Code provides for the death penalty for numerous offences, including murder preceded, accompanied or followed by another crime; poisoning; treason; espionage and various military crimes, including desertion to the enemy, incitement to desertion and unauthorized capitulation to the enemy. Pregnant women may not be executed.

Executions may be carried out only after prisoners have been convicted and sentenced by courts under the terms of the law and once pleas for clemency have been considered and rejected by the head of state who has the power to grant clemency.

Several executions were carried out before the present government took power in 1982: 15 people were executed in 1977 after being convicted of attempting to kill the head of state and overthrow the government, and in 1981 two soldiers were executed after being convicted of murder. All the executions were by firing-squad, as prescribed by the Penal Code.

The rule of law has been virtually suspended for many years. Since the government of President Hissein Habré came to power in 1982 numerous prisoners suspected of both armed and non-violent opposition to the government have been executed without any form of legal procedure (often, apparently, by order of the highest authorities). Some were killed as soon as they were captured in counter-insurgency operations, but many were executed after spending months in custody in the capital, N'Djamena, apparently after the authorities had decided to sentence them to death.

Chile

Status: Retentionist

Executions 1985 - mid-88: 2; murder

Other factors: Unfair trials; no right of appeal against sentences imposed by war councils

Method of execution: Shooting by firing-squad

In the 1980s the issue of the death penalty has received considerable attention in Chile, with the first death sentences passed by the courts since 1970 and the carrying out of four executions.

The death penalty has been provided in law since 1875 when the Penal Code was drawn up, and in the period to 1970 approximately 60 people were executed. The Popular Unity Government which came to power that year reduced the number of crimes punishable by death and the death penalty ceased to be mandatory. Since the military takeover in 1973 successive legislation has increased the number of offences punishable by death, and this penalty has once again been made mandatory for some offences during wartime.

Many people were summarily executed during the first few months after General Augusto Pinochet came to power, but no death sentences were passed by the ordinary courts between 1970 and 1980. Since then four former members of the security forces have been executed for common crimes, two in 1982 and two in January 1985. The former were executed for murder and the latter in a case involving a series of murders and rapes.

Between 1984 and mid-1988, death sentences were recommended by the prosecutor in the cases of 15 political prisoners mostly accused of participating in the killing of police or military authorities between 1980 and 1983. Of these, three political prisoners were subsequently sentenced to life imprisonment. Four political prisoners were sentenced to death. After a prolonged legal battle by defence lawyers the death sentence imposed on one of the four sentenced political prisoners, Carlos García, was commuted to life imprisonment in

November 1987. The Military Appeals Court failed to reach the required unanimous verdict (see below). The verdict was significant as it was the first case of a political prisoner facing a death sentence to reach the final stages of the judicial process. In the other three cases, the verdict of the Military Appeals Court was still pending at the time of going to press.

Several other political prisoners are also currently facing charges which could result in the imposition of death sentences. These include a group charged under the 1984 Anti-terrorist Law with involvement in an assassination attempt on General Pinochet in 1986.

The death penalty is provided for a number of offences contained in the Penal Code, the Code of Military Justice, the Anti-terrorist Law, the Arms Control Law and the State Security Law. Under the Penal Code the offences for which it can be imposed include treason, parricide and certain crimes resulting in the death, serious injury or rape of the victim, such as the abduction of minors and robbery with violence. Under the Code of Military Justice treason, espionage, and sedition resulting in death are among the capital offences listed. Under the 1984 Anti-terrorist Law certain crimes resulting in death or, in the case of kidnappings, serious injury may be punishable by death. The State Security Law provides for the death penalty for homicide and certain other crimes intended to subvert public order or intimidate the population. A range of crimes committed during wartime under the Code of Military Justice, the Arms Control Law and the State Security Law may be punishable by death.

In most cases the death penalty is optional, and if a death sentence is imposed the appeal court's verdict must be unanimous for it to be confirmed. However, when a judge of the Military Appeals Court voted in November 1987 against upholding the death sentence imposed on Carlos García "because a judge cannot order that the life of an individual be taken away", the prosecution, acting on behalf of the government, filed a complaint against him to the Supreme Court. The prosecution argued, unsuccessfully, that the judge's opposition to the death penalty had prevented an exemplary sentence from being upheld.

The death penalty is mandatory only under Article 5c of the State Security Law, which states that in wartime the penalties applicable to certain crimes "will be upgraded by one step and if the penalty is death, it must be applied".

The death penalty may not be imposed on individuals who acted in legitimate self-defence, through uncontrollable fear or while not in control of their mental faculties. Children aged under 16 are exempt, as are those aged under 18 if they acted "without judgment". A pregnant woman may be sentenced to death; however, both formal notification of the sentence and execution are delayed until 40 days after she has given birth.

Death sentences can be passed by civilian courts, military judges or war councils, depending on the legislation under which the accused is charged and whether it is in wartime. All except those sentenced to death by a war council have the right of appeal, either to an ordinary appeal court or to the Military Appeals Court. If the death sentence is confirmed, the defendant can ask the Supreme Court to annul it through various petitions of review, procedural complaints or cassation. There is no right of appeal to a higher court against death sentences imposed by war councils, which are subject only to review by a military commander.

In most cases prisoners can petition the President for clemency. General Pinochet has rejected all such petitions which have come before him during the 1980s. The Constitution stipulates that those sentenced to death for terrorist offences have no right to clemency or pardon, but it is unclear whether the President may still exercise his discretionary power to commute sentences or grant pardon. At the time of going to press no death sentence passed under the Anti-terrorist Law had reached the final stage of the judicial proceedings.

In nearly every capital case since 1982 there have been allegations of trial irregularities. The trials of political prisoners in particular often fall short of international standards for a fair trial. All political prisoners facing possible death sentences said they were tortured while held by the security forces. In addition, their defence lawyers have alleged that confessions extracted under torture have been used as evidence in trials, that their access to trial documents has been restricted or delayed, that there have been incomplete investigations, and

that prisoners have been convicted on the basis of supposition rather than proof. Such prisoners have been tried by military courts whose impartiality has frequently been called into question. There are further procedural limitations on defence rights in trials under the Anti-terrorist Law.

Execution is by firing-squad. A doctor is present to certify death and, if the first round of shots fails to kill the victim, the doctor "will indicate to the officer in charge of the firing-squad that it should shoot again". At a meeting in January 1987, however, doctors from the Chilean Medical College agreed that "the participation [of doctors] in executions is contrary to medical ethics".

▶ On 19 August 1988, the Military Appeals Court commuted to life imprisonment the death sentence against Jorge Palma Donoso, Carlos Araneda Miranda and Hugo Marchant Moya (convicted of the assassination of the regional governor of Santiago) after it failed to reach a unanimous agreement. The Court's president, Judge Enrique Paillas, voted against upholding the death sentences. The prosecution subsequently submitted a complaint about the court's ruling and a petition for cassation to the Supreme Court, arguing that it did not fulfil legal requirements. The petition also criticized the dissident vote of Judge Paillas. The Supreme Court rejected the complaint and the petition for cassation.

China

Status: Retentionist

Executions 1985 - mid-88: 500+; murder; rape; robbery; theft; embezzlement; corruption; bribery; smuggling; swindling; drug-trafficking; assault and battery; kidnapping and trafficking in women and children; leading a criminal gang; enticing or forcing women into prostitution; printing or showing pornographic material; illegal making and trading of firearms; organizing reactionary secret societies; use of poison or explosives

Other factors: Minimal safeguards for fair trial; public humiliation of prisoners before execution; public executions

Method of execution: Shooting

Since 1980 a large number of executions have been carried out in China during a series of official campaigns against crime. Legislation has been adopted on several occasions to increase the number of offences punishable by death and to speed up the procedures for trial, appeal, review and execution in some death penalty cases. Executions have been widely publicized in the national and local media and "mass sentencing rallies" attended by thousands of people have been held to expose offenders condemned to death to the public before being executed.

The death penalty has been used extensively since the founding of the People's Republic of China (PRC) in 1949. From the 1950s to the early 1970s it was often imposed for political offences, but most death sentences known to have been passed since 1979 (when China adopted for the first time a comprehensive criminal law) have been imposed for ordinary crimes. The Criminal Law states that the death penalty is to be applied only to "criminal elements who commit the most heinous crimes". It can be imposed as an optional punishment in particularly grave cases for both "counter-revolutionary" and ordinary criminal offences. These include offences against the person and property, such as murder, rape, arson, robbery and embezzlement, as well as

"counter-revolutionary" offences, such as treason, plotting to overthrow the government, organizing "armed rebellious assemblies", hijacking and espionage.

The number of offences punishable by death was increased substantially when China's legislature adopted amendments to the Criminal Law in 1982 and 1983. Economic offences such as smuggling, theft, bribery, drug-trafficking and illegal export of cultural relics became capital offences in 1982 when a campaign to eliminate corruption among state officials was launched.

In 1983 further amendments to the law were introduced after the start of an official nationwide campaign against crime. Seven more offences were made punishable by death, including "trafficking in human beings", enticing or forcing women to prostitution, and organizing reactionary secret societies. (Details of this legislation are provided in Amnesty International's report *China: Violations of Human Rights*, 1984, page 58.)

Under Chinese law, pregnant women and offenders aged under 18 at the time of the crime cannot be sentenced to death. However, a person aged between 16 and 18 who has committed a particularly serious offence may be sentenced to death with a two-year stay of execution, leaving the possibility of execution after that period if he or she does not reform satisfactorily.

Courts may impose death sentences with or without reprieve. In the case of the former, a death sentence may be imposed for which execution is suspended for two years. This system has existed since 1949 and is now maintained in the Criminal Law. During the two-year period of reprieve, offenders carry out compulsory labour. If they show evidence of "repentance" during this time, their sentence is commuted to a term of imprisonment. The proportion of suspended death sentences commuted compared to those carried out is not known, but Chinese officials have claimed that most are commuted. The best known cases of reprieve are those of Jiang Qing (Mao Zedong's widow) and Zhang Chunqiao, two members of the so-called "Gang of Four" who were given suspended death sentences in 1981 after being convicted of "counter-revolutionary" offences. Their sentences were commuted to life imprisonment by the Supreme

People's Court in 1983.

Defendants charged with offences punishable by death can be tried by Intermediate People's Courts or by High People's Courts in the first instance. They have the right to one appeal only against conviction and judgment. The law provides for an automatic review by a higher court if a defendant does not appeal. Although the right to defence is guaranteed by law, access to a lawyer is limited and there is no recognition of the right to be presumed innocent before being proved guilty in a court of law. In practice, few people are able to exercise effectively their right to defence.

In 1983 the legal safeguards for prisoners' rights were further curtailed for certain capital offences with the introduction of legislation aimed at speeding up the procedures for prosecution, trial, appeal and review. Defendants were denied the right to receive a copy of the indictment before trial and the time limit for appeal was reduced from 10 to three days. This measure applied to cases of murder, rape, robbery, explosions and "other activities that seriously threaten public security". Another amendment to the law suspended the automatic review of all death sentences by the Supreme People's Court, extending a provisional measure introduced in 1981 for a period of two years.

These provisions were applied immediately, and resulted in swift trials and executions. In several cases recorded by Amnesty International, people were sentenced and executed within a few days of arrest; for example, two men aged 18 and 19 were executed in Nanjing in September 1983 only six days after their arrest. An official court notice on their case indicated that the trial, sentencing, review by a high court and execution had all taken place within the six days. The legislation permitting these speedy procedures was still in force in mid-1988.

According to the Constitution, the President has the power to issue "special pardons", but the law does not contain any provision for condemned prisoners to seek such pardon. Amnesty International does not know of any case in which the President has commuted a death sentence.

The Criminal Law states that execution is by shooting. Before execution prisoners' hands are tied behind their backs and they are forced to kneel down by soldiers or police officers. They are then shot in the back of the head.

Some executions take place at designated execution grounds, while others are reportedly carried out in prisons. According to private sources, prisoners who are paraded publicly before execution sometimes have ropes fastened tight around their necks to prevent them from shouting. This was reportedly a method used to silence political prisoners during the Cultural Revolution, but the extent of its use, and whether it continues today, is not known.

According to the law, "the execution of the death sentence should be announced, but the condemned should not be exposed to the public". Despite this provision, public executions reportedly took place during the first few months of the 1983 anti-crime campaign and people sentenced to death are still subjected to public exposure and humiliation before execution.

Condemned offenders are often paraded in front of thousands of people at "mass sentencing rallies" held to publicize sentences. Prisoners are usually made to face the crowd with heads bowed and placards hanging around their necks while their crimes are denounced. Those sentenced to death without reprieve are executed immediately after the rally.

Sentencing rallies and the public parading of prisoners in trucks have long been practices in China, but in 1986 and 1987 Chinese officials indicated that the central authorities wished to put an end to such practices. In November 1987, for instance, an official from the Supreme People's Court was reported to have stated that local authorities had "exceeded their authority" by parading criminals in front of large crowds at mass rallies. He referred to such an event held in Beijing in August 1983, describing it as a mistake made by over-zealous police who had since been warned not to repeat such spectacles. Despite this, Amnesty International has recorded several instances of public sentencing rallies being held since late 1987.

The government does not publish statistics on death sentences or executions. Some cases are widely publicized by the official Chinese media, but the information provided by such official sources is fragmentary. Estimates by unofficial sources vary widely; some sources have estimated the number of executions to be as high as 30,000 during the four years between 1983 and 1987. The largest number of executions recorded during that period were carried out within three months of the launch of a nationwide anti-crime campaign in August 1983. During 1987 Amnesty International documented over 200 death sentences, of which 132 were carried out shortly after sentencing. Amnesty International believes the true total to be much higher. It recorded six death sentences and 59 executions during the first five months of 1988. Those executed since January 1987 include people convicted of drug-smuggling, corruption, producing and selling poisonous alcohol, robbery, theft, murder, rape, embezzlement, running a brothel and showing pornographic films.

▶ Between June and September 1988, Amnesty International learned of 35 death sentences (including four suspended for two years) and 19 executions for murder, robbery, theft, corruption, fraud, smuggling antiques and assault. One defendant was brought to trial four days after his arrest and executed six days later.

In September a state secrets law was adopted under which people convicted of gathering or revealing classified information may be sentenced to death.

Colombia

Status: Abolitionist

Executions 1985 - mid-88: None

Other factors: Not applicable

Method of execution: Not applicable

The last judicial execution took place in Colombia in 1909 when two men who attempted to assassinate the then President, General Rafael Reyes, were shot by firing-squad.

In 1910 the death penalty was abolished by legislative act and its prohibition was incorporated into the Constitution of 1886 which is still in force. Article 29 of the Constitution states, "The legislator may not impose the death penalty in any circumstances." This provision of the Constitution has been interpreted by successive Colombian governments to mean that

the introduction of new legislation on the death penalty is prohibited.

Comoros

Status: Abolitionist in practice

Executions 1985 - mid-88: None

Other factors: No right of appeal against sentences imposed by the State Security Court

Method of execution: Shooting by firing-squad

A number of offences, including treason, espionage, premeditated murder and the killing of a parent are punishable by death according to the Penal Code. The law stipulates that a pregnant woman cannot be executed until after her confinement. Defendants convicted and sentenced to death by criminal courts may appeal against their sentence to a higher court. However, people convicted by the State Security Court on charges of offences against the security of the state have no right of appeal or review before a higher court. The head of state is empowered to commute death sentences. The method of execution is shooting by firing-squad.

Since independence in 1975 no death sentences have been imposed by courts in the Comoros. Public opinion in the country appears to be generally opposed to the use of the death penalty.

Congo

Status: Retentionist

Executions 1985 - mid-88: None

Other factors: Unfair trials; no right of appeal against death sentences imposed by the Revolutionary Court of Justice

Methods of execution: Shooting by firing-squad; beheading by guillotine

Although the Penal Code provides for the death penalty for a variety of offences, few death sentences are known to have been passed since

1978. All death sentences imposed since then have been for murder or for related crimes resulting in loss of life. During the 1960s and 1970s a number of people were convicted of political offences, such as involvement in attempts to overthrow the government or in the assassination of President Marien Ngouabi in 1977, and were sentenced to death. Those executed included a former head of state, Alphonse Massamba-Débat, who was executed after a summary trial in March 1977. The last known executions for political offences were in February 1978, when 10 people were executed. One other person was sentenced to death *in absentia* at the same time; this sentence has never been commuted.

Under the Congolese Penal Code, which is based on a French code used during the reign of Emperor Napoleon III, premeditated murder is punishable by death. Murder in the course of another offence, and armed robbery are also capital offences, although no executions have been reported for the latter. A variety of political offences carry a mandatory death sentence including treason; espionage; insurrection; destruction of state property with explosives; and attempts to kill government or court officials or members of the security forces. The Penal Code also makes punishable by death a number of offences which are no longer applicable, such as attempting to kill "the Emperor". Children under the age of 16 at the time of the offence are exempted and execution of pregnant women is deferred until after childbirth.

Both ordinary criminal courts and a special Revolutionary Court of Justice, set up to try political cases, are empowered to impose death sentences. Those sentenced to death by ordinary courts may appeal to the Supreme Court but there is no right of appeal for those sentenced by the Revolutionary Court of Justice. All death sentences require confirmation by the head of state, who may commute them to terms of imprisonment. The Penal Code stipulates that those sentenced to death should be executed by guillotine, but in practice all executions since independence in 1960 have been by firing-squad.

Since 1985 only one death sentence is known to have been imposed. In August 1986 Claude-Ernest Ndalla was sentenced to death by the Revolutionary Court of Justice for involvement in causing a bomb explosion in 1982 in which several people were killed. The bomb explosion was said to be politically motivated. An Amnesty International observer attended the trial and the organization was concerned that the trial was unfair in a number of respects. Although Claude-Ernest Ndalla had no right of appeal, a petition for mercy was submitted on his behalf and in 1987 this was reported to be still under consideration.

In July 1981 six people convicted of murder were sentenced to death by the Criminal Court in Brazzaville. Two of the defendants were executed by firing-squad in October 1982. No other executions have been reported since 1978.

Costa Rica

Status: Abolitionist

Executions 1985 - mid-88: None

Other factors: Not applicable

Method of execution: Not applicable

The death penalty was abolished for all offences in 1877 by a decree issued during the dictatorship of General Tomas Guardia. Abolition was incorporated into Costa Rica's Constitution by another decree in 1882. Like the 1877 abolition decree, the current Constitution (1949) continues to declare that "human life is inviolable".

Under Spanish rule, the death penalty had been provided for a wide range of offences, but this was reduced after Costa Rica gained independence in 1821. Before abolition, death sentences had frequently been commuted to life imprisonment. The last known executions were in 1878 when two men convicted of treason were shot, although the death penalty had been abolished by decree in 1877.

Côte d'Ivoire

Status: Abolitionist in practice

Executions 1985 - mid-88: None

Other factors: None

Method of execution: Shooting by firing-squad

Under the Penal Code a number of offences, including murder and treason, are punishable by death. Desertion and capitulation by members of the armed forces also carry an optional death sentence. The law stipulates that pregnant women cannot be executed until at least eight weeks after giving birth, and that when a death sentence is confirmed on appeal, it cannot be carried out until a petition for presidential clemency has been reviewed and rejected. For those aged under 18, any death sentence is reduced to a term of imprisonment.

The only method of execution allowed for in the Penal Code is by firing-squad, out of public view. On 31 July 1981 the National Assembly voted to introduce a new Penal Code which among other things removed the death penalty for all political offences. Article 34 was amended to read, "The main penalties are: death, except in cases of political offences…"

On 13 October 1975, on the occasion of the 15th anniversary of independence, President Félix Houpouët-Boigny ordered the commutation to 20 years' imprisonment of the death sentences of all prisoners awaiting execution. It is believed that any subsequent death sentences have also been commuted by the President.

Cuba

Status: Retentionist

Executions 1985 - mid-88: 4; (includes 3 for murder, 1 not known)

Other factors: Defendants' rights curtailed during trial

Method of execution: Shooting by firing-squad

The 1979 Penal Code provided for the death penalty as an optional punishment for a wide range of crimes. Following a revision of the code in December 1987, however, it was abolished for "crimes against collective security", certain kinds of "crimes against peace and international law", and for robbery with violence or intimidation. The circumstances in which it can be imposed for rape and pederasty with violence have also been restricted. The death penalty continues to be provided for as an optional form of punishment in 23 articles, 19 relating to crimes against state security, two under Crimes against Life and Corporal Integrity (murder) and two under Crimes against the Normal Development of Sexual Relations and against the Family, Infancy and Youth (rape, and pederasty with violence).

The death penalty is also provided for in the 1979 Military Offences Law, and is established as an optional sentence for 19 offences, some of which apply only in time of war or during combat. There is no information available on how often it has been imposed or carried out, although unconfirmed reports suggest that executions of Cuban troops serving in Angola may have occurred.

According to the Penal Code "… the death penalty is of an exceptional nature and can only be applied by the court in the most serious cases of crime for which it has been established". It may not be imposed on anyone under 20 years old or on women who were pregnant either at the time of the offence or at the time of sentencing. Execution is by firing-squad.

Cases relating to capital offences that fall under the jurisdiction of civilian courts are heard first by a provincial people's court. The Attorney General told Amnesty International in March 1988 that it was current practice for him to approve all prosecution requests for the death penalty in advance. If the death penalty is requested by the prosecution, defendants undergo psychiatric observation for 45 days in order to establish whether they can be certified as sane. Sentence can be passed only after such an examination has taken place.

Death penalty cases are automatically sent for appeal to the People's Supreme Court. If that court confirms the death sentence, the Ministry of Justice then studies the case and makes recommendations to the Council of State, headed by President Fidel Castro. The Council has the power to decide whether a prisoner is executed or granted clemency; clemency takes the form of commutation to a maximum of 30 years' imprisonment.

Once sentenced to death by the court of first instance, the prisoner is held in an isolation cell while awaiting the result of the appeal process. Family visits are permitted every 21 days. If the Council of State confirms the death sentence the prisoner's family must be informed and allowed to visit the prisoner before the sentence is carried out. Executions are carried out at night and the body is buried in a cemetery by officials who must inform the family of its location.

There has been a decrease in the number of executions carried out in recent years. According to official figures given to Amnesty International, between 1959 and 1987 a total of 237 people were sentenced to death, mostly in the early years of the administration; in all but 21 cases the sentence was carried out. None of those executed were women. According to the Justice Minister, no one has been executed for crimes against state security since Luis Llanes Aguila in 1984, convicted of terrorism, sabotage and enemy propaganda. The official figures for executions of people convicted of crimes against state security between 1980 and 1984 are six in 1980, three in 1981, one in 1982, two in 1983 and one in 1984. Seven people convicted of common crimes were executed in 1984, one in 1985, none in 1986 and three in 1987. According to the Justice Minister, in 1986-7 11 people whose sentences had been suspended for several years pending a general judicial review had their sentences commuted.

In March 1988 five cases were awaiting the decision of the Council of State – one for crimes against state security and four for common crimes. Amnesty International requested that the sentences be commuted, and in April it was told that the Council had commuted the sentence of Arturo Suárez Ramos, accused of participating in an attempted hijacking and causing serious injury to several people in 1987. The four other death sentences pending decision were believed to relate to cases of murder.

The Justice Minister told Amnesty International in March 1988 that since about 1983 it had been official policy to reduce the use of the death penalty, partly because the Cuban Government did not feel currently threatened either internally or externally. However, the government wished to retain the option of its use in case such threats re-emerged.

Trials have been unfair in a number of ways, most notably in the lack, in practice, of judicial guarantees for political prisoners. Government officials have told Amnesty International that it is taking steps to improve defendants' rights, as in the past there have been allegations that access to defence counsel was severely limited, that lawyers were unwilling or unable to provide an adequate defence (partly because they received documents related to the case against the person only on the day of the trial), and that defendants were not kept informed of how their appeals were progressing. In some cases prisoners were reportedly not given written confirmation of their sentences, others had not been granted family visits following final confirmation of their death sentence and prior to execution, and in some cases relatives were not informed of when the execution was due to take place or where the body had been buried. However, recent measures to reinforce the role of the defence lawyer, such as earlier access to the prosecution case and to the client prior to the trial, are apparently intended to strengthen the rights of defendants in future.

No statistics on the use of the death penalty since 1959 are believed to have been published by the Cuban Government.

▶ No executions were reported in 1988.

Cyprus

Status: Abolitionist for all but exceptional crimes

Executions 1985 - mid-88: None

Other factors: None

Method of execution: Hanging

On 15 December 1983 the Council of Ministers voted in favour of the abolition of the death penalty for premeditated murder and its replacement with life imprisonment (Criminal Code [Amendment] Law 1983).

The Criminal Code retains the death penalty for treason (Section 36), instigating invasion (Section 37) and piracy with violence (Section 69). Certain offences against the state carry the death penalty under the Military Criminal Code. The death penalty may not be imposed on pregnant women or children under the age of 16 when the crime was committed.

The bill for the abolition of the death penalty for premeditated murder was initiated by the Parliamentary Law Committee who, in its explanatory memorandum of 14 June 1983, referred to resolution 727 of the Parliamentary Assembly of the Council of Europe (1980) calling on member states to abolish the death penalty for peacetime offences. The Law Committee stated that it believed, "Law and order is adequately protected by all other means offered and there is no sufficient reason for maintaining the death penalty in the case of premeditated murder."

Death sentences for offences under the ordinary criminal code may be imposed by the Assize Court, and by the military court for offences under the Military Criminal Code. Appeals against death sentences are passed by either court to the Supreme Court which consists of five judges. Both the President and the Vice-President have the right to exercise the prerogative of mercy, which allows them to commute death sentences to life imprisonment.

The last execution was carried out by hanging on 13 June 1962.

Czechoslovakia

Status: Retentionist

Executions 1985 - mid-88: 5+; murder

Other factors: None

Method of execution: Hanging (in a state of emergency also by shooting)

The CSSR Penal Code treats the death penalty as an exceptional punishment to be imposed only "if required for the effective protection of society", or "if there is no hope that imprisonment of up to 15 years will achieve the re-education of the perpetrator". Instead of the death penalty, the court can impose a prison term of 15 to 25 years, if it is "of the opinion that such a sentence is sufficient to achieve the aim of punishment". The death penalty may not be imposed on pregnant women nor on anyone under 18 years old at the time the crime was committed.

Under the Penal Code (1973), several crimes carry an optional death sentence, including murder (Article 219), crimes against the state (Articles 91-94, 97 and 105), hijacking (Articles 180A and 180C), genocide (Article 259), and any offences under Articles 92-94 and 97 if committed against an allied socialist state (Article 99). The Penal Code also lists several wartime and military offences that carry an optional death sentence.

An execution can take place only after the Supreme Court of the CSSR has examined the case and confirmed the verdict and after any petitions to the President for clemency have been denied. The judge, procurator, prison governor and a doctor must be present at the execution.

Between 1985 and 1988 Amnesty International received reports of five executions, all for crimes involving murder. There were three in 1985, three sentences and one execution in 1986, two sentences and one execution in 1987 and one death sentence passed during the first five months of 1988. Amnesty International believes the true total to be higher, however, as not all death sentences and executions are officially reported. The information on those that are reported and published in the Czechoslovak press is not always complete – sometimes only the initials of those sentenced to death or executed are used, and others are not identified at all.

In 1978, some 350 CSSR citizens signed a petition to the Federal Assembly of the CSSR calling for the abolition of the death penalty.

Denmark

Status: Abolitionist

Executions 1985 - mid-88: None

Other factors: Not applicable

Method of execution: Not applicable

The death penalty was abolished for ordinary offences under the Civil Penal Code of 15 April 1930 (Act No. 127), which came into force on 1 January 1933. The previous penal code had provided for the death penalty for murder and certain crimes against the state, the last execution for an offence committed in peacetime being carried out in 1892. The death penalty was retained under the Military Penal Code for certain crimes committed during wartime.

After World War II a special retroactive law was enacted which provided for the death penalty for certain crimes committed during the wartime German occupation of Denmark. Forty-six people were subsequently executed by shooting, the last execution being carried out in 1950.

In 1952 a law was enacted which provided for the death penalty during a state of war or foreign occupation. This law was repealed by the *Folketing* (parliament) in May 1978 by 100 votes to 46. The effect of this decision was to abolish the death penalty for all offences, including those in the Military Penal Code.

Djibouti

Status: Abolitionist in practice

Executions 1985 - mid-88: None

Other factors: No right of appeal against sentences imposed by the State Security Court

Method of execution: Shooting by firing-squad

After independence from France in 1977 the death penalty was retained in the Penal Code as an optional penalty for murder and for armed robbery causing death. These offences are tried by the Criminal Court. Appeals are allowed to the Supreme Court. If the Supreme Court quashes the verdict, the defendant is retried by a differently constituted criminal court. Offences against the security of the state, the most serious of which, such as treason, carry an optional death penalty, are tried by a special State Security Court. There is no right of cassation or review by a higher court from this court.

Members of the armed forces charged with a capital offence are tried by the Criminal Court, to which two military assessors of the same rank as the accused are added. Those convicted have the same right of appeal as civilians. All defendants are entitled to legal representation at all stages of the proceedings. Anyone condemned to death may petition the head of state for clemency, who may either commute or confirm the sentence, but the law does not require all death sentences to be automatically reviewed by the head of state. Execution is by shooting by firing-squad.

No death sentences have been passed in Djibouti since independence in 1977.

Dominica

Status: Retentionist

Executions 1985 - mid-88: 1; murder

Other factors: Executions resumed after an unofficial 13-year moratorium

Method of execution: Hanging

The law provides for a mandatory death penalty for murder (Offences against the Person Law, Chapter 44, Section 3). In 1984 the scope of the death penalty was extended to include a mandatory sentence for treason (Treason Act, Section 2). The death penalty may not be imposed on anyone aged under 18 at the time of the crime, nor on pregnant women.

Dominica is a member of the Organization of Eastern Caribbean States, together with six other countries (pending Grenada rejoining). All seven share a common judicial system known as the Eastern Caribbean Supreme Court which consists of a High Court of Justice and a Court of Appeal. Final appeal is to the Judicial Committee of the Privy Council (JCPC) in England which considers only cases involving constitutional matters or "matters of great public importance". The President may commute death sentences to a term of imprisonment of a minimum of two years.

On 8 August 1986 the first execution for 13 years was carried out, the previous one being in November 1973. Frederick Newton, a former Commander in the Dominica Defence Force, was convicted of the murder of a police officer killed during a military attack on a police station, and was sentenced to death in June 1983. His co-defendants, five soldiers, all had their death sentences commuted to life imprisonment in February 1986, five months before his execution.

In 1983 Eric Joseph, a Rastafarian, was convicted of murder and sentenced to death. When all appeals had been exhausted in Dominica, he was granted leave to appeal to the JCPC and the appeal was lodged in December 1985. However, in June 1986 the appeal was dismissed for "non-prosecution" (that is, a failure to pursue the case) because he was financially unable to continue to employ a lawyer. He was not permitted to pursue his case in *forma pauperis* (as a poor person) because there had been some reference to the fact that his family was trying to raise the money to cover the costs and that they had apparently already raised some. However, they could not, it seems, raise the full amount. The JCPC restored leave to appeal in early October 1986. In May 1988 it was still pending.

At the time of going to press there were three people under sentence of death.

▶ Eric Joseph's appeal was heard by the JCPC at the end of July 1988: it was rejected.

Dominican Republic

Status: Abolitionist

Executions 1985 - mid-88: None

Other factors: Not applicable

Method of execution: Not applicable

The death penalty was abolished in the current Constitution of the Dominican Republic which was promulgated in 1966. Article 8 guarantees "the inviolable right to life" and states that under no circumstances will it be possible to establish, pronounce or enforce the death penalty. It continues, "Therefore, neither the death penalty, torture, nor any other punishment or oppressive procedure or penalty that implies loss or diminution of the physical integrity or health of the individual may be established."

Ecuador

Status: Abolitionist

Executions 1985 - mid-88: None

Other factors: Not applicable

Method of execution: Not applicable

The death penalty was abolished for all offences in the Political Constitution of 1906. The current Constitution (promulgated in 1945 and amended in 1983) guarantees the inviolable right to life. Article 19 states, "There is no death penalty."

The abolition of the death penalty in 1906 was the culmination of a 50-year trend which had gradually restricted the number of crimes punishable by death. In 1851 Ecuador had banned the death penalty for "purely political crimes" and the Constitution of 1878 abolished the death penalty for both political and non-political crimes, with the exception of parricide.

Egypt

Status: Retentionist

Executions 1985 - mid-88: 12+; murder; abduction and rape

Other factors: None

Methods of execution: Hanging; shooting by firing-squad

The Penal Code provides for the death penalty for premeditated murder; murder in connection with other, unspecified, crimes; arson when death results; being accomplice to murder; causing the death of a child as a result of exposing it to danger or leaving it in a deserted place; giving false evidence resulting in a wrongful execution; and causing death through endangering a means of public transport. A public official who orders the torturing to death of a detainee or who tortures a detainee to death may be sentenced to death. Since 1976 hijacking has been a capital offence. The death penalty is not mandatory.

Rape, for which imprisonment with hard labour had previously been the maximum penalty, was made a capital offence by an amendment to the Penal Code passed by parliament in September 1980. It has been imposed and carried out for this offence on at least two people, in 1985.

Capital offences against the external security of the state include joining the armed forces of a country at war with Egypt; espionage; and conspiring with an enemy state to harm Egypt's defence or military operations. Offences against the internal security of the state which carry the death penalty include armed attacks on law enforcement authorities; attacks on public utilities or buildings resulting in death; remaining armed after being ordered to demobilize; instigation of, or involvement in, other acts of armed rebellion; and political murder. The death penalty is also provided for as an optional punishment for any offence against external or internal security intended to assist the enemy in time of war.

The Military Code lists a number of capital offences for serving members of the armed forces. These include collaboration with the enemy; maltreating the wounded or prisoners of war; sedition; neglect of duties in critical situations; looting; abuse of power; disobeying orders; and desertion during combat.

In practice, use of the death penalty has been extended to additional offences in the last decade, notably in 1980 for rape, and since 1985 for drug-trafficking (in the latter case, although previously provided for by law, it was not used by the courts). A suggestion made in October 1985 by the then Minister of the Interior, Ahmed Rushdi, that the death penalty should be made mandatory for drug-trafficking (reported in *Al Ahram* newspaper on 30 October 1985) has not been passed into law. Resistance to the suggestion, which could have substantially increased the number of death sentences each year, came from the legal profession and politicians belonging to various parties. Two of the arguments advanced against mandatory death sentences were firstly that they would encourage offenders to resort to violence in order to evade capture, thus endangering the lives of police and bystanders; and, secondly, the risk of offenders escaping punishment altogether, if the courts considered the death penalty inappropriate in a particular case, but were unable to impose any other form of punishment. Nevertheless, almost half the death sentences passed in Egypt since 1985 have been for drug-trafficking.

Exempted from any punishment, including the death penalty, are the insane, the mentally "deficient", and those who were under the influence of a drug which was not taken voluntarily or whose effect was unforeseen. Under the Criminal Procedure Code execution of a pregnant woman is deferred until two years after she has given birth. Anyone aged under 18 at the time of the offence is exempted from the death penalty.

A death sentence may be imposed only by

the unanimous decision of three judges in a criminal court. Such a recommendation must be approved by the *mufti*, the supreme Muslim religious authority in Egypt, who has 10 days to consider the trial dossier and the recommended sentence. If the *mufti* raises no objection the death sentence is approved. An appeal is lodged automatically before the Court of Cassation, and an application for a retrial may also be made by the defendant at this stage. After judicial remedies have been exhausted the Minister of Justice passes the case dossier to the President of the Republic who is empowered to grant clemency. If the President does not grant a pardon or order commutation within 14 days, the death sentence may be carried out. In practice, a period of at least a year usually elapses between sentence by the trial court and execution.

Hanging is the method of execution prescribed in the Penal Code; members of the armed forces are executed by firing-squad, in accordance with the Military Code. Execution takes place in a prison, and relatives of a condemned prisoner may visit the day before execution. The execution is attended by the prison governor, the prison doctor or another doctor appointed by the Prosecutor-General, and a representative of the Prosecutor-General.

There was a significant increase in the number of people sentenced to death in late 1985 and early 1986 after the Minister of the Interior urged the judiciary to impose the death penalty for drug-trafficking. Article 33 of Law No. 40, 1966 provides for the death penalty as an optional punishment for drug-trafficking, but no one had been sentenced to death for this offence until November 1985 when a death sentence was imposed *in absentia* on a Lebanese national. Since then at least 20 people convicted of drug-trafficking have been sentenced to death, although in a number of cases appeals and petitions for clemency are still pending. Fewer than 10 executions annually have come to Amnesty International's attention during the past 10 years, but this figure may increase in future if the death penalty continues to be imposed for drug-trafficking; most of those executed were convicted of murder.

In the 10-year period between 1 May 1978 and 31 May 1988 Amnesty International recorded 103 death sentences: 53 for murder; 26 for drug-trafficking; 12 passed *in absentia* in 1985 on men convicted of fighting against the Egyptian armed forces during a border dispute with Libya in 1977; and 12 for rape or abduction and rape. However, Amnesty International has not been able to obtain official statistics and the true figure may be higher. Twenty-five executions were recorded in the same 10-year period, although again, the true figure may be higher. All but two of these executions were for murder; the other two were for abduction and rape.

The largest number of executions carried out in one single case were those of Khaled Ahmed Shawqi Islambouli, Muhammad Abdul Salam Farag, Abdul Hamid Abdul Salam Abdul Al, Ata Tayel Rahel and Hussein Abbas Muhammad, all sentenced to death by the Supreme Military Court in 1982 for their part in the assassination of President Sadat in October 1981. The lengthy appeals procedure and review by the Court of Cassation normally followed in capital cases was not observed in this case – apparently because sentence had been passed by a military court. The five were sentenced on 6 March and executed on 15 April 1982. Neither their lawyers nor families were informed of the date of the execution and were not able to pay a final visit.

The Egyptian Bar Association and opposition political parties in Egypt have called for the abolition of the death penalty for political offences. At least 24 people were sentenced to death in 1985, 14 in 1986, four in 1987 and 17 in the first five months of 1988.

El Salvador

Status: Abolitionist for all but exceptional crimes

Executions 1985 - mid-88: None

Other factors: Public executions permitted

Method of execution: Shooting by firing-squad

Under Article 27 of the 1983 Constitution the death penalty can be imposed only during an international war on those convicted of certain offences defined in El Salvador's Military Code (1963, as amended). According to the code, treason, desertion, espionage and sedition are punishable by death. The penalty is not provided for in the Minors' Code, applicable to those under the age of 18, and does not apply during civil war. Under the Code of Criminal Procedure, the death penalty may be commuted by the executive. Executions are by firing-squad and are carried out in public.

When the 1983 Constitution was being drafted, in the context of El Salvador's continuing civil conflict, proposals were made both for total abolition of the death penalty and for its extension to cover treason, subversion, murder, kidnapping and arson leading to death. Some deputies who argued publicly against the death penalty reportedly received death threats from El Salvador's so-called "death squads".

The death penalty has been provided for in El Salvador since 1886, but has been applied only twice in the past 30 years. The last known judicial execution, for the rape of a young girl, was carried out in 1973.

Equatorial Guinea

Status: Retentionist

Executions 1985 - mid-88: 2+;
attempting to kill or overthrow the head of state; murder

Other factors: Unfair trials

Methods of execution: Shooting by firing-squad; hanging

Since the present government came to power in 1979 a total of 12 people have been sentenced to death for political offences, 11 of them before 1984 and one in 1986. They were convicted by military courts after unfair trials. Two people were sentenced to death for murder in 1987, one of whom was executed. However, it has not been possible to verify the total number of death sentences for murder.

When Equatorial Guinea gained independence from Spain in 1968 the Spanish Common Penal Code (1963) and the Spanish Code of Military Law (1945) became the basis of the new state's legal system. Under these codes, 43 offences carry an optional death sentence – 24 under the Code of Military Law and 19 under the Common Penal Code. These offences include crimes against the security of the state, rebellion, terrorism, sedition, and murder. All offences against the security of the state are subject to military jurisdiction. The crime of murder falls within the jurisdiction of the ordinary provincial courts and there is a right of appeal to the Supreme Court. Executions for sentences imposed by military courts are carried out by firing-squad; hanging is the method used under civil jurisdiction. Pregnant women may not be executed and children aged under 16 at the time of the crime may not be sentenced to death.

During the government of Francisco Macías Nguema (1968-1979) few trials were held. After one trial in June 1974 during which defendants had virtually no opportunity to defend themselves, 27 people were sentenced to death and publicly executed the same day.

After Francisco Macías Nguema was overthrown in a coup in August 1979, a special military court was established to try him and 10 other civilian and military officials for a number of crimes including treason and human rights violations. He and six others were sentenced to death and executed on the same day. Since then, after military trials in 1981, 1983 and 1986 involving a total of 87 defendants, five more people have been sentenced to death for plotting against the government. Four of them were executed almost immediately after their conviction, while the fifth (1983) had his sentence commuted to a term of imprisonment after a guarantee that he would not be executed had been given to a foreign embassy in which he had sought refuge.

Military trials held since August 1979 resulting in death sentences have been unfair in a number of respects. Defendants charged with certain offences, including crimes punishable by death, are tried by procedures known as the "most summary", which means that they have no right of appeal, and that presentation of the defence case is severely curtailed with no right to challenge the findings of the judge who carried out the pre-trial investigation. In addition to this, judges have no security of tenure since military courts are established for each particular case and dissolved after they have reached a verdict.

The fact that those who preside over military

courts are all serving members of the government has led some to question their independence and impartiality. In a trial in July 1983, for example, in which three people were sentenced to death for plotting to kill the President, the judge was the Minister of Defence. Two of the accused were subsequently executed. There were reports that both this group, and defendants sentenced to death in 1981, had been tortured during interrogation and that their convictions had been based on statements made under duress.

In August 1986 Eugenio Abeso Mondu's admission in court that he had attempted to overthrow the government was not adequately supported by corroborative evidence. Furthermore, the actions to which he had admitted in his statement and for which he was convicted appeared to amount to an offence defined in the Penal Code as "conspiracy", which carries a maximum penalty of 20 years' imprisonment, and not an "attempt" for which he was sentenced to death and executed.

Ethiopia

Status: Retentionist

Executions 1985 - mid-88: Not known

Other factors: Executions following secret summary trials; public executions permitted

Method of execution: Hanging; shooting by firing-squad

Under provisions of the 1957 Penal Code which are still in force, the death penalty is mandatory for armed robbery by a gang, and is optional for murder, other forms of armed robbery, looting and piracy. Defendants are tried by the High Court and have the right to legal representation and appeal to the Court of Appeal.

In addition, the Revised Special Penal Code (1981) provides for an optional death penalty for situations of "exceptional gravity" for a wide range of political offences. These include offences against the independence or territorial integrity of the state; engaging in armed uprising or civil war; counter-revolutionary acts; serious economic offences; and corruption. The "counter-revolutionary acts" which can be

punished by death include "committing treason against the country and the people by illegally leaving or attempting to leave the country".

Offences under the Revised Special Penal Code are tried by Special Courts, also established in 1981, which have civilian judges and provide for defendants to have the right to legal representation and to appeal to a Special Court of Appeal.

Members of the armed forces charged with offences against the Armed Forces Act, under which the death penalty is mandatory for mutiny and optional for certain other military offences, are tried by courts-martial. There is a right of appeal to a higher court-martial.

All people condemned to death have the right to petition the head of state for clemency. All death sentences must be reviewed by the head of state, who may confirm or commute the sentence. The 1987 Constitution provides for free state legal aid for defendants who cannot afford legal fees. The death sentence may not be imposed on anyone aged under 18 at the time of the offence, pregnant women or the insane.

Execution is by hanging or, in the case of members of the armed forces, shooting by firing-squad. Executions are carried out in prison; in exceptional circumstances they may take place elsewhere, for example, in public in a place appropriate to the crime.

The Revised Special Penal Code replaced the Special Penal Code of November 1974 which was introduced after the overthrow of Emperor Haile Selassie's government in September 1974 and made retroactive to February 1974, the beginning of the revolution. It replaced several articles of the 1957 Penal Code dealing with political offences, many of which were punishable by death, and also extended the range of use of the optional death penalty to include, among other offences, abuse of authority; causing famine or epidemic; and assisting in the escape of a prisoner awaiting trial for or convicted of these offences. Special Courts-Martial were established to try those charged with offences against the Special Penal Code. Judges were military officers and there was no right of appeal to a higher court. Death sentences required review by the chairman of the then ruling Provisional Military Administrative Council (PMAC, known as the *Dergue*).

The 1974 Special Penal Code was amended in 1976 to introduce further offences which carried an optional death penalty, including causing grave damage to the economy, committing counter-revolutionary acts and corruption.

The number of death sentences imposed or executions carried out between 1974 and 31 May 1988 is not known. No statistics about the use of the death penalty have been published. Between 1974 and 1981 there were several secret summary trials by Special Courts-Martial resulting in executions, for example in November 1976 when 50 students were executed. There were two executions in 1987 of local officials convicted of causing the deaths of prisoners in their custody. However, official reports of death sentences or judicial executions were exceptional and it was not known how many prisoners were under sentence of death at the time of going to press.

Fiji

Status: Abolitionist for all but exceptional crimes

Executions 1985 - mid-88: None

Other factors: None

Method of execution: Hanging

Fiji abolished the death penalty for murder in 1979 when a bill to make the death penalty mandatory for murder was amended in parliament to remove the death penalty and substitute life imprisonment in its place. The last execution took place in 1964, but death sentences were imposed in certain murder cases until its abolition. The death penalty is retained only for the crimes of treason, instigating foreigners to invade Fiji, and genocide.

A Royal Commission on Treatment of Offenders in 1980 recommended abolition of the death penalty for all offences, noting that public opinion appeared to favour its abolition, that criminal statistics in Fiji and elsewhere did not suggest that capital punishment had any greater deterrent effect than life imprisonment, and that there had never been any prosecutions for the exceptional crimes. No death sentences have been imposed since 1980.

Finland

Status: Abolitionist

Executions 1985 - mid-88: None

Other factors: Not applicable

Method of execution: Not applicable

The death penalty was abolished for peacetime offences in the Penal Code of 1949, and for all offences on 5 May 1972 by an amendment to the Penal Code of 1949 which came into force on 1 June 1972. In its preamble to the bill amending the Penal Code, the government stated that there was no convincing argument for preventive effects of the death penalty. The government also referred to the possibility of an innocent person being sentenced to death and executed. Furthermore, it was suggested by the government that abolition of the death penalty was as natural as abolishing the use of torture and other cruel punishments (as they had done earlier). The vote in parliament approving the government's proposal to abolish the death penalty was 140 in favour and 29 against.

Between 1939 and 1944, 500 people were sentenced to death for war crimes by courts-martial and executed by firing-squad. Most of these executions took place in 1942. The last execution for an ordinary criminal offence was carried out in 1826.

France

Status: Abolitionist

Executions 1985 - mid-88: None

Other factors: Not applicable

Method of execution: Not applicable

The death penalty was abolished for all offences, both civil and military, under Law No. 81-908 of 9 October 1981, which came into effect the following day. Article 1 states, "The death penalty is abolished."

The bill proposing abolition of the death penalty was presented to the National Assembly by the government of the new socialist President, François Mitterrand, who had been elected in May 1981.

France abolished the death penalty for political offences in 1848. However, two decree laws of June 1938 and July 1939 and an enactment (*ordonnance*) of June 1960 provided for the death penalty for a number of offences against state security.

Until October 1981, both the Penal Code and the Code of Military Justice authorized the use of the death penalty for a number of civil and military crimes. Between 1966 and 1977 nine people who had been convicted of criminal offences were executed by guillotine. The last execution was carried out on 10 September 1977, following a conviction for murder, rape and torture. Seven people were under sentence of death when the death penalty was abolished.

Gabon

Status: Retentionist

Executions 1985 - mid-88: 1; plotting to overthrow the government

Other factors: Special courts; public executions

Method of execution: Shooting by firing-squad

According to the Penal Code a number of offences are punishable by a mandatory death sentence, including premeditated murder, espionage and treason. However, in practice death sentences are rarely imposed.

Defendants sentenced to death have a right of appeal against the court's judgment. The law stipulates that when a death sentence is confirmed on appeal, it cannot be carried out until a petition for presidential clemency has been rejected.

In 1979 two people were executed in public in the centre of Libreville, the capital. In December 1982 three people convicted of murder by the criminal court, and whose appeals for clemency had been rejected by President Omar Bongo, were publicly executed on Libreville beach in front of a crowd

of several thousand people. The executions were televised.

The last known execution was carried out in August 1985. Alexandre Mandja Ngoucouta, an air force captain, was convicted and sentenced to death by a special military court. He was charged with plotting to overthrow the government and his appeal for clemency was denied.

In 1983 President Bongo declared in a press interview that he was "rather favourable" to abolition of the death penalty. Amnesty International wrote to him welcoming this statement, but no steps towards abolition have yet been taken by the Gabonese authorities.

In February 1985 two other people who had been found guilty of murder and sentenced to death by the criminal court benefited from presidential clemency; their sentences were commuted to life imprisonment with hard labour.

Gambia

Status: Retentionist

Executions 1985 - mid-88: None

Other factors: None

Method of execution: Hanging

The death penalty is provided for a large number of offences, including treason and murder. Pregnant women, children aged under 16, those certified insane and those who commit murder as a sudden response to provocation may not be executed. Defendants charged with capital offences have a right to defence counsel and those sentenced to death have a right of appeal. If a death sentence is confirmed on appeal, the defendant may submit a petition for mercy to the head of state, who is empowered to commute death sentences.

Following an unsuccessful attempt to overthrow the government of President Sir Dawda Jawara on 30 July 1981, in which many people were killed, the government-appointed Law Reform Commission proposed a new law. The law provides that any plot to overthrow the government by force, whether successful or not, will be regarded as treason; in addition, courts may base their verdicts on the evidence of one witness only. This proposal became law in May 1986, making the death penalty mandatory for a wide range of offences defined as treason.

A series of trials following the 1981 coup attempt resulted in death sentences being imposed by the Special Division of the Supreme Court. By May 1984, 63 people convicted of treason were under sentence of death, 26 of them convicted in the first four months of 1984.

Since 1984 the number of death sentences imposed has decreased. Meta Camara, a former corporal in the Gambian Field Force, was sentenced to death by the Supreme Court in December 1985 after being convicted of participating in the coup attempt. However, his sentence was reduced to 20 years' imprisonment by the Gambia Court of Appeal.

On 3 September 1981 the first execution in Gambia since independence in 1965 was carried out. Mustapha Danso was executed after he had been convicted in December 1980 of murdering the Deputy Commander of the Field Force. In 1986, Lamin Darbo, a businessman, was convicted of murder and sentenced to death by the Supreme Court.

Although a number of people have been sentenced to death since 1981, no executions are reported to have been carried out. In February 1984 President Dawda Jawara commuted the death sentences passed on 27 people, and in April 1984 the death sentences imposed on a further 16 people after conviction of involvement in the 1981 coup were also commuted. It appears that none of the remaining prisoners under sentence of death was executed. Many prisoners sentenced to death after December 1981 were kept in leg-irons and in solitary confinement. However, the use of leg-irons was banned by presidential order on 30 December 1982.

President Jawara stated publicly in September 1985 that he was personally opposed to the death penalty. Amnesty International welcomed this declaration and also the regular practice of granting clemency to people under sentence of death. The organization has expressed concern, however, about the new law which provides for a much broader definition of the crime of treason and makes it a capital offence, and has urged the Gambian Government to abolish the death penalty.

German Democratic Republic

Status: Abolitionist

Executions 1985 - mid-88: None

Other factors: Not applicable

Method of execution: Not applicable

The death penalty was abolished with immediate effect in a decree issued by the Council of State on 17 July 1987. The necessary legislative changes were approved by the People's Chamber on 18 December 1987.

The decree stated that the abolition was "in accordance with the recommendations ... of the United Nations for the gradual removal of the death penalty from the lives of nations", and that by abolishing the death penalty the GDR was declaring its position on "the right of humanity to a peaceful and dignified life, [and] on the preservation of human rights as a whole".

Before its abolition in 1987 the death penalty could be imposed for a number of crimes including murder, genocide, treason, espionage and sabotage, and for certain military offences when the country was in a "state of defence". Its use was not mandatory and the abolition decree stated that the death penalty had not been imposed "for years". To Amnesty International's knowledge no death sentences or executions in the GDR have been reported in the national media since 1974. However, sources outside the GDR have claimed that unreported executions have been carried out since then, most recently in 1980. Amnesty International has not been able to verify these claims.

Germany (Federal Republic of)

Status: Abolitionist

Executions 1985 - mid-88: None

Other factors: Not applicable

Method of execution: Not applicable

The death penalty was abolished for all offences under the Basic Law of the Federal Republic of Germany of 1949 (the equivalent of a constitution). Article 102 states, "The death penalty is abolished." Subsequent motions calling for the repeal of Article 102 in the 1950s were rejected by a clear majority of the *Bundestag* (lower chamber).

In 1945 the occupying authorities had abolished the death penalty for the large class of crimes for which it could be imposed under the previous National Socialist Government and had retained it only for murder. The last execution took place in 1949.

Ghana

Status: Retentionist

Executions 1985 - mid-88: 37+; armed robbery; murder; embezzlement; economic sabotage

Other factors: Special courts with deficient trial standards; no right of appeal against sentences imposed by Public Tribunals (until August 1984) or the Special Military Tribunal

Method of execution: Shooting by firing-squad

Following a change of government in 1979, the number of capital offences and executions in Ghana has increased. Most death sentences are passed by special courts which suffer from procedural deficiencies.

Under the Criminal Code of 1960, treason, murder and attempted murder in certain circumstances are punishable by death, with murder carrying a mandatory death penalty.

Such offences may be tried by the High Court, where the defendant has full rights of defence and a right of appeal to the Supreme Court. The head of state has the power to commute death sentences. Under the Armed Forces Act, No. 105 of 1962, the death penalty may be imposed for treason and mutiny by military personnel in time of war.

Within days of the coup on 4 June 1979 which brought a military government, the Armed Forces Revolutionary Council (AFRC), to power, three former heads of state and five other senior officers were executed by firing-squad, apparently for corruption and misuse of state funds. They had not been publicly or fairly tried.

On 29 June 1979 Special Courts were established under AFRC Decree 3 with the power to impose the death penalty for various "economic offences" committed since 1966, ranging from intent to sabotage the economy to hoarding. The Decree was declared to have been in force from the date of the coup. The Special Courts suffered from grave procedural deficiencies: members were not required to have legal training; the proceedings were hurried; allegations of ill-treatment by troops in pretrial detention were disregarded; and defendants were allowed neither defence counsel nor right of judicial appeal. The courts' decisions were subject only to review and confirmation by the AFRC. Nearly 70 former senior officials were sentenced to death or to long prison terms *in absentia*. None are known to have been executed. After a return to civilian rule in September 1979, the new head of state commuted all death sentences other than those imposed by the Special Courts.

A further coup in December 1981 brought to power the Provisional National Defence Council (PNDC), another military government. In July 1982 a further set of special courts was established under the Public Tribunal Law, PNDC Law 24. Public Tribunals were given the power to try any offence referred to them by the PNDC and to impose the death penalty for offences specified by the government or in cases in which the judges felt it was merited. In October 1982 the government reportedly directed Public Tribunals to impose the death penalty for treason (already a capital offence), and the following crimes: illegal importation of explosives and firearms; attempting to alter by force the "revolutionary path of the people of Ghana"; illegal currency dealing; attempted sabotage of the economy; smuggling of certain products; and corruption or extortion by certain senior government officials. Most of these offences had previously carried a prison sentence. It was not clear whether all were offences in law.

Trials before Public Tribunals were summary; under PNDC Law 24, there was no right of appeal. Members of the Tribunals were appointed by the PNDC and had no specific protection against dismissal, nor were they required to have any legal training. There appeared to be no clear criteria for referring cases to Public Tribunals rather than to the High Court, although defendants before Public Tribunals suffered disadvantages: Public Tribunals could pronounce heavier sentences than High Courts trying the same offences; the burden of proof was on the defendant; the standard of proof was not as rigorous as in the High Court; and not all defendants were represented by legal counsel.

In April 1984 the Special Military Tribunal (Amendment) Law, PNDC Law 77 of 1984, empowered special military courts set up in 1982 to impose the death penalty for offences against the security of the state. Members of the armed forces preside over the court, which sits *in camera*, and no judicial appeal may be made against its decisions. In April 1984, nine former army officers were convicted of treason *in absentia* by a Special Military Tribunal and sentenced to death.

In August 1984 a revised Public Tribunals Law, PNDC Law 78, established a National Public Tribunal as the highest court to which those convicted by lower Public Tribunals could appeal. It could also try cases itself and hear appeals against its own decisions. However, there was no guarantee that judges hearing the appeal would not be the same as those who presided over the National Public Tribunal whose decision was being challenged on appeal, and the independence of the appeal procedure was therefore not ensured.

A number of people have been executed after conviction by Public Tribunals of involvement in attempts to overthrow the government. In August 1983, seven people were executed following conviction, without benefit of legal counsel, in two trials. These concerned the murder of three High Court judges and a retired army officer in 1982, and an escape from jail in June 1983 by army officers suspected of involvement in earlier coup attempts, who had again attempted to overthrow the government. Three others sentenced to death *in absentia* for their involvement in the June 1983 coup attempt were among at least 11 people reported to have been executed summarily following a further coup attempt in March 1984. Six were executed in April 1985 and seven in June 1986 following conviction of further conspiracies against the government.

It is not always clear whether executions for criminal offences have resulted from conviction in the High Court or in Public Tribunals. At least 12 people were executed in 1985: five for armed robbery, three for embezzlement, one for murder and three for attempting to sabotage the economy. At least 14 were executed for murder and armed robbery in 1986, an unknown number in July 1987 for armed robbery and 11 in June 1988 for murder and armed robbery.

Greece

Status: Abolitionist in practice

Executions 1985 - mid-88: None

Other factors: None

Method of execution: Shooting by firing-squad

Following the national elections in 1981, the new government under Prime Minister Andreas Papandreou announced its intention to abolish the death penalty for peacetime offences. Although this intention has been reiterated since then, at the time of going to press no formal steps have been taken towards abolition.

Under the Greek Penal Code of 1950 an optional death penalty is provided for causing explosions resulting in death, for armed robbery resulting in death or severe injury, and for murder in certain circumstances, namely if the crime was particularly abhorrent in method and surrounding circumstances, and the criminal is considered dangerous to society.

Provision for the death penalty for military crimes and crimes against the state includes killing or attempting to kill the head of state, negotiating with a foreign government resulting in war against Greece, and colluding with the enemy in wartime and espionage. Article 138 of the Penal Code provides for a mandatory death penalty for "attempting to detach territory from Greece". In 1978 the Greek parliament passed a Law on Terrorism which provided for a mandatory death penalty for acts of terrorism resulting in loss of life.

The Greek Constitution limits the use of the death penalty for political offences. Article 7 (3) of the Constitution of Greece of 11 June 1975 states, "The death sentence shall not be imposed for political crimes, unless these are composite" (that is, unless there are aggravating factors).

The last execution was carried out on 25 August 1972 for a conviction of murder. Since then a number of death sentences have been imposed by Greek courts but no executions have been carried out. One death sentence was passed in June 1986 and another in February 1988, both of them for convictions of murder. Since 1972 all death sentences have been commuted to life imprisonment by the President.

Grenada

Status: Retentionist

Executions 1985 - mid-88: None

Other factors: None

Method of execution: Hanging

Under the Criminal Code of Grenada, a mandatory death penalty is provided for murder (Criminal Homicide and Similar Offences Title XVIII, 234) and treason (Offences Against the Safety of the State Act, Title XXIV). The death penalty cannot be imposed on anyone aged under 18 at the time of the crime.

Capital cases are tried by the High Court of Grenada before a judge and a 12-member jury; verdicts of guilty must be unanimous. Defendants may appeal to the Grenada Court of Appeal although this may change in the future (see below). The prerogative of mercy is exercised by the Governor General acting on the

advice of a minister. The minister is designated in the Constitution and operates in consultation with the Advisory Committee on the Prerogative of Mercy.

Until 1979 Grenada was a member of the Organization of Eastern Caribbean States together with six other countries. All seven shared a common judicial system known as the Eastern Caribbean Supreme Court (ECSC) which consists of a High Court of Justice and a Court of Appeal. Final appeal was to the Judicial Committee of the Privy Council (JCPC) in England. However, in 1979 the People's Revolutionary Government (PRG) established an independent court system and abolished the right of appeal to the JCPC (People's Law No. 84 of 1979, Privy Council [Abolition of Appeals] Law, 1979). Following the overthrow of the PRG in 1983, the 1974 Constitution was reinstated in November 1984 by the new authorities but the People's Laws passed by the PRG remained valid. This has caused some confusion which is still unresolved. Since reinstating the Constitution, the new government has announced its intention to return to the ECSC system.

In 1982 four people – three men and a woman – were sentenced to death on charges under the Terrorism (Prevention) Law which provides for the death penalty for those found guilty of causing death by explosives. The charge was made following an assassination attempt on the life of Prime Minister Maurice Bishop, in the course of which three children were killed by a bomb. The bomb had been planted under a platform where Prime Minister Bishop and other members of the government were to stand during a public meeting. The four prisoners were granted a full pardon by the Governor General in December 1983 and were immediately released.

Since 1984 at least 17 people have been sentenced to death. They include 14 members of the People's Revolutionary Government (PRG) and People's Revolutionary Army (PRA) convicted of the murder of eight people, among them Prime Minister Bishop, in October 1983. The defendants questioned whether the court before which they were tried – the Grenada Supreme Court – was constitutional. They maintained that reinstatement of the 1974 Constitution required a return to the former ECSC system which, among other things, provided a final right of appeal to the JCPC. The Court of Appeals (in Grenada) ruled that although the Constitution would entail an eventual return to the ECSC system it upheld the legitimacy of the Grenada Supreme Court for that trial. In April 1988 the case was still under appeal.

The last execution, of a prisoner convicted of murder, was carried out in October 1978.

Guatemala

Status: Retentionist

Executions 1985 - mid-88: None

Other factors: Unfair trials

Method of execution: Shooting by firing-squad

The Guatemalan Penal Code (1973) provides for the death penalty for aggravated homicide of the President (and for the Vice President when serving as President) or of a member of the culprit's immediate family, killing a kidnap victim, and rape of a girl under 10. The death penalty is optional for parricide, homicide and homicide of the Chief of State, but mandatory for rape and kidnapping when death results and the victim was under the age of 10. Under the 1985 Constitution the death penalty cannot be imposed on women, people over 70, those guilty of political crimes or related common crimes, or people extradited for political crimes or when a conviction is based on circumstantial evidence. A sentence can be imposed only after all appeals are exhausted. The Constitution states that Congress can abolish the death penalty.

When the 1985 Constitution was being debated, Monseñor Próspero Penados, the Archbishop of Guatemala, the Rector of the University of San Carlos, and some members of Congress called for total abolition on grounds such as Christian values, the possibility of error and international moves toward limiting its use. Other groups waged a public campaign for retention of the death penalty, particularly for kidnapping.

In practice, the judicial death penalty has rarely been carried out in Guatemala. Four judicial executions for criminal offences were reported in 1975. Among those executed were two former National Police officers, accused of killing a member of a prominent Guatemalan family who was apparently shot in the course of an attack on an opposition figure. The opposition called for a stay of execution to investigate claims by one of the men that he had been involved in the arrest of several opposition figures, who "disappeared" after he turned them over to his superior officers, and were later found dead.

The last judicial executions in Guatemala were carried out in 1982 (four) and 1983 (11), on charges such as kidnapping and subversion, under an emergency decree, Decree 46-82, promulgated during a state of siege imposed when General Efrain Ríos Montt seized power in 1982. The decree established secret military tribunals empowered to impose the death penalty for a wide range of political offences. There were inconsistencies in the evidence against those executed and strong indications that they had "confessed" under torture. Most had no access to defence counsel, and an appeals mechanism was instituted only after widespread international protest following the first executions under the decree.

The decree was rescinded after General Ríos Montt was overthrown in August 1983. There had been no executions under the decree since April 1983, when the Inter-American Commission on Human Rights asked the Inter-American Court whether Guatemala had failed to fulfil its obligations as a party to the American Convention on Human Rights by widening the range of crimes carrying the death penalty. In September 1983 the Court took the view that it had failed to fulfil its obligations.

Guinea

Status: Retentionist

Executions 1985 - mid-88: 2+

Other factors: Secret trials lacking elementary safeguards; no right of appeal against convictions or sentences imposed by the State Security Court and the Military Tribunal

Method of execution: Shooting by firing-squad

There were important changes in the use of the death penalty in 1984 following the death of the country's first President, Ahmed Sékou Touré, and a coup which brought a military government to power. In particular, the frequency of death sentences and executions diminished. However, the legal basis for the death penalty, a Penal Code enacted in 1975, has not changed. Both before and since 1984 most death sentences appear to have concerned offences which were in some way political, and in many prominent cases, again both before and since 1984, the government has refused to disclose whether executions have actually been carried out or not.

Under the Penal Code a wide range of offences carry a mandatory death penalty. These include premeditated murder; poisoning; the murder of either parent; murder when it is committed in the course of another offence; the destruction of buildings by arson or the use of explosives; and large-scale embezzlement of public funds. By far the largest number of capital offences, however, concerns the security of the state: working for a foreign power engaged in hostilities against Guinea, espionage, promoting civil war and leading a mutiny or other armed band. These offences were set out in considerable detail in the 1975 Penal Code after President Sékou Touré concluded that a "fifth column" was actively trying to bring about the downfall of his government.

Both ordinary criminal courts at the level of *tribunal de grande instance* (district courts responsible for trying serious cases) and a number of courts at national level are empowered to impose death sentences. On sever-al occasions before 1984 the government announced the creation of special courts; for example, in 1971, the entire National Assembly was transformed into a court and 91 death sentences were imposed on alleged "fifth columnists"; 58 of those concerned were publicly hanged. A special court for economic offences also imposed death sentences.

Since 1984 the criminal justice system has been reorganized, no special courts have been retained and no ordinary courts are known to have imposed death sentences. However, in August 1985, soon after an unsuccessful attempt to overthrow the government, two new courts with jurisdiction over political cases were established which have subsequently passed death sentences: a State Security Court which tries civilians, and a Military Tribunal for armed forces and police personnel. Those convicted by these courts have no right of appeal.

The law provides for a right of appeal for those sentenced to death by ordinary courts and stipulates that executions cannot be carried out until the head of state has considered and rejected petitions for clemency. In practice, trials at which death sentences have been imposed have been marked by serious flaws in procedures for appeals, and before April 1984 prisoners were frequently unable to petition for clemency. It is not clear whether any formal pleas for clemency were reviewed by the head of state after secret trials at which death sentences were imposed in 1986.

The law stipulates that death sentences are to be carried out by firing-squad, that pregnant women may not be executed until after giving birth and that those aged under 18 may not be sentenced to death. In practice, before 1984 many people condemned to death were killed by depriving them of all food and water (a process known as the "black diet"), and victims included teenagers of 14 or 15. This practice evidently started in the early 1970s and was used to kill large numbers of prisoners, probably hundreds. The most prominent victim was Diallo Telli, the former Secretary General of the Organization for African Unity (OAU), executed at the beginning of 1977.

Suspected political opponents of President Sékou Touré were frequently sentenced to death and executed. Although the number of executions declined in his last years in power, five people were executed in Mamou in March 1984, only a week before his death. They had been sentenced to death by a local court after violent protests against police action in the town and were not allowed to appeal to any higher court. A particular feature of executions of political prisoners from 1971 onwards was that executions and death sentences were rarely announced publicly, and prisoners' relatives were provided with no information whatsoever to indicate whether executions had been carried out.

After a coup in April 1984 and the arrest of relatives of President Sékou Touré and members of his administration, the new military government publicly undertook to respect human rights. In October 1984 the new head of state, President Lansana Conté, told foreign journalists that his government did not intend to use the death penalty. Nevertheless, after a coup attempt in July 1985, President Conté announced that those who had killed or wounded innocent people would themselves be killed. For almost two years following this announcement, there was no official news about those arrested either in July 1985 or earlier. However, unofficial sources claimed that at least 20 prisoners had been secretly executed shortly after the coup attempt, said to include both leaders of the coup attempt and relatives of President Sékou Touré arrested in April 1984.

In May 1987 the government announced the results of a series of secret trials, apparently held in 1986, and said that 58 people had been sentenced to death, 21 of whom were sentenced *in absentia*. Of the 37 who were present at their sentencing, the identity of 17 tried by the State Security Court was made public; the other 20 were sentenced by military court and no details other than their ranks were revealed. Similarly, the authorities did not disclose any details of the charges on which any of those tried had been convicted, and subsequently refused to make any information about the charges or judgments available to Amnesty International representatives who visited Conakry in June 1987.

Those sentenced to death included people arrested after the July 1985 coup attempt and others detained since April 1984. Among the civilians whose identity was revealed were a considerable number who were reported by

unofficial sources to have been already executed in 1985. In December 1987 President Conté told journalists that two prisoners who were widely believed to have been among the military personnel sentenced to death in 1986 had, in fact, died in custody in July 1985. He reportedly claimed that other prisoners sentenced to death were still alive. However, none had been seen by visitors since their arrest, and by April 1988 the relatives of prisoners convicted at the secret trials had not been given any information concerning the whereabouts or fate of the prisoners.

Although the government revealed few details about the secret trials, it is clear that they were marked by grave defects: not only did the accused not appear in court, but they were evidently unaware that they were being tried. The charges against them were not announced before or after the trials, making it impossible for anyone to contest the evidence admitted by the courts, a significant part of which seems to have consisted of statements made under duress by prisoners held incommunicado.

By May 1988 the situation of 35 people under sentence of death still remained to be clarified by the authorities. It was unclear how many were still alive or whether any had already been executed.

Guinea-Bissau

Status: Retentionist

Executions 1985 - mid-88: 7+; crimes against the security of the state; murder

Other factors: Unfair trials; no right of appeal

Method of execution: Shooting by firing-squad

Military courts are empowered to impose the death penalty in Guinea-Bissau for aggravated murder and offences against state security. After the present head of state took power in 1980 no executions were reported for five years. However, in 1986 at least 13 people were sentenced to death, seven of whom were executed.

The death penalty was introduced by the *Partido Africano da Independência da Guiné* e *Cabo Verde* (PAIGC), African Party for the Independence of Guinea and Cape Verde, during its war for independence from Portugal. Portuguese law did not provide for the death penalty except for certain military offences. Three years after the war began, the PAIGC adopted a Law of Military Justice of 19 September 1966 which made the death penalty mandatory for serious offences including treason and espionage. When Portugal recognized Guinea-Bissau's independence in September 1974 the new state adopted Portuguese legislation except where this conflicted with the Constitution which the PAIGC had promulgated in 1973 when it unilaterally declared independence.

While President Luis Cabral was in power from 1973 until 1980 at least 40 people were sentenced to death. Many others were executed without being tried.

The Law of Military Justice of 1966 was amended by Law No. 2/76 of 3 May 1976 which provided for imprisonment as an alternative to the death penalty for treason and espionage. However, Law No. 2/78 of 20 May 1978 extended the death penalty to other crimes. The Superior Military Tribunal was given exclusive jurisdiction over military personnel and civilians who were charged with aggravated premeditated murder and with a range of offences against the security of the state, including attempts on the life of leading PAIGC members, revealing state secrets, and armed attack against fortified places. An alternative 15-year prison sentence was applicable to all these crimes. The death penalty cannot be imposed on those aged under 18 at the time of the crime nor on pregnant women.

According to Article 6 of Law No. 2/78 the Council of State nominates the judges for each trial or series of trials. The judges therefore have no security of tenure, which calls into question their independence from the executive. The presiding judge must be a member of the General Staff of the Armed Forces and the panel of five judges should include a qualified lawyer to act as an assessor. Those sentenced to death have no right of appeal to a higher court against conviction and sentence. They may appeal to the Council of State for clemency or commutation of the sentence, but must do so within three days of being sentenced.

In 1980, when a new draft constitution was being discussed, a number of PAIGC and government officials reportedly objected that it had not abolished the death penalty. By contrast, in Cape Verde, where the same party was in power, the draft constitution had abolished it. Before the 1980 Constitution came into force the present government took power in a coup. The present Constitution was promulgated in May 1984 and does not forbid the death penalty.

In July 1986, 12 people, including former Vice-President Paulo Correia, were convicted of conspiring to overthrow the government and sentenced to death by the Superior Military Tribunal. The accused were held incommunicado for an extended period and only allowed to consult defence counsel a week before the trial, which was held *in camera*. There were reports that some of the defendants were convicted on the basis of confessions made under duress and in the absence of sufficient evidence against them. There was no right of judicial appeal. The Council of State later commuted six death sentences but Paulo Correia and five others were executed.

Five people have reportedly been sentenced to death and executed for aggravated murder since 1985.

Guyana

Status: Retentionist

Executions 1985 - mid-88: 9; murder

Other factors: Executions resumed after an unofficial 13-year moratorium

Method of execution: Hanging

A mandatory death penalty is provided for murder (Criminal Law [Offences], Chapter 8.01, 1973) and treason. Certain military offences – providing assistance to the enemy, participating in a mutiny or inciting others to participate, and failing to endeavour to prevent a mutiny or report that one is taking place or is intended – also carry an optional death sentence. These offences are tried by court-martial.

Murder cases are tried in the High Court before a judge and jury and appeals are heard by the Court of Appeal. The right to appeal to the Judicial Committee of the Privy Council in England was abolished by an act of Parliament in 1970.

Execution warrants are issued 48 hours before the date of execution. Since executions are normally carried out on a Tuesday, warrants are usually read at the weekend, reportedly causing difficulty for prisoners in contacting a lawyer to instruct him or her to lodge any final appeal or petition for mercy.

Between 1972 and 1985 death sentences were imposed but no executions were carried out. However, between 1985 and May 1988, nine prisoners convicted of murder were executed: four in October 1985; one in June 1986 and another four in April 1988. According to the government, the resumption of executions was a response to an increase in criminal activity. According to Amnesty International's records death sentences were imposed for convictions of murder every year between 1979 and 1987, except for 1981 and 1982; at least 10 of these sentences were passed between 1985 and 1987.

Following the four executions in April 1988, 22 prisoners remained under sentence of death, all of them convicted of murder.

Haiti

Status: Abolitionist

Executions 1985 - mid-88: None

Other factors: Not applicable

Method of execution: Not applicable

Abolition of the death penalty was enshrined in the 1987 Constitution which was approved by national referendum. Article 20 of the section relating to the fundamental rights of citizens states, "The death penalty is abolished in all cases." A governmental decree had already abolished the death penalty for all political offences except high treason in 1985, but it was still applicable for certain kinds of murder. Although the death penalty was imposed on a number of occasions, to Amnesty International's knowledge it has not been carried out since 1972. Execution was by firing-squad.

Following the departure of President-for-Life Jean-Claude Duvalier in February 1986, a number of former officials who had served under him or his father, François Duvalier, were charged with human rights abuses perpetrated in previous years, including murder. Luc Désir, Serge Gaston and Adherbal Lhérisson were arrested and sentenced to death in three separate trials in 1986 and early 1987, while Elois Maître and Jean Tassy were tried and sentenced to death *in absentia*. However, the new Constitution came into force in March 1987 before all legal procedures had been exhausted. Consequently, all pending death sentences are believed to have been commuted.

▶ Following the military coup in June 1988 President Namphy abolished the 1987 Constitution, but issued a decree on 12 July 1988 reaffirming abolition of the death penalty.

Honduras

Status: Abolitionist

Executions 1985 - mid-88: None

Other factors: Not applicable

Method of execution: Not applicable

The death penalty was abolished by decree in 1956. The National Constituent Assembly, which drew up a new Constitution in 1957, voted unanimously in favour of abolition (Article 61). Abolition was maintained in the 1965 Constitution and in the modified Constitution which has been in force since May 1985, which states, "The right to life is inviolable" (Article 65) and "The death penalty is prohibited" (Article 66). The last judicial execution was carried out in 1940 when a Costa Rican convicted of the murder of a Spaniard was shot by firing-squad.

Hong Kong

Status: Abolitionist in practice

Executions 1985 - mid-88: None

Other factors: None

Method of execution: Hanging

Treason and murder are punishable by death, with the latter carrying a mandatory death penalty. However, no executions have been carried out since November 1966, after the death penalty was provisionally abolished in the United Kingdom in 1965. Since 1966, over 200 people convicted of murder have had their death sentences commuted (the majority to life imprisonment) by the Governor of Hong Kong.

Defendants charged with murder are tried in the High Court, which sits with a judge and jury. If convicted, defendants may then lodge an appeal against their sentence with the Court of Appeal within 28 days of conviction. If the appeal is unsuccessful, appeal to the Judicial Committee of the Privy Council in England, which serves as the final court of appeal for Hong Kong, is also possible.

Once all channels of appeal have been exhausted, prisoners can petition the Governor for clemency. In reaching a decision, the Governor consults the Executive Council of Hong Kong, which is an advisory body to the Governor. According to a new procedure introduced in 1987, if prisoners fail to appeal to the Court of Appeal within 28 days of conviction, automatic consideration of commutation is given by the Governor one month thereafter.

Petitions for clemency (commutation) can also be sent to Queen Elizabeth II who, in reaching her decision, would take advice from the Secretary of State for Foreign and Commonwealth Affairs for the United Kingdom.

Between 1985 and May 1988, Amnesty International received reports of 45 people sentenced to death and six commutations of death sentences to life imprisonment; all sentences had been imposed for murder.

Hungary

Status: Retentionist

Executions 1985 - mid-88: 2+; murder

Other factors: None

Methods of execution: Hanging; shooting by firing-squad

Under the current Penal Code of 1978, the following crimes carry an optional death sentence: armed conspiracy or conspiracy in wartime (Article 139 paragraph 3); sabotage in wartime (Article 141 paragraph 3); aggravated cases of destruction or destruction in wartime (Article 142 paragraph 2); assassination of socialist officials (Article 143 paragraph 2); treason (Article 144 paragraph 2); genocide (Article 155); atrocities in wartime (Articles 158 paragraph 2, 160 and 163 paragraph 2); homicide (Article 166 paragraph 2); and hijacking an aircraft causing death (Article 262 paragraph 2). In addition the Penal Code lists 12 military offences carrying an optional death sentence.

The death penalty cannot be imposed on those who at the time of the crime were aged under 20; pregnant women or people classified as insane may not be executed. According to the Penal Code the death sentence is optional and courts may impose sentences of 10 to 15 years or life imprisonment as an alternative.

Defendants sentenced to death have the right of appeal to the Supreme Court, and if the sentence is upheld, the right to petition for clemency. This may be granted by the Presidential Council, which may commute the sentence. In such cases the court may decide to impose additional punishments, such as loss of civil liberties (confiscation of property is excluded).

Execution is by hanging or shooting the day after denial of the petition for clemency has been announced. Since the mid-1960s the death penalty has been imposed mainly in cases of premeditated homicide. In a July 1986 report to the Human Rights Committee (set up under the International Covenant on Civil and Political Rights), the Hungarian authorities stated that there had been 25 executions in the previous 10 years.

Although there are a number of officials known to favour abolition, there is apparently little public debate on the issue. In 1983 the Hungarian Lawyers Association organized a discussion on the death penalty which concluded that it was "wrong but necessary" and that it would eventually be abolished "as the penal system develops". The discussion also concluded that the use of the death penalty in peacetime should be distinguished from its use in wartime.

Amnesty International received reports of two executions between 1985 and 31 May 1988, both carried out in 1985, one for multiple murder and the other for double murder with robbery.

Iceland

Status: Abolitionist

Executions 1985 - mid-88: None

Other factors: Not applicable

Method of execution: Not applicable

The death penalty was abolished for all offences and replaced by life imprisonment in 1928 under the Law on Some Provisional Changes to the Penal Code of 25 June 1869 and Additions to It. This reform of the Penal Code was proposed by a private member of the *Althing* (parliament) during the reading of a government bill on the provision of more humane punishments for certain offences; the bill, however, had not included this change. The member proposing it cited changes introduced to the penal codes of Norway in 1902 and of Sweden in 1901. The proposal was accepted unanimously and the Penal Code of 1940 states that the maximum punishment is life imprisonment.

The last execution was carried out in 1830 when two people found guilty of murder were beheaded.

India

Status: Retentionist

Executions 1985 - mid-88: Not known

Other factors: Special courts with deficient trial procedures empowered to impose death sentences for "terrorist offences"

Methods of execution: Hanging; shooting

Dozens of people are believed to be sentenced to death every year, the majority for murder. However, since the government rarely publishes statistics the exact number of executions carried out in recent years is not known. According to figures announced in Parliament in November 1986, 35 people were executed in the three years 1982 to 1985.

The Penal Code provides for the death penalty for murder; attempted murder "if hurt is caused" when committed by a person serving life imprisonment; gang robbery with murder; abetting the suicide of a child or insane person; waging war against the government; abetting mutiny by a member of the armed forces; and fabricating false evidence with intent to secure the conviction of someone else for a capital offence when conviction ensues. Death sentences may be imposed for a number of offences committed by members of the armed forces under the Army Act, 1950, the Air Force Act, 1950 and the Navy Act, 1956. Under special "anti-terrorist" legislation introduced in 1984 and 1987, the death penalty can be imposed for certain "terrorist" acts tried by specially constituted courts with modified rules of procedure and restricted rights of appeal (appeals are to the Supreme Court only and must be lodged within 30 days). The death penalty is always optional except for the offence of murder committed by a person serving a sentence of life imprisonment.

In 1967 the Law Commission recommended that the Code of Criminal Procedure be amended to ensure that the death penalty was not imposed on any offender aged under 18 at the time of the offence; so far, that recommendation has not been implemented and only pregnant women are exempted from the death penalty – execution is stayed or the sentence may be commuted to life imprisonment. In practice, however, no woman has been executed since 1944, although some have been sentenced to death. In a recent case, the Supreme Court ordered prison authorities to satisfy themselves that a particular prisoner was in a "fit mental state" before executing him.

Death sentences may be imposed by a court of sessions or by the High Court acting as a court of first instance. If the death penalty is imposed by a court of sessions it must be confirmed by the High Court. Appeal is to the Supreme Court after leave has been obtained from either the High Court or the Supreme Court itself. If an acquittal has been reversed by the High Court and a death sentence has been imposed, the accused has automatic right of appeal to the Supreme Court.

Sentences passed by courts-martial set up under the Army, Air Force and Navy Acts must be confirmed by the central government which is empowered to commute sentences. There is no right of appeal to a higher court, but defendants may petition the central government for clemency. It is not known to what extent the death penalty is used by courts-martial.

Special courts established under the Terrorist Affected Areas (Special Courts) Act 1984 are empowered to impose the death sentence for certain offences committed by "terrorists" – a term which has been so broadly defined that it may include people who non-violently express their political opinions. These courts follow severely curtailed rules of procedure (including reversal of the burden of proof), and appeal is to the Supreme Court only. A similar system of "designated" courts has been set up under the Terrorist and Disruptive Activities (Prevention) Act 1987, which allows the death penalty to be imposed for widely defined "terrorist" acts. It is not known how many death sentences were imposed under these laws which were passed in the context of widespread unrest, including acts of political violence in various parts of the country, especially in the state of Punjab since 1984.

Both the President of India and state governors can grant clemency, but in practice they do so on the advice of the government. Under the Penal Code and the Code of Criminal Procedure, central and state governments are also empowered to commute death sentences.

Execution is usually by hanging. When this method was (unsuccessfully) challenged in the Supreme Court in 1983, the judgment was that hanging did not involve torture, brutality, barbarity, humiliation or degradation.

In May 1980 the Supreme Court ruled by a majority of four to one in the case of *Bachan Singh v. State of Punjab* that the death penalty was not unconstitutional. It did, however, reiterate that the penalty should be imposed only in the "rarest of rare cases". The effect of the Bachan Singh judgment was to oblige judges to be quite certain before passing a death sentence that in view of the nature and circumstances of the crime and criminal, the alternative penalty of life imprisonment could not, in all conscience, be imposed. In a dissenting judgment delivered in August 1982 Justice P.N. Bhagwati held that the death penalty in its application to murder violated Article 14 (the right to equality) and Article 21 (the right to life and personal liberty) of the Constitution. "The prevailing standards of human decency," he asserted, "are incompatible with [the] death penalty."

Recently the Supreme Court has dealt with an increasing number of people sentenced to death for "bride-burning". In December 1985 the Rajasthan High Court sentenced a man, Jagdish Kumar, and a woman, Lichma Devi, to death for two separate cases of killing two young women by setting them on fire. In an unprecedented move the court ordered both prisoners to be publicly executed. In a response to a review petition by the Attorney-General against this judgment the Supreme Court in December 1985 stayed the public hangings, observing that "a barbaric crime does not have to be met with a barbaric penalty".

In December 1987, following reports that a young woman in the state of Rajasthan had performed the ancient ritual of *sati* (self-immolation by a widow on her deceased husband's funeral pyre), the central government passed the Commission of Sati (Prevention) Act, 1987 which made the abetment of a successful *sati* punishable by death. A similar law had been passed previously by the Rajasthan Government and came into force on 1 October 1987.

Since the execution of V. N. Godse (who

assassinated Mahatma Gandhi in January 1948), several prisoners have been executed for politically motivated killings. Among them was Maqbool Ahmed Butt, a journalist and former President of the Jammu and Kashmir Liberation Front, who was convicted in 1969 of killing an Indian intelligence officer and executed in February 1984. On 22 January 1986 a special judge in New Delhi passed death sentences on three people – Satwant Singh, Kehar Singh and Balbir Singh – for participating in the assassination in October 1984 of former Prime Minister Indira Gandhi. The sentences were confirmed on appeal by the Delhi High Court on 3 December 1986. The Supreme Court, however, allowed a further appeal by the prisoners and granted a stay of execution on 14 April 1987.

Although there have been several moves to abolish the death penalty in India since 1930, they have so far been unsuccessful. In March 1983 when the death penalty was last discussed in Parliament, although the then Prime Minister Indira Gandhi said she was personally in favour of abolition, N. R. Laskar, Minister of State for Home Affairs, stated that the government was not considering any proposal to abolish the death penalty.

▶ Satwant Singh and Kehar Singh were executed on 6 January 1989 despite doubts about the evidence used for conviction. Balbir Singh had been acquitted by the Supreme Court in 1988.

Indonesia

Status: Retentionist

Executions 1985 - mid-88: 19; murder; subversion; rebellion

Other factors: None

Method of execution: Shooting by firing-squad

Use of the death penalty has increased sharply in recent years in Indonesia. Between 1975 and 1984 there were four executions; between 1985 and 1987 there were 19. Most of those executed had been under sentence of death for over 10 years. At least 30 prisoners remain under

sentence of death, but the true total may be higher: the government does not make such statistics available.

Few executions took place before the present government of President Suharto came to power following the failure of a coup attempt in 1965 which the government has blamed on the now banned *Partai Komunis Indonesia* (PKI), Indonesian Communist Party. After the present government came to power, some 60 people linked either to the PKI or to military units which supported the coup attempt were sentenced to death, including 14 of the 19 prisoners executed since the beginning of 1985. Six of the 14, charged with subversion under Presidential Decree 11/1963, were tried in special military courts from which there was no right of judicial appeal, only the right to petition the President for clemency. All 14 had been in detention for almost two decades at the time of their executions in 1985 and 1986 and had been under sentence of death for over 10 years.

Muslim activists convicted of violent crimes and people convicted of premeditated murder have also been executed. Two Muslim activists convicted of rebellion in connection with an attack in 1981 on a police station in West Java were executed in 1985 and 1986, and a third remains under sentence of death. In 1987 two men were executed for the murder of a young woman, 25 years after they were sentenced to death.

Most of the prisoners executed by the Suharto government had been convicted of subversion under Presidential Decree 11/1963. The death penalty may also be imposed for drug-trafficking, under Law 9/1976, and for a wide variety of offences in the Indonesian Criminal Code, including premeditated murder, other crimes against the person and certain crimes against the state, including rebellion. Although at least four death sentences for drug-trafficking have been imposed since the beginning of 1985 – two in 1985 and one each in 1986 and 1987 – no one has been executed for this offence. At least seven people were sentenced to death in the same period for murder.

Cases involving offences punishable by death are tried either in regular criminal courts, or, if the accused is a member of the armed forces or police, in a regular military court. (The special military courts set up after the 1965 coup attempt are no longer in operation.) The Criminal Procedure Code requires that defence counsel be provided in all cases where the death penalty may be imposed. The death penalty is optional in all cases and is imposed only if the judges decide there are no extenuating circumstances.

In both military and civilian courts of first instance, the defence or prosecution may appeal against the verdict to the relevant high court and then to the Supreme Court, a process which occasionally results in heavier sentences being imposed by the higher courts. For example, a sentence of life imprisonment imposed on Abdullah Umar, a Muslim activist convicted of murder, armed robbery and subversion, was changed to a death sentence in June 1985 by an appellate court in Yogyakarta, Central Java.

Delays in the appeals process are often lengthy. Two men allegedly involved in the 1965 coup attempt, Simon Petrus Soleiman and Athanasius Buang, were arrested on 5 October 1965 and sentenced to death four years later by the Regional Military Court in Jakarta. Both appealed to the Military High Court on the day their sentences were handed down, saying they had only been carrying out orders. They received no news about the status of their appeals until 3 February 1987 (18 years later), when they were informed that both their first and second appeals had been rejected. They were apparently unaware of having made a second appeal. Both have petitioned President Suharto for clemency.

A prisoner may request clemency from the President at any stage after the initial sentencing, but clemency following confirmation of a death sentence by the Supreme Court appears to be granted only rarely. If the prisoner refuses to submit a petition for clemency, the prosecutor may do so on his or her behalf. Executions are carried out only after petitions for clemency have been formally rejected.

Before a 1987 change in the law governing remission, a prisoner whose death sentence had been commuted to life imprisonment became eligible for remission of the sentence to a fixed term of 20 years and then for further reductions resulting eventually in the person's release. Under the revised law, once a sentence has been commuted to life imprisonment no further reductions are possible.

Over the years the question of the death penalty has been discussed several times in legal circles and in the popular press. An abolitionist group called *Hapus Hukuman Mati* (Abolish the Death Penalty), the abbreviation for which was HATI, the Indonesian word for "heart", was active in the late 1970s. Those calling for abolition of the death penalty have pointed to its irrevocability and the possibility of judicial error.

Iran

Status: Retentionist

Executions 1985 - mid-88: 743+; murder; drug offences; political violence; other political offences; adultery; prostitution; other "moral" offences; being corrupt on earth; being at enmity with God

Other factors: Unfair trials; secret executions; public executions; prisoners whipped before being executed; children executed

Methods of execution: Hanging; shooting by firing-squad; stoning

Thousands of people have been executed since the Islamic Republic came into being in 1979. Some were believed executed without trial, or after being sentenced only to prison terms, many after trials which failed to comply with international standards. Among those executed since 1979 are an unknown number of political opponents to the Iranian Government, many of whom were tried and executed in secret for their non-violent political opposition or religious beliefs. Others killed in large numbers include people convicted of murder, drug-trafficking and addiction, and political opponents convicted of armed opposition to the government. Thousands died in the wave of mass arbitrary executions which reached its peak in the early 1980s.

The Law of *Hodoud* (crimes against divine will, singular; *hadd*) and *Qisas* (retribution) forms a part of the Islamic Penal Code of Iran provisionally approved by the Islamic Consultative Assembly in 1982. It provides for the death penalty for a large number of offences including premeditated murder, rape, "moral" offences such as adultery, sodomy and repeated counts of drinking alcoholic liquor. The Law of *Hodoud* and *Qisas* also provides for the death penalty as a possible punishment for those convicted of being corrupt on earth or at enmity with God. Such broad terms can apply to political opponents, including those expressing their views in a non-violent manner.

Enforcement of the death penalty as an optional punishment for murder is determined by *qisas*. This derives from an interpretation of Islamic law and gives the right of retribution or bloodwite to the male next of kin of the murder victim. A person convicted of murder can only be executed with the consent of the victim's male next of kin who may choose to accept payment *(diya)* instead of enforcing the death penalty. Other exemptions from execution for murder include insane people, those under 18 at the time of the offence, and blind people. The Penal Code also stipulates that there is no penalty for the killing of certain types of people including those who have insulted the Prophet or the Holy Imams.

Certain crimes in the Penal Code such as adultery, sodomy and malicious accusation are regarded as crimes against God (*Hodoud*) and therefore liable to divine retribution, and carry a mandatory death sentence.

The death penalty may be imposed by either criminal courts or Islamic Revolutionary Courts (IRCs), each having jurisdiction over different types of offences. The IRCs have jurisdiction over the following crimes: all crimes against internal and external security, being corrupt on earth or being at enmity with God, attempts on the life of politicians, drug-trafficking, suppressing the struggle of the people of Iran, and plunder of the public treasury and profiteering.

According to regulations, IRCs should consist of three people, including two judges. In practice these courts have often consisted of just one person, a religious judge. In some cases a presumption of the guilt of the accused has meant that the trial consisted only of the reading out of the charge and the passing of sentence. Amnesty International has received reports of confessions, in political cases, which may have been extracted under torture, and of these being used to bring about the imposition of the death penalty. Amnesty International knows of no defendants before IRCs on political charges having been permitted to be represented by a lawyer.

In the early 1980s thousands of people were summarily executed after brief and inadequate trials before IRCs. Amnesty International understands that all death sentences passed by these courts are now referred for approval to the High Judicial Council, a committee of experts in Islamic jurisprudence, which may also refer the case back to the same court for reconsideration. This has led to some executions being deferred. However, in political cases, at least, there appears to be no provision for appeal against conviction and sentence to a higher tribunal, or for a fully informed review of possible errors by the trial court. In practice the majority of death sentences continue to be passed by IRCs.

The way in which guilt is established under the Penal Code in all capital offences relies heavily on the testimony of "righteous men"; such testimony may be proved by sworn oaths (*qassameh*). This system may also be used to prove guilt in capital cases tried before criminal courts, such as murder. Statements made as sworn oaths may not be challenged by the defendant, but they alone can constitute grounds for conviction. However, Amnesty International is not aware of any executions arising from such cases.

In cases tried before Criminal Courts, the right of appeal against conviction and sentence is lacking. The Supreme Court of Cassation is, however, required to review the application of the law in cases where criminal courts have passed sentences resulting in the death penalty or other serious punishments. No judgment comes into effect until the Supreme Court of Cassation has reviewed the lower court's recommendation.

In many cases which have resulted in execution, even these inadequate judicial procedures have not been observed, and many people are said to have been executed in secret either without trial or following summary proceedings.

The most common methods of execution are shooting by firing-squad and hanging. Many people have been hanged in public. Stoning to death, a particularly cruel method of execution, has also been used to punish certain offenders. The Penal Code stipulates, "In the punishment of stoning to death, the stones should not be so large that the person dies on being hit by one or two of them, nor should they be so small that they could not be defined as stones." Amnesty International recorded eight stonings in 1986, and this punishment continues to be imposed. Others have been sentenced to lashings prior to execution.

Between July and December 1981 Amnesty International recorded 2,444 executions; the actual figure is undoubtedly higher. This was a period when conflict between the ruling Islamic Republican Party and the outlawed opposition People's Mojahedine Organization was at a peak. Many members and supporters of the People's Fedayan Organization and other opposition groups have also been executed. Some of these may have been involved in armed opposition to the government, but many were not, and many others were executed merely on suspicion of involvement with opposition groups.

Hundreds of Iranians have been executed for narcotics offences, many after summary trials before IRCs. Between 10 June 1980 and 3 November 1981, for example, 459 people convicted of drug offences were executed, and according to official reports, a further 197 between March and April 1985. A major feature of the government's policy against drug abuse continues to be the imposition of the death penalty on offenders. People convicted of drug-trafficking made up over 25 per cent of the 158 executions recorded by Amnesty International in 1987, most of which were reported in the official Iranian press. A report in *Ettela'at* (a national daily newspaper) on 7 June 1987 quoted a statement by the Tehran Prosecutor's Office which said that 18,150 people had been arrested for drug-trafficking in the previous Iranian year (March 1986 to March 1987). Reportedly, 14,237 of those arrested were imprisoned and 37 were executed.

Children under 18 were among those executed in the early 1980s, and occasional reports of the executions of minors continue to reach Amnesty International.

▶ In August 1988 groups of alleged collaborators and members of the People's Mojahedine Organization of Iran (PMOI) were hanged in public in towns in Western Iran following an armed incursion into Iran by the PMOI backed National Liberation Army. At the same time there were unconfirmed reports that secret

executions of political prisoners had been stepped up. A ban on family visits to political prisoners, and speeches from senior officials advocating their execution, fuelled speculation that hundreds may have been executed. However, Amnesty International is unable to estimate the number of executions carried out in secret during this period.

Iraq

Status: Retentionist

Executions 1985 - mid-88: Hundreds reported every year; burglary and theft in time of war; premeditated murder; desertion from the army; treason; sabotage using arms and explosives; forgery of official documents and economic corruption

Other factors: Public executions; unfair trials; no right of appeal against sentences imposed by the Revolutionary Court and temporary special courts; retroactive legislation; children executed; prisoners executed after having been sentenced to a term of imprisonment

Methods of execution: Hanging; shooting by firing-squad

Iraq retains the death penalty as a mandatory or optional punishment for a wide range of criminal and political offences listed in the Penal Code (No. 111 of 1969), and in numerous resolutions having the force of law passed by the Revolutionary Command Council (RCC). Where extenuating circumstances prevail or there are grounds for clemency, a term of imprisonment may be imposed instead of the death penalty. If aggravating circumstances are proved, the death penalty may be imposed for an offence normally punishable by life imprisonment.

The Penal Code distinguishes between ordinary and political offences, and requires that a sentence of life imprisonment be imposed for the latter, instead of the death penalty. However, six types of offence are excluded from the category of political offences even if committed with a political motive. These are offences committed with a "base and selfish motive"; offences prejudicial to the external security of the state; premeditated murder or its attempt; an attempt on the life of the President of the Republic; terrorist offences; and "immoral" crimes such as theft, embezzlement, forgery, breach of trust, fraud, bribery, indecent assault and desertion from the army.

The amended Penal Code specifies numerous categories of capital offences deemed to be prejudicial to the external and internal security of the state, all of which carry a mandatory death penalty. These include certain non-violent political offences, such as the political activities of former and current members of the Arab Socialist Ba'th Party. Other capital offences under the Penal Code include publicly and flagrantly insulting the President of the Republic or his deputy, or members of the RCC, the Ba'th Party, National Assembly or the government.

Between 1978 and 1986, seven new capital offences were introduced by the RCC, including Resolution No. 461 of 1980 concerning membership of or affiliation to *al-Da'wa al-Islamiyya* (Islamic Call). This resolution may be applied retroactively, contrary to the provisions of the Penal Code and the Constitution. In March 1984 the Penal Code of the Popular Army was promulgated, providing the death penalty for 11 capital offences committed by members of the army.

Those aged under 18 at the time of the offence may not be sentenced to death. If the prisoner is pregnant execution must be stayed until four months after childbirth.

The courts competent to pass death sentences are the higher criminal courts, the permanent military courts, the Revolutionary Court, and temporary special courts set up on an *ad hoc* basis by the RCC to try particular groups of prisoners.

Judgments of the higher criminal courts must be referred automatically to the Court of Cassation within 10 days for review, even if no appeal has been lodged. Death sentences must be reviewed by a General Board comprising all the judges of the Court of Cassation. Those upheld by the Court of Cassation are referred to the Minister of Justice, who must have the sentence ratified by the President of the Republic.

Members of the armed forces are tried by permanent military courts. Death sentences imposed by these courts must be reviewed by the General Board of the Military Court of Cassation.

The Revolutionary Court is a permanent special court set up in 1968, and is competent to pass judgments for cases involving crimes against internal and external state security, and a wide range of other crimes. Its proceedings must be conducted in accordance with the Code of Criminal Procedure of 1971, but sentences passed by this court are final and are not subject to appeal or cassation. The Special Court of Kirkuk, another permanent special court set up in 1974 to try Kurds charged with political offences, was abolished in August 1982. Its decisions were not subject to appeal. Temporary special courts have also been set up in recent years to hear cases involving death sentences.

Execution is by hanging in prisons or in any other place in accordance with the law. Members of the armed forces are executed by firing-squad. Death sentences must be ratified by presidential decree before being carried out. The President is empowered to grant pardon or commute death sentences.

Hundreds of executions are reported to be carried out every year in Iraq. Many of the victims are said to have been executed without trial or after summary trials, and it has not always been possible to ascertain whether all of these executions were judicial. Amnesty International recorded the names of some 520 people reported to have been executed for political offences between 1978 and 1981. In March and April 1980 alone, about 100 executions were reported, and in 1982 and 1983 over 600 people were said to have been executed. Hundreds of executions have continued to be reported every year since 1984, but Amnesty International does not know the precise figure. Except in a few cases the government does not make public such executions, and many are reported to take place secretly in prisons, particularly of political prisoners and army deserters.

Among those executed have been members of banned political parties, suspected government opponents, students, army deserters and civilians arrested as hostages, including children. Those executed include Kurds, Arabs and Turcomans. According to available information, most political prisoners are tried by permanent or temporary special courts, and most death sentences are passed by such courts. The majority of these trials are held *in camera*, access to a government-appointed lawyer is severely restricted (and in some instances confined to the day of the trial) and confessions extracted under torture are frequently used as a basis for conviction.

Defendants charged with capital offences are frequently denied their legal right to call up witnesses on their behalf or to submit evidence refuting the charges. The role of the defence counsel is said to be often restricted to pleading for clemency or reduction of sentence. Some political prisoners have been sentenced to death by military courts following summary proceedings. In some cases, political prisoners are reported to have been executed after having been sentenced to terms of imprisonment. On 30 and 31 December 1987 over 150 political prisoners are reported to have been executed in Abu Ghraib Prison near Baghdad, some of whom were said to have been sentenced to imprisonment.

In mid-1986 a temporary special court sentenced to death seven defendants charged with economic corruption, and another in January 1987 sentenced to death seven Kurdish youths accused of committing "criminal and subversive acts using arms and explosives". Amnesty International did not have details of the trial proceedings followed in these two cases.

Children aged under 18 have been executed. In November and December 1987, five Kurdish children aged between 15 and 17 were among 31 Kurds reported to have been executed by firing-squad following summary military trials. Eight others aged between 14 and 17 were reported to have been executed in Abu Ghraib Prison on 30 and 31 December 1987. Amnesty International has been informed that in such cases, doctors have been asked to issue death certificates indicating that the victims had attained the age of 18 at the time of their execution.

Prisoners, including minors, are reported to have been tortured before being executed. Victims' bodies have been returned to their families bearing the marks of torture, including fingernails extracted and eyes gouged out. The body of one victim executed in 1985 was returned to his family with the head severed.

Upon receipt of the victims' bodies, families are asked to pay the customary "execution fees", normally ranging between 50 and 300 Iraqi dinars (approximately US$16 and US$96) per body to cover state expenses on items such as bullets, coffins and transportation. Families are also prevented from holding public mourning or burial ceremonies.

Ireland

Status: Abolitionist in practice

Executions 1985 - mid-88: None

Other factors: None

Method of execution: Hanging

Ireland abolished the death penalty in 1964 for all but three categories of offence. In doing so it created a new statutory offence: "capital murder". The three categories of offence for which the death penalty is retained are treason (Treason Act, 1939), capital murder and certain specified offences under the Defence Act, 1954. In the case of the first two the death sentence is mandatory, but the Defence Act allows the court-martial some discretion. Capital murder is the murder of a police or prison officer in the course of duty, murder committed in furtherance of certain offences under the Offences Against the State Act, 1939, and the politically motivated murder of a diplomatic official, member of the government or head of a foreign state. The Defence Act provides for the death penalty for military offences such as refusal to engage the enemy, aggravated desertion and violent mutiny.

Treason and capital murder offences may be tried by the Central Criminal Court, which sits with a judge and jury. Appeal is to the Court of Criminal Appeal and then to the Supreme Court on a "point of law of exceptional importance", for which leave is required. In practice, however, capital murder offences are tried by the Special Criminal Court, which sits with three judges and has no jury. This court is used mainly to try defendants charged with offences against the state and was reintroduced in 1972. The reason given for its reintroduction was that the ordinary courts were incapable of securing convictions because of intimidation of jurors. Appeal is to the Court of Criminal Appeal, and then, on a "point of law of exceptional importance" to the Supreme Court, for which leave is required.

Offences under the Defence Act are tried by courts-martial. These military tribunals can condemn members of the armed forces to death in wartime or in peacetime only when the offence has been committed by a member of the armed forces on active service abroad. There is a right of appeal to the Courts Martial Court of Criminal Appeal. Anyone sentenced to death may petition the President for clemency, who acts on the advice of the government.

The last execution was in 1954. In practice, since 1954 all death sentences have been commuted to a term of imprisonment. Recently, commutation has included a recommendation that the convicted person serve a minimum of 40 years.

Israel and the Occupied Territories

Status: Abolitionist for all but exceptional crimes

Executions 1985 - mid-88: None

Other factors: None

Method of execution: Hanging

The death penalty for murder was abolished in 1954. It is retained, however, for treason (Article 97 of the Israeli Penal Code); war crimes (the Nazi and Nazi Collaboration [Punishment] Law of 1950, and Crime of Genocide [Prevention and Punishment] Law of 1950); and for terrorist murder, attempted terrorist murder, sabotage and the use and unauthorized bearing of weapons (Article 58 of the Defence [Emergency] Regulations [DER] of 1945). The death penalty is not mandatory.

In the West Bank and Gaza, which Israel has occupied since 1967, terrorist murder and attempted terrorist murder are capital offences in accordance with DER and Article 51 (a) of Military Order 378. In 1968, however, Military Orders 268 (for the West Bank) and 72 (for Gaza) ruled that local courts, which hear criminal cases, should not pass death sentences. Local courts in the West Bank apply the Jordanian Penal Code, and Gaza local courts apply legislation introduced by the Egyptian authorities between 1948 and 1967.

In Israel capital cases are heard in the District Court presided over by a Supreme Court justice and two District Court judges. An automatic appeal is heard by the Supreme Court. The President of the State has the power to grant pardon or clemency. In Israel and the Occupied Territories offences under DER and Military Orders are heard in three-judge military courts. In Israel appeals against decisions of the Military Court can be made to the Military Court of Appeal and the Chief of Staff has the power to commute sentences. However, there is no such court in the Occupied Territories, although confirmation of the sentence is required by the Military Commander of the area who also has the power of commutation.

In all courts a death sentence can be imposed only when the judges' decision is unanimous. The minimum age at which a person can be sentenced to death is 17 for men and 18 for women.

The only execution to have been carried out since the foundation of the State of Israel in 1948 was that of Adolf Eichmann in 1962, who was hanged after being convicted of genocide perpetrated in Germany and territory under German occupation before and during World War II.

On 18 April 1988 John Demjanjuk was sentenced to death in Israel after having been convicted of war crimes and crimes against humanity and the Jewish people. He was identified as "Ivan the Terrible", a guard at the Treblinka camp where 850,000 people, most of them Jews, are estimated to have been killed during World War II. His appeal is scheduled to be heard in 1989.

Military prosecutors in Israel and the Occupied Territories have been directed by the Attorney-General not to request the death penalty without his authorization. However, in December 1983, two Israeli Arabs were sentenced to death for the premeditated murder of an Israeli soldier; the sentences were subsequently commuted by the Military Court of Appeal.

Italy

Status: Abolitionist for all but exceptional crimes

Executions 1985 - mid-88: None

Other factors: None

Method of execution: Shooting

The death penalty was abolished for all offences under a new Penal Code of 1889, but reintroduced for certain crimes against the state under Law No. 2008 of 25 November 1926, following a number of attacks on the life of the head of the Italian Government, Benito Mussolini. The new Penal Code of 1930, which came into force on 1 July 1931, increased the number of crimes against the state punishable by death and reintroduced the death penalty for certain serious common criminal offences.

On 10 August 1944 Decree Law No. 224 abolished the death penalty for all crimes in the 1930 Penal Code. However, it was retained under a separate Decree Law No. 159 of 27 July 1944 for serious crimes of fascism and collaboration with National Socialist fascists (*nazifascisti*). On 10 May 1945 Decree Law No. 234 introduced the death penalty as an exceptional and temporary measure for serious criminal offences such as participation in an armed band; robbery with violence; and extortion.

The death penalty was finally abolished for common criminal offences and military offences committed in peacetime under the new Constitution of the Republic of Italy of 27 December 1947. Article 27, which was implemented by Decree Law No. 21 of 22 January 1948, states, "The death penalty is not admitted save in cases specified by military laws in time of war." The Military Penal Code in Time of War retains the death penalty for a wide range of offences. The President is empowered by Article 87 of the Constitution to grant pardon or to commute a sentence.

Between 26 April 1945 and 5 March 1947, 88 people were executed for collaboration with the Germans during World War II. The shooting of three men in March 1947 were the last known executions carried out in Italy.

Jamaica

Status: Retentionist

Executions 1985 - mid-88: 30; murder

Other factors: None

Method of execution: Hanging

A mandatory death penalty is provided for murder (Section 3[1] of the Offences Against the Person Act, 1864 with amendments enacted in 1953 and 1958). Those under the age of 18 at the time of the crime and pregnant women are exempted.

Criminal cases are tried before a judge and 12-member jury in the circuit court in one of 14 judicial districts; the jury's verdict must be unanimous when returning a conviction for murder. The accused may appeal against conviction to the Court of Appeal of Jamaica. The final court of appeal is the Judicial Committee of the Privy Council in England (JCPC) which will consider only cases involving constitutional matters or points of law of "great public importance".

Under the Constitution, the Governor General, acting on the recommendation of the Jamaica Privy Council (also known as the Advisory Committee on the Prerogative of Mercy), may commute a death sentence to life imprisonment. The Jamaica Privy Council may receive information on a case at any time after the trial, but in practice it waits until appeals are exhausted before advising the Governor General on clemency.

In some cases, however, execution warrants have been issued before prisoners have been able to lodge appeals with the JCPC. This is very frequently due to the defendant's financial inability to employ a lawyer to prepare the case and file an appeal.

After an unofficial four-year moratorium on executions from April 1976, hangings resumed in August 1980. Since then, 59 prisoners have been executed: 29 between 1980 and 1984; nine in 1985; 13 in 1986; 6 in 1987 and two in February 1988. In July 1988 the number of prisoners under sentence of death had risen to 191, one of the highest per capita death row populations in the world. All prisoners had been convicted of murder.

During the moratorium on executions, Parliament considered the possibility of abolishing the death penalty. On 30 January 1979 the House of Representatives voted by a narrow majority to retain capital punishment but recommended that all existing death sentences be reviewed. On 9 February 1979 the Senate voted in favour of suspending the death penalty for a further 18 months while the issue was considered in more detail.

In June 1979 the Minister of Justice established a committee to consider whether the death penalty was an appropriate punishment for murder. The Committee on Capital Punishment and Penal Reform (known as the Fraser Committee, after its Chairperson Aubrey Fraser) submitted its report to the government in December 1981, stating that it was "... of the opinion that death as a penalty for murder should be abolished". However, it acknowledged that public sentiment was very much in favour of the death penalty. The committee recommended that moves towards abolition should be undertaken "as part of a comprehensive system of penal reform which should commence without delay". As a first step the committee recommended that, "All sentences of death imposed prior to December 31, 1980, which was the date originally prescribed for submitting the Committee's report ... should be statutorily commuted to sentences of life imprisonment." The committee further recommended that the application of the death penalty be modified to restrict it to a limited class of homicide, and that for an interim period of five years capital punishment should be retained only for murder committed by use of a firearm or explosive.

Although it had been submitted to the government in 1981, the Fraser Committee report was laid before Parliament for the first time by the Minister of Justice in March 1987, and then only for information. At the time of writing its recommendations had not been acted upon and Parliament had not debated the report.

The Fraser Committee's research team reviewed the cases of 40 of the 81 prisoners then on death row and found that they were almost all from the lower socio-economic sectors of society, that the majority had little or no education, that most were first offenders and that many appeared not to have had the benefit of adequate counsel. Amnesty International's own research, based on contact with lawyers representing prisoners under sentence of death and an examination of information on many prisoners' cases, supports these findings. Most prisoners are too poor to pay for private legal representation and are represented by court-appointed, newly qualified and inexperienced legal aid lawyers at trial and local appeal. The fees received by legal aid lawyers are extremely low and there is no legal aid for appeals to the JCPC. For pursuing such appeals, prisoners are therefore entirely dependent on lawyers providing their services free.

In 1982, by a majority of three to two, the JCPC dismissed appeals in the cases of Noel Riley and four others who had been sentenced to death in 1975 and 1976, the period during which executions had been suspended. The prisoners had argued that the issuing of warrants for their execution after the delay caused by the suspension of hangings amounted to "inhuman or degrading punishment or treatment" in violation of the Jamaican Constitution. The majority rejected the appeal on a point of law but two judges entered vigorous dissenting opinions in which they found that the appellants had been subjected to a "cruel and dehumanizing experience" and that their execution after such a delay would amount to "inhuman treatment". The five prisoners were executed three months after the decision was handed down.

Very few of the cases submitted to the JCPC are given a full hearing since they are normally rejected at the stage of seeking leave to appeal. However, in October 1987 the JCPC agreed to hear appeals in three separate cases of Jamaican prisoners who had been convicted and sentenced to death on the basis of poor identification evidence. This involved having been identified by only one witness in poor light, and at some considerable distance from the witness, and with no other evidence against the accused being presented. The appeals were based on claims that the trial judges had failed to direct the juries adequately on the weight they should attach to such evidence. In similar cases in the past, the JCPC has refused leave to appeal. However, it would seem that the growing number of cases raising this issue prompted the JCPC to consider it a point of law of general public importance, thereby bringing it within their jurisdiction. One of the prisoners whose appeal was to be heard, Junior Reid, had been scheduled for execution in June 1986 and granted a last-minute stay. Trevor Ellis, a prisoner convicted on the basis of similar evidence, had his petition for leave to appeal to the JCPC rejected in 1985 and came within hours of being executed in March 1988, before being granted a last-minute stay of execution.

In some cases there have been long delays between the hearing of an appeal by the Jamaican Court of Appeal and the delivery of the written reasons for judgment which prevented the prisoners from lodging any further appeals. A written decision from the Court of Appeal is the basis for a further appeal to the JCPC. Earl Pratt and Ivan Morgan, convicted and sentenced to death in January 1979 (the period during which executions were suspended while Parliament and the Fraser Committee considered the question of abolition), communicated their case to the Human Rights Committee set up under the International Covenant on Civil and Political Rights, according to the procedures of the Optional Protocol to that covenant. They alleged, among other things, that the long delays in the proceedings against them, particularly a delay of nearly four years in the issuing of the written judgment of the Jamaican Court of Appeals, violated their rights of due process under Article 14 of the Covenant. In dismissing their appeals in 1986, the JCPC expressed "disquiet" over the two having been under sentence of death for so long. Both came within hours of being executed on two occasions, in February 1987 and February 1988. In both instances a decision on their communication to the Human Rights Committee was pending.

There have been cases in which applications for leave to appeal to the Jamaica Court of Appeal have been treated as the full hearing of the appeal and dismissed orally, with no indication from the judges that they would put their reasons into writing. Such a practice prevents the prisoner from being able to pursue further appeals to the JCPC.

A number of prisoners are reported to have developed signs of mental illness while on death row, and at least one mentally ill prisoner has been executed. Stafford Pyne was executed on 28 June 1983, five days after a psychiatrist had diagnosed a schizophrenic illness. Pyne had a history of mental illness both in prison and before his arrest and had been treated in Bellevue Mental Hospital in Kingston at the age of 14.

Philip Grey, sentenced to death in March 1981 and declared insane by a consultant psychiatrist in February 1986, was scheduled for execution in November 1987. His sentence was commuted after the Jamaica Council for Human Rights (a local organization) sent a petition to the Governor General enclosing a copy of the psychiatrist's report.

Other prisoners with a history of mental illness before their arrest remain on death row. Ralph McKay, for example, convicted in April 1985, had been diagnosed as suffering from paranoid schizophrenia in 1964 and had received treatment for several years in a mental hospital in England; the diagnosis was confirmed by a psychiatrist who examined him after his arrest in 1983. This information was presented to the Governor General in a petition for clemency after McKay lost his local appeal, but at the time of going to press there had been no response to his petition and he was still on death row. Several other prisoners whose petitions for clemency have been submitted on grounds of their mental illness remain on death row.

Japan

Status: Retentionist

Executions 1985 - mid-88: 9; murder

Other factors: None

Method of execution: Hanging

After a significant decrease in the number of executions to one a year between 1979 and 1984, executions have since risen to two or three a year. As of June 1988 over 85 prisoners were known to be under sentence of death, of whom around 35 had had their sentences finalized by the Supreme Court and another 35 were waiting for a decision from the Supreme Court. All had been convicted of murder, some of them of politically motivated murder.

Japanese law provides for the death penalty for 18 offences. These include 13 crimes under the Penal Code, such as murder; causing death in the course of other offences such as robbery or rape; intentional damage to inhabited structures; and crimes against the state, including insurrection and giving military assistance to a foreign state. In addition, five other laws provide for the death penalty for various offences, including causing death during aircraft hijacking or by using explosives, and intentional hostage killing. The death penalty is optional except for the crime of inducing foreign aggression, for which it is mandatory. Since 1967 the death sentence has been imposed only for murder and death caused by explosives.

In 1974 the Legislative Council, an advisory commission of the Ministry of Justice, recommended that the number of offences carrying the death penalty should be reduced to eight in a revised Penal Code and that no offence should carry a mandatory death sentence. However, it is unlikely that the Penal Code will be revised in the near future.

Defendants aged under 18 at the time of the alleged offence may not be sentenced to death, and if the prisoner is insane or pregnant, executions must be stayed until recovery or childbirth. Executions take place in seven detention centres and death has to be confirmed by a medical doctor.

Capital offences are normally heard in the first instance by a district court. Decisions of a district court can be appealed to a high court and to the Supreme Court. Japanese law requires that all death sentences be reviewed by a higher court. After a sentence has been finalized by the Supreme Court, it is possible to reopen the procedure by requesting a retrial if new evidence indicating innocence is discovered or if evidence on which the original judgment is based is proved false. In 1983 and 1984, three prisoners sentenced to death for murder in the 1950s were acquitted after retrials. Another prisoner originally sentenced to death in 1958, Masao Akabori, also was granted a retrial which is expected to be completed in late 1988. Eight other prisoners have also applied for retrial.

Since March 1987 the Supreme Court has upheld 13 death sentences, and district courts are also imposing an increasing number. The increase follows the decision of the Tokyo High Court in March 1987 to reimpose a death sentence on Norio Nagayama. In its decision, the Tokyo High Court gave several criteria for the imposition of a death sentence: that more than one person is killed, that the murder is particularly cruel, and that the murderer does not show any repentance and has not been forgiven by the family of the victim.

Decisions on amnesty, commutation and reprieve are made by the cabinet and ratified by the Emperor. In deciding whether to grant clemency, the cabinet receives the advice of the National Offenders Rehabilitation Commission, an advisory body to the Ministry of Justice. The last general amnesty was in 1952; since then, only three prisoners have had their death sentences commuted in individual amnesties, in 1969, 1970 and 1975. The amnesties were granted on the grounds of illness, old age, repentance, and forgiveness on the part of the victim's family.

It is not uncommon for prisoners to remain under sentence of death for several decades. Sadamichi Hirasawa, for instance, was sentenced to death in 1950 and died, aged 95, in 1987. He had spent a large part of his existence not knowing whether he would be executed or whether his appeals for retrial would be granted.

An official of the Ministry of Justice told a visiting Amnesty International delegation in 1983 that prisoners who were calm and composed would be notified of their execution the previous day; those who were unstable would not be told. No public announcement is made of the executions and they are not reported in the press. The authorities do not confirm the names of executed prisoners and only release statistics periodically, claiming that such secrecy protects the family of the prisoner from the shame of having it known that their relative has been executed.

Jordan

Status: Retentionist

Executions 1985 - mid-88: 14+; murder

Other factors: No right of appeal against death sentences imposed by special courts

Methods of execution: Hanging; shooting by firing-squad

The Penal Code (Law No. 16 of 1960) provides for a mandatory death penalty for premeditated murder and other types of murder; crimes against the state, such as treason, attempts to change the Constitution by illegal means; attempts on the life or freedom of members of the royal family; and acts of terrorism, arson or sabotage in aggravated circumstances. Spying also carries a mandatory death penalty (Law No. 51 of 1971).

Under the Military Penal Code of 1952 certain acts of dishonourable behaviour in combat and cooperation with the enemy carry a mandatory death penalty. It is optional for other offences. According to a special law of 1952, possessing or dealing in weapons for illegal purposes is a capital offence.

In 1973 the sale of land to Israeli nationals in the Israeli Occupied West Bank became a capital offence. In 1988 the death penalty became mandatory for the rape of a girl aged under 15 and a new law on drugs greatly expanded the scope of the death penalty. The previous drugs law (1955) had provided for the death penalty for killing an official entrusted with the enforcement of that law.

Offenders aged under 18, people deemed insane at the time of the crime, and pregnant women are exempt from the death penalty. However, the code of criminal procedure (Law No. 9 of 1961) allows the execution of a woman three months after the birth of her child. A woman who murders her child may not be sentenced to death if her child was less than one year old and she killed it while incapacitated by birth or by breast-feeding.

Capital cases tried by ordinary criminal courts of first instance automatically go through two stages of review: first before the Court of Appeal, then before the Court of Cassation. Murder and rape cases are tried by the Court of Major Felonies, established in 1976, whose death sentences are automatically reviewed by the Court of Cassation.

Several military courts are authorized to try capital cases. Members of the armed forces and the General Intelligence Department (GID) are tried by internal tribunals applying the provisions of the ordinary and military penal codes. There is no right of appeal to a higher tribunal from these courts. Their decisions are reviewed by the Commander-in-Chief of the Armed Forces and the Director-General of the GID respectively. Members of the Public Security Department are tried by an internal tribunal, with reviews by the Court of Cassation.

People charged in connection with land sales to Israeli nationals, whether or not they are civilians, are tried by a special military court against whose verdict there is no right of appeal to a higher tribunal.

Since the declaration of martial law on 5 June 1967, a Martial Law Court, comprising three military officers, has tried several capital cases. Its jurisdiction has been expanded over the years and now includes offences against the security of the state; offences related to firearms and drugs; specific murder cases; and any other criminal cases referred to it by the General Military Governor (at present the Prime Minister). It is not bound by the code of criminal procedure or the law on evidence, and its proceedings sometimes deviate from international standards of fair trial. Its verdicts cannot be appealed to a higher tribunal but are reviewed by the General Military Governor.

According to the code of criminal procedure, once all appeals have been exhausted, death sentences must be ratified by the King who acts on the advice of the Council of Ministers and is empowered to commute sentences or grant a special pardon.

Prisoners under sentence of death are kept under constant surveillance, isolated from other prisoners as much as possible. Execution is by hanging, usually in al-Mahatta Central Prison in Amman at dawn. Members of the armed forces are executed by firing-squad in time of war.

Between 1973 and 1987 about 100 people were sentenced to death for land sales to Israeli nationals. All sentences, however, were passed *in absentia*, entitling defendants to a retrial if apprehended; no executions for this offence have been carried out. Six people were reportedly executed for murder in 1985, four in 1986, and one in 1988. In addition there were three executions following trials by the Martial Law Court (from which there is no right of appeal): one in January 1987 for a political assassination and two in January 1988 for murder in the course of robbery. One prisoner arrested in 1978 and convicted of a political crime reportedly remained under sentence of death in May 1988.

▶ On 19 July 1988 three other prisoners were executed after convictions by the Martial Law Court of crimes including premeditated murder. A fourth prisoner tried in the case had his death sentence commuted.

Kampuchea (Cambodia)

Status: Retentionist

Executions 1985 - mid-88: Not known

Other factors: Unfair trials

Method of execution: Shooting by firing-squad

The death penalty is provided for as an optional punishment under laws introduced in 1979 and 1980. A 1979 decree provided the death penalty for genocide, and its scope was extended to other offences in 1980 Decree Law No. 2 DL Punishments for the Offence of Treason Against the Revolution and Other Criminal Offences Generally. These include treason, which is variously defined as attempting to overthrow the government and systematic espionage, "wreck[ing] relations of solidarity among the people" or creating "disorder". The 1980 law also provides for an optional death penalty for theft of public property if it results "in bad consequences that are particularly serious"; for murder in "serious cases"; and for rape if the victim is an under-age girl or is killed.

The two laws indicate that people convicted of genocide or treason should not be sentenced to death if they vow political loyalty to the People's Republic of Kampuchea (PRK).

The judicial system does not adequately guarantee fair trials to political prisoners. There is provision for the right of defence counsel, but until 1985, no PRK law provided for judicial review. Since then there has been provision for a Supreme People's Tribunal before which appeals could presumably be heard, but in 1987 it was officially revealed that it was not functioning. A 1982 law gives the Minister of Justice and the Council of State (the country's supreme representative body) authority to overturn verdicts and order retrials and allows prisoners sentenced to death to petition the Council of State for commutation.

PRK tribunals have reportedly sentenced five defendants to death since 1979 for genocide or treason. Three of them were sentenced to death *in absentia*, including Pol Pot and Ieng Sary, both leading officials of the former Democratic Kampuchea (Khmer Rouge) Government. A political prisoner sentenced in 1983 was reportedly executed without judicial review, but there is no information about the fate of another political prisoner who was sentenced in 1986.

An official report to the National Assembly in 1984 revealed that since 1979 two people had been executed after being sentenced to death for convictions of murder, and rape of an under-age girl. In the second case the State Council refused clemency because the convicted man "had a bad curriculum vitae and would never be submissive to any advice". In a 1984 interview, a deputy minister of justice said two other people sentenced to death for ordinary criminal offences received commutations.

According to reports, executions are carried out by firing-squads composed of police officers.

Kenya

Status: Retentionist

Executions 1985 - mid-88: 32; treason; murder; robbery with violence

Other factors: None

Method of execution: Hanging

Under the Penal Code (revised 1970), the death penalty is mandatory for treason, which is interpreted in Kenya as acts or plans to kill, harm or depose the head of state or overthrow the government, or advocating such action. Murder also carries a mandatory death sentence. Robbery and attempted robbery carry a mandatory death penalty if the offender was armed with a dangerous or offensive weapon, or was in the company of others, or if violence was used.

People charged with treason or murder are tried by the High Court, after a preliminary inquiry by a lower court. Those convicted have the right of appeal to the Court of Appeal. Members of the armed forces charged with treason are tried by court-martial, with the right of appeal to the High Court and the Court of Appeal. Robbery with violence is tried in a magistrate's court by the Chief Magistrate or a Senior Resident Magistrate, with the right of appeal to the High Court and Court of Appeal. All defendants facing the death sentence have the right to legal representation, and in cases of treason and murder – but not robbery with violence – defendants are granted state legal aid if they cannot afford legal fees.

After exhausting the judicial appeals procedures, prisoners have the right to petition the head of state for clemency. All death sentences require presidential review, either to confirm or commute the sentence, upon advice from the Advisory Committee on the Prerogative of Mercy.

The death sentence may not be imposed on a pregnant woman, anyone aged under 18 at the time of the offence, or an insane person; no upper age limit is set. Execution is by hanging, usually carried out in Kamiti Prison in Nairobi, where all prisoners under sentence of death are held. Executions are not publicly announced and the government does not publish statistics on death sentences.

In 1985 at least 26 people were reported to have been executed. They included 12 former Kenya Air Force personnel tried *in camera* by courts-martial and convicted of treason in connection with a coup attempt in August 1982, who were executed secretly on 17 July 1985. These were the first death sentences and executions for treason since independence in 1963. Among the 12 were three men who had fled to Tanzania after the coup attempt. Despite having been given asylum there, they were forcibly returned to Kenya by the Tanzanian authorities in November 1983. Fourteen people convicted of murder or robbery with violence were also reportedly executed in 1985. At least six executions for the same offences are believed to have taken place in 1986, but it is not known if there were any executions in 1987 or early 1988.

Death sentences imposed by the courts between 1985 and 1987 numbered at least 25 each year. As of 31 May 1988 there were believed to be over 200 prisoners under sentence of death. They had been convicted of murder or robbery with violence in previous years and were awaiting the outcome of judicial appeals or petitions for clemency and presidential review.

The Penal Code adopted immediately after independence provided the death penalty for treason and murder. The main changes since then have been the broadening of the crime of treason in 1967 (even to the point of including speculation about who would succeed the then President, Jomo Kenyatta), and the introduction in 1975 of the death penalty for robbery with violence. The new legislation of 1975 provided that those charged with robbery with violence – the offence attracting the most death sentences and executions – would be tried by a lower court than those charged with other capital offences, and that they would not be eligible for state legal aid. Consequently most do not have legal defence representation and are also at a disadvantage with regard to filing an appeal within the statutory 14 days limit or petitioning the President for clemency.

Kiribati

Status: Abolitionist

Executions 1985 - mid-88: None

Other factors: Not applicable

Method of execution: Not applicable

Formerly known as the Gilbert Islands, Kiribati became independent from the United Kingdom in 1979. The 1965 Penal Code for the Gilbert and Ellis Islands had not provided for the death penalty for any crime, the maximum sentence being life imprisonment. Since independence there has been no legislation to introduce the death penalty.

Korea (Democratic People's Republic of)

Status: Retentionist

Executions 1985 - mid-88: Not known

Other factors: Not known

Method of execution: Shooting by firing-squad

The death penalty is retained in the Democratic People's Republic of Korea (DPRK), although the authorities release no details on the number of death sentences imposed or executions carried out. In 1981 the DPRK acceded to the International Covenant on Civil and Political Rights (ICCPR) and in 1984 a government representative presented its initial report concerning the implementation of the ICCPR to the Human Rights Committee (the body established by the ICCPR to monitor the implementation of its provisions by States Parties). The representative is recorded as saying that, "The death penalty is reserved for special offences such as espionage and premeditated murder."

Offences for which the death penalty may be imposed may be governed by the Penal Code which is believed to have been promulgated in 1976. Amnesty International has received no reply from the government in response to its

request for a copy of the code. However, the organization has received unconfirmed reports of executions carried out during the 1980s for rebellion, sabotage, murder, rape, adultery and embezzlement.

Korea (Republic of)

Status: Retentionist

Executions 1985 - mid-88: 23; murder and rape; rape and robbery

Other factors: None

Methods of execution: Hanging; shooting by firing-squad

The death penalty can be imposed for a wide range of criminal and political offences under the Criminal Code and various other laws. It is mandatory for nationals of the Republic of Korea (and foreigners on the Republic's territory) who fight for the enemy, and for offences under the Military Penal Code, such as leading an armed insurrection or desertion by a commanding officer.

In recent years most death sentences have been imposed for convictions of murder, murder or rape in the course of robbery, leading an "anti-state" organization (that is a group seeking to overthrow the government) and espionage for North Korea. In addition, some people were sentenced to death under the Act Concerning Additional Punishment for Specified Crimes. This law provides for the death penalty for aggravated or repeated offences such as habitual robbery, second-time robbery causing injury to a victim, and killing or causing the death of a kidnap victim.

At the end of June 1988 there were 29 prisoners whose death sentences had been finalized by the Supreme Court. They were believed to have been convicted of murder or of espionage for North Korea. Among them were two students, Yang Dong-hwa and Kim Song-man, who were found guilty of meeting North Korean officials either in North Korea or in a third country and receiving instructions to lead anti-government student activities.

The Code of Criminal Procedure requires that a defence counsel be present during the trial of capital offences. Most death sentences are tried in the first instance by district courts. All death sentences must be reviewed by a higher court and defendants sentenced to death may not waive their right of appeal. In practice, it is believed that all death sentences are reviewed twice: by a high court (or high court-martial in the case of military personnel) and by the Supreme Court.

The order to carry out a death sentence is signed by the Minister of Justice (or the Minister of National Defence in the case of military personnel). The order must be given within six months of the judgment becoming final and execution must then be carried out within five days. A death sentence is suspended if the prisoner is of unsound mind or is a pregnant woman; the suspension lasts until recovery or the birth of the child. Those aged over 16 may be sentenced to death, but according to official statistics no one under the age of 18 has been executed since 1971. Executions must be witnessed by officials of the prosecutor's office and of the detention centre (as well as by a military surgeon in cases under the Military Criminal Code), but they are not public. Executions of prisoners sentenced by civilian courts are carried out by hanging inside prisons. Members of the military are shot by a firing-squad.

Amnesty International does not have access to official statistics on executions. However, in October 1984 it was told by Ministry of Justice officials that in recent years there had been between five and 10 executions annually. Amnesty International has recorded 10 executions of political prisoners under the Anti-Communist Law or the National Security Law between 1975 and 1982. There were no executions between 30 June 1987 and 30 June 1988.

Some prisoners under sentence of death are reported to have been kept permanently handcuffed; the authorities have stated that only those thought to show suicidal tendencies are restrained in this way.

Between 1981 and 1984 President Chun Doo-hwan commuted a number of death sentences in political cases. These included Kim Dae-jung, whose death sentence for sedition was commuted in January 1981; three prisoners who had been convicted in connection with the Kwangju insurrection of May 1980; seven prisoners who had been convicted of espionage and "anti-state" activities; and

two students convicted of an arson attack in March 1982 on the US Cultural Center in Pusan. On the occasion of his inauguration, on 26 February 1988, President Roh Tae-woo commuted the death sentences of two prisoners; one had been convicted of murder, but maintained his innocence, the other had been convicted of espionage.

In January 1985, a committee of experts began working on a revision of the Criminal Code. Government officials have indicated to Amnesty International that under consideration are a reduction in the number of capital offences, and an amendment to the Juvenile Law which permits the execution of those aged between 16 and 18. At the same time, however, the authorities announced their intention to introduce the death penalty for people convicted of producing foodstuffs harmful to health.

Although a number of defence lawyers and judges are said to oppose the death penalty, there is no organized abolitionist movement. The only organization openly campaigning for abolition is the International Human Rights League of Korea. In late 1985 the League conducted a survey of one quarter of the country's judges. Sixty-four per cent said they believed that use of the death penalty should be more restricted, and eight per cent pronounced themselves in favour of its abolition.

▶ In December 1988 a presidential amnesty commuted the death sentences of Yang Dong-hwa, Kim Song-man and Shin Kwang-su.

Kuwait

Status: Retentionist

Executions 1985 - mid-88: 6+; premeditated murder

Other factors: No right of appeal against sentences imposed by the State Security Court; public executions

Methods of execution: Hanging; shooting by firing-squad

The Penal Code (Law No. 16 of 1960, amended in 1970) provides for a mandatory death penalty for offences against the security of the state, including attempts on the life, safety or freedom of the Amir (head of state) or the Crown Prince, and attempts to overthrow the government by force. The death penalty is mandatory for premeditated murder and murder by poisoning, and optional for other forms of murder, including death as a result of torture by public officials.

Other offences for which a mandatory or an optional death penalty is provided include aggravated kidnapping, rape in certain circumstances, false testimony leading to the execution of a defendant, and causing death by an attack on transport.

A special law passed in July 1985 introduced the death penalty for the use of explosives to kill, terrorize or commit sabotage, and made it mandatory if death results. Expansion of the use of the death penalty to include hijacking has also been discussed.

In September 1987 a new law on illicit drugs made the killing of an official entrusted with the enforcement of that law a capital offence. The same provision was contained in the previous 1983 law on illicit drugs. During the debate preceding the passing of the new law, the General Director of the General Administration for Criminal Investigations opposed any extension of the use of the death penalty, arguing that this would make the task of law enforcement officials more difficult as drug dealers would resist arrest "to the point of death".

Offenders who are mentally disturbed at the time of the offence are not considered criminally responsible; those aged under 18 at the time of the offence may not be sentenced to death. A man who kills a female relative or her partner upon finding them engaged in illicit sexual intercourse may not be sentenced to death, nor may a woman who kills her newborn infant in order to defend her honour. The death sentence passed on a woman found to be pregnant is automatically commuted if she gives birth to a living baby.

Ordinary death penalty cases are initially tried by the Criminal Court and automatically reviewed by the High Court of Appeal and the Court of Cassation. Capital cases involving offences against the security of the state and other offences such as those relating to explosives are tried by the State Security Court,

introduced in 1969. Most trials held in recent years before this court are conducted *in camera*, and no review by a higher tribunal against its verdicts is permitted.

The Penal Code allows the court to impose a prison sentence instead of the death penalty, on compassionate grounds. According to the 1985 law on explosives, however, this rule does not apply to the offences that fall within its remit. Defendants convicted *in absentia* by the Criminal Court or the State Security Court are entitled to a retrial. Death sentences must be ratified by the Amir, who is empowered to commute them or grant pardon.

Prisoners under sentence of death are held in solitary confinement. Relatives may visit them the day before execution, which is by hanging or shooting by firing-squad. The body is returned to the family if requested.

Since independence in 1961, 24 people – at least 14 of them foreign nationals – are reported to have been executed as of 31 May 1988. All were hanged after being convicted of premeditated murder or rape and murder.

Hangings used to be carried out in public in Nayef Palace Square, but since 1985 they have been carried out in Kuwait Central Prison. One Thai citizen, executed in 1981, died of suffocation as his body was not heavy enough to break his neck. Another Thai, executed with him, broke down in tears and protested his innocence before being led to the gallows. There were reportedly four executions in 1985 and two in 1986, all for premeditated murder. None were reported in 1987.

As of 31 May 1988, there were nine prisoners – four of them Kuwaiti nationals – who had received final death sentences passed by the State Security Court between 1984 and 1987 for political offences involving bombings and an attempt on the Amir's life. The sentences have not been ratified by the Amir.

▶ On 12 September 1988 four people, two men and two women, were executed following conviction for premeditated murder and other crimes.

Laos

Status: Retentionist (according to available information)

Executions 1985 - mid-88: Not known

Other factors: No constitution or legal code

Method of execution: Not known

The Lao People's Democratic Republic has had no constitution or penal code since its establishment in 1975. The government has reportedly promulgated interim rules and regulations for the arrest and trial of people accused of specific crimes, including armed resistance to the government. These instructions are allegedly applied capriciously and inconsistently, and it is said that government officials and their families can easily influence the judgments reached. The instructions reportedly include provisions for the death penalty, and require approval of death sentences by the Council of Ministers.

In 1980 the state news agency announced that four "hooligans" were sentenced to death "by the special jury of the People's Court of Vientiane Province" for having "implemented the subversive plan of the enemies, committed robberies, [and] disturbed the state of peace and security among the people". It is not known whether they were executed.

In a 1982 statement to the United Nations, the government said that "in actual practice" capital punishment was "invoked only in cases of extreme gravity ... crimes which testify to the unusually cruel character of the offender ... threatening the highest interests of the state."

Lebanon

Status: Retentionist

Executions 1985 - mid-88: Not known (16 by armed groups exercising *de facto* control of parts of Lebanon; murder; sabotage)

Other factors: None

Methods of execution: Hanging; shooting by firing-squad

In Lebanon the Penal Code provides for the death penalty for treason, murder in aggravating circumstances, and arson and attacks against means of transport and communication which result in death.

There are at least 12 articles in the Military Penal Code which provide for the death penalty, including offences such as desertion, bearing arms against the state and refusing to obey orders in time of war.

Courts competent to pronounce death sentences are the Criminal Court of Lebanon and the Military Court. Appeals against a death sentence can be addressed to the Court of Cassation or the Military Court of Cassation (which is headed by a magistrate). A death sentence cannot be finalized before it has been reviewed by the Amnesty Committee (consisting of five magistrates) and upheld by the head of state.

Thirteen years of civil war have left the Lebanese authorities with no effective control beyond Beirut, and the Criminal Court in Beirut is the only one now able to try murder cases. Between 1975 and 1983, 38 death sentences were passed by the Criminal Court. Eighteen of these were pronounced *in absentia*, 16 were commuted to between one and 12 years in prison or a sanatorium, and one prisoner, Ibrahim Tarraf, was executed on 3 March 1983 for murder. Of the other death sentences, two were confirmed but never carried out. A further death sentence was imposed by the Military Court in 1984, but it is not known whether the sentence was carried out.

On 27 April 1988 five death sentences were imposed *in absentia* for murder committed in 1980.

The four main militias in Lebanon – Amal, the Lebanese Forces, the Progressive Socialist Party and the South Lebanon Army – have carried out executions by firing-squad following some form of summary trial. Amnesty International has recorded 16 executions carried out in this way since the beginning of 1985. Most of those executed were accused of murder or acts of sabotage resulting in death.

Lesotho

Status: Retentionist

Executions 1985 - mid-88: None

Other factors: None

Method of execution: Hanging

Under the terms of the Criminal Procedure and Evidence Proclamation No. 59 of 1938 (with subsequent amendments), murder is punishable by a mandatory death sentence when the court concludes that there were no extenuating circumstances. Two other offences in common law – treason and rape – carry an optional death sentence.

Most death sentences known to have been imposed by the courts in Lesotho have been on people convicted of ritual murder or murder in the furtherance of robbery. The courts imposed death sentences on at least five people convicted of ritual murder: three in 1982 and two in 1984. However, few death sentences have been imposed during the last 10 years, and executions are rare. One person was sentenced to death in 1985 and pardoned the following year by the King. Tseliso Mona and Khopiso Mona were sentenced to death in 1986, and at the time of going to press their appeal had not been heard. No death sentences were imposed in 1987 or 1988. The last execution was in 1984.

Pregnant women, women convicted of killing their new-born children and anyone aged under 18 at the time of the offence may not be sentenced to death.

All capital cases are tried by the High Court in Maseru before a judge sitting with two assessors. The assessors, who are not necessarily legally trained, help decide questions of fact, including whether there are any extenu-

ating circumstances. Defendants facing capital charges who cannot pay for legal counsel are entitled to court-appointed counsel, who tend to be relatively inexperienced lawyers.

Those sentenced to death have automatic right of appeal to a higher court. Death sentences confirmed by the Court of Appeal are reviewed by the King, who has the prerogative to grant pardon or commute death sentences.

Members of the military government which took power in a coup in January 1986 are reported to have proposed publicly that armed robbery and theft of livestock should also be capital offences; however, no steps have been taken to implement these proposals.

There appears to be little discussion of the death penalty in Lesotho, perhaps because it is rarely used. Judges, both in the High Court and in the Court of Appeal, have generally interpreted "extenuating circumstances" broadly, with the result that death sentences have seldom been imposed or upheld on appeal.

Liberia

Status: Retentionist

Executions 1985 - mid-88: 1 +; murder
Other factors: Special courts with deficient trial standards; no right of appeal against sentences imposed by the Special Military Tribunal; public executions; retroactive use

Methods of execution: Hanging; shooting by firing-squad

Although no executions are known to have taken place since a return to constitutional rule in 1986, under the military government in power between 1980 and 1985, some 50 people were executed after trials in which defence rights were flagrantly denied, or without any trial at all.

The Liberian Penal Law of 1976 provides for an optional death penalty by hanging for treason and murder. In September 1986, armed robbery, hijacking and terrorism were reportedly made capital offences. Capital cases are heard before the Criminal Court with a right of appeal to the Supreme Court. Full defence rights are guaranteed by law but have often not been respected. The head of state has the power to grant clemency.

Under the government of President William Tolbert (1971-1980), 16 people were executed for murder, seven of them, including a woman, being publicly hanged in February 1979. After a change of government in 1980, seven people alleged to have been convicted of murder in the 1960s and 1970s were hanged in March 1981 although one case was still pending before the Supreme Court. Between August 1986 and May 1988, at least nine people were sentenced to death for murder but the outcome of their appeals is not known.

During a period of military rule from 1980 to 1985, all known death sentences were passed by a special military court. Following a successful coup on 12 April 1980, in which President Tolbert and at least 27 others were killed, the new military government, the People's Redemption Council (PRC), immediately issued PRC Decree No. 1 of 1980. This defined high treason, a capital offence, as including corruption, maladministration and the monopolizing of political power by public officials. PRC Decree No. 5 of 1980 made corruption involving a member of the security forces or a foreign resident punishable by death.

Shortly after the coup, a Special Military Tribunal was established with jurisdiction over both military personnel and civilians accused of treason or murder. Some 50 people, and possibly more, are believed to have been executed following conviction by this court sitting *in camera*, most of them soldiers convicted of political offences. In some cases, defendants were denied legal counsel and the right to cross-examine witnesses or present evidence in their defence. There was no right of appeal against the court's verdict and sentence, but all sentences had to be confirmed by the military government. It was not always clear whether those executed had received any trial at all or had simply been interrogated by the Special Military Tribunal or members of the government itself, nor whether executions had in fact been carried out.

Four people were publicly executed by firing-squad on the beach in Monrovia, allegedly for committing murder and looting, on 17 April 1980. It is not clear whether they had been tried at all. On 22 April 1980, after a hurried and secret trial before the Special Military Tribunal, 13 senior officials of the former government were also publicly executed on the beach. They were accused of high treason, corruption and human rights violations, and were denied all rights of defence. It was subsequently alleged that the court had acquitted some of the accused and sentenced only four to death, but that the new government had ordered them all to be executed. After widespread international protest, the government announced that there would be no further executions of former officials of the deposed government.

Thirteen soldiers were convicted by the Special Military Tribunal in June 1981 of plotting to overthrow the government and were reportedly shot in their cells. In August 1981, five leading PRC members were executed the day after a preliminary investigation by the Special Military Tribunal into an alleged plot to assassinate the PRC Chairman. Four soldiers were executed in February 1982 the day after reportedly confessing to murder and armed robbery. On 8 April 1985 an armed forces officer was executed shortly after confessing on television that he had attempted to assassinate the PRC Chairman. An unknown number of executions took place after an abortive coup in November 1985 but do not seem to have been preceded by any trials.

Following the return to constitutional rule in January 1986, the Special Military Tribunal was abolished, although military personnel continued to be tried by court-martial. At least one death sentence is believed to have been imposed by a court-martial sitting *in camera* in connection with the November 1985 coup attempt, but it is not known if the execution was carried out.

Libya

Status: Retentionist

Executions 1985 - mid-88: 9+; murder; other offences apparently politically motivated

Other factors: Televised executions; unfair trials

Methods of execution: Hanging; shooting by firing-squad

The death penalty is provided for numerous offences contained in the Penal Code of 1953, as amended by a number of special laws. However, a constitutional document entitled The Great Green Document on Human Rights in the Era of the Masses, adopted in June 1988, stated that the death penalty would be applied "only to he whose life constitutes a danger or corruption to society", and set abolition as an aim of society.

Under the Penal Code, the death penalty is mandatory for premeditated murder and other types of murder; acts against public safety such as causing epidemics or poisoning food or water resulting in death; and crimes against the state, including treason, attempting to change the form of government by violence or other illegal means, and advocating such change.

After Colonel Mu'ammar Gaddafi gained power in September 1969, a mandatory death penalty was introduced for taking up arms specifically against the new order (Revolutionary Command Council [RCC] Decision of 11 December 1969) and for forming or being involved in political parties or groups opposed to the principles of the new order (Law No. 71 of 1972).

The death penalty is also provided for causing the death of an official entrusted with the enforcement of the 1971 law on drugs; robbery resulting in death (1972); the destruction of an oil installation or a public storage facility (1979); and a number of military crimes punished by the Military Penal Code of 1974. In 1980 a policy of "physical liquidation" of political opponents was officially adopted.

Those deemed to have been mentally incapacitated at the time of the crime are either held not criminally responsible or are exempt from the penalty, depending on the degree of their incapacity. Those aged under 18 are also exempt, and pregnant women may not be executed until two months after giving birth. Defendants convicted in absentia are retried.

According to the Code of Criminal Procedure, capital offences are tried by the criminal section of courts of appeal which, until 1987 at least, were supposed to seek the opinion of the local mufti (Islamic religious authority) before issuing their verdict. The code provides for automatic review of death sentences by the Court of Cassation, but it also provides for the defence counsel or the defendant to request it. Judges may reduce a sentence on compassionate grounds. All death sentences require ratification by the Secretariat of the General People's Congress, Libya's highest authority since 1977. Executions are supposed to be by hanging and to take place in the prison or in other covered places. Military personnel are executed by firing-squad.

In 1969 a People's Court was introduced. Although intended for trying offences of "political and administrative corruption" committed by former senior civil servants, its jurisdiction was later expanded. The court was not bound by existing procedures and its verdicts were subject to review only by the RCC, the country's highest authority at the time. During the 1970s, the court tried political capital offences, often in camera. In several cases the RCC is reported to have abused its powers by amending prison sentences to death. In May 1988 a new People's Court was established with similar jurisdiction. The new court, however, is bound by the Code of Criminal Procedure and its decisions can be appealed to the Court of Cassation.

Permanent Military Courts and Temporary Military Courts are provided by law to try offences by military personnel. Death sentences are reviewed by the Supreme Military Court unless the defendant renounces this right. In the early 1970s, several special military courts specifically set up to try conspiracy cases reportedly imposed death sentences.

Following the declaration of the Jamahiriya (state of the masses) in 1977, and the establishment of revolutionary committees, a Permanent Revolutionary Court was introduced in 1980 to apply "the law of the revolution".

Other revolutionary courts appear to have been set up on an *ad hoc* basis by the revolutionary committees. In some instances, even Basic People's Congresses, Libya's main decision-making bodies, acted as tribunals. These courts violated international standards. Death sentences were imposed and a number of executions were carried out in apparent implementation of the policy of "physical liquidation".

The first known executions since September 1969 were carried out in April 1977 when 22 officers were shot and four civilians were publicly hanged, after conviction by military courts and the People's Court. The following years saw further executions – often in the month of April – for political offences. Prisoners of conscience were also executed.

In April 1983 a Libyan and four Palestinian teachers said to belong to the Islamic Liberation Party were publicly hanged in a university and in a school. In April and June 1984, 10 people, including students, were hanged in Tripoli University during sessions of Basic People's Congresses. Some of the hangings were televised. One student, al-Sadeq al-Shuwayhdi, was shown confessing and pleading for mercy in front of a crowd in a sports stadium before being hanged. He is said to have died slowly of suffocation. In February 1987 nine other executions were televised. Three military men were shot and six civilians were hanged after having been accused of politically motivated crimes. Some of the victims hanged were shown thrashing the air with their legs after stools were removed from under them.

Amnesty International has no information on death sentences imposed for common criminal offences, although official sources stated in 1988 that no executions for such offences had taken place since September 1969.

In March 1988 Colonel Gaddafi called for the abolition of the death penalty after having expressed reservations about its use on previous occasions. In further statements he said that his opposition to the penalty arose from having seen public executions, apparently those televised in June 1984. He also said that the policy of "physical liquidation" had ended. The death penalty was debated in May 1988 by the Basic People's Congresses, and on 12 June the General People's Congress adopted a con-

stitutional document setting abolition as an aim of Jamahiri society, affirming the right to commutation and outlawing certain methods of execution. Colonel Gaddafi regretted that the death penalty had not been totally abolished and pledged to continue working for that aim. On 13 June he intervened to commute all existing death sentences.

Liechtenstein

Status: Abolitionist

Executions 1985 - mid-88: None

Other factors: Not applicable

Method of execution: Not applicable

On 24 June 1987 the *Landtag* (parliament) adopted a new Penal Code which abolished the death penalty for all offences. The vote approving this proposal to abolish the death penalty was unanimous. The new Penal Code will come into force on 1 January 1989. When it was introduced in parliament, the commission set up by the government to reform the Penal Code stated that the death penalty should be abolished because its retention would be contrary to current European and international trends.

The death penalty was previously provided for murder, damage to property leading to the foreseeable death of a person, and high treason under the Austrian Penal Code of 1852 as applied in Liechtenstein. The last execution was carried out in 1785 by beheading.

Luxembourg

Status: Abolitionist

Executions 1985 - mid-88: None

Other factors: Not applicable

Method of execution: Not applicable

On 17 May 1979 the Chamber of Deputies approved a bill abolishing the death penalty for all offences by a majority of 32 votes to 14. The Penal Code was amended and no longer provides for the death penalty; the Constitution, however, does not explicitly rule out its use.

In 1948 the Penal Code was revised to replace beheading by shooting. After World War II, 18 people were sentenced to death, nine of whom were executed. The last execution for an ordinary criminal offence was on 7 August 1948. The last execution for war crimes was on 24 February 1949.

Madagascar

Status: Abolitionist in practice

Executions 1985 - mid-88: None

Other factors: None

Method of execution: Shooting by firing-squad

The Penal Code provides for the death penalty for certain offences against the security of the state, including provoking civil war, rebellion, sabotage of state property and treason. It is also mandatory for premeditated murder, torture, arson causing death or injury and armed robbery. In 1984 a new law was enacted under which people convicted of conspiracy against the government may be sentenced to death.

Defendants charged with capital offences are granted legal aid if they have no means of paying for legal representation. If convicted they have the right of appeal to the Supreme Court. If confirmed on appeal, a death sentence may not be carried out until a petition for presidential clemency has been considered and rejected. The law stipulates that minors and the mentally ill may not be executed. Execution of a pregnant woman must be deferred until after her confinement.

The last execution known to have been carried out was in 1958 when Madagascar was under colonial administration. Although the death penalty has been imposed on a number of occasions since independence in 1960, the head of state appears to have exercised his prerogative of mercy in every instance and there has been no case of the death penalty being imposed for political offences.

Malawi

Status: Retentionist

Executions 1985 - mid-88: Not known

Other factors: Unfair trials in traditional courts

Method of execution: Hanging

Under the Penal Code the death penalty is mandatory for prisoners convicted of murder or treason, and is optional for rape. Anyone convicted of robbery with violence, housebreaking or burglary must be sentenced either to death or to life imprisonment. Any of the offences carrying the death penalty may be tried in the "traditional courts" where the defendant does not have the benefit of many of the internationally recognized safeguards for a fair trial. Pregnant women and anyone aged under 18 at the time of the offence may not be sentenced to death.

Malawi has two parallel judicial systems. In the High Court and Court of Appeal people charged with a capital offence are allowed legal counsel and their cases are heard by a legally qualified judge. In the traditional courts, however, the defendant is not allowed a lawyer and cannot call witnesses, judges need not be legally trained, and the rules of procedure and evidence follow poorly defined notions of "custom" and "tradition" rather than any nationally or internationally accepted norms of legal procedure. The choice as to which judicial system will hear a case lies with the prosecution.

The "traditional court" system was developed by the British colonial authorities to deal with minor cases and disputes. Their jurisdiction was dramatically extended in 1970 when Life President Dr Hastings Kamuzu Banda objected to a High Court decision to acquit a group of people charged with murder. Their case was retried in the newly expanded traditional courts which were empowered to impose the death penalty for murder and rape. In 1976 the traditional courts were also empowered to impose death sentences for treason – shortly before the former secretary general of the ruling Malawi Congress Party, Albert

Muwalo Nqumayo, went on trial for treason in a traditional court in Blantyre. He was found guilty, sentenced to death, and executed in 1977. His co-defendant, former security police chief Focus Martin Gwede, was also sentenced to death but had his sentence commuted to life imprisonment. A large proportion of capital cases are apparently now heard by the traditional courts. Clemency may be granted by the President as head of state.

In 1983 Vera Chirwa, a law lecturer, and her husband Orton Chirwa, a former Minister of Justice and Attorney-General, were sentenced to death for treason by the Southern Region Traditional Court after allegedly being unlawfully abducted from Zambia. Both had been vocal critics of the Malawian Government while living outside the country and had formed an opposition political group. The National Traditional Court of Appeal later commented that some of the lower court's rulings had been "wrong in law" and that "the record is littered with unnecessary abuse which is not part of the traditional law", but nevertheless upheld the verdict and death sentences. In June 1984, after many international appeals, President Banda commuted the Chirwas' sentences to life imprisonment.

Death sentences are carried out by hanging at Zomba Central Prison. Usually, groups of prisoners are executed on the same day by a visiting executioner from South Africa. It is not known whether any executions took place between 1985 and 1987, though it is known that death sentences were regularly imposed and carried out during the 1970s. In 1983 Golden Mandondo and Lawrence Kananji were sentenced to death by the Southern Region Traditional Court for the murder of a volunteer aid worker in Zomba. It is not known whether the sentences were carried out.

Malaysia

Status: Retentionist

Executions 1985 - mid-88: 52+; drug-trafficking; unauthorized possession of firearms, ammunition or explosives; murder; kidnapping

Other factors: None

Method of execution: Hanging

The death penalty was retained from the colonial period when the country became independent in 1957. The number of death sentences and executions has increased since March 1980 when seven men were hanged under a 1975 amendment to the Internal Security Act (ISA), 1960 which made the death penalty mandatory for unauthorized possession of firearms, ammunition or explosives. In 1975 the Dangerous Drugs Act, 1952 was also amended, making the death penalty the maximum sentence for drug-trafficking; in April 1983 it became mandatory. Under the Firearms (Increased Penalties) Act, 1971 (discharging a firearm with the intention of causing death or hurt in the commission of a scheduled offence) the death penalty is also mandatory. The death penalty is also provided for other offences under the Penal Code (for example, murder, for which it is mandatory; aiding the suicide of a child or insane person); the Firearms (Increased Penalties) Act, 1971 (discharging or being an accomplice in discharging a firearm with the intention of causing death or injury in the commission of a scheduled offence); the Kidnapping Act, 1961; the Armed Forces Act, 1972 (mutiny); and the Arms Act, 1978 (waging war against the government). Amnesty International has learned from press reports that 36 death sentences were imposed in 1985, 48 in 1986, 41 in 1987 and 24 up to 31 May 1988.

Under the 1975 amendment of the ISA, the mandatory death penalty applies to those convicted of possessing or consorting with the possessor of firearms, ammunition or explosives without valid reason, in any area proclaimed by the Yang di-Pertuan Agong (King) as a "security area". A proclamation to this effect was issued in May 1969 rendering all areas in

Malaysia as "security areas". The ISA also provides for a mandatory death penalty for other firearms offences. At least 40 people have been executed under the act since 1975, 13 of them between 1985 and May 1988. The identity and offence of those executed is not always made public by the authorities.

Since April 1983 the death penalty has been mandatory for drug-trafficking on conviction of possession of 15 grams of heroin or morphine, 200 grams of cannabis, or 1,000 grams of opium. Between 1975 (when the death penalty became the maximum punishment for drug-trafficking) and May 1988, at least 62 people were executed for drug-related offences, 29 of them between 1985 and May 1988. During 1987 alone, 14 executions for drug offences were reportedly carried out. At least 31 new death sentences were announced in 1987, although in May an anti-narcotics officer gave a much larger figure of 67 death sentences imposed for drug-trafficking during the first four months alone. In the same year, the Supreme Court dismissed appeals of 15 others already convicted.

More than 100 people have been hanged since 1975, the majority of whom were convicted under the Dangerous Drugs Act and the ISA. This number includes 11 foreigners convicted of drug-trafficking and a 69-year-old Malaysian woman who was hanged in July 1987 after being found guilty three years previously of trafficking 55 grams of morphine. The precise number of prisoners who are awaiting trial on charges of drug-trafficking or whose case is under appeal is not known, but it is believed to be several hundred. Some 1,526 people were detained between 1985 and 1987 for suspected drug-trafficking. Since 1975 about 200 people have been convicted and sentenced to death, but it usually takes at least three years for a case to come to court and the majority are still awaiting the outcome of their appeals. In July 1985 the then Deputy Minister for Home Affairs was reported to have complained about appeal procedures which could "stretch out the time between sentencing and execution" by as much as two years, and announced at the same time that the authorities "plan to hang one person every week".

Capital cases are tried in the High Court and there is a right of appeal to the Supreme Court. Death sentences upheld by the Supreme Court are automatically reviewed by a Pardons Board. As head of state, the King, with the rulers of each of the 13 individual states, has the authority to grant pardon or suspend or commute sentences, acting on the advice of the Pardons Board. Some prisoners have appealed successfully to the Supreme Court, but Amnesty International knows of only two cases in which a death sentence was commuted by the head of state. The first was in March 1984 when a former government minister, who had been sentenced to death for murder, had his sentence commuted to life imprisonment. The second case was in January 1988 when Jamaludin bin Ahmad was released after six years in jail when the state Pardons Board granted his request for clemency. He had been arrested in February 1981 and sentenced to death in December 1986 under the Internal Security Act for the illegal possession of three pistols in a security area.

There has been widespread criticism – in which the Malaysian Bar Council has taken part – of the mandatory death penalty imposed under the ISA. Criticism increased in 1985 when Sim Kie Chon, a factory worker, was due to be executed for the illegal possession of firearms (Section 57 [1] of the ISA). He was granted a last-minute stay of execution in August 1985 to pursue a court application challenging as unconstitutional the rejection of his clemency petition by the Pardons Board. He did so on the grounds that a rejection of his petition violated the Constitution's provision of equality and non-discrimination in view of the earlier commutation of the death sentence of the former government minister. Sim Kie Chon was nevertheless executed in March 1986, one month after the Supreme Court had dismissed his application.

Maldives

Status: Abolitionist in practice

Executions 1985 - mid-88: None

Other factors: None

Method of execution: Not known

The Maldives still retains the death penalty in its Penal Code, but has reportedly not carried out an execution since 1952. The only offences known to be punishable by death are premeditated murder and treason.

Mali

Status: Retentionist

Executions 1985 - mid-88: None

Other factors: Special courts with deficient trial standards

Method of execution: Shooting by firing-squad

The death penalty is provided for in law for a wide range of offences and death sentences continue to be passed, but no executions are known to have been carried out since 1980.

Under the Penal Code of 1961 the death penalty may be imposed for treason and other crimes against the security of the state; premeditated or aggravated murder; torture committed in the course of a crime and certain other crimes against the person; aggravated theft; and certain other crimes against property. There is a right of appeal from the Assizes Court to the Court of Appeal and then, on questions of law only, to the judicial section of the Supreme Court. All death sentences are reviewed by the head of state who has the power to grant clemency.

The last known executions were carried out in August 1980 on two people convicted of murder committed in the course of an armed robbery. Amnesty International received no further reports of death sentences passed in the Assizes Court in the early 1980s. In 1986 and 1987 at least eight death sentences were imposed, five of them *in absentia*, for aggravated theft, premeditated murder, arson, and murder committed in the course of armed robbery. None of these recent sentences are known to have been carried out, nor is it clear whether they have been formally commuted by the head of state.

In February 1976 a special military court was created – the Special State Security Court. This is presided over by trained judges and armed forces officers and has the power to impose the death penalty for offences against the security of the state. Later in the year it was further empowered to impose the death penalty for offences against state property above a certain value (in 1987 that amount was 10 million CFA francs, US $36,000). There is no right of appeal to the Court of Appeal but those convicted may appeal to the Supreme Court on questions of law.

In October 1978 the Special State Security Court sentenced to death two former members of the military government for conspiring to overthrow the government. In a related trial of former security officials on corruption charges in June 1979, one of them received a second death sentence and another armed forces officer was also sentenced to death. None of these sentences was carried out but in 1983 the two former government members died at the remote desert prison in Taoudénit where very severe conditions have led to the deaths of a number of prisoners over the years.

At least 19 death sentences are known to have been passed by this court, three of them *in absentia*, between 1985 and 1987: one in August 1986 for treason (*in absentia*) and the others for embezzlement of public funds. It is not known whether any of these sentences have been carried out.

Malta

Status: Abolitionist for all but exceptional crimes

Executions 1985 - mid-88: None

Other factors: None

Method of execution: Not known

Malta abolished the death penalty in 1971 for all offences in the Criminal Code (Criminal Code [Amendment] [Number 2] Act). However, it is retained under the Armed Forces Act of 1970 for a series of offences committed by those subject to military law, such as aiding the enemy, communicating intelligence to the enemy, or taking part in a mutiny. Trial is by court-martial.

Under the Constitution of 1964, the President has the power to grant pardon, and to reprieve or commute death sentences after receiving the advice of the Cabinet.

The last execution was carried out in 1943.

Marshall Islands

Status: Abolitionist

Executions 1985 - mid-88: None

Other factors: Not applicable

Method of execution: Not applicable

The Marshall Islands became an independent republic in free association with the United States of America in October 1986. The Constitution states, "No crime under the law of the Marshall Islands may be punished with death" (Article III).

Mauritania

Status: Retentionist

Executions 1985 - mid-88: 3; offences against state security

Other factors: Special courts with deficient trial standards; no right of appeal from Special Court of Justice; public executions

Methods of execution: Shooting by firing-squad (under jurisdiction of the Special Criminal Court: stoning; beheading by sword; by means of the weapon used)

In 1980 Islamic law (*Shari'a*) was introduced for the trying of criminal offences, resulting in at least four executions. Seven people have been executed since 1981 for involvement in conspiracies or attempts to overthrow the government.

Under the Penal Code of 1983, the death penalty may be imposed for treason and other crimes against the security of the state, premeditated and other types of murder, certain other crimes resulting in death, torture committed in the course of a crime, certain armed robbery offences and other offences against property.

Certain types of murder, homicide and armed robbery, which were specified as capital offences in the previous Penal Code of 1972, are not included in the 1983 code. However, the death penalty was extended to the killing of a newborn child by its mother, torture committed in the course of a crime, and *hadd* offences (offences against divine will) specified in Islamic law. Muslims may be sentenced to death for unrepentant apostasy and in certain cases of adultery, homosexuality and rape. Under military law, treason and several other serious offences committed by members of the armed forces in time of war carry the death penalty. The death penalty may not be passed on children aged under 16 or on pregnant women. The head of state has the power to grant clemency.

Capital cases may be tried before the ordinary criminal courts from which there is a right of appeal to the Court of Appeal and, on questions of law only, to the Judicial Chamber of the Supreme Court. No death sentences are known to have been passed by the ordinary criminal courts in recent years. Execution is by firing-squad. The 1983 Penal Code provides for execution by stoning for certain cases of adultery and homosexuality, but no such execution is known to have been carried out.

The introduction of Islamic law to try criminal offences brought about changes to the judicial system and increased the scope of the death penalty. In May 1980 a Special Criminal Court was established to try, under rules of evidence according to Islamic law, certain offences against the person and property specified in the 1972 Penal Code. It was empowered to impose the penalties for those offences specified in Islamic law, including the death penalty. The court was presided over by a judge qualified in Islamic law. The only right of appeal for those convicted by this court was on questions of law to the Chamber of Islamic Law of the Supreme Court. An ordinance of August 1980 specified that executions should be in public and that the head of state should decide whether the condemned person was to die by means of the weapon used in the crime, or by sword or firing-squad.

Two death sentences were imposed on defendants convicted of murder by the Special Criminal Court in July 1980 but it is not known whether they were carried out. In September 1980 a man convicted of murder was executed by firing-squad near Nouakchott before a crowd of thousands. He died only after a second volley had been fired. It was alleged that he suffered from mental illness and that his victim's heir had not been given the opportunity to pardon him or to accept compensation instead, as required under Islamic law. Following convictions by the Special Criminal Court, further public executions by firing-squad were carried out – one in December 1980 after a death sentence passed in August for murder was upheld by the Supreme Court and was confirmed by the head of state and the victim's son. There was one execution in February 1982 for armed robbery, and one in February 1983 for murder.

In June 1983 an ordinance was issued which transferred the jurisdiction of the Special Criminal Court to the ordinary criminal courts. Since then, no further death sentences are known to have been passed for criminal offences.

Since the first of a series of military coups in July 1978, a special military court has tried political cases and passed death sentences. In September 1978 a Special Court of Justice was established with jurisdiction over offences against the security of the state or involving members of the armed forces. In 1985 the court was divided into three chambers with jurisdiction over security, military and corruption cases.

The state prosecutor, investigating magistrate and presiding judge in the State Security Chamber are all armed forces officers. Cases are heard under a summary procedure and defendants are denied access to legal counsel throughout the pre-trial investigation by a magistrate. Counsel may consult the prosecution dossier and their client only just before the trial begins. State security cases have usually been heard in camera at a military barracks, although the press was allowed to attend the most recent such trial in late 1987. There is no right of appeal to any higher court but the head of state may be petitioned for clemency.

In March 1981 the Special Court of Justice sentenced four armed forces officers to death for involvement in an attempted coup in the same month. They were executed shortly afterwards. Three of the officers had previously been sentenced to death in absentia for treason and desertion. It is not known whether further death sentences passed in absentia on three civilians allegedly involved in the coup attempt were carried out. In December 1987 the court sentenced three armed forces officers to death after convicting 44 people of involvement in a coup attempt in October. The majority of those convicted were current or former members of the security services, and all were from the black community. The officers sentenced to death were executed three days later.

Mauritius

Status: Retentionist

Executions 1985 - mid-88: 1; murder

Other factors: Executions resumed after an unofficial 23-year moratorium

Method of execution: Hanging

No one was executed in Mauritius for more than 20 years up to 1984, but since then two prisoners convicted of murder have been executed and the scope of the death penalty has been extended. Four more prisoners were under sentence of death at the end of May 1988.

The death penalty has long been in force for murder, treason and mutiny. These offences are tried in the Court of Assizes before a judge and jury of nine citizens. The accused has the right to legal counsel and can appeal automatically to the Supreme Court. At the Supreme Court's discretion, the defendant may appeal to the Judicial Committee of the Privy Council in England (JCPC) which serves as the final court of appeal for Mauritius. Finally, all death sentences are reviewed by an advisory committee on the prerogative of mercy which recommends whether or not clemency should be shown. In practice, the decision as to whether to grant clemency lies with the Prime Minister.

In September 1986 the Dangerous Drugs Act was passed. Section 38 introduced a mandatory death sentence for any person convicted of importing "dangerous drugs", including opium, heroin, cannabis and coca leaves. These cases are heard by a judge sitting alone without a jury. In December 1987 two Indian nationals became the first people to be sentenced to death under Section 38. Their appeal was turned down in June 1988.

In 1984 Leopold Myrtillé was hanged in Beau Bassin Prison, making him the first person to be executed since 1961, when the country was still under colonial rule. He had been convicted of murder. In October 1987 a second execution took place, of Eshan Nayeck, also convicted of murder. In 1987 the Supreme Court turned down appeals from two other prisoners convicted of murder and sentenced to death, who then announced that they would appeal to the JCPC.

A large section of public opinion in Mauritius has been shocked by the revival of the death penalty after a long period without its imposition, and many senior political figures have stated their opposition to it. Many members of parliament belonging to the opposition *Mouvement militant mauricien* (MMM), Mauritian Militant Movement, are opposed to the death penalty. Although it is the government which has recently extended the scope of the death penalty, the leaders of two minority parties in the ruling coalition, Sir Gaëtan Duval of the *Parti mauricien social-démocrate* (PMSD), Mauritian Social Democratic Party, and Sir Satcam Boolell of the Labour Party, have both stated that they favour its abolition. When the Dangerous Drugs Bill was before Parliament, Sir Gaëtan Duval, at that time Minister of Justice and Deputy Prime Minister, unsuccessfully proposed an amendment substituting a 30-year prison sentence as the penalty for drug-trafficking.

Mexico

Status: Abolitionist for all but exceptional crimes

Executions 1985 - mid-88: None

Other factors: None

Method of execution: Shooting by firing-squad

The 1917 Constitution prohibits the death penalty for political offences and states, "...it can only be imposed for high treason committed during a foreign war, parricide, murder that is treacherous, premeditated, or committed for profit, arson, abduction, highway robbery, piracy and grave military offences."

The death penalty was included in the 1871 Penal Code, but was excluded from the 1929 and subsequent penal codes. None of Mexico's 32 states currently retain the death penalty in their penal codes and it has not been used for several decades. The last execution was in 1937 in the state of Puebla, there having been seven other executions in the preceding 26 years.

In January 1937 the Attorney-General of the

Republic argued forcefully against a parliamentary move to reintroduce the death penalty, "The extraordinary sanction of the death penalty cannot be justified as a measure of deterrence by example ... and is unnecessary for the defence of society." Over the years the Mexican Government has remained opposed to reintroduction. In 1982 its report to the Human Rights Committee under Article 40 of the International Covenant on Civil and Political Rights stated, "...the death penalty is not a typical feature of ordinary criminal proceedings and only exists as a dead letter in the Military Code of Justice ... This demonstrates a trend towards abolition ... from which it may be assumed that it will not be restored."

In April 1988 presidential candidate Carlos Salinas de Gortari of the ruling Institutional Revolutionary Party reportedly told journalists that, if elected, and if he felt the public so required, he would consider holding a referendum on reintroduction of the death penalty. The statement provoked widespread opposition to reintroduction, both from the general public and from Mexican bishops, political leaders, senators and prominent lawyers.

Micronesia (Federated States of)

Status: Abolitionist

Executions 1985 - mid-88: None

Other factors: Not applicable

Method of execution: Not applicable

The Federated States of Micronesia became an independent republic in free association with the United States of America in November 1986. Article IV, Section 9 of its Constitution states, "Capital punishment is prohibited."

Monaco

Status: Abolitionist

Executions 1985 - mid-88: None

Other factors: Not applicable

Method of execution: Not applicable

The death penalty was abolished for all offences in 1962 under Article 20 of a new Constitution of 17 December 1962. Article 20 states, "No one may be subjected to cruel, inhuman or degrading treatment. The death penalty is abolished." The last execution was by guillotine in 1847.

Mongolia

Status: Retentionist

Executions 1985 - mid-88: Not known

Other factors: Not known

Method of execution: Not specified in current criminal code (the Criminal Code of 1929 states that execution is by shooting)

Under the Criminal Code (1961) of the Mongolian People's Republic, several crimes carry an optional death penalty, although Article 18 of the Criminal Code states that it is an "exceptional measure of punishment" permitted "if this is specified in the Criminal Code". The following crimes are punishable by death: espionage (Article 46); sabotage (Article 48); terrorist acts (Article 47); intentional homicide under aggravating circumstances (Article 70); large-scale stealing of state or social property (Article 63); aggravated theft of private property (Article 109); and aggravated assault with intent to rob (Article 168). Women, men aged over 60 and anyone under 18 at the time of the crime may not be sentenced to death.

Trial is by "people's courts" and defendants may file an appeal against the judgment within 10 days of the sentence being imposed. Appeals are heard by courts higher than those which pass sentence, and according to the Constitution, right of pardon is exercised by the Presidium of the Great People's Khural (the highest organ of state power).

Little information is available on the application of the death penalty, apart from that given by official sources. In 1980 a representative of Mongolia stated at the Human Rights Committee, set up under the International Covenant on Civil and Political Rights, that the death penalty was rarely used in practice, and that during the previous 10 years it had been used only in grave cases of premeditated murder and "the large-scale misappropriation of socialist property". The number of death penalties imposed amounted to "an average of three a year". The representative explained that the death penalty was not applicable to women because "in the first place women were mothers above all and required particularly humane treatment, and secondly, because it was considered that the exemption of women from the death penalty was a significant step towards its complete abolition". He also said that a draft law to repeal the death penalty for theft and robbery had been submitted to the Presidium of the Great People's Khural, but by 1985 no changes had been made to legislation concerning the death penalty.

In 1986, the Mongolian Vice-Minister of Justice indicated at the Human Rights Committee that the Mongolian Criminal Code was being amended and that the number of offences liable to incur the death penalty might be reduced. He also stated that the carrying out of death penalties had decreased since 1980.

Montserrat

Status: Abolitionist in practice

Executions 1985 - mid-88: None

Other factors: None

Method of execution: Hanging

The Penal Code provides for a mandatory death sentence for murder (Part XII, Homicide and other offences against the person). Those aged under 18 at the time of the crime and pregnant women are exempt from the death penalty.

Montserrat is a member of the Organization of Eastern Caribbean States together with six other countries (pending Grenada rejoining). All seven share a common judicial system known as the Eastern Caribbean Supreme Court which consists of a High Court of Justice and a Court of Appeal. Final appeal is to the Judicial Committee of the Privy Council in England. However, the Privy Council will consider only cases involving constitutional matters or "matters of great public importance". Death sentences may be commuted to a term of imprisonment by the Governor General.

The last execution was carried out in 1961. There are no prisoners under sentence of death.

Morocco and Western Sahara

Status: Retentionist

Executions 1985 - mid-88: None

Other factors: None

Method of execution: Shooting by firing-squad

Under the Penal Code the death penalty is retained for a number of crimes, including crimes against the person, such as premeditated murder; murder in the course of other crimes; parricide; taking the life of another person by poisoning; use of violence against a public official that led to his or her death intentionally; death resulting from use of torture or acts of savagery in order to commit a felony; armed robbery; arson; and certain crimes against the internal and external security of the state and public order, including treason, damaging the territorial unity (in time of war), and taking up arms for or inciting civil war. The death penalty is also provided for under the Code of Military Justice for crimes such as desertion to the enemy. According to the Penal Code, judges may take extenuating circumstances into account when reaching a decision. The death penalty is mandatory for attempts on the life of the King.

The execution of a pregnant woman is deferred until 40 days after she has given birth. Children aged under 16 may not be executed.

Courts competent to try capital cases are the Criminal Chamber of Appeal Courts and the military courts. Military courts try military personnel and anyone accused of an offence against the external security of the state. Judgments of both courts are subject to a review only by the Supreme Court which may quash the sentence on a point of procedure. Once a sentence is finalized by the Supreme Court, the public prosecutor must report it immediately to the Minister of Justice and present a petition for clemency on behalf of the prisoner. No death sentence may be carried out until a petition for clemency has been presented and refused. The right to grant clemency is the prerogative of the King who may commute a sentence to life imprisonment or grant pardon.

Execution is carried out inside the prison where the prisoner is detained, or in any other designated place. Executions are not public, unless otherwise decided by the Minister of Justice, but are carried out in the presence of certain competent authorities as stated in the Penal Code.

There were 28 death sentences between 1985 and mid-1988, 16 of them imposed *in absentia*. There were no executions, but some cases have exhausted all judicial remedies and, at the time of going to press, are awaiting the King's decision to grant or refuse pardon. Most of these prisoners were convicted by the Criminal Chamber of Appeals Courts of plotting to overthrow the monarchy; they are also accused of belonging to various unauthorized Islamic movements. Most of the defendants have alleged that they were tortured during pre-trial incommunicado detention to extract information and that the court based its prosecution on such evidence. These allegations do not appear to have been investigated by the court.

Mozambique

Status: Retentionist

Executions 1985 - mid-88: 4+; treason; armed rebellion

Other factors: Unfair trials; no right of appeal (until a change of law in 1988); retroactive use

Method of execution: Shooting by firing-squad

Between 1979 and April 1983, 68 people were sentenced to death and executed. Ten more were sentenced between April 1983 and May 1986, four of whom are reported to have been executed. No death sentences are reported to have been imposed between May 1986 and the time of going to press.

There was no provision for the death penalty for the first four years after Mozambique became independent from Portugal in 1975. It was introduced in 1979 to punish crimes against the security of the state and certain military offences. In 1983 it was extended to include other crimes against the security of the state and ordinary offences, and to additional military crimes in 1988 (Law 17/87). Automatic right of appeal against death sentences imposed for offences under military law was also introduced in 1988.

According to Law No. 2/79 of 1 March 1979 entitled *Crimes against the People and the People's State*, the death penalty was introduced to "repress and discourage" the activities of armed government opponents. The law was introduced at a time when the *Resistência Nacional Moçambicana* (RNM or RENAMO), Mozambique National Resistance, had been carrying out guerrilla attacks in various parts of the country. The new law provided for a mandatory death sentence for five offences and for an optional death sentence for 10 other offences (including espionage, mercenarism and sabotage), the alternative sentence being 12 to 30 years' imprisonment to be imposed when the court believed that a culprit could be rehabilitated. The death penalty could also be applied to anyone who attempted a crime punishable by death or knowingly assisted a person guilty of such a crime.

According to this law, defendants charged with offences against the security of the state are to be tried by a Provincial People's Tribunal with the right of appeal to the Supreme People's Tribunal. However, since neither court had been established at the time the law was introduced, a special Revolutionary Military Tribunal was set up on 29 March 1979. The law establishing this court stipulated that those convicted by it were to have no right of appeal. When Provincial People's Tribunals and a High Court of Appeal were subsequently established, the Revolutionary Military Tribunal, the only court empowered to impose the death penalty, retained full jurisdiction over crimes against the security of the state.

On 30 March 1979 the newly formed Revolutionary Military Tribunal began to try 10 alleged RNM supporters accused of committing violent crimes. The following day all 10 were found guilty and were promptly executed. Neither they nor any of the other 68 people sentenced to death between 1979 and May 1986 have been able to appeal against their conviction or sentence.

In March 1983, when levels of both ordinary and politically motivated crime were reportedly rising, the death penalty was extended to include offences such as murder, blackmarketeering and the preparation of armed rebellion and acts of terrorism. One week later six people were sentenced to death, two of them for smuggling. They were executed before an invited audience on 9 April 1983.

Besides those sentenced to death by the Revolutionary Military Tribunal, a total of seven people were sentenced and executed after two public rallies in the small towns of Macia and Magude, north of Maputo (the capital), in January 1983. During the rallies, which the local press referred to as "trials", senior government officials questioned captured RNM members who admitted to having carried out violent acts. The watching crowds called for them to be put to death and they were promptly executed by army firing-squads. Following national and international protests, no further rally executions or death sentences for economic offences have been reported.

Trials have been unfair. Not only have those sentenced to death had no right to appeal but many defendants have had little opportunity to present their defence. Some have had no legal counsel whatsoever, while others have had no contact with any counsel until their trial began, with no opportunity to call witnesses in their defence. In some cases members of the defence counsel, themselves soldiers representing civilians before military judges, have reportedly confined themselves to making pleas for mitigation without challenging weak prosecution evidence. Furthermore, in 1979 and again in 1983, people were sentenced to death and executed for crimes which were not punishable by death when they were committed.

Although the law does not specifically exempt any category of person from the death penalty, in practice only adult males have been sentenced to death. The People's Assembly has the power of commutation but has not commuted any death sentences.

Since May 1986 no death sentences have been passed. In September 1987 a senior party official addressing the People's Assembly said that the execution of a smuggler in 1983 had not had any deterrent effect.

▶ In October 1988 Amnesty International was told by government officials that new legislation would go before the People's Assembly before the end of the year abolishing the Revolutionary Military Tribunal and establishing a Supreme People's Tribunal, to which those sentenced to death in future would have automatic right of appeal.

Namibia

Status: Retentionist

Executions 1985 - mid-88: 9; murder

Other factors: None

Method of execution: Hanging

Under South African administration the death penalty has remained in force in Namibia for offences similar to those punishable by death in South Africa. The South African Criminal Procedure Act of 1977 is in force in Namibia, making offences such as murder, rape and aggravated robbery or housebreaking punishable by death. The death penalty is mandatory for murder, unless the court concludes that there are extenuating circumstances (in which case it may be imposed on an optional basis), and it may also be used to punish treason and a range of political offences. Security laws such as the Terrorism Act of 1967, the Internal Security Amendment Act of 1976, and Section 21 of the General Laws Amendment Act of 1962 all remain in force in Namibia, although they have been repealed in South Africa itself. These laws provide for the death penalty to be imposed for sabotage, participation in "terroristic activities" and undergoing, or encouraging others to undergo, any form of training aimed at achieving the aims of "communism", as broadly defined in the legislation.

All capital cases are tried by the Supreme Court, which sits in Windhoek, the capital, by a single judge sitting with two assessors. The assessors are usually trained lawyers, and have an equal vote with the judge on questions of fact, such as the existence of extenuating circumstances, but defer to the judge on points of law. Defendants accused of committing capital offences are assisted by legal counsel, who may be appointed by the court if the defendant cannot afford to pay for it.

Those convicted and sentenced to death in Windhoek may apply to the trial judge for the right to appeal to a higher court. If this is refused, the convicted person can either appeal to a full bench of the Supreme Court in Windhoek, or petition the Chief Justice in Bloemfontein in South Africa. Appeals are heard by the South African Appeal Court in Bloemfontein. If a death sentence is confirmed on appeal, the condemned person may petition the State President of South Africa for clemency.

The death penalty may not be imposed on a woman convicted of murdering her newly-born child, nor on anyone aged under 18 at the time of the offence; a pregnant woman may not be executed. Execution is by hanging.

Virtually all death sentences in Namibia appear to have been imposed for murder, including in cases for which the court has decided that there were extenuating circumstances. In April 1988, for example, Gert Eiman was sentenced to death for murder although the court had acknowledged that psychiatric evidence given at the trial constituted extenuating circumstances. Gert Eiman was, however, given leave to appeal.

Thirty-one people were sentenced to death between August 1977 and May 1988, of whom 14 were executed and 12 reprieved. Ten people were sentenced to death between 1985 and 1987: four in 1985, three in 1986 and three in 1987. Four others were sentenced to death between January and May 1988. The majority of those sentenced were black Namibians. Twelve of the 14 people executed between 1977 and mid-1988 were black, as were all of the 12 who had their death sentences commuted. Five cases were pending at the time of going to press.

A number of defendants have alleged that they were tortured or ill-treated in police custody to make them confess. In May 1988, for example, farm labourer Sagarias Ariseb was hanged for the murder of the manager of the farm where he worked. At his trial he claimed to have been whipped and given electric shocks by police to make him confess to the killing; this claim was rejected by the Supreme Court.

One person has been sentenced to death for a politically motivated offence in recent years, but the sentence was later commuted on appeal to 17 years' imprisonment. Markus Kateka was one of two men tried in 1980 on charges of assisting South West Africa People's Organization (SWAPO) guerrillas who had attacked the farm where they were working. Although there had been no loss of life, a death sentence was imposed on Markus Kateka. The presiding judge is reported to have said that "the punishment must…serve to draw farmworkers' attention to their particular duties…not to collaborate with terrorists…" The South African Appeal Court reduced the sentence to imprisonment in July 1981.

In 1984 Jonas Paulus, a black member of the police counter-insurgency unit *Koevoet* (Crowbar), which has been widely accused of human rights violations, was convicted of murder and sentenced to death. He was hanged in 1985.

In certain cases the South African State President has intervened to prevent the prosecution of security force personnel accused of capital offences. Using his powers under the South African Defence Act, President P. W. Botha ordered the termination in June 1986 of the trial of four white Defence Force members accused of murdering Franz Uapota, a black civilian who had allegedly been kicked, struck with rifle butts and beaten to death in November 1985. In March 1988 the President again intervened to prevent the prosecution of six other Defence Force members, including two white colonels, accused of murdering former political prisoner Immanuel Shifidi, stabbed to death during a SWAPO rally in 1986. In both cases the President said that the SADF action had been "in good faith in the combating of terrorism".

Nauru

Status: Abolitionist in practice

Executions 1985 - mid-88: None

Other factors: None

Method of execution: Not known

According to official figures no executions have been carried out since Nauru gained independence from Australia in 1968. However, the death penalty is mandatory for murder under the Criminal Code Act, 1899 of the Australian state of Queensland, which remains in force in Nauru, even though it was later repealed in Queensland. It is not known if any prisoners have ever been sentenced to death in Nauru.

Nepal

Status: Retentionist

Executions 1985 - mid-88: None

Other factors: Special courts; retroactive use of law

Methods of execution: Hanging; shooting

No executions have taken place in Nepal since 1979. The death penalty for murder was abolished in 1946 under the legal code, but reintroduced in October 1985 for murder in certain circumstances, including during hijacks or kidnappings, by using toxic substances, or when "subjecting any person to prolonged torture . . . or recklessly using weapons". Two other laws introduced that year also provide for the death penalty. Following a number of bomb explosions outside the National Assembly building and elsewhere in June 1985 in which several people were killed, the Destructive Crimes (Special Control and Punishment) Act, passed in August for an initial three-year period, made the death penalty applicable to anyone convicted of causing death by using explosives or weapons in a public place "with the motive of harming or disturbing the security, tranquillity or order" of the country. The Nepal Special Services Act, 1985, which established a Nepali intelligence service, provides for the death penalty for employees breaking conditions of employment – for example, misusing their position or divulging secret information – "depending on the extent of ... guilt".

The death penalty is also available under the Treason (Crime and Punishment) Act of 1961 for a number of offences against the state and Royal Family. The death penalty may be imposed on anyone who assaults or, by use of force, obstructs the movements of the King or other members of the Royal Family. Attempting to overthrow the government by armed force is also punishable by death. The law gives the government discretionary powers to decide which court should hear cases involving these capital offences. On the rare occasions when such trials have taken place (none during the last decade), they have been held before special courts, sometimes in closed session. Appeal against the court's decision may be made to the Supreme Court. The 1959 Army Act also provides for the death penalty.

Only three executions are known to have taken place since 1946, one by hanging in 1962 and two by shooting in 1979, all following trials under the Treason (Crime and Punishment) Act.

In 1987, four people held responsible for the bombings which occurred two years earlier were sentenced to death under the Destructive Crimes (Special Control and Punishment) Act. The law was applied retroactively since it came into effect two months after the bombings. All four were convicted *in absentia*. The trial took place before a special court and was held in closed session. Under the Act, procedures for the investigation of offences substantially reduced legal safeguards for prisoners. Suspects may be kept in police custody for 90 days before being brought to court, and for a further 90 days with court permission.

To date no death sentences have been imposed under the 1985 amendments to the legal code.

The Nepal Bar Association has been outspoken in its criticism of the reintroduction of the death penalty for murder, and has issued a press statement listing seven reasons why the death penalty for murder should not be restored. These include the irrevocable and cruel nature of the punishment, and the lack of any figures or studies undertaken in Nepal that indicate that the death penalty has an actual deterrent effect. Lawyers in Nepal also criticized the passing of death sentences on those convicted in the 1985 bombings trial, and drew particular attention to the retroactive application of the law.

Under the Constitution of Nepal, the King is empowered to commute death sentences or grant pardon.

Netherlands

Status: Abolitionist

Executions 1985 - mid-88: None

Other factors: Not applicable

Method of execution: Not applicable

On 11 April 1982 the Dutch Parliament adopted by a large majority a constitutional provision which abolished the death penalty for all offences. On 17 February 1983 the new Constitution of the Kingdom of the Netherlands came into effect. Article 114 states, "The death penalty may not be imposed."

The death penalty was abolished for common criminal offences under a statute of 1870 but it was retained under the Military Penal Code for certain wartime offences. In the Netherlands Antilles and Aruba the death penalty was not abolished for common criminal offences until the introduction of Law No. 156 of 28 November 1957. It was retained as an optional punishment under the Penal Code of the Netherlands Antilles and Aruba for collaboration with a foreign power leading to the outbreak of hostilities or war and for serious wartime offences.

The last execution for a peacetime offence was in October 1860. The last executions under military jurisdiction were in 1945.

During World War II the Dutch Government in exile in London issued a special royal decree on war crimes, the *Buitengewoon Besluit Oorlogsmisdrijven* of 22 December 1943. This decree provided for the death penalty for certain war crimes committed during the German occupation; its provisions were incorporated into a statute on war crimes in July 1952. After the war, 39 people were executed under the provisions of the decree (a fortieth prisoner committed suicide before the execution could be carried out). The last execution took place in 1952.

Under the new Constitution of 1983, laws contradicting its provisions will be maintained until they can be changed by parliament. A bill abolishing the death penalty, insofar as it is still provided for under Dutch military law and legislation governing wartime offences, has been before parliament since 1981.

New Zealand

Status: Abolitionist for all but exceptional crimes

Executions 1985 - mid-88: None

Other factors: None

Method of execution: Hanging

The death penalty for murder was abolished in 1961 under the Crimes Act. Since then the only crime for which civilians may receive the death penalty is treason. During the 20th century no civilian has ever been convicted of treason. A justice ministry committee of inquiry into violence in 1987 concluded that "capital punishment is without justification. It is ineffective as a deterrent and morally repugnant". A Crimes Amendment Bill which would abolish the death penalty for all offences was under discussion in the government's 1988 legislative program.

Military personnel may be sentenced to death under the Armed Forces Discipline Act of 1971 for aiding the enemy or engaging in conduct likely to imperil the success of any operation against the enemy (Clause 23); communicating or giving intelligence to the enemy (Clause 24); spying (Clause 26); and mutiny

(Clause 32). No-one in the armed forces has been sentenced to death or executed in peacetime.

The last executions of soldiers were carried out during World War I. The last civilian executed in New Zealand was hanged in Mount Eden prison, Auckland, in 1957.

Nicaragua

Status: Abolitionist

Executions 1985 - mid-88: None

Other factors: Not applicable

Method of execution: Not applicable

The death penalty was abolished on 21 August 1979 when the Statute on Rights and Guarantees of Nicaraguan Citizens was promulgated. Article 5 stated, "The right to life is inviolable and inherent in the human person. In Nicaragua there is no death penalty."

The previous Constitution of 1974, which was abrogated immediately after the fall of the government of Anastasio Somoza Debayle in July 1979, retained the death penalty for serious military and criminal offences, although there are no records of it having been imposed.

On 25 September 1979 Nicaragua ratified the American Convention on Human Rights which states that "the death penalty shall not be re-established in states that have abolished it". In 1985 the Nicaraguan Government informed the UN Secretary-General that its decision to abolish the death penalty had been based on adherence to international human rights instruments upholding the right to life.

In the new Constitution, which was widely discussed at all levels of society before it came into force in January 1987, abolition was affirmed in the same terms as in the August 1979 decree.

The last judicial executions took place in Managua in August 1930. Three men were sentenced to death and executed for "atrocious murder".

Niger

Status: Abolitionist in practice

Executions 1985 - mid-88: None

Other factors: Special courts with deficient trial standards; secret trials; no right of appeal against sentences imposed by special courts

Method of execution: Shooting by firing-squad

The death penalty is provided for in law but no executions are known to have been carried out since 1976.

Under the Penal Code of 1961, offences which carry the death penalty are treason and other crimes against the state; premeditated murder; torture and other crimes against the person; and aggravated theft with violence. Although the Supreme Court was suspended following a coup in April 1974, the ordinary courts have continued functioning. There is a right of appeal from the criminal courts to both the Court of Appeal and to the State Court, a court of cassation established in August 1974. The head of state has the power to grant clemency.

The April 1974 coup brought a military government to power which established special courts to try treason cases. A State Security Court set up in November 1974 was convened as a court-martial in April 1976 to try more than 40 people suspected of involvement in a coup attempt in March 1976. The trial was held in secret under summary procedures. There was no right of judicial appeal although death sentences had to be confirmed by the head of state. Nine people were sentenced to death, two *in absentia*, and the seven in custody were executed by firing-squad on 21 April 1976.

Twelve people were sentenced to death in July 1985 by a special military court following an alleged attack on government buildings in May. They are believed to have been tried in secret under summary procedures and with no right of appeal. In October 1985 the head of state ordered a stay of execution, and in November 1987, seven of the death sentences were commuted to life imprisonment by a new head of state. It was not clear what had happened to the other five prisoners, although unconfirmed reports suggested that they had died in detention.

The Special Court of Justice was created in September 1985 to try offences against state property. It may impose the death penalty for offences involving over 200 million CFA francs (US$ 720,000). It is not clear whether there is any right of appeal. No death sentences are known to have been imposed by this court.

Two men were sentenced to death between 1979 and 1983, but are not known to have been executed. Details of the convictions were not made available. A former gendarme, sentenced to death for murder in April 1986, benefited when the new head of state announced in December 1987 that he was commuting all death sentences. It is not known whether any other prisoners benefited from this measure.

Nigeria

Status: Retentionist

Executions 1985 - mid-88: 439+; armed robbery

Other factors: Special courts with deficient trial standards; no right of appeal against sentences imposed by the Special Military Tribunal or Robbery and Firearms Tribunals; public executions; retroactive use

Methods of execution: Shooting by firing-squad; hanging

There were relatively few executions under a civilian government in the early 1980s, but in 1984, after a military government had taken power, 355 death sentences were carried out. In 1985 there were 301 executions. After another government change in August 1985, the number of executions is believed to have declined. Amnesty International knows of at least 64 in 1986, 45 in 1987 and 29 in the first five months of 1988, but the real figures are undoubtedly higher.

Most executions are of people convicted of armed robbery by special courts, not under the ordinary criminal law. Although individual government officials are known to be personally opposed to the death penalty and to believe that it leads to more violence from armed robbers, there appears to be widespread support for summary trials and public executions, not just in an attempt to deter crime but also to punish the wrongdoers.

Nigeria is a federation of 21 states, each with its own government, laws and judiciary. Under the ordinary criminal law applicable throughout the federation, offences punishable by death include treason, murder and certain other offences against the state or resulting in loss of life. Such cases may be tried by the High Court in each state. Those convicted may appeal to the Court of Appeal and then to the Supreme Court both of them federal courts. The death penalty may not be passed on children aged under 17 nor on pregnant women. The relevant State Military Governor may grant clemency on the advice of the State Advisory Committee on the Prerogative of Mercy.

Although hangings continue to take place within prisons they are not officially reported. Relatively few of the death sentences imposed in the High Courts under the ordinary criminal law are believed to have been carried out in recent years, apparently because facilities for carrying out hangings are not readily available. However, Nasiru Bello, sentenced to death in the High Court for armed robbery, was executed in 1981 before his appeal could be heard by the Court of Appeal. In 1986 the Supreme Court held that his constitutional right to an appeal had been infringed. In January 1987 a meeting of state attorney-generals agreed to recommend that prisoners sentenced to hang by the High Court should be executed by firing-squad, out of public view.

Since 1966 various military governments have introduced the death penalty for a range of other crimes, in particular for armed robbery and economic offences, and have set up special courts, at both state and federal level, to try these offences under summary procedures. The presiding judges have been armed forces officers or serving or retired High Court judges, usually assisted by other members who are not required to have any legal training. Defendants have usually had no right of appeal to a higher court and their sentences have been subject to review only by the head of state – or, in the case of Robbery and Firearms Tribunals, the relevant State Military Governor – acting on the advice of Advisory Committees on the Prerogative of Mercy. Trials before these courts could not be considered fair by international standards.

In 1979, a 1974 decree giving special courts power to hand down death penalties for certain kidnapping and lynching offences was repealed, and jurisdiction in armed robbery cases was restored to the High Court. The civilian government, which took office in September, announced that all death sentences for armed robbery which had not been confirmed by September 1979 would not be carried out, and it ended public executions. Relatively few executions took place during the period of civilian government from 1979 to 1983: for example, eight in 1980, 14 in 1981.

At the end of 1983, a military government took power under Major-General Muhammadu Buhari. Under the Robbery and Firearms Decree No. 5 of 1984, it re-established special courts in every state with the power to impose a mandatory death penalty for armed robbery. In 1986 the Armed Forces Ruling Council (AFRC) decreed that each stage of the prosecution of an armed robbery case was to be completed within seven days. In some cases, the review, confirmation and execution of sentences have been so swift as to cast doubt on the thoroughness of review.

The Supreme Military Council issued further decrees in 1984 which increased the number of capital offences considerably, but they were amended after another change of government in 1985. The Special Tribunal (Miscellaneous Offences) Decree and the Counterfeit Currency Decree established special courts with the power to impose the death penalty for 17 offences previously punishable by imprisonment, including illegal dealing in petroleum products, drugs or counterfeit currency. In April 1985 three people were executed following conviction under the Miscellaneous Offences Decree for drugs offences; in at least one of these cases the offence had been committed before the decree was introduced. In 1985 the AFRC, led by Major-General Ibrahim Babangida, came to power. It set up a special appeals court which commuted seven outstanding death sentences imposed by the Miscellaneous Offences Tribunal, and the death penalty was replaced by life imprisonment as the most severe punishment for those convicted under these decrees.

The AFRC has, on many occasions, publicly proclaimed its commitment to human rights. However, 10 armed forces officers were executed in March 1986 following a trial which lacked procedural safeguards. They were sentenced to death by a special military court established under the Treason and Other Offences Decree, No. 1 of 1986. They were charged with complicity in a plot to overthrow the government in December 1985. The decree allowed no judicial appeal to a higher court, only a plea for clemency to a member of the government – the Chairman of the Joint Chiefs of Staff – and then to the AFRC, the supreme executive body.

Most of those executed in recent years have been convicted by Robbery and Firearms Tribunals and executed in public by firing-squad. In some states, executions are attended by thousands of people, including children. In July 1986 it was reported that the Military Governor of Niger State had ordered that people convicted of armed robbery should be executed slowly, by being wounded so that their deaths took a long time. In response to protests about this particularly cruel method of execution, a state official said that the aim had been to cause suffering to the condemned men and to deter other criminals, and that two people had been executed by firing-squad in this way.

Most of those sentenced to death by Robbery and Firearms Tribunals have been men. In January 1988 it was reported that a woman convicted of armed robbery was not hanged because the gallows in the prison at Jos were defective. It appeared that the Robbery and Firearms Tribunal which convicted her had specifically ruled that as a woman, she should not be executed by firing-squad in public, but should be hanged in a prison, out of public view.

The large number of prisoners under sentence of death, and prison overcrowding in general, have been cited as reasons for carrying out executions on some occasions. In November 1984, 55 prisoners in Anambra State were reportedly executed to reduce prison overcrowding. At least 70 prisoners under sentence of death were involved in rioting in Benin City Prison in May 1987. The disturbances apparently started after an unsuccessful attempt to prevent the hanging of two condemned men and resulted in the deaths of 24 prisoners. Further trouble at the prison in January 1988 was followed by the public execution of 12 prisoners; officials reportedly said that the executions were carried out to help reduce overcrowding, one of the causes of unrest inside the prison.

Norway

Status: Abolitionist

Executions 1985 - mid-88: None

Other factors: Not applicable

Method of execution: Not applicable

The death penalty was abolished for premeditated homicide and other ordinary offences under the Civil Penal Code of 22 May 1902, which came into force on 1 January 1905. It was retained in the Military Penal Code of 22 May 1902 until 1979 when the death penalty was abolished for all offences.

In its proposal to parliament to abolish the death penalty for all offences, the government stated that it is an inhumane, punitive measure, that the government was taking a principled stand against the death penalty for humanitarian reasons, and that abolition would be a contribution to international work for the worldwide abolition of this kind of punishment. Eighty-five members of parliament voted in favour of abolition, and 49 voted against it.

After World War II, 37 people convicted of treason and other serious war crimes connected with the German occupation were executed – the last on 29 August 1948. The last execution for an ordinary criminal offence was carried out in 1876 by beheading.

Oman

Status: Retentionist

Executions 1985 - mid-88: Not known

Other factors: Not known

Method of execution: Not known

The death penalty is retained in Oman. The legal system is based on Islamic law (*Shari'a*), but it is not known to Amnesty International for what offences the death penalty may be imposed, or whether there have been any death sentences or executions in recent years.

Pakistan

Status: Retentionist

Executions 1985 - mid-88: 115+; murder

Other factors: Public hanging; special courts with curtailed procedures; no right of appeal against sentences imposed by special military courts; children executed

Methods of execution: Hanging; stoning

Pakistan has one of the highest "death row" prison populations in the world. The official figure in December 1984 was 2,105. Unofficial reports put the figure at 1,467 for prisoners held in October 1987 in Punjab Province alone, where half the country's population lives. During 1987 Amnesty International recorded 71 death sentences. The true number, however, was believed to be significantly higher. The number of executions is not known.

The death penalty has been provided for in law since the country's creation in 1947. The latest period of martial law (1977-1985) was marked by a considerably higher number of executions than previously. At least 41 prisoners were executed between mid-1985 and mid-1986 in Punjab Province. Two men were publicly hanged in Punjab during January 1988, the first public executions for about 10 years. Both prisoners were hanged in front of thousands of people. Two more public executions before large crowds took place in Punjab in February 1988.

The death penalty is most regularly imposed for murder. The death sentence is mandatory only when murder is committed by a prisoner already serving a life sentence. Other offences punishable by death include kidnapping a child under the age of 10, abetting mutiny, dacoity (gang robbery), hijacking, and defiling the name of the Prophet Mohammad.

In addition to ordinary criminal courts and special military courts during martial law, the death penalty can also be imposed by the Federal *Shari'a* Court which follows the Islamic Code of Justice and by Special Courts for Speedy Trials that pass sentences in a matter of days.

In 1978 *Shari'a* benches were established in the High Courts and the Supreme Court to examine whether any laws passed were incompatible with Islam. Further amendments to the Constitution in 1979 and 1980 established the Federal *Shari'a* Court as a separate judicial institution parallel to the civil court system. The Federal *Shari'a* Court can impose death sentences for sexual offences and murder in the course of robbery and may specify the method of execution in accordance with Islamic law. Stoning to death is one such method.

In the face of widespread concern about stoning, including opposition voiced by some Islamic scholars, the Federal *Shari'a* Court ruled in 1981 that the penalty was "repugnant to the injunctions of Islam". The government appealed against this ruling before the *Shari'a* Bench of the Supreme Court, but before a hearing could be arranged further amendments to the Constitution gave the Federal *Shari'a* Court the power to review its own decisions. The court was reconstituted after the government appointed a new Chief Justice. It overturned its earlier judgment and declared stoning to death lawful.

Amnesty International does not know if any people have been executed by stoning. In November 1987 Shahida Parveen and Mohammad Sarwar were sentenced by the Federal *Shari'a* Court to be stoned to death on charges of illegal marriage, a judgment which was criticized as inhuman by women's organizations in the country, the Executive Committee of the Pakistan Medical Association and others.

Ever since martial law was imposed, death sentences passed by civilian courts have followed an established judicial procedure. All death sentences imposed by lower courts require confirmation by a High Court, regardless of whether the prisoner appeals. If a sentence is confirmed by a High Court, the prisoner may appeal to the Supreme Court, but only within a seven-day period as opposed to the 30 days allowed in other criminal cases. The Supreme Court may decide not to hear the case. There is a large backlog of appeals pending and the majority of prisoners under sentence of death are awaiting appeals, a process which often takes several years.

In February 1979 the Supreme Court upheld by four to three the death sentence imposed on former Prime Minister Zulfikar Ali Bhutto, whose government was overthrown by a military coup in 1977. Some members of the court expressed serious doubts about his conviction on charges of conspiracy to murder a political opponent and argued that he should be acquitted. Zulfikar Ali Bhutto was executed in April 1979, despite international appeals. It was the first execution known to have taken place in Pakistan following a split Supreme Court decision.

Under the Criminal Procedure Code, all death sentences may be commuted at any stage by the provincial or federal governments. The Constitution also empowers the President to grant clemency.

Although some prisoners charged with capital offences continue to be tried by ordinary courts, many are now tried by special courts using procedures which depart from the customary legal safeguards contained in the Code of Criminal Procedure. These courts were established under the Special Courts for Speedy Trials Ordinance, for a trial period of one year, beginning in October 1987. Cases deemed "gruesome, brutal and sensational" or which have "led to public outrage" may be tried by a special court set up by the provincial government. The provincial government also has the authority to transfer to a special court any cases pending before an ordinary court, in the "public interest".

There are some procedural irregularities; for example, the court may not adjourn for more than two days, a fact that can adversely affect the presentation of witnesses before the court. The period in which an appeal may be filed to a

High Court is reduced to only seven days. During the first six months of their establishment in October 1987, special courts were reported to have sentenced over 50 people to death, in some cases after trials lasting only two to three days.

Special courts have also been established to try capital offences under the Suppression of Terrorist Activities (Special Courts) Act, 1975, although these are less frequently used. This law also departs from customary legal safeguards in that the accused may be presumed guilty until proved innocent.

Since martial law was lifted in December 1985, special military courts have ceased to function. However, dozens of prisoners convicted by these courts remain under sentence of death. Trials before special military courts were unfair due to their lack of independence from the executive and their acceptance of evidence given in statements extracted under duress. They also gave no right of judicial appeal as trial proceedings were subject to review only by the martial law authorities. In at least two cases, sentences of imprisonment were increased to the death penalty on the instructions of the martial law authorities during the review process. Three prisoners executed following trials by military courts were reported to be aged under 18 at the the time of their offences.

It was announced in February 1988 that the government would reconsider the cases of some prisoners convicted by special military courts. At that time, the Supreme Court was also hearing the government's appeal against a decision by the Lahore and Sind High Courts to hear petitions challenging verdicts of the special military courts.

▶ In August 1988 Shahida Parveen and Mohammad Sarwar were acquitted on the grounds that there was neither a confession from the accused nor an eyewitness to the crime.

On 6 October 1988 Amnesty International was officially informed that President Ishaq Khan had commuted the death sentences of six prisoners.

After being sworn in on 2 December 1988, Benazir Bhutto, Prime Minister of Pakistan, requested that the Acting President Ghulam Ishaq Khan commute all death sentences in Pakistan. He immediately stayed all executions and began to commute over 2,000 death sentences.

Panama

Status: Abolitionist

Executions 1985 - mid-88: None

Other factors: Not applicable

Method of execution: Not applicable

Panama has never used the death penalty. The 1972 Constitution (as amended in 1978 and 1983) states that there is no death penalty, "*No hay pena de muerte…*" (Article 30).

Panama came into existence in 1903, when it separated from Colombia, and it then adopted much of Colombia's legislation. It is not clear precisely when Panama definitively abolished the death penalty, but the Penal Code of 1922 stipulated that the death penalty was abolished for all offences.

The last known execution on Panamanian territory took place in 1903 when a Liberal general was executed by firing-squad. He had been convicted under military jurisdiction on unsubstantiated charges of mass murder, apparently to remove him as a popular indigenous leader. However, as the execution took place before Panama became an independent nation, it was carried out under Colombian jurisdiction. It was also illegal under the "Wisconsin Agreement" of 1902 between the USA and Colombia, which had declared an amnesty for the Liberals, who had lost a debilitating civil war with the Conservatives in the years preceding Panama's independence.

Papua New Guinea

Status: Abolitionist for all but exceptional crimes

Executions 1985 - mid-88: None

Other factors: None

Method of execution: Hanging

The death penalty has been abolished for ordinary crimes since Papua New Guinea became independent in 1975. The Criminal Code Act of 1974, adopted shortly before independence, provides for the death penalty for treason and attempted piracy with personal violence, but it has never been imposed for these offences. The last execution by hanging was carried out in 1950.

In 1980 a bill to restore the death penalty as a discretionary punishment for wilful murder was defeated in Parliament. A move in parliament in 1985 to introduce the death penalty for gang-rape and murder was unsuccessful.

Paraguay

Status: Abolitionist in practice

Executions 1985 - mid-88: None

Other factors: None

Method of execution: Shooting by firing-squad

Article 65 of the National Constitution (1967) states that the death penalty will not be applied, under any circumstances, for political reasons. Under the Penal Code of 1914 the death penalty is provided for certain categories of homicide: parricide, homicide for a reward or contract, and homicide in the course of stealing (Article 62). The death penalty may also be applied for a wide range of crimes when they result in death, including arson; acts endangering public safety; sabotage; unjustified manufacture, handling and possession of explosives; and acts committed by a Paraguayan national to induce or help a foreign power to undertake hostilities against Paraguay when these acts lead to a declaration of war. The death penalty may not be imposed on those aged under 22.

The last officially recorded executions were carried out in 1928. Gaston Gadin was sentenced to death for the murder of his parents with Cipriano León, his paid accomplice. The two men were executed by firing-squad.

Death sentences imposed by courts of first instance and upheld by the Appeals Court must be confirmed by the Supreme Court of Justice. According to Article 112 of the Penal Code, only the President of the Republic can commute a death sentence upheld by the Supreme Court; commutations are always to 30 years' imprisonment and conditional release without completion of three quarters of this sentence is prohibited.

The Military Penal Code of 1980 provides for the death penalty for any military personnel guilty of treason or desertion in time of war. Sentence may be commuted by the Executive Power to 25 years' imprisonment.

Since the last judicial executions in 1928, about 14 death sentences have been imposed but none have been carried out. In 1985 the public prosecutor recommended that the death sentence be imposed on Remigio Gimenez, accused of several offences committed between 1958 and 1960, including murder and participation in guerrilla activities. The judge, however, handed down a sentence of 30 years' imprisonment. In 1987 José Gil Portillo and Leonardo Lezcano were found guilty of killing a minor in order to rob him. The trial judge sentenced them to death but this was commuted to 30 years' imprisonment on appeal.

Peru

Status: Abolitionist for all but exceptional crimes

Executions 1985 - mid-88: None

Other factors: None

Method of execution: Shooting by firing-squad

The death penalty was first abolished in Peru in the National Constitution of 1856. Abolition was, however, short-lived and the death penalty was reintroduced in the constitutional reform of 1860 for aggravated homicide. It was extended in the 1920 Constitution to include treason. The 1924 Penal Code, however, substituted life imprisonment for crimes previously punishable by death and the country became abolitionist once again. However, in 1949 the death penalty was again incorporated into the Penal Code by decree law, and successive military governments in power between 1968 and 1980 extended the range of capital offences to include terrorist acts.

Under the new Constitution which was approved in 1979 and which came into force in

July 1980, the death penalty was abolished for peacetime offences. Article 235 states, "There is no death penalty except for treason in times of external war." A new military penal code was introduced in July 1980 retaining the death penalty in times of war as punishment for a series of crimes against the state committed by military personnel.

Since the restoration of civilian government in 1980, there have been several proposals by both the executive branch and members of Congress to modify the Constitution to provide for the death penalty for acts of terrorism in peacetime. These proposals have generally coincided with a significant upsurge in the violent activities of armed opposition groups. None of these proposals has been put to a vote in the Congress.

The last execution took place in January 1979 when a non-commissioned officer in the Peruvian air force was convicted of selling military secrets to the Chilean Government.

Philippines

Status: Abolitionist

Executions 1985 - mid-88: None

Other factors: Not applicable

Method of execution: Not applicable

The death penalty was abolished in the 1987 Constitution of the Philippines. The Bill of Rights states, "Excessive fines shall not be imposed, nor cruel, degrading or inhuman punishment inflicted. Neither shall the death penalty be imposed, unless, for compelling reasons involving heinous crimes, the Congress hereafter provides for it. Any death penalty already imposed shall be reduced to *reclusion perpetua* [life imprisonment]" (Article III, Section 9). The 1987 Constitution, which replaced the 1973 Constitution of President Ferdinand Marcos, was drafted by a Constitutional Commission in 1986 and ratified by an overwhelming majority of voters in a national referendum in February 1987.

No executions were carried out in the decade before the death penalty was abolished, the last execution, by electrocution, having been in 1976. Nevertheless, death sentences continued to be handed down by the courts until late 1986. Over 500 prisoners, most of whom had been sentenced to death by military tribunals during the martial law period (1972-1981), were reported to be still under sentence of death in 1987 when President Corazon Aquino announced in April that she would commute all these death sentences to life imprisonment. In January 1988, however, according to the records of the Department of Justice, over 360 prisoners were still under sentence of death, and an official statement said that an act of Congress was needed to put the commutations into effect.

In August 1987 General Fidel Ramos, then Chief of Staff of the Armed Forces, called publicly for the reintroduction of the death penalty for rebellion, murder and drug-trafficking. The military also pressed for its reinstatement in a series of recommendations submitted to the President and Congress for combating the insurgency of the New People's Army, an armed opposition group. Meanwhile, when the newly elected Congress convened in mid-1987, a bill was introduced to reinstate the death penalty for 12 "heinous crimes", including murder, rebellion and the import or sale of prohibited drugs. The bill cited a recent coup attempt as an example of "the alarming deterioration of the peace and order condition throughout the country" and argued for the death penalty both as an "effective deterrent against heinous crimes" and "as a matter of simple retributive justice". In an amendment early the following year (1988), rebellion was removed from the list, but four new offences were added.

In October 1987 Amnesty International testified before a Congressional joint committee that the death penalty was a violation of human rights, and presented evidence from Asia and the Pacific to show that it was often unfairly imposed. Although some representatives questioned whether the death penalty had any deterrent effect, the bill passed all three readings in the House of Representatives by large majorities.

Several prisoners under sentence of death for many years had their convictions overturned following reviews of their sentences by the Supreme Court after President Aquino came to power. Alberto Opida and Virgilio Marcelo, for example, had been under sentence of death for murder since 1976, but their convictions were overturned by the Supreme Court in June 1986 when it ruled that the original trial judge had been prejudiced against the defendants.

In several case reviews, the Supreme Court suggested that the prisoners might have been convicted of crimes they did not commit. The following are some cases in point. Manuel Navoa was convicted of arson with multiple homicide and sentenced to death in 1979. He was acquitted in August 1986 when the Supreme Court decided that his confession had been extracted under duress (he claimed it had been extracted at gunpoint and after beatings), and accepted the testimony of his university teachers that he had been in class at the time of the crime. Similarly, in August 1986 the Supreme Court reversed a conviction of murder and a death sentence imposed in 1983 on Florencio Poyos on the grounds that his confession was invalid. The court suggested that two other people who had fled from the scene of the crime and who were still at large were probably guilty of the murder. Zosimo Crisologo, a deaf-mute who was arrested in 1977 and sentenced to death for robbery with homicide, was acquitted in June 1987 when the Supreme Court concluded that there was insufficient evidence against him and that in the absence of a sign-language interpreter he had not understood the proceedings at his original trial.

In July 1987 the Supreme Court ordered the release of Senen Ola, who had been imprisoned since 1970 and sentenced to death for "frustrated robbery with homicide", declaring that the evidence was insufficient for conviction and implicated someone else as the more likely murderer.

Poland

Status: Retentionist

Executions 1985 - mid-88: 11+; murder

Other factors: None

Methods of execution: Hanging; shooting by firing-squad

The Penal Code of 1889 abolished the death penalty after lengthy parliamentary discussion which had begun early in the 19th century.

After the establishment of an independent Polish Republic in 1918, the death penalty was reintroduced in 1926 by Decree No. 2008. In 1930 the application of the death penalty was extended by decree to cover serious crimes against the state.

The Penal Code of 1932, which remained in effect until 1970, provided for the death penalty for several offences. A decree of August 1944, made public in 1946, introduced the death penalty for grave atrocities during World War II; collaboration with the German occupation forces; and causing loss of life or serious damage to the Polish State. A decree of January 1948 introduced the death penalty for political offences and certain crimes against property committed in peacetime.

The current Penal Code of 1969 states that the death penalty is "exceptionally provided for the most serious crimes" (Article 38). Offences carrying an optional death sentence include murder and crimes against the state such as aggravated treason; espionage; aggravated economic sabotage; and disturbing the national economy. The Penal Code specifies one military crime punishable by an optional death sentence: failing to carry out an order during combat. A law of 21 November 1967 concerning the obligation to defend the Polish People's Republic also provides for an optional death sentence for certain crimes during conditions of immediate serious threat to state security, mobilization or war. The death penalty is not imposed on those under 18 at the time of the offence nor on pregnant women.

The defendant has the right of appeal to the Supreme Court. In the Supreme Court the defendant is not present and it is possible for a person sentenced to 25 years' imprisonment to be subsequently sentenced to death *in absentia* by the Supreme Court following a prosecutor's appeal. This happened in May 1984 to Zdzislaw Czeslaw Kubiak. After a death sentence has been upheld by the Supreme Court, the defendant has the right to petition for clemency. This may be granted by the State Council (chaired by the head of state) which may commute the death sentence to 25 years' imprisonment. Execution is by hanging; military personnel, however, are shot by firing-squad.

In practice, the death penalty is imposed almost exclusively for murder. According to reports in the official press in 1985 there were seven executions carried out and eight death sentences imposed. In 1986 the figures were two and seven respectively. In 1987 there were two executions; one death sentence was reported in the first quarter of 1988. Every case involved the crime of murder.

Abolition, or at least a significant reduction in the number of crimes carrying the death penalty, has been repeatedly promoted in Polish legal literature. In the period when the trade union Solidarity existed legally, work was started both by the government and by Solidarity to amend the Penal Code. The so-called social draft of amendments to the Penal Code was put forward in May 1981 by a committee of legal experts headed by Wladyslaw Wolter, and sponsored by Solidarity. The draft proposed the complete abolition of the death penalty, leaving 25 years' imprisonment as the most severe penalty. The position of an official committee appointed by the government for the same purpose was never made known.

Amendments to the Penal Code since the imposition of martial law in December 1981 did not touch the articles relating to the death penalty. Public opinion polls carried out between 1964 and 1977 showed that not more than one third of the population favoured abolition and a poll in January 1988 reported 60.3 per cent of the population in favour of retention.

A congress in October 1983, representing Poland's 5,600 barristers, called for the abolition of the death penalty for all crimes and in February 1988 the Chairman of the Supreme Bar Council stated that the Bar had "no doubts" in calling for total abolition. However, on 25 February 1988 the authorities refused permission to found an association called "the Social Committee for the Abolition of the Death Penalty", reportedly on the grounds that it "constituted a threat to security, peace and public order".

Portugal

Status: Abolitionist

Executions 1985 - mid-88: None

Other factors: Not applicable

Method of execution: Not applicable

The death penalty was abolished for all offences in a new Constitution which was approved by the Constituent Assembly in 1976. The Assembly voted unanimously in favour of Article 25 of the Constitution which states, "1. Human life is inviolable. 2. In no case will there be the penalty of death."

Portugal abolished the death penalty for political offences in 1852, and for common criminal offences in 1867. In 1911 the death penalty was abolished for all offences, but it was reinstated in 1916 for military crimes committed in wartime "in a theatre of war".

The last execution for a common criminal offence was in April 1846. The last known recorded execution under military jurisdiction was carried out in May 1849. However, death sentences were imposed by military courts on a number of occasions until 1905. Although several of these sentences are known to have been commuted, it has not been possible to verify that none were actually carried out.

Qatar

Status: Abolitionist in practice*

Executions 1985 - mid-88: None

Other factors: None

Methods of execution: Hanging; shooting by firing-squad; beheading by sword

The death penalty is retained in law for a number of offences, the principal legal source of which is Islamic law *(Shari'a)*. These offences are codified principally in Qatar's Penal Code No. 14 of 1971. The Amended Provisional Constitution of 19 April 1972 contains provisions relating to the commutation of death sentences and the granting of clemency.

Offences punishable by death include the following: murder; murder in the course of other crimes; crimes against the state; and giving false information leading to the conviction and execution of an innocent person. In April 1987 a law was promulgated which introduced the death penalty for recidivist drug-trafficking (Law No. 9). No death sentences under this law have been reported. Pregnant women and anyone under the age of 18 at the time of the offence are exempted from the death penalty. If the prisoner is pregnant, the death sentence is commuted to life imprisonment.

The courts competent to pass death sentences are the criminal courts. In criminal cases, the jurisdiction of the *Shari'a* courts is restricted, although they are competent to pass sentences on Muslims committing offences specified in certain parts of the Penal Code, including premeditated murder. Death sentences passed by the criminal courts are automatically referred for review to the Court of Appeal, while those passed by *Shari'a* courts are referred to the Supreme *Shari'a* Court. Sentences upheld by these courts must be ratified by the head of state before being carried out. The accused has the right to seek pardon from the head of state, who is empowered to commute death sentences or grant pardons. Execution is by hanging, firing-squad, or beheading by sword.

According to information provided by the government to the United Nations, restriction on the use of the death penalty is present policy in Qatar. No executions have been reported in the country for over 10 years.

* Amnesty International learned of two executions carried out by beheading by sword in October 1988. These were the first known executions for over 10 years (see status).

Romania

Status: Retentionist

Executions 1985 - mid-88: 2+

Other factors: None

Method of execution: Shooting by firing-squad

After the formation of a socialist government in Romania at the end of World War II, Law No. 16, 1949, introduced the death penalty for a number of civil crimes. Previously it could only be used in wartime. Decree Nos. 469 and 318 of 1957 and 1958 considerably extended the range of crimes punishable by death. The death penalty was mandatory for a number of offences until 1968, when alternative punishments were introduced.

Although the death penalty is treated in theory as an "exceptional punishment" (Article 3 of the 1969 Penal Code), a large number of offences carry an optional death sentence. They include crimes against the state, such as treason, sabotage and espionage; economic crimes not involving loss of life such as undermining the economy; embezzlement of public property by an official if very serious consequences result; major theft of public property; murder "when committed with cruelty"; and cruel and inhuman treatment of prisoners. The Penal Code also lists seven military offences punishable by an optional death sentence.

The death penalty may not be imposed on anyone aged under 18, pregnant women or mothers of children under the age of three when the offence was committed or judgment pronounced (Article 54). In such cases the penalty is 25 years' imprisonment. Under Article 55 a death sentence is commuted to 25 years' imprisonment if it has not been carried out within two years of the date of sentencing and the defendant was present at the trial, or, if not present at the trial, within two years of the defendant's apprehension, or seven years from the date the sentence became final.

The death penalty may be imposed by regional courts or by district courts, which have local jurisdiction. An appeal against a death sentence passed by a district court may be made to the regional court; if the sentence is upheld a further appeal may be made to the Supreme Court. Appeals against death sentences imposed in the first instance by a regional court are to the Supreme Court. If a death sentence is upheld by the Supreme Court, the prisoner may petition the State Council within five days.

According to Article 424 of the Code of Penal Procedure, if a death penalty is upheld after all avenues of appeal, review and petition for clemency are exhausted, the case is to be referred back to the court that first passed the sentence and execution is to be carried out by the order of the president of that court. The State Council may grant clemency after an appeal has been submitted via the Ministry of Justice. Execution is by firing-squad.

The Romanian Government informed the United Nations Secretariat that between 1974 and 1978, 22 death sentences were imposed and 16 executions carried out, each involving crimes against the person. Amnesty International, however, learned of additional death sentences imposed during this period for offences other than those against the person: Bucharest Radio reported on 27 August 1976 that the Bucharest Territorial Military Court had sentenced Nicolae Ilies and Bogdan Jordanescu to death for treason and divulging state economic secrets, and that the sentences had been confirmed on appeal to the Supreme Court. It was later reported that these sentences had been commuted in November 1976.

In April 1979 a Romanian representative told the Human Rights Committee set up under the International Covenant on Civil and Political Rights, that during the past 15 years the death penalty had not been applied in a single case involving an offence against state property, and that its scope had been considerably reduced in new legislation being drafted. He also said that the penalty "... would be applied exclusively as an exceptional measure and as an alternative in cases of homicide, treason, espionage and aerial piracy having particularly serious consequences".

After these official statements were made, however, Amnesty International noted an apparent increase in the number of death sentences imposed. In 1983 at least 13 death sentences were passed, five for stealing large quantities of meat and another two for theft of public property with particularly serious consequences – none of these seven cases involved loss of life. In several cases, the sentences were reported to have been confirmed by the Supreme Court and petitions for clemency to have been rejected by the State Council.

In 1984 Amnesty International wrote to the Romanian authorities expressing concern at this apparent increase in the number of death sentences imposed and in the range of offences for which it was applied. To its knowledge, no death sentences have been reported in the Romanian press since then, although the organization understands that the courts have continued to impose them. On 28 March 1986 Florentin Scaletchi was reportedly sentenced to death by the Bucharest Military Court for treason and other offences, after having tried to sail to Turkey without authorization. His sentence was commuted by the Supreme Court on 1 July 1986 to 20 years' imprisonment. In an amnesty on 26 January 1988 to mark President Ceausescu's 70th birthday, all people sentenced to death had their sentences commuted to 20 years' imprisonment.

Amnesty International received an unofficial report that two people (names unknown) were executed in late 1985 in Calea Rahovei Prison in Bucharest, where all executions are reportedly carried out.

There seems to be little debate on the death penalty in Romania. However, in February 1988 President Ceausescu proposed re-examining death penalty legislation in order to restrict it to "exceptional cases involving a limited number of very serious offences against state security and Romania's sovereignty".

Rwanda

Status: Retentionist

Executions 1985 - mid-88: None

Other factors: Lack of legal representation

Method of execution: Shooting by firing-squad

The Penal Code provides for a mandatory death sentence to be imposed for a wide range of

195

offences, including premeditated murder; murder of a person's parents or children, whether or not the offence was premeditated; and incidents in which other offences, such as rape, robbery, kidnapping, sorcery or torture have been committed and in the course of which a death is caused. Other offences punishable by death include treason or revealing state secrets in time of war; attempts to overthrow the government with violent means or to kill the head of state; attacks on public officials when murder is intended; and some cases of criminal association when the same offence has been committed before.

A considerable number of death sentences are imposed by the courts, although no executions have been reported since 1982. Those sentenced to death by ordinary courts have a right of appeal and may also seek review of their cases by the Cassation Court. Those convicted by the State Security Court, which has jurisdiction over all cases of a political nature, have no general right of appeal but may appeal on points of law to the Cassation Court. Under the terms of the law it is the duty of the prosecuting authorities to submit all death sentences to the head of state for review. The results are not known to be made public. Those who commit a capital offence when aged under 18 may not be sentenced to death, and execution of pregnant women is deferred until after they have given birth.

During the 1980s executions have been reported on only one occasion. This was on 15 September 1982 when 43 prisoners under sentence of death, mostly for murder, were executed by firing-squads at prisons in Butare and Kigali. The executions occurred only two months after the head of state had announced that he was commuting the death sentences imposed by the State Security Court in 1981 on two prominent political prisoners, and were interpreted by many as a restatement of the government's willingness to use the death penalty. From 1982 onwards the number of prisoners under sentence of death increased gradually until 1986, when the total was reported by government officials to exceed 500. However, in July 1987 President Juvénal Habyarimana commuted to life imprisonment all death sentences which had already been confirmed on judicial appeal; 537 prisoners were reported to have benefited from this measure.

In June 1985 five people were sentenced to death after being found guilty of involvement in the murder of 56 political prisoners in the mid-1970s. They and seven others had been tried *in camera* by an ordinary criminal court. It is difficult to establish whether their trial was fair, and it is not known whether their appeals have been heard.

A particular characteristic of trials which result in death sentences is that virtually no one tried on capital charges is assisted by legal counsel. A similar absence of defence counsel is noted at all levels in Rwanda's court system. The absence may be due to the lack of people with legal training. However, in several cases defendants in politically sensitive cases are reported to have been refused access to legal counsel, for example at a trial before the State Security Court which resulted in two death sentences in late 1981. The effect of the lack of legal representation is that more prisoners appear to be convicted on capital charges and sentenced to death than would be the case if they were represented by trained lawyers, who would be better able to contest points of law with state prosecutors and ensure proper presentation of defence cases, including pleas of extenuating circumstances. Trained lawyers would also be able to ensure that appeals containing appropriate legal arguments were submitted to higher courts on behalf of all those sentenced to death.

St Christopher and Nevis

Status: Retentionist

Executions 1985 - mid-88: 1; murder

Other factors: Executions resumed after an unofficial 11-year moratorium

Method of execution: Hanging

Under the Offences Against the Person Act (Chapter 56) a mandatory death penalty is provided for murder. The law exempts those who were aged under 18 at the time of the crime and pregnant women.

St Christopher and Nevis is a member of the Organization of Eastern Caribbean States together with six other countries (pending Grenada rejoining). All seven share a common judicial system known as the Eastern Caribbean Supreme Court which consists of a High Court of Justice and a Court of Appeal. Final appeal is to the Judicial Committee of the Privy Council in England which will consider only cases involving constitutional matters or "matters of great public importance". The Governor General may commute a death sentence to a term of imprisonment.

The last execution, of a prisoner convicted of murder, was carried out on 11 May 1985. At the time of going to press, there were no prisoners under sentence of death. Four death sentences were imposed between 1982 and 1987 all of which were commuted to life imprisonment.

St Lucia

Status: Retentionist

Executions 1985 - mid-88: 1; murder

Other factors: Executions resumed after an unofficial 10-year moratorium

Method of execution: Hanging

Under the Criminal Code, a mandatory death penalty is provided for murder (Offences Affecting Persons, Cap. 250, Section 178), murder or attempted murder while serving a prison sentence of three years or more (Section 177), and treason. The death penalty may not be imposed on anyone aged under 18 at the time of the crime or on pregnant women.

St Lucia is a member of the Organization of Eastern Caribbean States together with six other countries (pending Grenada rejoining). All seven share a common judicial system known as the Eastern Caribbean Supreme Court which consists of a High Court of Justice and a Court of Appeal. Final appeal is to the Judicial Committee of the Privy Council in England which will, however, consider only cases involving constitutional matters or "matters of great public importance".

After a period of 10 years when no executions were carried out, two men convicted of murder were hanged in September 1982, and another in April 1986.

At the time of going to press there were no prisoners under sentence of death.

St Vincent and the Grenadines

Status: Retentionist

Executions 1985 - mid-88: 2; murder

Other factors: None

Method of execution: Hanging

Under the Penal Code a mandatory death penalty is provided for murder (Offences Against the Person and Reputation Act Part VIII) and treason. The death penalty may not be imposed on anyone who was under 18 at the time of the crime or on pregnant women.

St Vincent and the Grenadines is a member of the Organization of Eastern Caribbean States together with six other countries (pending Grenada rejoining). All seven share a common judicial system known as the Eastern Caribbean Supreme Court which consists of a High Court of Justice and a Court of Appeal. Final appeal is to the Judicial Committee of the Privy Council in England which will, however, consider only cases involving constitutional matters or "matters of great public importance".

After three executions were carried out in 1978, there were no more until March 1987 when two men convicted of murder were hanged.

In July 1985, in his Throne Speech to Parliament, the Governor General announced that the government intended to stimulate the widest possible discussion on the abolition of the death penalty. However, Amnesty International is not aware of any such discussion nor of its outcome.

The number of prisoners currently under sentence of death, if any, is not known.

San Marino (Republic of)

Status: Abolitionist

Executions 1985 - mid-88: None

Other factors: Not applicable

Method of execution: Not applicable

The death penalty was first abolished for all offences in 1848. Between 1853 and 1858 it was reintroduced for exceptional crimes. The first Penal Code of the Republic, introduced in 1865, made no provision for the death penalty. The last known execution was carried out in 1468.

São Tomé and Príncipe

Status: Abolitionist for all but exceptional crimes

Executions 1985 - mid-88: None

Other factors: No right of appeal against sentences imposed by the Special Court for Counter-Revolutionary Acts

Method of execution: Not known

Abolition of the death penalty is currently under debate in the National Assembly and a decision is expected in early 1989. Although São Tomé and Príncipe retains the death penalty, no death sentences have ever been imposed.

When São Tomé and Príncipe gained independence from Portugal in 1975, Portuguese law, which retained the death penalty for certain military crimes in time of war, was adopted as the basis of the country's legal system, and mercenarism was made punishable by death under Law 41/79 of 17 July 1979. Mercenarism was defined as the crime committed by a foreigner (or a national of São Tomé and Príncipe in the pay of a foreigner) of organizing or carrying out armed actions, acts of sabotage or any other acts endangering the country's peace and security.

The law on mercenarism was introduced shortly after a trial by the Special Court for Counter-Revolutionary Acts in March 1979, when several people were convicted of complicity in a plot to overthrow the government which involved an invasion of the country. All crimes against the security of the state, including mercenarism, fall under the jurisdiction of the Special Court for Counter-Revolutionary Acts from which there is no right of appeal. According to the Constitution the President has the power to grant pardons and to commute sentences.

Saudi Arabia

Status: Retentionist

Executions 1985 - mid-88: 140; murder; robbery with violence; drug offences; adultery

Other factors: Public executions; no clemency for *hadd* offences

Methods of execution: Beheading; stoning

There is no Penal Code or Code of Criminal Procedure in Saudi Arabia. The official law is Islamic law (*Shari'a*) with particular reference to the Hanbali school of Islamic jurisprudence. If an issue is not covered in the six classic works of Hanbali scholars, jurists are first to refer to the texts of other schools of Islamic jurisprudence and thereafter to exercise their own reasoning (*ijtihad*). To supplement Islamic law, the state also issues regulations in the form of Royal Decrees and delegated orders, codes and bye-laws.

The death penalty is provided for in law for various types of murder. It is mandatory for the following *hadd* offences (offences against divine will): certain sexual crimes, such as adultery committed by a married person; apostasy; certain acts of sabotage involving loss of life; and treason or conspiracy against the state. The death penalty is not mandatory for the *hadd* offence of robbery with violence for which it may only be applied in cases involving aggravating circumstances.

On 18 February 1987 the Council of Senior Ulema (senior religious scholars entrusted with interpreting Islamic law) issued Decision No. 138 which extended the death penalty to include those convicted of drug smuggling or receiving and distributing drugs from abroad.

The ruling was approved by the King in March, and in the ensuing 12-month period at least 10 people were executed for drug-related offences.

Use of the death penalty has continued to increase in recent years. Amnesty International recorded 74 executions between 1981 and 1984, 45 in 1985, 24 in 1986 and 54 in 1987. The organization has received reports of 17 executions having taken place in the first five months of 1988.

Most of these executions were carried out as *qisas* (retribution) punishments for various types of murder. The family or heirs of the victim may demand *qisas* in the form of the death of the culprit, or by financial settlement, or they may waive any claim to *qisas*. In a few cases, such as those of previously convicted murderers, the authorities may insist on a death sentence being carried out in the public interest.

A person convicted of murder may be held in prison for several years until the murder victim's heir reaches maturity (aged 18) and can decide whether the execution should proceed. Muhammad bin Mahdi bin 'Abd Allah Mahyab, a Yemeni national, for example, was executed in 1985 some 12 years after he was convicted of murder. In 1987, in four cases involving six offenders, executions were carried out between 18 months and 15 years after sentencing.

Cases involving offences punishable by death are tried in the General Courts of First Instance. According to the amended Regulation on the Judiciary of 5 December 1975, cases before the General Courts of First Instance are usually heard by a single judge who cross-examines the two parties and their witnesses and decides both guilt or innocence and the amount of damages. Judgments in death penalty cases, however, are passed by a three-judge panel and are automatically referred to a Court of Appeal.

A death sentence may not be imposed on anyone who, at the time of the offence, was aged under 18 or was deemed insane. If the prisoner is pregnant execution must be stayed up to a maximum of two years after childbirth. The death penalty for apostasy applies only to Muslims.

The Courts of Appeal are divided into three departments: criminal law, personal status and cases not falling into these categories. The departments are bound by their own prior reasonings and by those of the other departments. Appeals are heard by a panel of five judges.

A Court of Appeal may affirm the judgment or ask the trial judge to modify or reverse it. If the trial judge does not agree to modify or reverse the judgment and the Court of Appeal stands by its position, the Court of Appeal may annul the decision and refer the case to another trial judge whose decision in turn will be open to appeal.

Decisions of the Courts of Appeal are final except in death penalty cases when they are referred to the permanent body of the Supreme Judicial Council for review and approval. The permanent body is composed of five members of the rank of Head of Court of Appeal. Final ratification is by Royal Decree.

There can be no clemency in the case of proved *hadd* offences. However, since confessions carry great weight in *Shari'a* courts and may result in conviction in the absence of witnesses or other evidence, withdrawal of confessions at any stage of the judicial process may result in non-applicability of the *hadd* punishments. If the heirs of the victim of a murder waive their claims on the culprit, the state may rule that the offender spend between two and five years in prison.

Executions are public and are usually carried out by beheading with a sharp sword or, in the case of sexual crimes, by stoning to death (using moderate-sized stones). They are carried out in major towns and cities, often in a square in front of the Provincial Governor's Palace.

▶ On 24 August the Council of Senior Ulema issued a ruling extending the death penalty to those convicted of acts of sabotage or being corrupt on earth that undermine security, whether or not loss of life is involved.

Senegal

Status: Abolitionist in practice

Executions 1985 - mid-88: None

Other factors: No right of appeal against death sentences imposed by the State Security Court

Method of execution: Shooting by firing-squad

Although the death penalty is provided for in law there have been no executions since 1967. According to the Penal Code a number of offences are punishable by a mandatory death penalty, including premeditated murder; poisoning; acts of barbarism; and hostage-taking. Espionage and treason are also punishable by a mandatory death sentence.

Defendants sentenced to death for criminal offences by the Assize Courts have a right of appeal to the Supreme Court. Death sentences confirmed on appeal may not be carried out until a petition for presidential clemency has been rejected (Article 41 of the Constitution). However, people sentenced to death by the State Security Court on charges against the security of the state have no right of appeal to a higher court. The State Security Court was created on 4 December 1973 to replace the Special Court set up in 1961 to try political offences.

The method of execution is by firing-squad, out of public view. Execution of a pregnant woman must be deferred until after her confinement.

Since independence in 1960 only two death sentences have been carried out. Abdou Faye was executed after being found guilty by the Special Court in Dakar of murdering (in February 1967) a member of the National Assembly. Moustapha Lô was sentenced to death by the same court on 15 June 1967 and later executed. He was convicted of attempting to assassinate the then head of state Leopold Sedar Senghor, who in both cases rejected the condemned prisoners' petitions for clemency. In July 1978 Jacques Gomn was sentenced to death by the Assize Court after being found guilty of murder. However, his sentence was reduced to life imprisonment after he was retried by the same court in 1980.

On several occasions the Assize Courts and the State Security Court have convicted people of capital crimes but have not imposed the death penalty because of extenuating circumstances.

Seychelles

Status: Abolitionist for all but exceptional crimes

Executions 1985 - mid-88: None

Other factors: None

Method of execution: Not known

No executions have been carried out for more than 40 years. In 1976 the government of the newly independent Seychelles provisionally abolished the death penalty for murder. It had previously been provisionally abolished for murder under an amendment to the Penal Code in 1966 while Seychelles was under British colonial rule. In 1980 the Seychelles Government informed the UN Secretariat, as reported in the UN Secretary-General's five-yearly report on capital punishment in 1980, that the death penalty was retained only for treason.

Anyone accused of a capital offence has a right to legal counsel of their own choosing and the right of appeal to the Court of Appeal. They may subsequently appeal for clemency to the President.

In 1981 a number of people were arrested in the course of an attempted overthrow of the Seychelles Government by foreign mercenaries. Four of them were convicted of treason in the Supreme Court and sentenced to death in 1982. President France-Albert René subsequently commuted their sentences to life imprisonment and they were later released. In 1982 the head of the Seychelles armed forces, James Michel, was reported as saying that the government abhorred the death penalty.

Sierra Leone

Status: Retentionist

Executions 1985 - mid-88: Not known

Other factors: None

Methods of execution: Hanging; shooting by firing-squad

The death penalty has been provided for in law since independence in 1961 for various offences, including murder, robbery with violence, mutiny, and treason. Trials are normally held in the High Court before a judge and a jury, which must reach a unanimous verdict for conviction. However, there is no provision for jury trials in military courts. Defendants have a right to legal counsel and representation and anyone convicted by the High Court is allowed 21 days to file an appeal with the Court of Appeal. Further appeals can be made to the Supreme Court (the highest court) which is presided over by the Chief Justice.

Before the death penalty may be carried out a Committee for the Prerogative of Mercy, appointed by the Cabinet and chaired by the First Vice-President, advises the President on whether or not to commute the death sentence. Executions are by hanging although an amendment to the Criminal Procedure Act in 1973 provides also for execution by firing-squad. Among the first to be executed by firing-squad in 1973 were a former Minister of Information and Broadcasting and three others who had been convicted of murder. Places of execution are not specified, but all executions known to Amnesty International since 1973 have been carried out at Pademba Road Prison in Freetown. Pregnant women and those aged under 18 may not be sentenced to death but are instead given custodial sentences.

In 1975 six civilians and two soldiers were hanged at Pademba Road Prison after being convicted of treason. Amnesty International has received no information on executions which may have been carried out since then, but the organization is concerned about death sentences that continue to be imposed by various courts.

In 1983 five people were sentenced to death for murder by the High Court in Freetown. Three others, Ahmed Turay, aged 21, Saliu Bangura, aged 19, and Michael Turay, aged 30, were found guilty of armed robbery and sentenced to death by firing-squad by the High Court in Makeni in northern Sierra Leone, despite claims by the three in court that they had confessed under duress and on false promises of immunity from prosecution. No investigation of their claims was reported to have been ordered by the court. Another eight people were convicted of murder and sentenced to death by the High Court in 1984.

In 1986 two people were convicted of murder and sentenced to death. One of these, a police officer who was convicted of murdering a prisoner in a police cell, had his sentence set aside by the Court of Appeal which ordered a retrial. It is not known whether the retrial has taken place.

Following a major treason trial in 1987, 16 people were convicted of treason and sentenced to death by the High Court in Freetown. They were accused of involvement in a conspiracy to overthrow the government of President Joseph Saidu Momoh by violent means in March 1987. Among those convicted were Francis Mischeck Minah, who at the time of his arrest was First Vice-President, Minister of Justice and Attorney-General; Gabriel Mohamed Tennyson Kaikai; a former Assistant Superintendent of Police; and Haruna Vandy Jimmy, a former member of Parliament. All 16 filed appeals which were scheduled to be heard by the Court of Appeal in mid-1988.

Singapore

Status: Retentionist

Executions 1985 - mid-88: 2+; drug-trafficking

Other factors: None

Method of execution: Hanging

The death penalty was in use during the colonial period and was retained after Singapore became an independent republic in August 1965.

Death sentences may be imposed for a number of offences under the Penal Code; the

Internal Security Act, 1960; the Misuse of Drugs Act, 1973 as amended in 1975; and the Arms Offences Act. Capital offences include murder; treason; hurting or imprisoning the president; offences relating to the unlawful possession of firearms and explosives; and perjury resulting in the execution of a person indicted on a capital charge. The 1975 amendment to the Misuse of Drugs Act made the death penalty mandatory for possession of over 15 grams of heroin or fixed amounts of other drugs.

At least 20 people convicted of drugs offences have been executed since 1975, the last one in January 1986. At least 11 others have been sentenced to death since 1985 – three in 1985, one in 1986, three in 1987 and four up until May 1988; all await the outcome of their appeals. Three other prisoners were sentenced to death in 1987 on conviction of murder. In addition, nine people were reported to have been executed between 1973 and 1980 under the Arms Offences Act which provides for a mandatory death penalty for discharging a firearm in the course of a crime.

Capital offences are tried before the High Court. The defendant has the right of appeal against conviction to the Court of Criminal Appeal and legal counsel is guaranteed by law. On dismissal of the appeal, prisoners may seek permission to appeal to the Judicial Committee of the Privy Council in England, which serves as the final court of appeal for Singapore. If a sentence is upheld by the Privy Council, prisoners may submit a clemency petition to the President of Singapore. Once a death sentence has been imposed by the High Court, prisoners are held on "death row" in Changi Prison, where all executions are carried out. It was reported in 1978 that a total of 102 men and one woman had been hanged there since 1949.

▶ In November 1988, two women and a man were executed. They had been convicted of murder in May 1983. Sek Kim Wah, convicted of murder in 1983, was executed in December 1988.

Solomon Islands

Status: Abolitionist

Executions 1985 - mid-88: None

Other factors: Not applicable

Method of execution: Not applicable

There has been no provision for the death penalty in the laws of the Solomon Islands since the country became independent in 1978. The death penalty appears to have been abolished by the colonial government in 1966 through an amendment to the Penal Code. The amendment changed the punishment for premeditated murder from death to life imprisonment.

Somalia

Status: Retentionist

Executions 1985 - mid-88: 150+; organizing a subversive organization; organizing an armed band for subversion; espionage; murder; embezzlement

Other factors: Prisoners of conscience sentenced to death and executed; unfair trials by special security courts or military courts with no right of appeal; public executions

Method of execution: Shooting by firing-squad

The law provides for the death penalty for a wide range of political and non-political offences. All capital offences are tried by special security courts or military courts, where procedures are often summary or informal, and where international standards of fair trial are ignored. There is no right of appeal nor are death sentences automatically subject to review by the head of state. Many executions were carried out in the northern regions – particularly in or around Hargeisa – in the context of armed conflict between government forces and the Somali National Movement (SNM), an opposition organization based in

Ethiopia which launched attacks across the border in these areas.

The 1962 Penal Code, enacted shortly after independence (1960), prescribed a mandatory death penalty for several offences against the state, and for murder. After the assumption of power in 1969 by the army, the Supreme Revolutionary Council enacted the National Security Law (1970), which extended the range of the death penalty, making it mandatory for 20 separate offences against the security of the state. These include treason, espionage, subversion, sabotage, publishing or distributing "anti-state propaganda", and several offences involving non-violent political, religious or trade union activities, for which prisoners of conscience could be, and have been, executed. The latter include "exploiting religion for creating national disunity", and "organizing strikes, walk-outs, stoppages, etc".

In 1975 a mandatory death penalty was introduced for embezzlement of public funds exceeding 100,000 Somali shillings (US$600 equivalent in 1988). The death sentence is also mandatory for members of the security forces who have been convicted by court-martial of serious military offences such as mutiny or desertion.

Execution is deferred for pregnant women, nursing mothers (until one year after the birth) and the insane. There appear to be no lower or upper age limits for imposition of death sentences or executions. Condemned prisoners are held separately in special cells in Mogadishu central prison and several regional prisons. Executions are carried out by firing-squad inside the prison or in public. In Mogadishu, public executions have been carried out at the Police Academy.

Except for military offences, which are tried by courts-martial, the National Security Court, established in 1970, has exclusive jurisdiction over all capital cases. The court consists of a president, who must be a member of the armed forces, and four counsellors, who must be members either of the armed forces or security service, or judges or law graduates. The President of the National Security Court since 1970 has been Brigadier General Mahmoud Ghelle Yusuf, who has also been a member of the government since 1970. The court has a Special Prosecutor, who is not under the authority of the Attorney General or Minister of Justice. The court's independence and impartiality are open to serious doubt.

The law allows defendants in capital cases to have legal representation and the court must assign a defence lawyer to any defendant who cannot afford legal fees. However, there have been reports of cases in which defendants facing the death penalty were denied legal representation.

Prisoners suspected of offences against the National Security Law are held incommunicado for an unrestricted period, sometimes for years, until they are formally charged shortly before trial. Many prisoners have been tortured during this incommunicado detention. Once charged, prisoners have access to defence counsel only in the presence of a representative of the Prosecutor. Trials may be held *in camera* for security reasons but otherwise a limited number of defendants' relatives is usually allowed to attend the trial.

As with courts-martial, in which defendants also have restricted rights to legal representation, there is no right of appeal against the verdict of the National Security Court, but convicted prisoners do have the right to petition the head of state for clemency. The head of state may confirm or commute the sentence, but there is no automatic executive review of all death sentences. Many death sentences have been carried out within hours of conviction, suggesting that the right to petition for clemency was ignored.

Few death sentences have been reported by the news media, which is state-controlled. Statistics on the use of the death penalty are not published by the government. Between 1985 and mid-1988 over 200 death sentences are believed to have been imposed, and the majority carried out. Several death sentences were imposed for murder and there were also executions for political offences. Many people were condemned after being convicted of having links with the SNM, including school students demonstrating against the government, and business people accused of giving funds to the SNM.

In April 1987, nine teachers of Islam (known as *sheikhs*) were condemned to death by the National Security Court in Mogadishu for "exploiting religion for creating national disunity or subverting or weakening state authority".

Ten *sheikhs* had been condemned to death for this offence in 1975 and executed within hours. The April 1987 trial started without prior notice and lasted only a few hours. The defendants had been arrested in May 1986 after criticizing state restrictions on religious activities and calling for the introduction of "moderate Islamic laws". They were denied legal counsel of their choice and refused to accept any counsel appointed by the court. The nine death sentences were all commuted to unspecified prison terms in August 1987.

In February 1988, former Vice-President Ismail Ali Abokor, former Foreign Minister Omar Arteh Ghalib, Abdi Ismail Yunis, a former university dean, Suleiman Nuh Ali, an architect, and four others, were condemned to death by the National Security Court in Mogadishu. Arrested in 1982 for alleged treason, they had been held incommunicado and were not formally charged until shortly before their trial. They were convicted of "organizing a subversive organization" (namely the SNM) and other offences. Amnesty International regarded them as prisoners of conscience imprisoned for their non-violent political views. Some days later, after international appeals for clemency, President Mohamed Siad Barre commuted all eight death sentences: Ismail Ali Abokor and Omar Arteh Ghalib were to serve unspecified prison terms under house arrest and the six others received 24-year prison sentences.

At the time of going to press, the number of people held under sentence of death was not known, but it was believed to be considerable.

▶ Ismail Ali Abokor and Omar Arteh Ghalib were released on 21 October 1988.

South Africa

Status: Retentionist

Executions 1985 - mid-88: 537+; murder; rape; aggravated robbery; aggravated housebreaking; treason

Other factors: Death sentences imposed disproportionately on the black population by an almost entirely white judiciary

Method of execution: Hanging

Over the last 10 years there has been an almost unbroken upward trend in the annual number of executions. Between 1978 and the end of 1987 the courts sentenced 1,593 people to death (including at least 98 people in the four nominally independent "homelands" – Bophuthatswana, Ciskei, Transkei and Venda), and the annual total of executions exceeded 100 in every year except for 1983. In 1987 at least 172 people were executed, the highest annual figure since South Africa's political independence from the United Kingdom in 1910. Of these 172, at least eight were executed in the nominally independent "homelands", whose executions are not included in the statistics issued by the authorities in Pretoria. Nine of those executed in 1987 were white. In one week in December 1987, 21 people were executed in groups of seven.

In February 1988, 267 people were under sentence of death, and by mid-June, 71 people had been executed since the beginning of the year. Neither of these figures include an unknown number of sentences and executions in the nominally independent "homelands".

Most death sentences are imposed on people convicted of murder. Under the Criminal Procedure Act, 1977 (CPA) the death penalty is mandatory for murder unless the court concludes that there are extenuating circumstances. It is optional for kidnapping, childstealing, rape, aggravated robbery or attempted robbery, aggravated housebreaking or attempted housebreaking, and treason. In addition, the Internal Security Act, 1982 (ISA) provides for the death penalty for "terrorism", which is very broadly defined and includes acts or threats of violence and attempted acts of violence, carried out with intent to, among other things, "overthrow or endanger the state authority ... or bring about or promote any constitutional, political, industrial, social or economic change in the Republic". Any person convicted of assisting a person convicted of "terrorism" is liable to the same sentence. The ISA replaced security legislation on sabotage and other security laws which had provided for the death penalty for a wider range of offences.

There are 10 "homelands", four of which are nominally independent and have similar death penalty laws to the rest of South Africa. In the Transkei, however, propagating or disseminating the view that Transkei forms part of another country was made a capital offence in 1977, the year after the "homeland" was declared independent.

Those aged under 18 at the time of the commission of a murder, pregnant women and a woman convicted of murdering her newly-born child are exempted from the death penalty.

Capital cases are tried in the Supreme Court before a judge with two assessors. Assessors are usually trained lawyers and they participate in deciding questions of fact, including the existence of aggravating or extenuating circumstances. The judge alone decides questions of law and has sole discretion over sentencing. If the accused is unrepresented, defence counsel is appointed by the court.

There is no automatic right of appeal against the decision of the Supreme Court. Defendants must first apply to the trial judge for leave to appeal. If this is denied, the convicted person may petition the Chief Justice for leave to appeal. The Chief Justice's decision is final.

The Appellate Division of the Supreme Court is the final court of appeal. With the exception of Venda, the nominally independent "homelands" have constituted their own final courts of appeal, consisting of retired white South African judges or judges still serving in the provincial divisions of the Supreme Court.

If an appeal is rejected, defendants can petition the President for clemency. The President may commute a sentence or direct the original trial court to examine new evidence which might affect the conviction or sentence. The proportion of death sentences thus reprieved rose from just under 10 per cent in 1978

to 45 per cent in 1983. Since then the rate has fallen steadily, with only 12 per cent of death sentences being reprieved in 1987.

One of the most notable aspects of the use of the death penalty in South Africa is its disproportionate imposition on the black population (including people officially described as "coloureds") by an almost entirely white judiciary. All judges are white, except for one black judge in the Bophuthatswana "homeland". Assessors are also white, with a few exceptions in the Natal and Cape Provincial Divisions.

Recent research, corroborating that carried out in the late 1960s by Professor Barend van Niekerk of Natal University, has shown that black defendants stand a greater chance than white defendants of receiving the death penalty, especially when the victim is white. For example, between June 1982 and June 1983, of 81 blacks convicted of murdering whites, 38 were hanged; of 52 whites convicted of murdering whites, only one was hanged. None of the 21 whites convicted of murdering blacks was hanged, but 55 of the 2,208 blacks convicted of murdering blacks were hanged.

In 1987 two white men, Johannes Wessels and George Scheepers, were executed for the murder and rape of two black women. The case attracted public attention primarily because very few whites have been executed for murdering black people and none had previously been executed for raping black women. Similar public attention has attended the death sentences imposed in May 1988 on two white police officers, both members of the Eastern Cape Riot Squad, for the murder of a black youth, and those imposed in April 1988 on two Robbery Squad officers in Johannesburg convicted of murdering two black men.

As a consequence of poverty most black defendants in capital cases are represented by lawyers appointed by the court, who are usually the most junior members of the bar and are paid at a substantially lower rate and for a shorter period than privately hired counsel. This arrangement does not permit the appointment of a solicitor, who is crucial for the proper preparation of a case.

Trials are conducted in one of the two official languages, English or Afrikaans; neither is the mother tongue of most black people. Accordingly, black defendants must often rely on interpreters and may be put at a disadvantage as a result.

The last 10 years have seen an increasing number of death sentences imposed at political trials held under the security laws, and at trials of people accused of politically related murders committed during the nationwide protests which began in the urban black townships in 1984. Defendants in these cases are frequently held incommunicado for many months, under the ISA. In addition to the psychological effects of prolonged isolation and intensive interrogation, these defendants may also be subject to torture.

Before the CPA was amended in 1977, the prosecution was required to show that a confession was freely and voluntarily made before it could be admitted as evidence. Since then, however, if defendants claim during a trial that their confession was made under duress, the onus is upon them to prove it. Moreover, in many cases potential prosecution witnesses are also held in prolonged incommunicado detention before giving evidence in court; during their detention they too may be subject to duress. If such witnesses refuse to testify for the prosecution, they may be imprisoned for up to five years for contempt of court, or they may be charged with perjury if their evidence in court differs from statements which they made to the police while in detention. A number of death sentences have been imposed after trials conducted in such circumstances.

Several members of the banned African National Congress have been sentenced to death in recent years for treason and other offences committed in the course of guerrilla activities. In 1983, three were hanged for treason – the first people to be executed for treason since 1914. In other cases, those sentenced to death for treason or other political offences have had their sentences commuted by the President if there was no loss of life resulting from their offences.

Between 1985 and the end of 1987, 69 people were sentenced to death and nine people executed after being convicted of politically related murders. Among those under sentence of death at the time of going to press are those known as the Sharpeville Six, convicted of involvement in the murder in September 1984 of the deputy mayor of Sharpeville by a crowd protesting at rent increases. Eight people alleged to have been in the crowd were tried for murder, six of whom were sentenced to death. During the trial some of the defendants said that they had been assaulted and tortured by the police while kept in incommunicado detention. The court, however, rejected these allegations.

In December 1987 the Appeal Court upheld the convictions and sentences and, in a controversial decision, confirmed the appropriateness of convicting the six for murder on the basis of "common purpose" with the "mob", which was "directed at killing the deceased". The court, however, acknowledged that "it has not been proved in the case of any of the six ... that their conduct had contributed causally to the death of the deceased". The Appeal Court's interpretation of the doctrine of common purpose spreads the net of criminal liability very widely, and raises the prospect of many death sentences being imposed in future trials arising out of political conflict.

Following the President's denial of clemency to the Sharpeville Six in March 1988, a lengthy legal battle ensued in an attempt by the defence lawyers to have the trial reopened, primarily on the grounds that at least one key prosecution witness may have committed perjury because of police coercion.

The increasing number of executions, particularly for offences arising out of political protests, has stimulated renewed discussion of the death penalty within South Africa. Opposition by religious, trade union and political organizations, human rights groups and members of the legal profession has become more active. In July 1988, for example, the South African Council of Churches expressed publicly its total opposition to the use of the death penalty and urged the government both to declare a moratorium on executions and to appoint an independent commission to consider abolition of the death penalty in South Africa. The parliamentary opposition Progressive Federal Party has also called for a commission of inquiry into the death penalty and has urged a moratorium on executions. In 1988 the Society for the Abolition of the Death Penalty in South Africa, operative in the early 1970s, was re-established.

▶ On 23 November 1988, President P.W. Botha granted clemency to the Sharpeville Six shortly after the Appeal Court had turned down their application for a retrial. Their sentences were commuted to terms of imprisonment of between 18 and 25 years. Despite the commutation of the sentences of the Sharpeville Six, the precedent set in terms of the use of the "common purpose" doctrine and the failure of the court to find extenuating circumstances in such a case, remains unchallenged as a basis for bringing convictions for murder and sentences of death. Clemency was also granted to four white police officers and two other people under sentence of death. All sentences were commuted to terms of imprisonment.

Spain

Status: Abolitionist for all but exceptional crimes

Executions 1985 - mid-88: None

Other factors: None

Method of execution: Shooting by firing-squad

The death penalty was in use until 1932 when it was abolished for common criminal offences when the Penal Code was reformed under the Second Republic. However, it was reinstated for certain crimes of terrorism in 1934 and reintroduced for murder and other common crimes in 1938.

Three years after the death of the Head of State, Generalisimo Francisco Franco, in 1975, a new Constitution was approved by popular referendum in December 1978. This abolished the death penalty for peacetime offences but retained it for offences under the Military Penal Code in time of war. A new Military Penal Code, which retained the death penalty as an optional punishment for a wide range of wartime offences, came into force in June 1986. While the new Military Penal Code was under consideration, members of the *Cortes* (parliament) introduced a motion to remove the death penalty, but the motion was defeated. As head of state, the King has the constitutional power to grant clemency.

The last executions were on 17 September 1975 when five men convicted of murdering public order officials were shot by firing-squad

despite worldwide appeals for clemency.

Sri Lanka

Status: Abolitionist in practice

Executions 1985 - mid-88: None

Other factors: None

Method of execution: Hanging

During the past 10 years there have been a number of changes in law which have expanded the scope of the death penalty to include it for drug offences, among others. However, since the present United National Party (UNP) Government assumed office in July 1977, no judicial executions are known to have been carried out. The last hanging was on 23 June 1976. According to prison statistics at least 533 death sentences were imposed between 1977 and 1987, the highest number being in 1985 when there were 81 sentences; 50 death sentences were imposed in 1986, and 79 in 1987.

Under the Penal Code a mandatory death penalty is provided for murder (Section 296), abetment of suicide (Section 299) and the giving or fabrication of false evidence leading to the conviction and execution of an innocent person (Section 191). In addition, an optional death penalty is provided for attempts to overthrow the government; attempts to murder the President or a member of parliament, the police or the armed forces or a public officer (under Emergency Regulation 23); destroying property, causing or attempting to cause death, looting and trespassing (under Emergency Regulation 24); and unauthorized transport or possession of offensive weapons or offensive substances (under Emergency Regulation 36). In 1984 the death penalty was introduced for possession of drugs or their manufacture, under the Poisons, Opium and Dangerous Drugs (Amendment) Act No. 13 of 1984. Amnesty International has received reports of four death sentences imposed for offences under this act. The majority of people sentenced to death have been convicted of murder.

There have been several moves for the abolition of the death penalty in Sri Lanka, some of them based on the Buddhist objection to the taking of life. From April 1956 all death sentences for murder were commuted, and two years later the death penalty was suspended, pending a full investigation by the Commission on Capital Punishment. In its report published on 19 June 1959, the majority of the commission members recommended that the death penalty remain suspended. The commission concluded that there was no evidence that imposing the death penalty on a few was a greater deterrence to potential murderers than imprisoning all those convicted of murder. However, the death penalty was reintroduced in 1959 after the assassination of the then Prime Minister S. W. R. D. Bandaranaike, and in the early 1970s several executions were carried out each year.

The Sri Lanka Committee for the Abolition of the Death Penalty was formed in April 1977. In 1983 a book by Donovan Moldrich, a member of the Committee, was published. Entitled *Hangman – Spare the Noose*, it includes a historical and analytical survey of the death penalty in Sri Lanka with the focus on the "need formally and legally to abolish capital punishment which is a stain on the ... image of Sri Lanka".

The death penalty can be imposed only by the High Court. Prisoners have the right of appeal to the Court of Appeal and the Supreme Court. The President has the power to grant clemency. Clemency usually takes the form of commutation of the death sentence to 20 years' imprisonment or less, the majority the result of presidential amnesty on special occasions or for reasons of health. Sirimavo Bandaranaike's government, for example, granted a general amnesty to 144 men and three women on 22 May 1977. One hundred and ninety six men have reportedly been reprieved between July 1977 and 4 February 1983.

Sudan

Status: Retentionist

Executions 1985 - mid-88: 9; subversion and apostasy; murder

Other factors: Public executions; prisoner of conscience executed; unfair trials; prisoners under sentence of death kept in chains

Methods of execution: Hanging; shooting by firing-squad; stoning

The law provides for the death penalty for a wide range of offences. Several new capital offences were introduced in the Penal Code of September 1983 on the basis of their existence in Islamic law (*Shari'a*), although certain parts of the 1983 September Laws were repealed or effectively suspended after the overthrow of President Gaafar Mohamed Nimeiri's government in April 1985. The death penalty is mandatory for murder, mutiny by a member of the armed forces, and a number of political offences including subversion, initiating war against the state, treason, espionage and subversion of the national economy. The death penalty for murder may be set aside by a court and the convicted person released if the murder victim's family agrees to this and is paid compensation (*diya* or "bloodwealth") by the convicted person's family. The victim's family can alternatively demand that the condemned person be executed.

The Penal Code also contains *hadd* offences (offences against divine will) and penalties derived from Islamic law. Thus adultery, certain other sexual offences and bearing false witness carry a mandatory death penalty. The death penalty is optional for armed robbery, organizing or participating in a criminal organization, and repeated brothel-keeping. The death penalty may not be imposed on those aged under 18 or over 70, pregnant women, nursing mothers and the insane.

Defendants facing the death penalty have the right to legal representation and appeal to a higher court. Civilians are tried by the High Court, with the right of appeal to the Court of Appeal. Military personnel are tried by court-martial, with the right of appeal to a higher court-martial. The courts are required to appoint a lawyer at the state's expense for any defendant who cannot afford legal fees. Death sentences require review by the Supreme Court and also by the head of state, who may either confirm them or grant clemency. Since April 1985 a five-member Supreme Council of State has exercised the functions of head of state.

Under the Prisons' Regulations, 1976, condemned prisoners are kept permanently chained by the hands and legs. Execution for murder, treason and other political offences is by hanging. Members of the armed forces are executed by firing-squad. Executions take place inside a prison. The prescribed methods of execution for *hadd* offences are stoning for adultery, and execution with crucifixion for other offences. This has been interpreted to mean hanging followed by post-mortem crucifixion. No execution by crucifixion or stoning has been carried out. Between 1984 and 1985 the public were invited to attend at least two executions for armed robbery in Kober Prison.

Following the overthrow of President Nimeiri's government in April 1985, the section of the Judgments (Basic Rules) Act (1983) allowing general implementation of Islamic law was repealed. It had empowered judges to apply Islamic law in cases where the offence was not specified in the Penal Code.

Under President Nimeiri's government, there were executions for treason, mutiny and murder. Many people were executed after summary trials by courts-martial or following coup attempts in 1971, 1975 and 1976. According to the government's reply to the United Nations Secretariat as reported in the UN five-yearly report on capital punishment in 1985, there were 83 executions in the Sudan, all for murder, between 1979 and 1983. During a state of emergency from April to September 1984, special "Emergency Courts" (later renamed "Decisive Justice Courts") sentenced over 10 people to death for murder or armed robbery.

The most significant case of an unfair trial and wrongful execution, which provoked international condemnation, was that of 76-year-old Mahmoud Mohamed Taha who was publicly hanged inside Kober Prison on 18 January 1985. A frequent critic of the government and leader of the Republican Brothers, he had just been released from 18 months' detention without trial when he was rearrested on 5 January 1985 with four other members of the Republican Brothers. They were accused of distributing pamphlets advocating the repeal of the 1983 September Laws and a peaceful solution to the internal armed conflict in the south of the country. The five were charged with subversion and brought to court two days later. After two short hearings in which they refused to participate or be legally represented, they were convicted and sentenced to death. Two weeks later the Court of Appeal, in an automatic review of the trial, upheld the convictions and ruled that they were also guilty of apostasy – an offence for which they had not been charged or tried – and it added death sentences for this offence under the Judgments (Basic Rules) Act. The court gave Mahmoud Mohamed Taha's four co-defendants a month to repent of apostasy or be executed, but the next day President Nimeiri confirmed all five death sentences, ordering Mahmoud Mohamed Taha's immediate execution and giving his four co-defendants three days to repent or die. The legal prohibition against sentencing to death anyone over 70 years old was ignored. The four were forced to watch their leader's hanging the next day, 18 January. Apparently on his wishes, they later signed declarations of repentance – and were then freed.

After President Nimeiri's overthrow in April 1985, death sentences for murder continued to be imposed but there was a halt to executions. However, on 15 October 1987, eight prisoners condemned to death for murder in the previous two or three years were executed in Kober Prison.

As of 31 May 1988, there were believed to be over 100 prisoners condemned to death, including about 70 in Kober Prison.

Suriname

Status: Retentionist

Executions 1985 - mid-88: None

Other factors: Executions resumed after an unofficial 50-year moratorium

Method of execution: Shooting by firing-squad

Under the Criminal Code the death penalty is provided for as an optional sentence for murder and aggravated homicide (Articles 349 and 348). Under the Military Criminal Code it is provided for crimes against the security of the state, such as attempting to subject the territory of the state to foreign domination. Pregnant women and children under 18 at the time of the crime are exempted from the death penalty.

There had been no executions for over 50 years until 1982 when one was carried out under Decree A-7 (Maintenance of National Security during a State of War or a State of Emergency). This decree was introduced on 11 March 1982, and as long as the accused was granted a hearing, empowered military courts to impose death sentences on any person considered a serious danger to national security during wartime or a state of emergency. No right of appeal was provided. Only one such death sentence was actually imposed under this decree – Sergeant Major Wilfred Hawker was executed by firing-squad on 13 March 1982 after being convicted of attempting to overthrow the military government (which had itself come to power as a result of a coup in 1980), at a summary one-day trial. The Decree was rescinded on 23 March 1982.

At a meeting of the Human Rights Committee (set up under the International Covenant on Civil and Political Rights) in 1980, a government representative had stated that the death penalty had not been carried out for more than 50 years and that he "doubted whether it ever would be again". The death penalty remained in the Code of Criminal Procedure, he said, because some members of parliament had been unwilling to abolish it, arguing that it acted as a deterrent.

Swaziland

Status: Retentionist

Executions 1985 - mid-88: None

Other factors: None

Method of execution: Hanging

The Criminal Law and Procedure Act No. 67 of 1938, as amended in 1975, provides for a mandatory death sentence to be imposed for murder when there are no extenuating circumstances; an optional death sentence is provided for treason. Murder does not include the deliberate killing by a woman of her own baby if the child is less than a year old and it is considered that the mother is still recovering from breast-feeding and giving birth. Pregnant women and anyone aged under 18 at the time of the offence may not be sentenced to death.

Capital cases are tried by the High Court in Mbabane by a judge and two assessors who are not trained lawyers. The assessors participate in deciding questions of fact, such as the existence of extenuating circumstances. If the accused person cannot afford defence counsel, the court will appoint one in capital cases.

All death sentences are automatically referred to the Court of Appeal, which is not a permanently constituted court, but is composed of visiting judges and senior barristers from South Africa. If the sentence is confirmed on appeal, the convicted person has the right to appeal to the King for mercy. The King is advised by the Committee on the Prerogative of Mercy which consists of the Minister of Justice and two other ministers, as well as the Attorney-General. If the King confirms the death sentence, he is required to sign a death warrant before the execution is carried out.

Death sentences have been imposed in particular on those found guilty of ritual murder – that is, killings, often of children, intended to influence events by magical means. On a number of occasions public figures have urged expansion of the scope of the death penalty to include any involvement with a ritual killing. In 1985, for example, a member of the House of Representatives urged that a mandatory death sentence should be imposed on anyone found in possession of human flesh for ritual purposes. The law was not, however, subsequently amended.

From 1985 to mid-1988, 13 people have been sentenced to death – there were three sentences in 1985, seven in 1986 and three in 1987. At the time of going to press there were still two people under sentence of death. In 1985 Mjoniseni Mkhabela was sentenced to death after being convicted of selling his nephew to be ritually murdered. In May 1986 two men were sentenced to death after being convicted of murdering a 10-year-old boy, allegedly for ritual purposes.

The last known executions were in July 1983 when seven men and one woman were hanged at Matsapha Central Prison. All had been convicted of murder. Their death warrants were signed by the Queen Regent, as King Sobhuza II died in 1982 after a 60-year reign. The coronation of King Mswati III in April 1986 was marked by the commutation of all death sentences, but it is not known how many prisoners were under sentence of death at the time and therefore benefited from this measure.

Sweden

Status: Abolitionist

Executions 1985 - mid-88: None

Other factors: Not applicable

Method of execution: Not applicable

The death penalty was abolished for peacetime offences on 3 June 1921 (Act 1921:288), a proposal to this effect being approved by a large majority in the *Riksdagen* (parliament). Abolition of the death penalty for wartime offences followed some 50 years later, in an act adopted in 1972 which came into force on 1 July 1973 (Act 1973:20). The effect of this decision, voted by 266 to 37, was to abolish the death penalty for all offences.

The prohibition of the death penalty is enshrined in the Instrument of Government of the Swedish Constitution, which came into effect on 1 January 1975. Chapter 8, Article 1 originally stated, "No law or other regulation may imply that a sentence for capital punish-

ment can be pronounced." In 1976 this statement was moved to Chapter 2 on Fundamental Liberties and Rights, where Article 4 states, "Capital punishment may not occur." By placing the statement in this Chapter, it applies not only to Swedish citizens but also to alien residents who are thus protected against expulsion or extradition to states where the death penalty is still practised.

The last execution was carried out in 1910.

Switzerland

Status: Abolitionist for all but exceptional crimes

Executions 1985 - mid-88: None

Other factors: None

Method of execution: Shooting

Switzerland abolished the death penalty for political offences in 1848, and for all offences except those committed under the Military Penal Code in time of war under the new Federal Constitution of 1874. However, the relevant article of the 1874 Constitution (Article 65) was amended five years later in 1879 so that the death penalty was once again prohibited for political crimes only. This provision is still part of the present Constitution.

Following this amendment, between 1880 and 1894, 10 Swiss cantons reintroduced the death penalty into their penal codes for serious, non-political offences and in some cantons it remained in effect until the end of 1941. The last execution under cantonal penal legislation was in 1940 in the Canton of Obwalden.

The Swiss Penal Code of 21 October 1937 (which came into force on 1 January 1942) centralized the legislation on civil penal law throughout the cantons of the Swiss Confederation. It made no provision for the death penalty and had the effect of overturning those provisions which had existed in cantonal penal codes, thus effectively abolishing the death penalty for peacetime offences.

The death penalty is, however, retained under the Military Penal Code of June 1927 which came into force in 1928, and is applicable in time of war or imminent threat of war for a wide range of offences. The death penalty is mandatory for "desertion to the enemy" but optional for all other offences.

During World War II, the Federal Council (the executive of the Confederation) introduced the death penalty in a temporary, emergency law in 1940 for revealing military secrets and for treason. Between 1942 and 1945, of the 33 people who were sentenced to death, 17 were executed (by shooting). The last execution was on 7 December 1944.

A new Federal Constitution was drafted in 1977, providing for the abolition of the death penalty for all offences but it has never been debated by parliament. In 1991 the government is due to present a revised Constitution for parliament's consideration which is expected to propose the prohibition of the death penalty for all peace time offences.

Syria

Status: Retentionist

Executions 1985 - mid-88: 31; espionage; rape of minors; premeditated murder; attempted premeditated murder; incitement to commit murder; drug-trafficking; causing car bomb explosions; robbery leading to loss of life

Other factors: Public executions; no right of appeal against sentences imposed by state security courts

Methods of execution: Hanging; shooting by firing-squad

Under the 1949 Penal Code the death penalty is provided for a variety of offences. The 1950 Military Penal Code and the 1966 Penal Code for Economic Crimes also provide for the death penalty. Several other laws passed by legislative decree have increased the number of capital offences.

The Penal Code distinguishes between criminal offences of a political nature and ordinary offences, the maximum penalty for the former being life imprisonment. However, the provisions of this code do not apply to crimes against the external security of the state. For ordinary crimes, a term of imprisonment may be imposed instead of the death penalty in certain circumstances – if, for example, the judge decides that the motive for a capital offence is "honourable". Under the Penal Code a mandatory death penalty is provided for premeditated murder; death in the course of other crimes; aggravated rape; arson resulting in death in certain circumstances; and deliberate destruction of means of communication or transport leading to loss of life. The death penalty may also be imposed for a wide range of offences against the external and internal security of the state.

The provisions of the Penal Code apply to both civilians and the military. The Military Penal Code also provides for the death penalty (mostly as the mandatory punishment) for over 28 offences committed by members of the armed forces. These include fleeing to enemy ranks in wartime; disobeying military orders; violently disarming or robbing an injured or sick comrade; treason; and espionage.

In January 1965 the scope of the death penalty was expanded to include communicating with or accepting benefits from any foreign state or agency for the purpose of carrying out acts hostile to the aims of the revolution; attacking places of religious worship, military and government establishments and private and public property; and inciting sectarian or racial strife. The same decree provided for the death penalty as an optional punishment for publicly carrying out acts incompatible with the implementation of the Socialist order of the State, and committing other offences deemed by law to be connected with the Socialist transformation. The death penalty was also introduced for membership of the prohibited *al-Ikhwan al-Muslimun,* Muslim Brotherhood (Law No. 49 of 1980) and for recidivist drug-trafficking (Law No. 182 of 1960 as amended).

Those aged under 18 at the time of the crime may not be sentenced to death. If the prisoner is pregnant, execution must be stayed until after childbirth.

The courts competent to pass death sentences are the criminal courts, the permanent military courts, the state security courts and the economic security courts. Civilians may be tried by any of the four types of court in certain circumstances. Death sentences passed by criminal courts and economic security courts may be reviewed only by the Supreme Court of Cassation, and those passed by military courts by the Military Court of Cassation. Prisoners convicted by the state security courts may not appeal.

Death sentences imposed on civilians may be carried out only after consultation with the Pardons Committee at the Ministry of Justice, and after ratification by the President. Death sentences imposed on members of the armed forces by the permanent military courts are referred to the President for ratification by the Minister of Defence, who makes comments on each case after taking into account the views of the Defence Council, which fulfils the role of the Pardons Committee for ordinary crimes. Sentences passed by the state security courts must be ratified by the President, who may also revoke the verdict and either order a retrial or suspend the case, or reduce the penalty. The decision of the President is irrevocable and cannot be contested or revised.

Execution of civilians is by hanging in prison or any other place designated by law. Members of the armed forces are executed by firing-squad in a place designated by the Minister of Defence and in the presence of various people, including a doctor.

Since 1985 Amnesty International has learned of 31 officially confirmed executions: 15 in 1985, eight in 1986, five in 1987 and three in January 1988. Those executed include civilians and soldiers convicted of spying for Israel and jeopardizing state security, and others convicted of offences which included premeditated murder, incitement to commit murder, drug-trafficking, aggravated rape and causing car-bomb explosions. Many of the executions were carried out in public. In September 1987 the Economic Security Court in Damascus sentenced to death five people convicted of economic corruption, reportedly the first death sentences to be passed for such offences in Syria. It is not known whether the executions were carried out.

▶ In August 1988 three people were hanged after having been convicted of murder.

Taiwan (Republic of China)

Status: Retentionist

Executions 1985 - mid-88: 17+; murder; robbery; rape and murder; armed robbery; narcotics and firearms-trafficking

Other factors: None

Method of execution: Shooting

A large number of offences are punishable by death, but in practice the courts impose death sentences for less than 10. Under the Criminal Code, three categories of offence carry a mandatory death penalty: rape and intentional killing of the rape victim; piracy and arson or other specified offences; and intentional killing of a victim kidnapped for ransom. Mandatory death sentences are also provided for under the Statute for the Punishment of Sedition and under the Criminal Law of the Armed Forces for offences including rebellion, espionage and helping the enemy. Under the law, execution is suspended if the prisoner is insane or pregnant.

Until martial law was lifted in July 1987, civilians charged with sedition and certain serious criminal offences were tried by military courts. The authorities publicly justified this as a means to combat what it regarded as an increase in violent crimes. Amnesty International was concerned about some unfair aspects of these military trials. The last prisoner sentenced to death for sedition was Wu Tai-an, executed in May 1979.

All death sentences imposed by district courts must automatically be referred for review to the Taiwan High Court and the Supreme Court. In at least one case in recent years a prisoner's death sentence has been annulled on appeal. In 1983 the Supreme Court twice sent Chang Ming-chuan's case back to the High Court for review on the grounds that his conviction for murder and robbery was based on unsatisfactory evidence. Chang's lawyer pointed out several discrepancies in the evidence against him, and the fact that he said his confession had been extracted under torture.

A presidential amnesty on 22 April 1988 (marking the 100 days of the death of President

213

Chiang Ching-kuo) commuted to life imprisonment the death sentences of some categories of convicts. Prisoners found guilty of certain crimes, such as multiple or repeated murders, kidnap for ransom, rape and robbery, group robbery and crimes involving firearms were, however, excluded from the amnesty. This group included the 100 or so prisoners sentenced to death since 1984 about whom Amnesty International has some information. Amnesty International has no information on cases of individual commutations of death sentences and these are believed to be rare.

In September 1987, after the lifting of martial law, the government confirmed to Amnesty International its intention to retain the death penalty.

Tanzania

Status: Retentionist

Executions 1985 - mid-88: None

Other factors: None

Method of execution: Hanging

Although Tanzanian courts continue to impose death sentences for murder, executions have seldom been carried out in recent years. In 1987 the scope of the death penalty in the semi-autonomous islands of Zanzibar was reduced when a law which had provided for the execution of clove smugglers was amended.

The Penal Code provides for the death penalty for treason and murder; for the latter offence it is mandatory. Serious cases are heard in the High Court where defendants have the right to be represented by their own lawyer or counsel provided by the state. If convicted and sentenced to death they have the right of appeal to the Court of Appeal, and to petition the President for clemency if that appeal fails. Pregnant women and anyone under the age of 18 may not be sentenced to death.

According to figures provided by the Tanzanian Government to the Secretary-General of the United Nations, there was one execution between 1974 and 1978, although 65 people had been sentenced to death in the same period. At least four people were sentenced to

death for murder in 1985, 10 in 1986, seven in 1987 and one up to 31 May 1988; no executions are known to have been carried out, however.

The islands of Zanzibar have a separate legislature and judicial system from mainland Tanzania. In 1985 Zanzibar adopted a new Constitution and judicial system which introduced a number of important guarantees of a fair trial. Judges, for example, were now required to have legal training, rules of procedure and evidence established, and defendants given the right to legal counsel. Previously none of these safeguards existed. The final right of appeal for prisoners sentenced to death in Zanzibar is to the Tanzanian Court of Appeal in Dar es Salaam.

A second important reform was the amendment in March 1987 of Decree No. 3, passed in 1969, which provided a mandatory death penalty for anyone convicted of smuggling cloves, the islands' main cash crop. The amended law provides for a prison term of between five and seven years. No one is known to have been executed under the law.

Opposition to the death penalty has been expressed by some prominent individuals, including a High Court judge who said it was alien to Tanzania, but the government has made no move to abolish it in law. Before he left office in 1985 former President Julius Nyerere is reported to have told police and prison officers that the country aspired to build a prisons department whose duty it was to reform, not to torture. He said that he had found it very difficult to order the hanging of convicted murderers during his presidency because "You will be killing two people instead of one".

Thailand

Status: Retentionist

Executions 1985 - mid-88: 34+; drug-trafficking; premeditated murder; aggravated rape; aggravated homicide

Other factors: No right of appeal against sentences imposed by military courts

Method of execution: Shooting

A mandatory death penalty is provided for premeditated murder, the murder of an official on government business and regicide. The death penalty is optional for robbery, rape, kidnapping, arson and bombing if death results, insurrection, treason and espionage. Children aged under 15 and the King cannot be sentenced to death.

New legislation has extended the application of the death penalty. The Royal Act on Harmful Habit-Forming Drugs, 1979 introduced an optional death penalty for possession of more than 100 grams of heroin, while maintaining a mandatory death penalty for its production, import or export. The 1978 Royal Act On Certain Offences Related to Air Travel introduced an optional death penalty for aircraft hijacking.

Most death sentence cases are tried in ordinary criminal courts under the Criminal Procedure Code, which guarantees the right of appeal to the Appeals Court and then the Supreme Court. However, military courts may also impose death sentences, and they allow no appeal. They may try civilians for almost all capital offences under the Penal Code if committed where martial law is in effect. Martial law is currently in force in a few places declared insecure because of insurgent activities or foreign military threat. Military courts are also empowered to try defendants accused of capital offences if committed in conjunction with "communistic activities".

Prisoners sentenced to death are allowed 60 days to petition the King for commutation once all appeals have been exhausted. The Ministry of Interior makes a recommendation on the request. Ministerial guidelines suggest recommending against commutation in cases of multiple death sentences or particularly violent capital crimes, but favour clemency for women, young people, civil servants, soldiers and prisoners from countries with whom Thailand has friendly relations. They also suggest taking account of extenuating circumstances and "inflexibility" in the law, such as there being no distinction between possession of 100 grams and 100 kilograms of heroin.

The government rarely makes its statistics on executions available to the public, but insists that few executions take place. About 10 people are believed to have been executed in 1985, 10 more in 1986, and between 14 and 16 people in 1987. However, many prisoners under sentence of death have received commutations by Royal Pardon. The death sentences of 48 people who had exhausted all opportunity for judicial appeal were commuted in 1983 to mark the bicentennial of the reigning dynasty. A further 65 finalized death sentences were commuted on the King's 60th birthday in December 1987. All executions are believed to take place at Baang Khwaang Central Prison in Bangkok.

However, the number of people under sentence of death and the number of executions have been gradually increasing. In May 1981, 121 people were reportedly under sentence of death; by February 1987 the figure had reached 314. In 1980 four people were executed, but Ministry of Interior officials said in 1987 that between 14 and 16 people had been executed that year.

Buddhist prisoners are permitted a visit by a Buddhist monk before execution, but in 1985, Phra Amornvethi, the senior monk who had been visiting condemned prisoners, resigned. This was in protest over inadequate prison facilities for last religious rites which, he said, made it impossible "for a death convict to get his mind settled".

There have been cases of civilian prisoners being executed for ordinary offences, without appeal, after trial by military courts; for example, Wara Woradilok, Chuchart Meksuthas and Charoon Chaiwong were shot in February 1986 after conviction without appeal for murder. However, most prisoners sentenced to death who cannot appeal or have exhausted all opportunity for appeal receive a royal pardon (commutation to a term of imprisonment). Ministry of Interior officials said in 1987 that the King grants a royal pardon to 90 per cent of the prisoners who petition individually for clemency. On his birthday in 1986 the King commuted the death sentence of a political activist convicted, without appeal, of killing a police officer. The King has also granted several general pardons commuting all finalized death sentences to a term of imprisonment.

Togo

Status: Abolitionist in practice

Executions 1985 - mid-88: None

Other factors: No right of appeal against death sentences imposed by the State Security Court

Method of execution: Shooting by firing-squad

Under the Penal Code the death penalty is the mandatory punishment for a large number of offences, including premeditated murder; the killing of a parent; and various offences against the internal and external security of the state, such as treason, armed rebellion and espionage. The law stipulates that execution of pregnant women is deferred until after childbirth, and that even when a death sentence has been confirmed by the courts it may not be carried out until a petition for presidential clemency has been reviewed and rejected. The method of execution is by firing-squad, out of public view.

Although those convicted by ordinary courts have a general right of appeal and may appeal on points of law to a cassation court, those sentenced to death by the State Security Court have no right of appeal. The State Security Court has general jurisdiction over all politically motivated offences and over crimes against the security of the state. The court comprises four judges and a president appointed annually by cabinet decree.

According to the Constitution the President is empowered to commute death sentences and has done so on various occasions. In December 1986, for example, 13 people were sentenced to death, three of them *in absentia*, by the State Security Court in Lomé. They were charged with participation in an attempt to overthrow the government in September 1986 and it appears that their trial was very brief. Since their arrest they have been held at a military camp in Tokoin, Lomé, and are not allowed visits from their family. However, on 21 October 1987 President Gnassingbé Eyadéma commuted the death sentences to life imprisonment of the 10 who had been present at their trial.

Death sentences were also imposed by the State Security Court at a previous trial in August 1979 at which 10 people (eight of whom had been tried *in absentia*) were sentenced to death. In reaching its verdict and pronouncing sentence the court appeared not to take into consideration defendants' claims that confessions admitted as evidence had been made in custody under torture. Indeed, there did not appear to be substantial evidence that the two defendants who were present at their trial had been involved in a conspiracy to overthrow the government by force. Furthermore, none of the defendants had adequate access to their defence counsel before the trial, and two of the judges had already stated publicly before the trial began that they believed the accused to be guilty. The death sentences imposed on the two who had been present in court were later commuted to life imprisonment by President Eyadéma. They were released in 1985 before their sentences had expired.

Tonga

Status: Retentionist

Executions 1985 - mid-88: None

Other factors: None

Method of execution: Hanging

Tonga retains the death penalty for treason and murder under Articles 43 and 82 of its Criminal Offences Act. All death sentences must be reviewed by the King of Tonga and his Privy Council who have the power to commute them. Pregnant women and children under 15 cannot be sentenced to death.

The last executions took place in September 1982 when three men were hanged for murder, despite appeals for clemency from local religious leaders. In 1983 the Tongan Legislative Assembly was reported to have voted to retain the death penalty and in September 1984 the Minister of Police suggested that it be introduced as an optional punishment for drug-trafficking; it is not known if any additional legislation resulted. No death sentences were reported between 1985 and 1988.

Trinidad and Tobago

Status: Retentionist

Executions 1985 - mid-88: None

Other factors: None

Method of execution: Hanging

A mandatory death penalty is provided for murder (Offences Against the Person Act, 1925, Chapter 11.08) and treason (Chapter 11.03). The death penalty is also provided for as an optional sentence for a number of offences under military law (Defence Act, 1962). The death penalty may not be imposed on those who were under 18 at the time of the crime nor on pregnant women.

Capital trials are held in the High Court before a judge and a 12-member jury; a unanimous verdict for the conviction or acquittal of the accused is required. Appeals are heard by the Court of Appeal. Final appeals may be submitted to the Judicial Committee of the Privy Council in England (JCPC) which will consider only cases involving constitutional matters or "matters of great public importance".

The President of Trinidad and Tobago may exercise his prerogative of mercy by commuting a death sentence to life imprisonment. The President acts on the advice of the Advisory Committee on the Power of Pardon (also known as the Privy Council). An automatic stay of execution comes into force for the period between sentencing and giving notice of appeal, and also until the final determination of all appeals.

According to official figures given by the Minister of National Security on 12 April 1988 during a debate in the Senate, there were 46 prisoners under sentence of death. At least two death sentences were imposed in 1985, four in 1986 and two in 1987. There was a marked increase in the number of death sentences imposed during the first quarter of 1988 when 14 were passed, two of them in retrials. Of the 46 prisoners mentioned by the Minister, three had exhausted all their legal appeals; 25 cases were pending before the Court of Appeal, 11 cases were pending before the JCPC and seven

prisoners had filed constitutional motions in the local court. Another two death sentences were passed on 14 April 1988. The longest serving prisoner had been under sentence of death since 1974. There have been no executions since November 1979.

Among the prisoners on death row is Lalchan Nanan who was convicted of murder in July 1977. The day after the end of the trial the foreman of the jury approached the defence lawyer and informed him that the jury had been divided eight to four in its verdict, and that they were not aware that all members of the jury had to be in agreement. He also said that he had misunderstood the word "unanimous" to mean "majority", when asked by the clerk of the court whether the jury had reached a unanimous verdict. The trial judge dismissed a motion submitted to him by the defence lawyer to redress the situation. The Court of Appeal dismissed his appeal in June 1979; an appeal to the JCPC was denied in July 1986. Lalchan Nanan then submitted a constitutional motion to the High Court of Trinidad and Tobago which is still pending. He remains on death row.

On 29 July 1987 the High Court annulled the death sentences of Andy Thomas and Kirkland Paul on the grounds, among other things, that their prolonged confinement on death row in conditions of "appalling barbarity" and the circumstances in which death warrants were read to them only hours before their scheduled executions, constituted "cruel and unusual treatment or punishment" in violation of the Constitution. Both prisoners, who had been under sentence of death since 1975, were released in August 1987 as a result of a presidential amnesty during celebrations of the country's 25th independence anniversary. Kitson Branche, another prisoner under sentence of death, also benefited from the presidential amnesty and was released on the same date after spending over 15 years on death row.

The death penalty has been the subject of much debate in recent years. The Commission of Inquiry into Prisons appointed in 1972 devoted a chapter of its 1980 final report to capital punishment. The majority of the commission's members were "of the view that the death penalty should be retained ... but reserved for certain kinds of homicide where the act is particularly heinous and/or where the killing takes place with premeditation and malice aforethought". For crimes of passion, which accounted for 53 per cent of murder convictions between 1970 and 1975, the committee recommended life imprisonment or lesser penalties, depending on the circumstances of the crime. The commission suggested that these changes should be instituted for a trial period of five years, after which the situation should be reviewed. Its members acknowledged that they had been influenced by the belief that "the public at large and the law makers, at this stage, would support the retention of the death penalty". A minority had felt that the death penalty should be abolished for a trial period of five years, with life imprisonment being the punishment for "murder in the first degree". However, the recommendations of the commission were not implemented.

In May 1982 the Council of the Bar Association passed a unanimous resolution calling upon the Attorney-General to establish a commission of inquiry into the way the judicial system was dealing with capital cases. The Council also requested a moratorium on executions pending the report of the proposed commission. The Bar Council was reported by its president in June 1982 to be "overewhelmingly against the use of the death penalty".

Trinidad and Tobago's Permanent Representative in Geneva reported to the Human Rights Committee (set up under the International Covenant on Civil and Political Rights) in October 1984 that some consideration was being given to the abolition of the death penalty, and that public debates regarding this question indicated that opinion was divided almost equally on the subject.

In December 1984 the National Coalition Against the Death Penalty, a local organization, presented a petition to the Prime Minister urging the government to abolish the death penalty. This petition had the backing of more than 40 national organizations representing, among other bodies, churches, trade unions, professional organizations and schools. It also requested the authorities to reduce the sentences of those already under sentence of death to life imprisonment.

In March 1988 an independent senator filed a motion in the Senate to initiate a discussion in Parliament on the issue of the death penalty.

The Senate discussed the motion in early April and voted 22 to three in favour of setting up a commission of inquiry to study the penalty. The approved motion requested that the government set up the commission as a matter of urgency and that the commission should report back as promptly as possible.

▶ In October 1988 Lalchan Nanan was released on humanitarian grounds.

Tunisia

Status: Retentionist

Executions 1985 - mid-88: 30; premeditated murder; rape; aggravated robbery

Other factors: Special courts; no right of appeal against sentences imposed by the High Court

Methods of execution: Hanging; shooting by firing-squad

Following a change of government in November 1987 there have been no executions. In April 1988 President Zine al-Abidine Ben Ali told Amnesty International that he is personally opposed to the death penalty. Since he came to power three death sentences have been commuted.

Under the Penal Code the death penalty is provided for a number of offences including attempts against the external security of the state, such as treason and spying; crimes against the internal security of the state, such as attempts on the life of the head of state; looting; destruction by explosion of arsenals or other state property; conspiracy to change the government; and crimes against the individual such as premeditated murder and parricide. In March 1985 the Penal Code was amended to make certain kinds of rape punishable by death: rape of minors (in the case of children under 10) and rape with the use of violence. Use or threat of violence against a magistrate in court was also made a capital offence. The Code of Military Justice also provides for the death penalty for a number of military offences and wartime crimes committed by military personnel.

The death penalty is mandatory unless there are extenuating circumstances. Those aged under 18 at the time of the crime and people who are insane may not be sentenced to death. Execution of pregnant women is deferred until after childbirth.

The Military Court, ordinary courts (Criminal Chamber of Appeals Courts) and special courts such as the High Court (and until its abolition in December 1987, the State Security Court) have jurisdiction in trials involving capital offences. There is no appeal against High Court decisions. Sentences imposed by the Military Court and the Criminal Chamber of Appeals Court may be appealed to the Military Court of Cassation and the ordinary Court of Cassation respectively. When reviewing sentences imposed by the Criminal Chamber of Appeals Court, the Court of Cassation may annul a decision and order a retrial on the grounds of incompetence, "excess of power", irregularities in procedures or questions of law. The Military Court of Cassation may annul a Military Court decision on the grounds of incompetence or other reasons, and request that the case be heard again by a competent jurisdiction, or it may simply annul the decision without ordering a retrial if it believes that the facts do not constitute a felony.

When a death sentence is imposed by the ordinary courts the case dossier is immediately submitted to the Public Prosecutor of the Court of Cassation. The sentence is finalized once the Court of Cassation has confirmed it. In all cases, executions may not be carried out before a petition for clemency has been rejected by the President of the republic.

Execution is by hanging for those convicted by ordinary courts, and by firing-squad for those convicted by military courts. Article 292 of the Code of Civil and Commercial Procedures specifies certain national and religious days when executions may not be carried out.

Between 1985 and mid-1988, 30 executions were carried out and 13 people were sentenced to death, four in absentia. Most death sentences have been imposed for premeditated murder, aggravated robbery or theft, murder, aggravated rape and rape of minors.

Death sentences in 1987 included six imposed by the State Security Court (four in absentia) in the trial of members and alleged members of the Mouvement de la tendance islamique (MTI), Islamic Tendency Movement. The two who were present at their trial were executed before the change of government in November 1987. The trial fell short of international standards for fair trial and cast doubts on the impartiality of the court. Defendants were reportedly subject to irregular pre-trial and trial procedures including arbitrary arrest, incommunicado detention, torture and ill-treatment in custody. Several of them contested confessions introduced in court as evidence against them on the grounds that they had been extracted under torture. Defence lawyers' pre-trial access to their clients was severely restricted and the impartiality of the President of the Court was questioned. Following the change of government, the State Security Court was abolished in December 1987 and two individuals sentenced to death in absentia were retried: one had his sentence commuted and the other received a sentence of five years' imprisonment. Amnesty International knows of no death sentences imposed since then.

Turkey

Status: Retentionist

Executions 1985 - mid-88: None

Other factors: Unfair trials

Method of execution: Hanging

Sixteen articles of the 1926 Penal Code, as amended, provide for a mandatory death penalty for crimes against the state, the government and the Constitution. In addition, eight articles provide for a mandatory death penalty for common criminal offences such as murder or crimes leading to the unjustified execution of another person. Twenty articles of the Turkish Military Penal Code, two articles of the Law on Treason and one article of the Law on Smuggling also provide for a mandatory death penalty. Under Article 55 of the Penal Code anyone aged under 18 at the time of the offence may not be sentenced to death. Article 12 states that execution of a pregnant woman must be deferred until she has given birth, and that an insane person may not be executed.

Under Article 12 of the Penal Code death

sentences are to be carried out after being confirmed by the Civilian or Military Court of Cassation and approved by an act of parliament. Death sentences are reviewed by the parliamentary Judicial Committee which makes a recommendation to parliament to vote on. The act of parliament must be ratified by the President who is empowered to commute death sentences on grounds of age or ill-health. Once the act is ratified and has been announced in the official gazette (*Resmi Gazete*), the Ministry of Justice is responsible for carrying out the execution.

Between October 1980 and October 1984, 50 people were executed: 27 of them had been convicted of politically related offences, all but one involving killings, and 23 for common crimes. Since 25 October 1984 there have been no executions, but both civilian and military courts have continued to impose death sentences. The exact number of death sentences imposed by military courts since the introduction of martial law in December 1978 is not known, but is estimated to be well over 700. The number of people under sentence of death who had exhausted all legal remedies was 192 as of 31 May 1988. If confirmed by parliament and the President, death sentences may be carried out immediately.

Since a military coup in 1980 the majority of death sentences have been imposed by military courts trying offences that "led to the announcement of martial law". Almost all political prisoners sentenced to death have been tried by military courts. Such courts are not independent of the executive, either in law or in practice. They have repeatedly failed to investigate allegations that statements introduced in court as evidence against defendants were extracted under torture. Lawyers defending political prisoners have been harassed and impeded in many ways.

In recent times executions have generally followed military coups. After the coup of 1960 Prime Minister Adnan Menderes and two of his ministers were hanged. After the 1971 coup three leaders of a radical student movement were executed. Between 1973 and 1980 there was a *de facto* moratorium on executions: death sentences were still imposed but were not ratified by parliament. This moratorium came to an end shortly after the military coup of 12 September 1980, and in the next four years 50 people were executed.

The two most recent executions were carried out on 7 and 25 October 1984 under the civilian government which came to power in December 1983.

A number of political prisoners were sentenced to death without sufficient access to defence counsel, and some without any legal representation at all.

Serdar Soyergin was charged with killing Erdogan Polat and Captain Bülent Angin on 14 September 1980 in Gaziantep. The verdict was announced on 19 September 1980 at the end of a court hearing which lasted only three hours in Adana Military Court. Serdar Soyergin was not represented by a lawyer. He admitted having killed Erdogan Polat in self-defence but denied killing the Captain. All the witnesses said that they had not seen Serdar Soyergin shooting at the Captain. The legal proceedings in this case were quickly completed and Serdar Soyergin was executed on 26 October 1980.

Erdal Eren was executed on 13 December 1980 after lengthy hearings in Ankara Military Court. The death sentence was twice quashed by the Military Court of Cassation but finally confirmed. There are serious doubts about whether Erdal Eren was guilty of killing a police officer, the crime of which he was convicted, and about whether he was 18 years old at the time of the alleged offence.

The opposition Social Democrat Populist Party (SHP) advocates abolition of the death penalty, and the other main opposition party, the True Path Party, has proposed holding a referendum on the issue. Important professional organizations, such as the Turkish Medical Association and the Union of Turkish Bars, have repeatedly stated that they are in favour of abolition. The Human Rights Association founded in 1986 gathered 130,000 signatures between September and December 1987 on a petition in support of abolition.

By April 1988 none of the legislative initiatives to abolish the death penalty had resulted in any changes. A draft law to commute to life imprisonment all death sentences pending with the Judicial Committee for more than a year was submitted to the committee in February 1988. It was withdrawn on the recommendation of the Prime Minister. In February 1988 deputies from the SHP submitted a draft law to abolish the death penalty – even though it was unlikely to get a majority in the Judicial Committee or parliament.

In April 1987 Turkey applied for full membership of the European Community. The European Parliament passed resolutions in 1984, 1985 and 1988 opposing the use of the death penalty in Turkey. On 11 October 1984, following the first of two executions that month, the European Parliament adopted a resolution calling on the Turkish authorities "to suspend the carrying out of any further death sentences with immediate effect". On 21 January 1988 the European Parliament called on the recently re-elected Government of Turkey "to take the necessary steps to commute all death sentences pending in the country, until such time as this abominable penalty is abolished".

Turks and Caicos Islands

Status: Abolitionist in practice

Executions 1985 - mid-88: None

Other factors: None

Method of execution: Hanging

The death penalty is provided for murder (Offences Against The Person Act, Chapter 21, Part II). Those aged under 18 at the time of the crime and pregnant women are exempted.

After the trial, and if the local court has dismissed the appeal, the prisoner can lodge a final appeal with the Judicial Committee of the Privy Council in England which will consider only cases involving constitutional matters or "matters of great public importance".

The death penalty "had not been imposed or carried out since July 31, 1945", according to a letter from the Governor General Mr C. J. Turner to Amnesty International. However, a death sentence was imposed in April 1988 on a man from the Dominican Republic for the murder of a local man. His appeal will be heard in October 1988 and an issue to be raised is the wording of the Act ("Whoever shall be convicted of murder shall be liable to suffer death") and whether the word "liable" means mandatory or discretionary.

Tuvalu

Status: Abolitionist

Executions 1985 - mid-88: None

Other factors: Not applicable

Method of execution: Not applicable

Formerly known as the Ellis Islands, Tuvalu became independent from the United Kingdom in 1978. The 1965 Penal Code for the Gilbert and Ellis Islands had not provided for the death penalty for any crime, the maximum sentence being life imprisonment. Since independence there has been no legislation to introduce the death penalty.

Uganda

Status: Retentionist

Executions 1985 - mid-88: 11+; murder; armed robbery

Other factors: Summary trials by military courts with no right of appeal; public executions

Methods of execution: Hanging; shooting by firing-squad

Under the Penal Code the death penalty is mandatory for treason, murder, armed robbery and armed smuggling. Death sentences may also be imposed for mutiny and various related offences and kidnap with intent to murder. The most recent extension of the scope of the death penalty came in 1987 when the National Resistance Council, the country's interim legislature, passed an amendment to the Penal Code introducing a mandatory death sentence for armed smuggling. By June 1988 no one was known to have been sentenced to death under this new provision.

Death sentences may be imposed either by the High Court or by one of the various tribunals responsible for administering discipline within the National Resistance Army (NRA). Civilians accused of capital offences are tried in the High Court where they have access to legal counsel of their choice and the right of appeal to the Supreme Court. If conviction and sentence are upheld, the case is then considered by the Advisory Committee on the Prerogative of Mercy which recommends to the President whether or not the sentence should be carried out. No execution can take place without the President signing the death warrant. From 1981 to 1987 this advisory committee did not exist, which partly accounts for the fact that no judicial executions took place during that period. By early 1988 the committee had still not reviewed the cases of any of the 70 or more prisoners under sentence of death at Luzira Upper Prison near Kampala, some of whom had been sentenced in the mid-1970s.

In March 1988 Davis Ssozi Ntambi, Aloysius Ndibowa and Mubiru Mukasa were sentenced to death by the High Court after being found guilty of treason for allegedly plotting to overthrow the government. At the time of going to press they are apparently exercising their right of appeal. Nobody has been executed after being convicted of treason in the High Court since Uganda's independence in 1962. There were a large number of quasi-judicial executions after unfair and summary trials under the government of President Idi Amin in the 1970s, and further summary and arbitrary executions while the Amin government and the governments of President Milton Obote (1980-85) and Major General Tito Okello (1985-86) were in power.

Two codes of conduct governing the behaviour of NRA soldiers were incorporated into Ugandan law after the NRA took power in 1986. The Code of Conduct for the National Resistance Army provides for a mandatory death sentence for murder, treason, rape and disobedience of a lawful order resulting in loss of life. Soldiers are tried before a unit disciplinary committee chaired by the unit second-in-command. They have no right to legal representation and no right of appeal. All death sentences must be confirmed by the chairman of the High Command, who is also the President of Uganda.

The NRA's Operational Code of Conduct defines a series of offences related to the army's operations in the field, including desertion, disobeying lawful orders, misuse of arms and failure to execute one's duties. All the offences in this code carry a maximum penalty of death. Defendants may be tried in a unit tribunal, a field court-martial or the general court-martial, all of which may hand down a death sentence. There is no automatic right to a lawyer and no right of appeal. Death sentences handed down by a unit tribunal or general court-martial must be confirmed by the High Command. The High Command advises its Chairman on how to exercise his prerogative of mercy. Execution is normally by firing-squad.

No one has been executed within the civilian justice system since 1977, but in 1987 seven soldiers were executed by the NRA for murder and armed robbery, and at least another four were executed during the first five months of 1988. In some cases these executions were carried out publicly; according to the government this was to reassure the civilian population of the government's commitment to enforcing proper standards of behaviour within the army. It appears that the executions were usually carried out very soon after the alleged offence was committed, apparently for the same reason. Private Richard Onen, for example, was publicly executed in Soroti on 25 December 1987 after being convicted of a murder committed the previous day.

In February 1988 the Minister of Justice informed an Amnesty International delegation visiting Kampala that a new army code of conduct being drafted at that time would provide for an automatic right of appeal. He also stated that defendants were entitled to representation by military lawyers, although no such right is specified in either of the codes of conduct and it does not appear that in practice such a right is automatically available.

Union of Soviet Socialist Republics

Status: Retentionist

Executions 1985 - mid-88: 63+; large-scale theft of social property; aggravated bribe-taking; aggravated rape; aggravated murder; aggravated hijacking; attempting to take the life of a police officer; war crimes; espionage

Other factors: None

Methods of execution: Shooting; hanging (for war criminals only)

Although the USSR announced its intention to restrict the scope of the death penalty in February 1987, the number of reported executions and death sentences has not decreased since then. By 31 May 1988 at least 15 people had been executed and another 71 sentenced to death.

Since the announcement in February, the Soviet media have, for the first time in decades, reported the views of people who want the death penalty abolished and have exposed cases in which innocent people were sentenced to death. One of the most notable of these involved 14 Belorussians who between 1971 and 1984 were forced to confess to a series of rapes and murders they did not commit. At least one was subsequently executed, but the fate of the others has not been disclosed.

In keeping with socialist doctrine, Soviet penologists have traditionally preferred correction and re-education to retribution as a way of treating offenders. Although the USSR is formally committed to abolishing the death penalty, it has been in use throughout the history of the Soviet state, except for short periods in 1917, 1920 and 1947-1950.

The criminal codes of the 15 republics of the USSR are based on Fundamentals of Criminal Legislation of the USSR and Union Republics, adopted in 1958. The same crimes are punishable by death throughout the USSR; for simplicity, this report will refer to the code of the Russian Republic (RSFSR). Article 23 stresses that the death penalty is "an exceptional measure of punishment" in force only "until its complete abolition", but no fewer than 18 peacetime offences are now punishable by death, including some which do not involve violence. Death sentences may be imposed for nine crimes against the state (including disrupting the work of prisons); four against life or person (including aggravated homicide and hijacking an aircraft with loss of life); and five economic crimes (including large-scale theft of state property and aggravated bribe-taking).

The death penalty is optional for all but one of the capital crimes listed in the RSFSR Criminal Code. The exception is "taking, or attempting to take the life of a police officer, or of a people's guard" (Article 191-2), which carries a mandatory death sentence if committed under any of a list of 12 specified aggravating circumstances.

A reduction in the scope of the death penalty would reverse a 30-year trend. Amendments to the criminal code doubled the number of capital crimes in the 1960s and 1970s and increased the circumstances in which existing capital offences could be punished by death. In 1980 the death penalty was abolished for rape in some circumstances, but otherwise the trend continued. In 1984, any prisoner became liable to be sentenced to death for terrorizing other convicts or prison staff, whereas previously only "especially dangerous recidivists" and others convicted of "grave crimes" were so liable (Article 77-1). The law on economic speculation (Article 88) was also amended. Previously this was punishable by death only when carried out by a recidivist as "a form of business or in large amounts", but in 1984 this qualification was removed. In 1986 the death penalty for bribe-taking was extended to include officials who had committed the offence more than once, or in an organized manner, or on a large scale (Article 73).

A death sentence may not be passed on anyone under 18 at the time of the offence or when sentence is passed, or on a pregnant woman. In the case of a woman who is pregnant when due for execution, the death sentence must be commuted. The death penalty may not be imposed on anyone ruled to have been insane when the crime was committed or when judgment was passed.

Most capital cases are tried before ordinary courts but suspected spies go before military tribunals – as do members of the armed forces,

KGB officers and prison and labour camp staff. The same codes of law apply in both courts.

Capital cases cannot be tried by the lowest courts but are automatically assigned to courts at the intermediate (city, region, or territory) or higher level. In cases of "extreme complexity" or "particular national importance" the Supreme Court of any republic, or the USSR Supreme Court can act as a court of first instance. In the five republics that have no intermediate courts – Estonia, Latvia, Lithuania, Moldavia and Armenia – the republican Supreme Court generally acts as court of first instance.

As in other criminal cases, a bench of three judges tries capital cases and passes sentence by majority verdict. Only one of the three is professionally trained. The others are lay judges known as "People's Assessors" who sit at most for four weeks in two years.

A defence lawyer must assist in capital cases, but unless the defendant is deaf, dumb or blind, the lawyer may not take part until after the preliminary investigation is complete – a period that may legally last as long as nine months. Prisoners can appeal against the verdict or sentence to the next highest court within seven days of receiving a written copy of the judgment. Because their cases are heard at a higher level at first instance, prisoners under sentence of death have fewer opportunities to appeal than many other prisoners. Since 1980 at least seven prisoners have been sentenced to death without right of appeal. They included a 25-year-old, Gennady Kalinin, sentenced in 1984 by the RSFSR Supreme Court for theft and murder. The outcome of his case is not known.

Death sentences may also be reduced by judicial review. Under this procedure a higher court re-examines the case after it has received a protest against the judgment of the court of first instance or the court of appeal. A protest may be lodged only by a Procurator or a Court President, and their levels of authority in this area are set forth in the Code of Criminal Procedure. Although death sentences are suspended pending appeal, they may still be carried out before a judicial review has been completed.

If these remedies fail, prisoners under sentence of death can petition for clemency, which may be granted by the Presidium of the USSR Supreme Soviet and by the Presidium of a republican Supreme Soviet. The procedure is secret, but reported cases show that clemency is considered only if prisoners petition for it, or if relatives or social organizations do so on their behalf. If clemency is granted the death sentence is commuted to imprisonment of up to 20 years in the harshest type of corrective labour colony.

The Soviet press reports death sentences with approval and often prints prejudicial articles about people who are still awaiting trial for capital crimes. However, in what is officially described as a campaign for *glasnost* (openness), some Soviet lawyers have questioned the fairness of trials, particularly in capital cases. They argue that defendants are powerless during the investigation of their case because they cannot see a lawyer. Judges are predisposed to convict, because the official who prosecutes the case, the Procurator, is also responsible for overseeing "the correct application of the law", and few judges are willing to flout the opinion of such an official. Judges in their turn influence the People's Assessors, who have little or no experience of the law.

Soviet scholars have argued that capital and other trials would be fairer if judges were not dependent on local Communist Party officials for their election, homes and cars. Often judges have been under pressure to choose People's Assessors who will vote with them in controversial cases, and even fix sentences in advance with the judges who will hear the appeal.

It is not known how many people are sentenced to death and executed in the USSR each year because such statistics have been secret since 1934. Press reports indicate, however, that the punishment is used regularly. In 1985 at least 67 death sentences and 34 executions were reported. Another 35 death sentences and at least 14 executions were reported in 1986. In 1987, 61 people were reportedly sentenced to death and another nine were executed. Between January and May 1988 Amnesty International learned of 10 more death sentences and six executions. Only two commutations have been reported since 1985. In 108 cases the final outcome was not known.

More than half the death sentences reported were for murder, or atrocities committed during World War II. However, six officials from Uzbekistan and Kazakhstan were executed for taking bribes and another 21 death sentences were reported for economic crimes. In late 1985 international news agencies stated that 21 Soviet soldiers serving in Afghanistan had been executed for insubordination in combat, but this was not reported in the Soviet press.

A death sentence was passed in at least one political case. Adolf Tolkachev, convicted of being a United States spy, was executed in October 1986.

The reported execution in 1985 of a Georgian former priest, Teymuraz Chikhladze, may also have been politically motivated. He was convicted – on evidence that many Georgians consider suspect – of directing a hijack attempt in which he had not taken part. Reports of public protests at his death sentence were suppressed, and a man suspected of sending the reports abroad received 12 years' imprisonment and exile for "anti-Soviet agitation and propaganda".

▶ In December new draft Fundamentals of Criminal Legislation were published in the Soviet press for discussion. They are due to be adopted by the USSR Supreme Soviet on 15 March 1989. The draft legislation reduces the scope of the death penalty from 18 to six peacetime offences. The six offences which remain punishable by death are treason, espionage, terrorist acts, sabotage, intentional homicide under aggravating circumstances, and rape of minors. Furthermore, women are exempt from the death penalty, as are men who were under 18 at the time of the crime or are 60 when sentence is passed.

United Arab Emirates

Status: Retentionist

Executions 1985 - mid-88: 7; murder; rape; armed robbery

Other factors: Public executions; no right of appeal against sentences imposed by the Federal Supreme Court

Methods of execution: Shooting by firing-squad; stoning; beheading

The death penalty is retained as a mandatory or optional punishment for a number of offences,

the principal legal source of which is Islamic law *(Shari'a)*. Certain capital offences have also been introduced through laws and decrees passed by the Federal National Council. In addition to Islamic law, the Provisional Constitution of 1971 contains a number of provisions relating to the ratification and commutation of death sentences and the granting of clemency.

Offences punishable by death include murder; adultery; rape; armed robbery; certain offences against public and private property; treason; apostasy; and drug-related offences. No death sentences for drug offences had been passed under this law at the time of going to press.

A draft penal code came before the country's Federal National Council for approval during its 1984-1985 session. According to Amnesty International's information, this draft code provides for the death penalty for 15 offences and expands its scope to include offences such as espionage and forming armed factions. However, at the time of going to press no decision on the code had been taken by the council.

Those under the age of 18 at the time of the crime may not be sentenced to death. If the prisoner is pregnant, execution must be stayed until after childbirth.

Death sentences may be imposed by *Shari'a* courts and the federal courts of first instance and are not automatically referred to a higher tribunal for review. However, the accused may appeal to the court of appeal in each emirate or to the High Court of Appeal within 15 days of sentence being passed. The Federal Supreme Court is empowered to hear cases involving crimes affecting the interests of the state (such as crimes relating to the security of the state), and may also impose the death penalty. Federal Supreme Court judgments are not subject to appeal or cassation, although the accused does have the right to seek pardon from the head of state.

Death sentences upheld by the courts of appeal and those passed by the Federal Supreme Court must be ratified by the head of state who is also empowered to commute such sentences or grant pardons, taking into account recommendations made by the Minister of Justice. Death sentences may be commuted to life imprisonment or to a term of imprisonment with additional penalties. Execution is by firing-squad, stoning or beheading by sword.

According to Amnesty International's information, 28 death sentences were passed between 1977 and 1988, of which 13 were known to have been carried out and three commuted. Nine of the sentences were passed in 1985, two in 1986 and two in May 1988. Most of the death sentences were passed by *Shari'a* courts, and were for murder, rape, adultery and armed robbery.

The 13 known executions were all carried out by shooting by firing-squad, although in the case of an Indian executed in 1981 for murder, the original sentence passed by a *Shari'a* court specified that execution was to be by beheading. Ten of the executions were carried out in Abu Dhabi, two in 'Ajman and one in Ra's al-Khaimah. Altogether, 10 executions were reported to have been carried out in public.

The three death sentences that were known to be commuted had been passed in Abu Dhabi for adultery. One death sentence (by stoning) passed on an Indian was commuted to 100 lashes and deportation (July 1982), and in February 1984 an Indian man and a Sri Lankan woman were sentenced to death (also by stoning) by a *Shari'a* court, with a stay of execution in the latter case as the woman was pregnant. Both sentences were subsequently commuted by Shaikh Zayed Ibn Sultan al-Nahayyan to a term of imprisonment, flogging and deportation. According to Amnesty International's information, both these convicted people were deported without being flogged.

United Kingdom

Status: Abolitionist for all but exceptional crimes

Executions 1985 - mid-88: None

Other factors: None

Method of execution: Hanging

The Murder (Abolition of Death Penalty) Act, 1965 abolished the death penalty for murder for a five-year experimental period. Abolition of the death penalty for murder in Great Britain was made permanent by resolutions of both Houses of Parliament on 18 December 1969.

The death penalty is retained for high treason both in peacetime and in wartime under the Treason Act, 1914, and in England and Wales for piracy with violence under the Piracy Act, 1837.

The death penalty is retained for a number of offences committed by members of the armed forces in wartime such as treason and espionage, under the Army Act, 1955; the Air Force Act, 1955; and the Naval Discipline Act, 1957. Under the Armed Forces Act adopted in 1981, the death penalty was abolished for civilians convicted of spying on board a naval ship or at an overseas naval establishment.

A death sentence may not be imposed on anyone who was aged under 18 at the time of the offence nor on a woman pregnant at the date of the imposition of the sentence.

The Royal Prerogative of Mercy is exercised by the monarch on the advice of the Secretary of State for Home Affairs.

The Northern Ireland (Emergency Provisions) Act 1973 abolished the distinction previously used in Northern Ireland between murder and "capital murder" – that is, the murder of a police officer or prison officer in the course of duty – and provided a maximum penalty of life imprisonment for murder.

Several United Kingdom Crown Dependencies – the Channel Islands (Guernsey and Jersey) and the Isle of Man – are internally self-governing and have their own legislatures and legal systems. Jersey retains the death penalty for murder, and the Isle of Man for murder, treason and genocide. Guernsey, however, abolished the death penalty under Section 1 of the Homicide (Guernsey) Law 1965. All recent death sentences imposed in Jersey and the Isle of Man have been commuted by the Queen to life imprisonment.

Since the death penalty was abolished for murder, motions to reintroduce it have been defeated in the House of Commons (lower House of Parliament) on a number of occasions. Most recently a vote on an amendment to the Criminal Justice Bill to reintroduce the death penalty for murder was held on 7 June 1988. The proposed amendment was defeated by 341 votes to 218.

The last executions – of two men convicted of murder – were on 13 August 1964.

United States of America

Status: Retentionist

Executions 1985 - mid-88: 66; murder

Other factors: Children under 18 at the time of the crime executed

Methods of execution: Electrocution; lethal injection; lethal gas; hanging; shooting by firing-squad

The USA is a federation of 50 states which have their own laws, judiciary, elected legislature and state government. In the late 1960s a number of key cases affecting the death penalty statutes of various states were awaiting decisions by the US Supreme Court; this had led to an unofficial moratorium on executions. In what was a crucial case, the US Supreme Court ruled in *Furman v. Georgia* (1972) that the death penalty was being applied in an "arbitrary and capricious" way and constituted "cruel and unusual punishment" in violation of the Constitution. The ruling led to states revising their statutes while the moratorium continued. The first major test case of the new laws was in 1976 in *Gregg v. Georgia*. The Supreme Court upheld the revised laws of a number of states and the death penalty in practice was reintroduced. Since *Furman*, 36 states have revised their statutes and currently authorize the death penalty to be imposed for aggravated murder.[1]

The death penalty is provided for under federal (civilian) law for deaths resulting from aircraft hijacking under the Air Piracy Act, 1974 (49 U.S.C. 1472-3). It is also provided for crimes committed by members of the US armed forces under the Uniform Code of Military Justice (UCMJ), including first-degree murder and a number of other offences, such as espionage and desertion, when committed in wartime.

[1] They are: Alabama, Arizona, Arkansas, California, Colorado, Connecticut, Delaware, Florida, Georgia, Idaho, Illinois, Indiana, Kentucky, Louisiana, Maryland, Mississippi, Missouri, Montana, Nebraska, Nevada, New Hampshire, New Jersey, New Mexico, North Carolina, Ohio, Oklahoma, Oregon, Pennsylvania, South Carolina, South Dakota, Tennessee, Texas, Utah, Virginia, Washington and Wyoming.

The Department of Defense Authorization Act, 1986, amended the UCMJ to provide a maximum sentence of death for members of the armed forces convicted of espionage in peacetime. Although the death penalty remains on the statute books for a number of other federal offences, the laws concerned have not been revised in the light of US Supreme Court rulings in the 1970s and cannot be enforced in their present form.

In June 1988, 30 prisoners in 14 states were under sentence of death for crimes committed when they were under 18 years of age. This is permitted by 25 states, either by not specifying a minimum age or by setting one below 18. Until February 1987 the US Supreme Court had never ruled on whether imposing the death penalty on juvenile offenders was unconstitutional, but it agreed to do so in the case of William Wayne Thompson who was aged 15 at the time of the crime (he was convicted with three adults in Oklahoma of the murder of his former brother-in-law). On 29 June 1988 the Supreme Court ruled by five votes to three to overturn William Thompson's death sentence; however, it left unanswered the key question of whether executing any juvenile offender violated the Constitution.

Most states have legislation providing for the suspension of a death sentence passed on a pregnant woman until the termination of pregnancy. A 1983 study found, however, that 10 states permitted the execution of pregnant women, although in practice it was improbable that this would happen.

As of 1 May 1988 there were 2,048 prisoners under sentence of death in 35 states, including three sentenced under military law. Ninety-eight prisoners, including three juvenile offenders (two in Texas and one in South Carolina), were executed between 1977 (which marked the end of the unofficial 10-year moratorium on executions) and 31 May 1988. Since 1984 the number of executions has fluctuated between 18 and 25 a year. There were 21 executions in 1984, 18 in both 1985 and 1986, and 25 in 1987.

In most states, the only capital offence is aggravated murder (usually first-degree murder). The death penalty is optional and is most commonly imposed for murders committed during the course of an additional serious offence, such as robbery or rape; these are known as "felony murders". There are, however, wide regional disparities in the numbers of death sentences imposed and carried out: just four southern states (Florida, Georgia, Louisiana and Texas) have accounted for more than three-quarters of all executions since 1977.

Trials of capital offences are in two phases: first a verdict of guilty or innocent is reached, then, if found guilty, there is a sentencing (or penalty) phase during which the court considers aggravating and mitigating circumstances. In most states it is the jury who imposes sentence, but in Alabama, Florida and Indiana the jury recommends sentence to the trial judge who is not, however, bound by their recommendation. In four states (Arizona, Idaho, Montana and Nebraska) the judge alone passes sentence.

Capital convictions are appealed automatically to the state supreme court. Further appeals raising constitutional issues may then be made in the state and federal courts. Power to commute death sentences and stay executions normally rests with the state governor or the state Board of Pardons and Paroles (BPP), whose members are usually appointed by the governor. In some cases the BPP makes clemency recommendations to the governor. In recent years, few sentences have been commuted.

The most common methods of execution are electrocution, injection of poison and asphyxiation by gas. A few states provide for execution by firing-squad or hanging.

Although the present laws contain guidelines intended to eliminate arbitrary sentencing in trials of capital offences, research by various US lawyers and academics has shown that whether a death sentence is imposed or not is largely determined by decisions taken by prosecutors at an early stage of the judicial process. Prosecutors have considerable discretion over whether or not to seek the death penalty in a given case, and in practice, only a minority of crimes for which death is a possible penalty are tried as capital offences. Decisions leading to an eventual death sentence may be based on factors beyond the circumstances of the crime itself, including financial and community pressures, the race and social status of the offender and victim, and where the crime was committed. In 1985, 273 prisoners were sentenced to death. In 1986, 330 death sentences were passed. In 1987 some 300 death sentences were passed.

Jury selection procedures in most states allow prosecutors to exclude committed opponents of the death penalty from sitting as jurors in capital trials. This provision was laid down in a 1968 US Supreme Court ruling, *Witherspoon v. Illinois*, and clarified in a 1985 ruling, *Wainwright v. Witt*. Studies have indicated that this practice has created "death-prone" juries more disposed to the imposition of the death penalty, and less impartial when giving their verdict than juries selected under the normal procedures for criminal trials. In 1985 the Eighth Circuit Court of Appeals ruled in an Arkansas case that the exclusion of death penalty opponents from jury service in capital trials was unconstitutional. However, this ruling was challenged by the state of Arkansas and was reversed by the US Supreme Court in *Lockhart v. McCree* (1986).

Black defendants, especially in the southern states, have often been convicted by all-white juries after prosecutors have used their powers of peremptory challenge to exclude black prospective jurors. A US Supreme Court ruling in April 1986 (*Batson v. Kentucky*) made it easier for black defendants to challenge the exclusion of blacks from their trial juries, but this was not retroactive and cannot be a basis of appeal on past decisions.

There is widespread concern about the quality of legal representation given to defendants accused of capital crimes. Many are assigned court-appointed or legal-aid lawyers who are frequently inexperienced, ill-equipped to handle such cases and severely limited in their resources. As most states do not provide funds for the legal representation of capital defendants after their death sentences have been upheld following direct appeal to the state supreme court, in order to file further appeals on constitutional grounds, they must rely on volunteer lawyers working without payment. A shortage of volunteer lawyers, especially in the southern states, means that some defendants may not be represented at this important stage of the judicial process. Although a relatively large number of death sentences are overturned on appeal, the courts are limited in their ability to redress fundamental inconsistencies in the system, especially where these result from discretionary decisions taken by the prosecutor at an early stage of the judicial process.

Blacks comprise 12 per cent of the national population but 41 per cent of prisoners under sentence of death. The evidence suggests that race – especially that of the victim – has an important bearing on the likelihood of a death sentence being imposed, particularly in the southern states. Although blacks and whites are the victims of homicide in almost equal numbers, most offenders who are sentenced to death are convicted of murdering whites (86 per cent in 1987). Forty-five of the 98 prisoners executed between January 1977 and May 1988 were black or Hispanic, and 84 of the 98 had been convicted of killing white victims.

In an important ruling on race discrimination and the death penalty (*McCleskey v. Kemp*) the US Supreme Court considered a detailed study which, after measuring for over 230 non-racial factors, showed that in Georgia white-victim homicides were over four times more likely to result in death sentences than black-victim homicides. In this ruling, issued in April 1987, the Court ruled by five votes to four that Georgia's death penalty statute was constitutional, although the risk of race being a factor in death sentencing was acknowledged. Four of the nine justices gave strongly-worded dissenting opinions arguing that there was a risk of racial discrimination in the application of Georgia's death penalty statute which was unconstitutional.

Evidence suggests that many prisoners under sentence of death in the USA may be mentally handicapped or suffer from mental illness. A June 1987 report by the Clearinghouse on Georgia Jails and Prisons estimated that 20 per cent of prisoners under sentence of death in the state may have below-average intelligence or be severely mentally handicapped. Although states have procedures for testing prisoners' mental competence, most tests evaluate sanity and mentally handicapped prisoners are usually found to be sane.

Since 1984 at least six prisoners diagnosed as mentally handicapped or as borderline cases have been executed. In April 1988 Georgia became the first state to prohibit the imposition of the death penalty on those convicted of murder found "guilty but mentally retarded". The new law came into effect in July 1988. Most US states with provision for the death penalty forbid the execution of insane prisoners, either by statute or by case law. Nevertheless, at least three prisoners suffering from mental illness have been executed in recent years and others have come close to being executed. (In 1986 the US Supreme Court held in *Ford v. Wainwright* that Florida's procedures for determining sanity at the time of execution were inadequate.)

The death penalty has been imposed on prisoners who have later been found to be innocent and have been cleared of the charges against them. Some prisoners have been executed even though new evidence brought to light by lawyers and investigators had cast doubt on their guilt. A study published in 1987 cited 349 US cases in which innocent people were wrongly convicted of crimes punishable by death between 1900 and 1985; 23 of them were executed. Since 1985 at least two prisoners who may have been innocent have been executed: Willie Jasper Darden was executed in Florida on 15 March 1988 despite evidence from two independent alibi witnesses suggesting that he could not have been at the scene of the crime when the murder was committed. International appeals, including messages from the Pope, Andrei Sakharov and the Reverend Jesse Jackson, failed to persuade Governor Martinez to grant clemency. The other was Edward Earl Johnson, executed in Mississippi on 20 May 1987 for the murder of a white police officer. Following Edward Johnson's arrest, an eye-witness to the crime (who knew him personally) at first told the police that he was not the assailant. Edward Johnson, who always maintained that he was innocent, alleged that the police had threatened him and coerced him into signing a confession on the basis of which he was sentenced to death. Since his execution, an alibi witness has stated that she was with Edward Johnson at a pool hall at the time the murder was committed.

Puerto Rico, a self-governing US territory with Commonwealth status, abolished the death penalty for all offences in 1929. The death penalty had been permitted since 1879, during the period of Spanish rule. It was retained in a statute of 1902 when Puerto Rico came under US domination. In 1917 a law was passed suspending use of the death penalty for a four-year period ending in April 1921. In April 1929 the death penalty was abolished by Law 42. This prohibition was enshrined in the Bill of Rights of the Constitution of the Commonwealth of Puerto Rico in 1952, which states, "There will be no death penalty" (Article II, Section 7).

The last executions were carried out in 1902 when four men were executed for murder. The method of execution used was the garrotte.

▶ On 30 June 1988 the US Supreme Court said it would again review the constitutionality of the death penalty for juveniles. It is hoped that the court will rule for the first time on whether the execution of anyone who was under 18 at the time of their offence violates the US Constitution's ban on cruel and unusual punishment.

Two executions were carried out in June 1988 (Arthur Gary Bishop in Utah, and Edward Byrne in Louisiana), and one in July (James Messer in Georgia).

Uruguay

Status: Abolitionist

Executions 1985 - mid-88: None

Other factors: Not applicable

Method of execution: Not applicable

The death penalty was abolished by law for all offences, including those subject to military law, on 23 September 1907. The 1889 code of practice to the 1830 Constitution had stated that the death penalty should be applied only "with the greatest discretion" for "atrocious crimes". Prohibition was enshrined in Article 163 of the 1918 Constitution, and repeated in subsequent versions. The 1967 Constitution, currently in force, states, "The death penalty will not be applied to anybody" (Article 26). The last execution took place at the end of the nineteenth century.

Vanuatu

Status: Abolitionist

Executions 1985 - mid-88: None

Other factors: Not applicable

Method of execution: Not applicable

Vanuatu, which had previously been the joint British-French dominion of the New Hebrides, became independent in July 1980. Before independence, the Code of Criminal Law, 1973, had made no provision for the death penalty, the maximum sentence being life imprisonment. This was retained in Vanuatu's Penal Code of 1981.

Vatican City State

Status: Abolitionist

Executions 1985 - mid-88: None

Other factors: Not applicable

Method of execution: Not applicable

In June 1929, offences committed within Vatican City State were placed under the jurisdiction of the Italian Penal Code and related laws under Article 4 of the Vatican Law on the Sources of Legislation (see under *Italy*). Article 4 stated that attacks on the life, person or liberty of the Pope were punishable in accordance with Article 1 of Italian Law No. 2008 of 25 November 1926, which provided the death penalty for attacks on the head of state. Article 4 also stated that in the case of an attack on a foreign head of state within Vatican City State, the penalty would be that applicable in the victim's own state.

On 21 June 1969, however, a Vatican law was promulgated which amended Vatican penal law and procedure and repealed the provisions of Article 4, thereby abolishing the death penalty for all offences.

Venezuela

Status: Abolitionist

Executions 1985 - mid-88: None

Other factors: Not applicable

Method of execution: Not applicable

The death penalty was abolished for political offences in 1849 and for all offences in 1863 under the government of General Juan Crisostomo Falcón. Article 58 of the Venezuela Constitution (1961) states, "The right to life is inviolate. No law can impose the death penalty, nor any authority apply it."

Viet Nam

Status: Retentionist

Executions 1985 - mid-88: 3+; treason and espionage

Other factors: None

Method of execution: Shooting by firing-squad

The death penalty has been in use since the colonial era. It was retained first by the Democratic Republic of Viet Nam (DRV) in 1945, again applied in the DRV and the Republic of Viet Nam (RVN) following the partition of the country in 1954, and again following the end of hostilities and reunification of the country in 1976, under the newly constituted Socialist Republic of Viet Nam.

Although no official statistics on the use and application of the death penalty since 1976 appear to have been made public, Justice Minister Phan Hien was reported in 1985 as saying "several dozen executions are carried out each year", mainly for violent crimes but sometimes for economic offences considered to constitute crimes against state security. He said the government saw a need to "set examples" in order to "educate the population". To Amnesty International's knowledge only eight new death sentences and three executions were reported by the official media between 1985 and May 1988, but it is believed that the actual figure may be considerably higher.

The three known executions took place in January 1985 after appeals for clemency had been dismissed by the Council of State following conviction of the accused on charges of treason and espionage. In 1985 two death sentences were imposed, one on conviction of "plotting to overthrow the government", and the other reported as the first death penalty imposed for an "economic crime". In 1986 three death sentences were imposed for armed robbery; the murder of a public security official while attempting to flee the country; and "counter-revolutionary" activities. During 1987 three death sentences were reported, two for embezzlement and one for armed robbery and attempted murder.

A Code of Criminal Law, representing the first systematic codification of laws since the formation of the DRV in 1945, came into force in January 1986. Prior to this, most laws in Viet Nam were issued as separate decrees, ordinances or resolutions by the Council of Ministers and were supplemented by decisions and circulars issued by the Supreme People's Court and the Supreme People's Organ of Control. As such, decrees providing for the death penalty for offences considered a threat to the state were introduced from 1946 and were extended further in the following decades.

The new Code of Criminal Law incorporates most of these earlier provisions, particularly those pertaining to crimes formerly described as "counter-revolutionary acts" which are punishable by death in especially serious cases. These include high treason; espionage against the independence and territorial integrity of the Socialist Republic of Viet Nam; acts of terrorism; banditry; sabotage; and hijacking or other acts aimed at the overthrow or subversion of the socialist system. Thirteen out of the total 18 provisions of the Code dealing with Especially Dangerous Crimes against National Security retain the death penalty as a form of punishment (Articles 72-79, 84, 87, 94, 95 and 98).

Apart from offences against national security, the Code of Criminal Law contains a further 16 articles out of a total of 280 which allow for the imposition of the death penalty for crimes against the life, health, dignity and honour of humankind, including murder, rape and armed robbery; crimes against social ownership, including theft and embezzlement; crimes against a citizen's right of ownership; economic crimes; crimes against the obligation and responsibility of military personnel; and undermining peace, war crimes and crimes against humanity.

Defendants are usually tried in courts of first instance by provincial or municipal People's Courts and have the right to appeal to the Supreme People's Court. On dismissal of the appeal, they may petition the Chairperson of the Council of State to commute any death sentence.

Article 27 of the Code of Criminal Law stipulates that the death penalty may not be imposed on children below the age of 16 at the time of the crime, and that executions of pregnant women or women raising a child aged under one year will be delayed. The same article states that in "special cases specifically stipulated by law" the death penalty can be carried out immediately after the trial. This appears to have been enforced in January 1985 when three people were executed within 20 days of their first hearing before the Supreme Court, which sentenced them (and two others whose sentences were subsequently commuted to life imprisonment) to death upon conviction of counter-revolutionary activities and espionage. It appears that there was no review of their conviction and sentence by any other court, which was upheld by the Council of State in dismissing their applications for clemency.

▶ In 1988 five death sentences were imposed, two of them on Buddhist monks convicted of "counter-revolutionary activities". These two sentences were commuted later in the year.

Western Samoa

Status: Abolitionist in practice

Executions 1985 - mid-88: None

Other factors: None

Method of execution: Hanging

The death penalty is mandatory for treason and murder under Articles 28 and 66 of the Crimes Ordinance, 1961, but it is not used in practice. Since independence in 1962, all death sentences have been commuted to terms of imprisonment by the head of state. The Constitution empowers the head of state to grant pardons and reprieves and to commute any sentence passed by the courts, after consultation with government ministers (Article 110). The law provides that death sentences may not be imposed on pregnant women or anyone under the age of 18 at the time the crime was committed.

Yemen (Arab Republic)

Status: Retentionist

Executions 1985 - mid-88: 34+; murder; aggravated robbery

Other factors: Public executions; corpses may be crucified following execution

Methods of execution: Beheading; shooting by firing-squad; stoning

Although the Yemen Arab Republic (YAR) has no penal code, a draft penal code issued in 1978 appears to reflect existing practice and sometimes to be referred to by the courts, even though it is not law. A Code of Criminal Procedure was adopted in Law No. 5 of 1979.

The draft penal code provides for a mandatory death penalty for *hadd* offences (offences against divine will according to *Shari'a*, Islamic law), including illicit sexual intercourse and sodomy; aggravated robbery; and apostasy from Islam. Crimes against the state, aggravated murder or kidnapping and certain military offences are also punishable by death. The death penalty as *qisas* (retribution, in accordance with the wishes of a murder victim's family or heirs) may be imposed for the murder of a Muslim only. According to the draft penal code, the *hadd* punishment lapses if the offender converts to Islam or repents following apostasy. The head of state may waive or delay punishment of a *hadd* offence if this would be in the "public interest".

Those deemed insane, and children aged under 15 at the time of the crime are not considered criminally responsible. Women may not be executed while pregnant nor until two years after giving birth, and there must be others who can support the child thereafter.

Death penalty cases are tried by courts of first instance and later by one of several provincial courts of appeal. They are automatically appealed to the Supreme Court of Cassation. If upheld, death sentences are finally reviewed by the Supreme Council of Justice, presided over by the head of state. No death sentence can be carried out unless ratified by the head of state.

According to the Code of Criminal Procedure, executions are carried out in a prison or place designated for this purpose. Visits by relatives are allowed on the day of execution provided they are away from the place of execution.

Executions are to be carried out "without drama or torture", by beheading by sword or by shooting; stoning is used for certain sexual offences. For aggravated robbery the method is as indicated in the verdict and may be followed by crucifixion of the corpse for up to three days. The body is buried at government expense if no relatives request it to be returned to them.

In 1987 at least 25 people were executed, in public, 22 in implementation of *qisas* for murder, and three for aggravated robbery. By 31 May 1988 a further nine people had been executed in implementation of *qisas* for murder. Amnesty International has little information on the use of the death penalty in previous years, but has learned that in 1986 a man was executed for murder after receiving 100 lashes for sexual offences, and a former Sana'a University professor was sentenced to death *in absentia* for apostasy from Islam on the basis of his writings. Between 1973 and 1978 Amnesty International recorded over 100 executions for sabotage or treason, including some carried out after trials by a special military court.

▶ Between June and December 1988 at least 15 people were executed in implementation of *qisas* for murder.

Yemen (People's Democratic Republic of)

Status: Retentionist

Executions 1985 - mid-88: 5+; treason

Other factors: None

Method of execution: Shooting by firing-squad

The People's Democratic Republic of Yemen's Penal Code (Law No. 3 of 1976) stipulates that the death penalty is an "exceptional temporary measure" to be imposed, pending total abolition, for the most serious crimes "when it is necessary for the protection of society and there is no hope of reforming the offender through the penalty of imprisonment". Its imposition is not mandatory for capital offences included in the Penal Code except, apparently, in one instance (see below).

Crimes punishable by death under the Penal Code include crimes against peace and humanity, such as initiating a war of aggression and persecuting or exterminating specific groups of people; war crimes; and crimes against the state and the people, such as treason, spying, and acts of terrorism or sabotage aimed at undermining the existing order.

Capital crimes that affect society or public safety include forming or participating in armed bands, hijacking aircraft (if this leads to serious harm to life or property), polluting air or water and arson or other acts of destruction committed in aggravating circumstances.

Murder is punishable by death if aggravated by several circumstances, including greed, revenge, use of cruel means, and if the victim is a pregnant woman or a public official murdered on account of his or her position. Other crimes against the person punishable by death include the rape of a female if it leads to her death or suicide.

A person giving false testimony leading to a death sentence is to be punished with the same penalty as that imposed on the offender. This is the only instance in the Penal Code in which the death penalty appears to be mandatory.

There are also a number of crimes against public property and the national economy which are punishable by death, such as theft, burglary, and destruction of or damage to public property, in aggravating circumstances.

Neither the Military Penal Code nor the Military Code of Criminal Procedures are published. Amnesty International does not know which offences, if any, involve capital punishment.

Those under 18 at the time of the crime cannot be sentenced to death, and people whose actions were impaired by mental illness or were unintentionally affected by alcohol or drugs at the time the crime was committed are not considered criminally responsible. A woman who was pregnant at the time of the crime or the sentence cannot be sentenced to death, nor can a woman who kills her child while giving birth or immediately after its delivery.

Defendants tried *in absentia* are entitled to a retrial. Ordinary death penalty cases are tried by one of six Governorate (province) Courts and death sentences are automatically sent for review by the Supreme Court of the Republic.

Death penalty cases of particular gravity are tried in the first instance by the Supreme Court, composed of three judges. The Code of Criminal Procedure provides for a form of appeal against decisions of this court, which allows any party to question the application of the law or possible substantial flaws in the proceedings. Such an appeal must be examined by a body which includes all the Supreme Court judges.

It is not known whether military courts, which try offences by members of the armed forces, have death penalty jurisdiction. It appears that there are at least three military courts linked to the Ministries of Defence, Interior and State Security.

The Constitution of 1978 formally prohibits the establishment of special courts. Previously, special courts with death penalty jurisdiction were in operation, such as the People's Courts, for trying mainly security offences.

A death sentence cannot be carried out until it is ratified by the head of state (Chairman of the Presidium of the Supreme People's Council) who may also commute it, pardon the offender or grant a reprieve.

A prisoner condemned to death is kept in solitary confinement under a 24-hour watch. Visits by relatives are permitted the day before the execution, which is carried out by firing-squad, apparently always in al-Mansura Prison in Aden. According to law, the body is buried by the prison administration and is not returned to the family.

In December 1987 five people were executed 17 days after having been convicted by the Supreme Court of offences which included treason and were related to the civil war in January 1986. Recorded executions before that, carried out in 1982, were of 10 people convicted of sabotage by the Supreme Court. Amnesty International has no information on executions for ordinary criminal offences, but at least two death sentences are known to have been ratified by the head of state as of 31 May 1988.

Yugoslavia

Status: Retentionist

Executions 1985 - mid-88: 4; murder

Other factors: None

Method of execution: Shooting by firing-squad

The Constitution of the Socialist Federal Republic of Yugoslavia describes the death penalty as an "exceptional" measure. It is always an optional punishment. Although the law provides for the death penalty for a wide range of offences, over the last 10 years its imposition has been limited largely to cases of aggravated murder (such as multiple or particularly brutal murders).

The eight criminal codes of the country's six constituent republics and two autonomous provinces, all enacted in 1977, provide for the death penalty for the following crimes: aggravated forms of murder; armed robbery resulting in loss of life (except for the republics of Croatia and Slovenia); and aiding or inciting anyone under 14 or of unsound mind to commit suicide (except for Kosovo province).

In addition, a person who aids anyone under 18 in perpetrating aggravated murder may be punished by death under the criminal codes of Serbia and Kosovo province, a measure designed to discourage families from using minors (exempt from the death penalty) to carry out vendetta killings.

Almost a third (45) of the 141 articles of the Federal Criminal Code of 1977 prescribe the death penalty. A person who commits murder "out of motives hostile to Yugoslavia" may be punished by death as may a Yugoslav citizen who "signs or recognizes capitulation or who accepts or recognizes the occupation of Yugoslavia or any part of it". Article 139 defines the circumstances which can make certain political offences capital: these include not only loss of life but also "danger to human life", "great violence or great destruction", when the security or the economic or military strength of the country is jeopardized, "or in other particularly grave cases". These circumstances apply not only to offences such as terrorism and armed revolt, but also to offences which do not involve violence or loss of life, such as espionage and "association for the purpose of hostile activity", or which concern damage to property (the destruction of important economic objects out of motives hostile to Yugoslavia). Genocide and other war crimes, certain military offences (when committed in wartime) and hijacking resulting in loss of life are also punishable by death.

Those aged under 18 at the time of the offence and pregnant women cannot be sentenced to death. A pregnant woman cannot be executed during pregnancy or for a year after she has given birth. Severely physically and mentally ill people cannot be executed while their illness lasts.

Civilians charged with capital crimes are tried in ordinary courts, from which appeal may be made to the Supreme Court of the republic or autonomous province. Final appeal is to the Federal Court for federal offences and to a different panel of the Supreme Court for other cases. Military personnel are tried by military courts, from which appeal may be made to the Supreme Military Court and to the Federal Court. Once all the avenues of appeal have been exhausted, defendants have the right to petition for clemency to the Presidency of the respective republic or autonomous province or to the Federal Presidency in the case of federal offences. These bodies automatically review death sentences even if no petition for clemency is filed by the defendant. Amnesty International knows of only two cases since 1978 in which clemency was granted.

According to official statistics, between 1973 and 1987, 49 death sentences were upheld in the final court of appeal. These comprised three imposed for armed robbery resulting in loss of life, two for war crimes and one for sabotage; the other 43 were imposed for aggravated murder. These figures do not include death sentences imposed by military courts: according to a 1979 *Reuters* report, three Croatians involved in an armed incursion into the country were executed in 1973.

Amnesty International learned of six death sentences imposed in 1985, four in 1986, three death sentences and three executions in 1987 and four death sentences and one execution in the first five months of 1988. All those executed had been convicted of aggravated murder.

Sentencing policy differs widely from one part of the country to another. To promote greater uniformity, legislative changes were proposed in 1988 whereby the Federal Court would review all death sentences in final instance.

In its report submitted in 1983 to the Human Rights Committee, set up under the International Covenant on Civil and Political Rights, the government stated that the "prevailing view is that it [the death penalty] should not be abolished for the time being". However, it declared that "the Yugoslav self-management socialist society is oriented towards abolishing capital punishment".

Despite this orientation, the authorities have blocked attempts to legalize an abolitionist movement in the country. In 1981 the Society to Campaign for the Abolition of the Death Penalty was refused official registration (and thus the right to act publicly). The Society for the Dissemination of Knowledge about the Death Penalty met with a similar refusal in 1987.

In 1984 a petition to abolish the death penalty was submitted to the Federal Assembly; it had received some 1,500 signatures. After debate, the Assembly concluded that there were as yet "no constitutional or other prerequisites for abolition". Nonetheless, further proposals for the abolition of the death penalty were under discussion in 1988. In March 1988 the President of the Supreme Court of Slovenia announced that the death penalty in Slovenia (where the last execution was reportedly in 1957) would soon be abolished. In April 1988 it was officially announced that the Federal Assembly would soon be presented with changes to the Federal Criminal Code which would reduce the number of offences punishable by death.

▶ On 29 July 1988 the Yugoslav press reported the execution of Laszlo Egete, aged 35, who had been convicted of the rape and murder of a nine-year-old girl.

Zaire

Status: Retentionist

Executions 1985 - mid-88: 4+; armed robbery with murder; armed rebellion

Other factors: None

Methods of execution: Shooting by firing-squad; hanging

The death penalty is mandatory for a wide range of offences and a considerable number of death sentences are imposed by the courts on those convicted of murder and armed robbery. However, there appear to have been relatively few executions in recent years.

Under the Penal Code the death penalty is mandatory for premeditated murder; some offences against the person involving loss of life, such as rape or kidnapping; armed robbery; treason; and a number of other political offences, such as attempts on the head of state's life, and leading an insurgency. Those convicted of criminal association may also be sentenced to death. The Code of Military Justice provides for members of the armed forces to be sentenced to death for a variety of offences, especially those committed during times of war or in the course of military operations, such as desertion and unnecessary surrender, and also genocide and abuses against non-combatants such as pillage and reprisal killings.

Capital cases are tried by *tribunaux de grande instance* (district courts responsible for trying serious cases), rather than local courts. Those sentenced to death have a right of appeal to a provincial appeal court. Those convicted by the State Security Court, which tries civilians charged with political offences, have no right of appeal but, like civilians whose death sentences are confirmed upon appeal, they may seek a review of their trial on points of law by the Judicial Section of the Supreme Court. No death sentences are known to have been imposed by the State Security Court since 1977. Before 1980 those convicted by military courts had no right of appeal, but in 1980 the Code of Military Justice was amended to allow a right of appeal for those convicted by military courts in peacetime.

Women who are pregnant at the time they are sentenced to death cannot by law be executed until after delivery. Children aged 15 or under cannot be sentenced to death.

State prosecutors must refer all death sentences confirmed on appeal to the head of state for review and possible commutation. It is not known how the review process is carried out and long periods sometimes elapse before decisions are announced; for example, a petition for clemency concerning a prisoner whose death sentence had been confirmed on appeal in 1977 was eventually rejected in January 1986. Even when petitions for clemency are rejected, death sentences are not necessarily carried out. Furthermore, President Mobutu Sese Seko has occasionally ordered the commutation of all death sentences confirmed on appeal. The last such commutation was announced in October 1980, but the number of prisoners who benefited is not known.

Methods of execution are not fixed by law, except in the case of those sentenced to death by military courts, who are executed by firing-squad. However, other executions are reported to have been by hanging. The main legal text governing the way executions are carried out dates from 1898, but there have been numerous changes in practice, as in 1966, when four government opponents were publicly hanged in the capital. A 1936 law forbids the photographing of executions and makes it an offence to be in possession of a camera within 150 metres of a place where an execution is occurring.

No official statistics concerning the number of death sentences or executions are published, but the results of clemency petitions are printed in the government gazette. These indicate that in 1985 only one sentence was confirmed, and that during the first half of 1986 nine petitions for clemency were rejected.

The number of death sentences confirmed by the head of state and the number of executions appears to have been significantly lower in the mid-1980s than in earlier years. A considerable number of death sentences was imposed by military courts in the late 1970s, after armed rebellions in Shaba region and after the discovery of an alleged conspiracy against the President. Many of those sentenced to death were executed: for example, in March 1978 13 people were executed the day after they were convicted of plotting against the President.

During the 1980s death sentences have been imposed in particular to punish certain types of crime, such as armed robbery and abuses by soldiers. Soldiers convicted of killing or robbing civilians have been sentenced to death, although relatively few are known to have been executed. Executions have been announced on only two occasions, in 1981 and 1986: in both cases the victims had been convicted of armed robbery and murder in widely-publicized cases. At least 17 prisoners were hanged in March 1981 and four were executed in 1986. The rope used in the 1981 hangings at Luzumu prison was made of nylon and when some of the victims did not die immediately on the gallows they were shot dead by guards.

The number of executions carried out without being announced officially is not known. Prisoners sentenced to death by the courts are known to have been executed in secret, but such executions have been difficult to distinguish from extrajudicial executions, which have also often occurred. In 1981 a non-commissioned officer sentenced to death *in absentia* in 1978 was executed in secret some time after he had surrendered to the authorities in the hope of benefiting from an amnesty announced for government opponents in 1979. In 1984 and 1985 executions were reported in the aftermath of an insurgency in northeast Shaba region. Official sources indicated subsequently that some insurgents had been tried and sentenced to death by military courts. No details of any trials were made public, however, and it appeared that many of those killed had been victims of extrajudicial executions.

▶ Six prisoners were reportedly executed in Bukavu in August 1988.

Zambia

Status: Retentionist

Executions 1985 - mid-88: 11; murder; aggravated robbery

Other factors: None

Method of execution: Hanging

Under the Penal Code the death penalty is mandatory for murder, treason and aggravated robbery – the latter being defined as theft involving actual or threatened use of violence. Zambia has been seriously affected by violent crime in recent years and at least 50 death sentences were imposed between 1985 and 1987 for murder and aggravated robbery. According to some reports, at least 140 prisoners were under sentence of death at the end of 1987.

The latest executions were carried out on 27 December 1985, when 11 prisoners convicted of murder and aggravated robbery were hanged at Kabwe Maximum Security Prison. Apparently one of those executed had been under sentence of death since 1975.

Capital offences are tried in public in the High Court, where defendants have the right to a defence lawyer of their choice. There is an automatic right of appeal to the Supreme Court. If the higher court upholds the death sentence, the case is referred to the Advisory Committee on the Prerogative of Mercy which makes recommendations to the President concerning clemency. Pregnant women and children aged under 18 at the time of the offence may not be sentenced to death.

There have been no executions of prisoners convicted in politically related cases since independence in 1964. In 1983 the High Court sentenced seven men to death for their alleged part in a plot to overthrow the government in 1980. The Supreme Court quashed the conviction of two of them in 1985, but confirmed the conviction and upheld the death sentences imposed on Edward Shamwana, a former High Court Commissioner, and four others. However, in November 1986 President Kenneth Kaunda commuted all five sentences to life imprisonment.

While under sentence of death Edward Shamwana brought a number of suits to the High Court against the prison authorities, alleging torture, solitary confinement, harassment and denial of access to medical treatment and a priest. The courts did not rule in favour of any of these cases, although Edward Shamwana did receive an apology from the prison authorities for the denial of access to a priest. Edward Shamwana also complained that he was denied food on occasions when he was transferred to Lusaka for court hearings. Amnesty International has received reports that the conditions for condemned prisoners in Kabwe Prison are very poor, with severe overcrowding, inadequate food and frequent punishments for alleged disciplinary offences. Some prisoners are apparently unable to obtain pens and paper in order to draft their appeals for clemency.

There has been little public statement of opposition to the use of the death penalty in Zambia, although one High Court judge made a speech in 1986 in which he recommended its abolition. A letter to the official *Times of Zambia* later the same year criticized the death penalty as a violation of Zambia's ruling doctrine of humanism: "Punishment must be seen as a form of school. It is therefore unthinkable that a convict would reform once sent to the gallows."

Zimbabwe

Status: Retentionist

Executions 1985 - mid-88: 24; murder

Other factors: None

Method of execution: Hanging

The death penalty is in force for a wide variety of offences, many of them relating to armed political opposition. After independence in 1980 no executions were carried out for two years and in 1981 the President commuted all death sentences. Since 1982, however, there have been an increasing number of executions, totalling 24 up to 31 May 1988. The Rhodesian Government which held power before 1980 often executed political prisoners, sometimes

in secret after trials which were held *in camera*. The insane, children under 16 and pregnant women may not be sentenced to death.

People accused of capital offences are tried in the High Court, where they have the right to a defence counsel of their own choice. Those sentenced to death can automatically appeal to the Supreme Court, consisting of the Chief Justice and at least two other judges of appeal. If the sentence is confirmed the President has the power to grant clemency. At least 39 people were sentenced to death between 1985 and 1987 – 14 in 1985, 18 in 1986 and 7 in 1987 – although in some cases the Supreme Court later reduced their sentences.

The death penalty may be imposed for treason; murder; attempted murder; conspiracy and incitement to murder; rape and attempted rape; robbery and attempted robbery where there are aggravating circumstances; any offence dangerous to life in which murder took place; and a variety of offences related to political opposition, including unlawful possession of arms, arson, interfering with an essential service, causing substantial financial loss to any person or the state and sabotage of the railways. Many of these offences are contained in the Law and Order (Maintenance) Act, introduced by the former Rhodesian Government and retained by independent Zimbabwe. Since 1980, however, people have been executed only for murder. Murder carries a mandatory death sentence unless the court finds that there are extenuating circumstances.

Executions are carried out by hanging and groups of prisoners are periodically hanged on the same day. Ten people were executed in the space of a week in August 1985, another five on a single day in April 1986, and nine within a week in May 1987. Announcing these last executions, the Sheriff of Zimbabwe, an official of the High Court, described them as "in line with the government's desire to rid society of undesirables".

In May 1984 President Robert Mugabe, then Prime Minister, was reported to have stated that the government would consider abolishing the death penalty once the problem of armed insurgency in the southwest of the country had ended. The Minister of Justice made a similar statement in December 1984, only weeks after the Provincial Governor of Matabeleland South had called for the public execution of armed rebels by firing-squad. However, only nine of the 24 prisoners executed between 1985 and 1987 were described by the semi-official press as being "dissidents" or armed rebels.

A number of prominent voices have been raised against the use of the death penalty in Zimbabwe. In a speech in December 1987 the Chief Justice, Enoch Dumbutshena, called on the government to review the use of the death penalty – in particular the imposition of mandatory sentences for murder – and stressed the need for rehabilitation of offenders. Later the same month Chenjerai Hove, a prominent poet, took up the theme of rehabilitation in an article in the semi-official *Herald* newspaper, "If the human race is to claim to be more civilized than any other species, it is time our civilizations were based not on how sophisticatedly we can kill our neighbours, but rather on how efficiently we are able to ennoble human and other life around us … the death sentence is abominable, as abominable as the crime itself. Our state must be based on love, not hatred and victimization. Our penal code must be based on rehabilitation rather than annihilation."

Appendices

The following appendices give the texts of the main international standards on the death penalty. Also included are several statements and documents from Amnesty International and other organizations.

As described in Chapter 3, international human rights standards provide for restrictions and safeguards in countries where the death penalty has not yet been abolished. The UN and other intergovernmental organizations have set up machinery for attempting to ensure that the agreed safeguards and restrictions are observed.

The Human Rights Committee set up under the ICCPR regularly receives reports from states parties to the Covenant on the measures they have taken to give effect to the rights contained therein. The Committee can also receive complaints from individuals alleging that their human rights have been violated by any state which has become a party to the Optional Protocol to the Covenant.

The UN Special Rapporteur on summary or arbitrary executions, appointed in 1982, has developed a system of sending urgent messages to governments on the basis of appeals from various sources alleging imminent or threatened summary executions, including executions in cases where the 1984 ECOSOC safeguards have not been observed. Some of these involve extrajudicial executions where the victims have not been charged or tried for an offence punishable by death, but the majority are in death penalty cases where safeguards may have been lacking.

The UN Secretary-General can use his "best endeavours" to intercede with governments in death penalty cases where the safeguards provided for in Articles 6, 14 and 15 of the ICCPR appear not to have been respected.[1] Individuals and organizations who have known of such impending cases have presented their information to the Secretary-General with a view to seeking his intercession, and while his appeals are normally kept confidential, he is free to make his concerns public.[2]

Finally, in the Americas and in Western Europe, institutions have been created to examine complaints of violations of the human rights set forth in the respective regional human rights treaties. These are the Inter-American Commission on Human Rights and the Inter-American Court of Human Rights with regard to the American Convention on Human Rights, and the European Commission of Human Rights and the European Court of Human Rights for the European Convention on Human Rights.

1 He was requested to do so by the UN General Assembly in resolution 35/172 of 15 December 1980 (see Appendix 9).

2 Rodley, *op. cit.* pages 187-190.

Appendix I

Universal Declaration of Human Rights (extracts)

Article 3
Everyone has the right to life, liberty and security of person.

Article 5
No one shall be subjected to torture or to cruel, inhuman or degrading treatment or punishment.

Appendix 2

International Covenant on Civil and Political Rights (extracts)

Article 6

1. Every human being has the inherent right to life. This right shall be protected by law. No one shall be arbitrarily deprived of his life.

2. In countries which have not abolished the death penalty, sentence of death may be imposed only for the most serious crimes in accordance with the law in force at the time of the commission of the crime and not contrary to the provisions of the present Covenant and to the Convention on the Prevention and Punishment of the Crime of Genocide. This penalty can only be carried out pursuant to a final judgment rendered by a competent court.

3. When deprivation of life constitutes the crime of genocide, it is understood that nothing in this article shall authorize any State Party to the present Covenant to derogate in any way from any obligation assumed under the provisions of the Convention on the Prevention and Punishment of the Crime of Genocide.

4. Anyone sentenced to death shall have the right to seek pardon or commutation of the sentence. Amnesty, pardon or commutation of the sentence of death may be granted in all cases.

5. Sentence of death shall not be imposed for crimes committed by persons below eighteen years of age and shall not be carried out on pregnant women.

6. Nothing in this article shall be invoked to delay or to prevent the abolition of capital punishment by any State Party to the present Covenant.

Article 14

1. All persons shall be equal before the courts and tribunals. In the determination of any criminal charge against him, or of his rights and obligations in a suit at law, everyone shall be entitled to a fair and public

hearing by a competent, independent and impartial tribunal established by law. The Press and the public may be excluded from all or part of a trial for reasons of morals, public order (*ordre public*) or national security in a democratic society, or when the interest of the private lives of the parties so requires, or to the extent strictly necessary in the opinion of the court in special circumstances where publicity would prejudice the interests of justice; but any judgment rendered in a criminal case or in a suit at law shall be made public except where the interest of juvenile persons otherwise requires or the proceedings concern matrimonial disputes or the guardianship of children.

2. Everyone charged with a criminal offence shall have the right to be presumed innocent until proved guilty according to law.

3. In the determination of any criminal charge against him, everyone shall be entitled to the following minimum guarantees, in full equality:

(a) To be informed promptly and in detail in a language which he understands of the nature and cause of the charge against him;

(b) To have adequate time and facilities for the preparation of his defence and to communicate with counsel of his own choosing;

(c) To be tried without undue delay;

(d) To be tried in his presence, and to defend himself in person or through legal assistance of his own choosing; to be informed, if he does not have legal assistance, of this right; and to have legal assistance assigned to him, in any case where the interests of justice so require, and without payment by him in any such case if he does not have sufficient means to pay for it;

(e) To examine, or have examined, the witnesses against him and to obtain the attendance and examination of witnesses on his behalf under the same conditions as witnesses against him;

(f) To have the free assistance of an interpreter if he cannot understand or speak the language used in court;

(g) Not to be compelled to testify against himself or to confess guilt.

4. In the case of juvenile persons, the procedure shall be such as will take account of their age and the desirability of promoting their rehabilitation.

5. Everyone convicted of a crime shall have the right to his conviction and sentence being reviewed by a higher tribunal according to law.

6. When a person has by a final decision been convicted of a criminal offence and when subsequently his conviction has been reversed or he has been pardoned on the ground that a new or newly discovered fact shows conclusively that there has been a miscarriage of justice, the person who has suffered punishment as a result of such conviction shall be compensated according to law, unless it is proved that the non-disclosure of the unknown fact in time is wholly or partly attributable to him.

7. No one shall be liable to be tried or punished again for an offence for which he has already been finally convicted or acquitted in accordance with the law and penal procedure of each country.

1. No one shall be held guilty of any criminal offence on account of any act or omission which did not constitute a criminal offence, under national or international law, at the time when it was committed. Nor shall a heavier penalty be imposed than the one that was applicable at the time when the criminal offence was committed. If, subsequent to the commission of the offence, provision is made by law for the imposition of the lighter penalty, the offender shall benefit thereby.

2. Nothing in this article shall prejudice the trial and punishment of any person for any act or omission which, at the time when it was committed, was criminal according to the general principles of law recognized by the community of nations.

Appendix 3

General comment on Article 6 of the International Covenant on Civil and Political Rights, adopted at its 378th meeting (16th session) on 27 July 1982 by the Human Rights Committee set up under the International Covenant on Civil and Political Rights (extracts)

1. The right to life enunciated in Article 6 of the Covenant has been dealt with in all State reports. It is the supreme right from which no derogation is permitted even in time of public emergency which threatens the life of the nation (Article 4) ... It is a right which should not be interpreted narrowly.

6. While it follows from Article 6 (2) to (6) that States parties are not obliged to abolish the death penalty totally, they are obliged to limit its use and, in particular, to abolish it for other than the "most serious crimes". Accordingly, they ought to consider reviewing their criminal laws in this light and, in any event, are obliged to restrict the application of the death penalty to the "most serious crimes". The article also refers generally to abolition in terms which strongly suggest (paras. 2 (2) and (6)) that abolition is desirable. The Committee concludes that all measures of abolition should be considered as progress in the enjoyment of the right to life within the meaning of Article 40, and should as such be reported to the Committee. The Committee notes that a number of States have already abolished the death penalty or suspended its application. Nevertheless, States' reports show that progress made towards abolishing or limiting the application of the death penalty is quite inadequate.

7. The Committee is of the opinion that the expression "most serious crimes" must be read restrictively to mean that the death penalty should be a quite exceptional measure. It also follows from the express terms of Article 6 that it can only be imposed in accordance with the law in force at the time of the commission of the crime and not contrary to the Covenant. The procedural guarantees therein prescribed must be observed, in-

cluding the right to a fair hearing by an independent tribunal, the presumption of innocence, the minimum guarantees for the defence, and the right to review by a higher tribunal. These rights are applicable in addition to the particular right to seek pardon or commutation of the sentence.

Appendix 4

Safeguards Guaranteeing Protection of the Rights of Those Facing the Death Penalty, adopted by the UN Economic and Social Council in resolution 1984/50 at its 1984 Spring session on 25 May 1984 and endorsed by the UN General Assembly in resolution 39/118, adopted without a vote on 14 December 1984

1. In countries which have not abolished the death penalty, capital punishment may be imposed only for the most serious crimes, it being understood that their scope should not go beyond intentional crimes, with lethal or other extremely grave consequences.

2. Capital punishment may be imposed only for a crime for which the death penalty is prescribed by law at the time of its commission, it being understood that if, subsequent to the commission of the crime, provision is made by law for the imposition of a lighter penalty, the offender shall benefit thereby.

3. Persons below 18 years of age at the time of the commission of the crime shall not be sentenced to death, nor shall the death penalty be carried out on pregnant women, or on new mothers or on persons who have become insane.

4. Capital punishment may be imposed only when the guilt of the person charged is based upon clear and convincing evidence leaving no room for an alternative explanation of the facts.

5. Capital punishment may only be carried out pursuant to a final judgment rendered by a competent court after legal process which gives all possible safeguards to ensure a fair trial, at least equal to those contained in Article 14 of the International Covenant on Civil and Political Rights, including the right of anyone suspected of or charged with a crime for which capital punishment may be imposed to adequate legal assistance at all stages of the proceedings.

6. Anyone sentenced to death shall have the right to appeal to a court of higher jurisdiction, and steps should be taken to ensure that such appeals shall become mandatory.

7. Anyone sentenced to death shall have the right to seek pardon, or commutation of sentence; pardon or commutation of sentence may be granted in all cases of capital punishment.

8. Capital punishment shall not be carried out pending any appeal or other recourse procedure or other proceeding relating to pardon or commutation of the sentence.

9. Where capital punishment occurs, it shall be carried out so as to inflict the minimum possible suffering.

Appendix 5

American Convention on Human Rights (extract)

Article 4. Right to Life

1. Every person has the right to have his life respected. This right shall be protected by law and, in general, from the moment of conception. No one shall be arbitrarily deprived of his life.

2. In countries that have not abolished the death penalty, it may be imposed only for the most serious crimes and pursuant to a final judgment rendered by a competent court and in accordance with a law establishing such punishment, enacted prior to the commission of the crime. The application of such punishment shall not be extended to crimes to which it does not presently apply.

3. The death penalty shall not be reestablished in states that have abolished it.

4. In no case shall capital punishment be inflicted for political offenses or related common crimes.

5. Capital punishment shall not be imposed upon persons who, at the time the crime was committed, were under 18 years of age or over 70 years of age; nor shall it be applied to pregnant women.

6. Every person condemned to death shall have the right to apply for amnesty, pardon, or commutation of sentence, which may be granted in all cases. Capital punishment shall not be imposed while such a petition is pending decision by the competent authority.

Appendix 6

Geneva Conventions and Additional Protocols (extracts)

a. Geneva Convention relative to the Treatment of Prisoners of War of 12 August 1949

Article 100

Prisoners of war and the Protecting Powers shall be informed, as soon as possible, of the offences which are punishable by the death sentence under the laws of the Detaining Power.

Other offences shall not thereafter be made punishable by the death penalty without the concurrence of the Power upon which the prisoners of war depend.

The death sentence cannot be pronounced on a prisoner of war unless the attention of the court has, in accordance with Article 87, second paragraph, been particularly called to the fact that since the accused is not a national of the Detaining Power, he is not bound to it by any duty of allegiance, and that he is in its power as the result of circumstances independent of his own will.

Article 101

If the death penalty is pronounced on a prisoner of war, the sentence shall not be executed before the expiration of a period of at least six months from the date when the Protecting Power receives, at an indicated address, the detailed communication provided for in Article 107.

b. Geneva Convention relative to the Protection of Civilian Persons in Time of War of 12 August 1949

Article 68

Protected persons who commit an offence which is solely intended to harm the Occupying Power, but which does not constitute an attempt on the life or limb of members of the occupying forces or administration, nor a grave collective danger, nor seriously damage the property of the occupying forces or administration or the installations used by them, shall be liable to internment or simple imprisonment, provided the duration of such internment or imprisonment is proportionate to the offence committed. Furthermore, internment or imprisonment shall, for such offences, be the only measure adopted for depriving protected persons of liberty. The courts provided for under Article 66 of the present Convention may at their discretion convert a sentence of imprisonment to one of internment for the same period.

The penal provisions promulgated by the Occupying Power in accordance with Articles 64 and 65 may impose the death penalty on a protected person only in cases where the person is guilty of espionage, of serious acts of sabotage against the military installations of the Occupying Power or of intentional offences which have caused the death of one or more persons, provided that such offences were punishable by death under the law of the occupied territory in force before the occupation began.

The death penalty may not be pronounced on a protected person unless the attention of the court has been particularly called to the fact that since the accused is not a national of the Occupying Power, he is not bound to it by any duty of allegiance.

In any case, the death penalty may not be pronounced on a protected person who was under eighteen years of age at the time of the offence.

Article 75

In no case shall persons condemned to death be deprived of the right of petition for pardon or reprieve.

No death sentence shall be carried out before the expiration of a period of at least six months from the date of receipt by the Protecting Power of the notification of the final judgment confirming such death sentence, or of an order denying pardon or reprieve.

The six months period of suspension of the death sentence herein prescribed may be reduced in individual cases in circumstances of grave emergency involving an organized threat to the security of the Occupying Power or its forces, provided always that the Protecting Power is notified of such reduction and is given reasonable time and opportunity to make representations to the competent occupying authorities in respect of such death sentences.

c. The Four Geneva Conventions of 12 August 1949

Common Article 3

In the case of armed conflict not of an international character occurring in the territory of one of the High Contracting Parties, each Party to the conflict shall be bound to apply, as a minimum, the following provisions:
1. Persons taking no active part in the hostilities, including members of armed forces who have laid down their arms and those placed *hors de combat* by sickness, wounds, detention, or any other cause, shall in all circumstances be treated humanely, without any adverse distinction founded on race, colour, religion or faith, sex, birth or wealth, or any other similar criteria.

To this end, the following acts are and shall remain prohibited at any time and in any place whatsoever with respect to the above-mentioned persons:

. . . (d) the passing of sentences and the carrying out of executions without previous judgment pronounced by a regularly constituted court, affording all the judicial guarantees which are recognized as indispensable by civilized peoples.

d. Protocol Additional to the Geneva Conventions of 12 August 1949, and relating to the Protection of Victims of International Armed Conflicts (Protocol I)

Article 76, paragraph 3

To the maximum extent feasible, the Parties to the conflict shall endeavour to avoid the pronouncement of the death penalty on pregnant women or mothers having dependent infants, for an offence related to the armed conflict. The death penalty for such offences shall not be executed on such women.

Article 77, paragraph 5
The death penalty for an offence related to the armed conflict shall not be executed on persons who had not attained the age of eighteen years at the time the offence was committed.

e. Protocol Additional to the Geneva Conventions of 12 August 1949, and relating to the Protection of Victims of Non-International Armed Conflicts (Protocol II)

Article 6, paragraph 4
The death penalty shall not be pronounced on persons who were under the age of eighteen years at the time of the offence and shall not be carried out on pregnant women or mothers of young children.

Appendix 7

Protocol No.6 to the Convention for the Protection of Human Rights and Fundamental Freedoms ("European Convention on Human Rights") concerning the abolition of the death penalty (extracts)

The member States of the Council of Europe, signatory to this Protocol to the Convention for the Protection of Human Rights and Fundamental Freedoms, signed at Rome on 4 November 1950 (hereinafter referred to as "the Convention"),

Considering that the evolution that has occurred in several member States of the Council of Europe expresses a general tendency in favour of abolition of the death penalty;

Have agreed as follows:

Article 1
The death penalty shall be abolished. No one shall be condemned to such penalty or executed.

Article 2
A State may make provision in its law for the death penalty in respect of acts committed in time of war or of imminent threat of war; such penalty shall be applied only in the instances laid down in the law and in accordance with its provisions. The State shall communicate to the Secretary General of the Council of Europe the relevant provisions of that law.

Article 3
No derogation from the provisions of this Protocol shall be made under Article 15 of the Convention.

Article 4

No reservation may be made under Article 64 of the Convention in respect of the provisions of this Protocol.

Article 5

1. Any State may at the time of signature or when depositing its instrument of ratification, acceptance or approval, specify the territory or territories to which this Protocol shall apply.

2. Any State may at any later date, by a declaration addressed to the Secretary General of the Council of Europe, extend the application of this Protocol to any other territory specified in the declaration. In respect of such territory the Protocol shall enter into force on the first day of the month following the date of receipt of such declaration by the Secretary General.

3. Any declaration made under the two preceding paragraphs may, in respect of any territory specified in such declaration, be withdrawn by a notification addressed to the Secretary General. The withdrawal shall become effective on the first day of the month following the date of receipt of such notification by the Secretary General.

Article 6

As between the States Parties the provisions of Articles 1 to 5 of this Protocol shall be regarded as additional articles to the Convention and all the provisions of the Convention shall apply accordingly.

Article 7

This Protocol shall be open for signature by the member States of the Council of Europe, signatories to the Convention. It shall be subject to ratification, acceptance or approval. A member State of the Council of Europe may not ratify, accept or approve this Protocol unless it has, simultaneously or previously, ratified the Convention. Instruments of ratification, acceptance or approval shall be deposited with the Secretary General of the Council of Europe.

Article 8

1. This Protocol shall enter into force on the first day of the month following the date on which five member States of the Council of Europe have expressed their consent to be bound by the Protocol in accordance with the provisions of Article 7.

2. In respect of any member State which subsequently expresses its consent to be bound by it, the Protocol shall enter into force on the first day of the month following the date of the deposit of the instrument of ratification, acceptance or approval.

Article 9

The Secretary General of the Council of Europe shall notify the member States of the Council of:

a. any signature;

b. the deposit of any instrument of ratification, acceptance or approval;

c. any date of entry into force of this Protocol in accordance with Articles 5 and 8;

d. any other act, notification or communication relating to this Protocol.

List of Member States of the Council of Europe with dates of signature and ratification of the Sixth Protocol to the European Convention on Human Rights (as of 1 January 1989)

Member state	Signature	Ratification
Austria	28 April 1983	5 January 1984
Belgium	28 April 1983	
Cyprus		
Denmark	28 April 1983	1 December 1983
France	28 April 1983	17 February 1986
Germany (Federal Republic)	28 April 1983	
Greece	2 May 1983	
Iceland	24 April 1985	22 May 1987
Ireland		
Italy	21 October 1983	29 December 1988
Liechtenstein		
Luxembourg	28 April 1983	19 February 1985
Malta		
Netherlands	28 April 1983	25 April 1986
Norway	28 April 1983	25 October 1988
Portugal	28 April 1983	2 October 1986
San Marino		
Spain	28 April 1983	14 January 1985
Sweden	28 April 1983	9 February 1984
Switzerland	28 April 1983	13 October 1987
Turkey		
United Kingdom		

Appendix 8

United Nations General Assembly resolution 32/61 of 8 December 1977 (extract)

Capital punishment

The General Assembly,

Having regard to Article 3 of the Universal Declaration of Human Rights, which affirms everyone's right to life, and Article 6 of the International Covenant on Civil and Political Rights, which also affirms the right to life as inherent to every human being,...

1. *Reaffirms* that, as established by the General Assembly in resolution 2857 (XXVI) and by the Economic and Social Council in resolutions 1574 (L), 1745 (LIV) and 1930 (LVIII), the main objective to be pursued in the field of capital punishment is that of progressively restricting the number of offences for which the death penalty may be imposed with a view to the desirability of abolishing this punishment...

Appendix 9

United Nations General Assembly resolution 35/172, adopted without a vote on 15 December 1980

Arbitrary or summary executions

The General Assembly,

Having regard to the provisions bearing on capital punishment in the International Covenant on Civil and Political Rights, particularly its Articles 6, 14 and 15,

Recalling its resolution 2393 (XXIII) of 26 November 1968, in which it invited Governments of Member States, *inter alia*, to ensure the most careful legal procedures and the greatest possible safeguards for the accused in capital cases in countries where the death penalty obtains,

Alarmed at the incidence in different parts of the world of summary executions as well as of arbitrary executions,

Concerned at the occurrence of executions which are widely regarded as being politically motivated,

1. *Urges* Member States concerned:

(a) To respect as a minimum standard the content of the provisions of Articles 6, 14 and 15 of the International Covenant on Civil and Political Rights and, where necessary, to review their legal rules and practices so as to guarantee the most careful legal procedures and the greatest possible safeguards for the accused in capital cases;

(b) To examine the possibility of making automatic the appeal procedure, where it exists, in cases of death sentences, as well as the consideration of an amnesty, pardon or commutation in these cases;

(c) To provide that no death sentence shall be carried out until the procedures of appeal and pardon have been terminated and, in any case,

not until a reasonable time after the passing of the sentence in the court in the first instance;

2. *Requests* the Secretary-General to use his best endeavours in cases where the minimum standard of legal safeguards referred to in paragraph 1 above appears not to be respected;

3. *Further requests* the Secretary-General to seek from Member States, specialized agencies, regional intergovernmental organizations and concerned non-governmental organizations in consultative status with the Economic and Social Council views and observations concerning the problem of arbitrary executions and summary executions, and to report to the Committee on Crime Prevention and Control at its seventh session.

Appendix 10

Checklist of main restrictions and safeguards on the death penalty

Restriction/ safeguard	International Covenant on Civil and Political Rights[1]	ECOSOC Safeguards (1984)	American Convention on Human Rights[2]	European Convention on Human Rights[3]	African Charter on Human and People's Rights[4]	Geneva Conventions and Additional Protocols
Restriction to the most serious crimes	X	X	X			X[5]
No use against people under 18 years old at the time of the offence	X	X	X			X[6,7,8]
No use against people over 70 years old at the time of the offence			X			
No execution of pregnant women	X	X	X			X[6,7]
No execution of the insane		X				
Right to a fair trial	X	X	X	X	X	X[9]

253

Restriction/ safeguard	International Covenant on Civil and Political Rights[1]	ECOSOC Safeguards (1984)	American Convention on Human Rights[2]	European Convention on Human Rights[3]	African Charter on Human and People's Rights[4]	Geneva Conventions and Additional Protocols
Right of appeal or review by a higher court	X	X	X			X[9]
Right to petition for clemency	X	X	X			X[8]
No retro active use	X	X	X	X	X	X[8]

1 Articles 6, 14, 15.
2 Articles 4, 8, 9.
3 Articles 6, 7.
4 Article 7.
5 With reference to protected civilians under the Fourth Geneva Convention of 12 August 1949, the death penalty may be imposed only for espionage, serious acts of sabotage against the military installations of the occupying power, or intentional offences which have caused the death of one or more persons.
6 Applies in international armed conflicts under Additional Protocol I to the Geneva Conventions.
7 Applies in non-international armed conflicts under Additional Protocol II to the Geneva Conventions.
8 Applies to protected civilians under the Fourth Geneva Convention.
9 Common Article 3 of the four Geneva Conventions restricts the use of the death penalty to judgments by a regularly constituted court, "affording all the judicial guarantees which are recognized as indispensable by civilized peoples".

Appendix II

Statute of Amnesty International (extracts)

As amended by the 18th International Council, meeting in Águas de Lindóia, Brazil, 30 November – 6 December 1987

1 ... the object of AMNESTY INTERNATIONAL shall be to secure throughout the world the observance of the provisions of the Universal Declaration of Human Rights, by:...
(c) opposing by all appropriate means the imposition and infliction of death penalties and torture or other cruel, inhuman or degrading treatment or punishment of prisoners or other detained or restricted persons whether or not they have used or advocated violence...

2. In order to achieve the aforesaid object, AMNESTY INTERNATIONAL shall:...

(k) oppose the sending of persons from one country to another where they can reasonably be expected to become prisoners of conscience or to face torture or the death penalty...

Appendix 12

Declaration of Stockholm

Amnesty International conference on the abolition of the death penalty, 11 December 1977

The Stockholm Conference on the Abolition of the Death Penalty, composed of more than 200 delegates and participants from Africa, Asia, Europe, the Middle East, North and South America and the Caribbean region,
RECALLS THAT:
– The death penalty is the ultimate cruel, inhuman and degrading punishment and violates the right to life.
CONSIDERS THAT:
– The death penalty is frequently used as an instrument of repression against opposition, racial, ethnic, religious and underprivileged groups,
– Execution is an act of violence, and violence tends to provoke violence,
– The imposition and infliction of the death penalty is brutalizing to all who are involved in the process,
– The death penalty has never been shown to have a special deterrent effect,
– The death penalty is increasingly taking the form of unexplained disappearances, extrajudicial executions and political murders,
– Execution is irrevocable and can be inflicted on the innocent.
AFFIRMS THAT:
– It is the duty of the state to protect the life of all persons within its jurisdiction without exception,
– Executions for the purposes of political coercion, whether by government agencies or others, are equally unacceptable,
– Abolition of the death penalty is imperative for the achievement of declared international standards.
DECLARES:
– Its total and unconditional opposition to the death penalty,
– Its condemnation of all executions, in whatever form, committed or condoned by governments,
– Its commitment to work for the universal abolition of the death penalty.
CALLS UPON:
– Non-governmental organizations, both national and international, to work collectively and individually to provide public information materials directed towards the abolition of the death penalty,
– All governments to bring about the immediate and total abolition of the death penalty,

– The United Nations unambiguously to declare that the death penalty is contrary to international law.

The Declaration of Stockholm was adopted by Amnesty International in March 1978 as a statement of principle on the death penalty.

Appendix 13

Amnesty International Declaration on the Participation of Health Personnel in the Death Penalty

Amnesty International,
RECALLING that the spirit of the Hippocratic Oath enjoins doctors to practise for the good of their patients and never to do harm,
CONSIDERING that the Declaration of Tokyo of the World Medical Association provides that "the utmost respect for human life is to be maintained even under threat, and no use made of any medical knowledge contrary to the laws of humanity",
FURTHER CONSIDERING that the World Medical Association, meeting in Lisbon in 1981, resolved that it is unethical for physicians to participate in capital punishment,
NOTING that the United Nations' Principles of Medical Ethics enjoin health personnel, particularly physicians, to refuse to enter into any relationship with a prisoner other than one directed at evaluating, protecting or improving their physical and mental health,
CONSCIOUS of the ethical dilemmas posed for health personnel called on to treat or testify about the condition of prisoners facing capital charges or sentenced to death, where actions by such personnel could help save the prisoner's life but could also result in the prisoner's execution,
MINDFUL that health personnel can be called on to participate in executions by, *inter alia*:
– determining mental and physical fitness for execution,
– preparing, administering, supervising or advising others on any procedure related to execution,
– making medical examinations during executions, so that an execution can continue if the prisoner is not yet dead,
DECLARES that the participation of health personnel in executions is a violation of professional ethics;
CALLS UPON health personnel not to participate in executions;
FURTHER CALLS UPON organizations of health professionals:
– to protect health personnel who refuse to participate in executions,
– to adopt resolutions to these ends, and
– to promote worldwide adherence to these standards.

This declaration was formulated by the Medical Advisory Board of Amnesty International in 1981 and revised in 1988 in light of developments on the issue.

Appendix 14

Joint statement by 42 international non-governmental organizations concerned with human rights in consultative status with the UN Economic and Social Council, submitted to the Sixth United Nations Congress on the Prevention of Crime and the Treatment of Offenders (Caracas, Venezuela, 25 August – 5 September 1980)

ABOLITION OF THE DEATH PENALTY

A joint statement by 42 international non-governmental organizations concerned with human rights in consultative status with the Economic and Social Council

The resolution which follows is supported by the international non-governmental organizations listed overleaf. It is submitted by them to the Congress for consideration under item 5 of agenda: *United Nations Norms and Guidelines: From Standard-Setting to Implementation.* The organizations, which represent a substantial body of informed public opinion from all parts of the world, hope that the Congress will be able to support the proposals contained in the resolution.

THE UNDERSIGNED INTERNATIONAL NON-GOVERNMENTAL ORGANIZATIONS CONCERNED WITH HUMAN RIGHTS,

Affirming their unswerving commitment to the protection of the right to life of every human being,

Reiterating their total opposition to any form of cruel, inhuman or degrading treatment or punishment,

Considering that the death penalty is in violation of both the above principles,

1. *Call on* all governments that retain capital punishment to cease employing it;

2. *Call on* the General Assembly of the United Nations to promulgate a declaration that would urge its total worldwide abolition;

3. *Call on* all non-governmental organizations concerned with human rights to make every effort at the national and international level to secure the abolition of capital punishment.

Submitted by
Amnesty International
Anti-Slavery Society
Arab Lawyers Union
Caritas Internationalis
Commission of the Churches on International Affairs of the World
    Council of Churches
Friends World Committee for Consultation (Quakers)
International Alliance of Women
International Association for Religious Freedom
International Association of Democratic Lawyers
International Confederation of Free Trade Unions

International Council of Jewish Women
International Council of Women
International Federation of Free Journalists
International Federation of Human Rights
International Federation of Women Lawyers
International League for Human Rights
International Movement for Fraternal Union among Races and Peoples
International Organization – Justice and Development
International Peace Bureau
International Social Service
International Union for Child Welfare
International Union of Judges
International Young Christian Workers
International Youth and Student Movement for the United Nations
Minority Rights Group
Pax Christi
Pax Romana
Socialist International Women
Société Internationale de Prophylaxie Criminelle
Union of Arab Jurists
War Resisters' International
Women's International League for Peace and Freedom
Women's International Zionist Organization
World Alliance of Young Men's Christian Associations
World Assembly of Youth
World Confederation of Labour
World Federation of United Nations Associations
World Jewish Congress
World Muslim Congress
World Student Christian Federation
World Union of Catholic Women's Organizations
World Young Women's Christian Association

Appendix 15

Abolitionist and retentionist countries and territories (as of 1 January 1989)

1. Abolitionist for all crimes

(Countries whose laws do not provide for the death penalty for any crime.)

Country	Date of abolition	Date of abolition for ordinary crimes	Date of last execution
Australia	1985	1984	1967
Austria	1968	1950	1950
Cape Verde	1981		1835
Colombia	1910		1909
Costa Rica	1877		
Denmark	1978	1933	1950
Dominican Republic	1966		
Ecuador	1906		
Finland	1972	1949	1944
France	1981		1977
German Democratic Republic	1987		
Germany (Federal Republic)	1949		1949
Haiti	1987		1972*
Honduras	1956		1940
Iceland	1928		1830
Kiribati			**
Liechtenstein	1987		1785
Luxembourg	1979		1949
Marshall Islands			**
Micronesia (Federated States)			**
Monaco	1962		1847
Netherlands	1982	1870	1952
Nicaragua	1979		1930
Norway	1979	1905	1948
Panama			1903*
Philippines	1987		1976
Portugal	1976	1867	1849*
San Marino	1865	1848	1468*
Solomon Islands		1966	**
Sweden	1972	1921	1910
Tuvalu			**
Uruguay	1907		
Vanuatu			**
Vatican City State	1969		
Venezuela	1863		

Total: 35 countries

Note: The date given for abolition is the date when the decision to abolish the death penalty was taken, unless that decision only came into effect years later, in which case the latter date is given.

2. Abolitionist for ordinary crimes only

(Countries whose laws provide for the death penalty only for exceptional crimes such as crimes under military law or crimes committed in exceptional circumstances such as wartime.)

Country	Date of abolition	Date of last execution
Argentina	1984	
Brazil	1979	1855
Canada	1976	1962
Cyprus	1983	1962
El Salvador	1983	1973*
Fiji	1979	1964
Israel	1954	1962
Italy	1947	1947
Malta	1971	1943
Mexico		1937
New Zealand	1961	1957
Papua New Guinea	1974	1950
Peru	1979	1979
São Tomé and Príncipe		**
Seychelles		**
Spain	1978	1975
Switzerland	1942	1944
United Kingdom	1973	1964
Total: 18 countries		

* Date of last known execution
** No executions since independence

3. Abolitionist in practice

(Countries and territories which retain the death penalty for ordinary crimes but have not executed anyone during the past 10 years or more.)

Country	Date of last execution (if known)
Andorra	1943
Anguilla	1820s
Bahrain	1977
Belgium	1950
Bermuda	1977

Country	Date of last execution (if known)
Bhutan	1964*
Bolivia	1974
British Virgin Islands	
Brunei Darussalam	1957
Cayman Islands	1928
Comoros	**
Côte d'Ivoire	
Djibouti	**
Greece	1972
Hong Kong	1966
Ireland	1954
Madagascar	1958*
Maldives	1952*
Montserrat	1961
Nauru	**
Niger	1976*
Paraguay	1928
Senegal	1967
Sri Lanka	1976
Togo	
Turks and Caicos Islands	
Western Samoa	**

Total: 27 countries and territories

* Date of last known execution
** No executions since independence

Note: All of these countries and territories can be considered abolitionist in practice in that they have not carried out executions for the past 10 years or more. However, death sentences have continued to be imposed in a number of these countries, and not all of them have a policy of regularly commuting death sentences.

4. Retentionist

(Countries and territories which retain and use the death penalty for ordinary crimes.)*

Afghanistan	Benin	Chad
Albania	Botswana	Chile
Algeria	Bulgaria	China (People's Republic)
Angola	Burkina Faso	
Antigua and Barbuda	Burma	Congo
Bahamas	Burundi	Cuba
Bangladesh	Cameroon	Czechoslovakia
Barbados	Central African Republic	Dominica
Belize		Egypt

Equatorial Guinea	Libya	South Africa
Ethiopia	Malawi	Sudan
Gabon	Malaysia	Suriname
Gambia	Mali	Swaziland
Ghana	Mauritania	Syria
Grenada	Mauritius	Taiwan (Republic of
Guatemala	Mongolia	China)
Guinea	Morocco	Tanzania
Guinea-Bissau	Mozambique	Thailand
Guyana	Namibia	Tonga
Hungary	Nepal	Trinidad and Tobago
India	Nigeria	Tunisia
Indonesia	Oman	Turkey
Iran	Pakistan	Uganda
Iraq	Poland	Union of Soviet Socialist
Jamaica	Qatar	Republics
Japan	Romania	United Arab Emirates
Jordan	Rwanda	United States of
Kampuchea	Saint Christopher and	America
Kenya	Nevis	Viet Nam
Korea (Democratic	Saint Lucia	Yemen (Arab Republic)
People's Republic)	Saint Vincent and the	Yemen (People's
Korea (Republic)	Grenadines	Democratic Republic)
Kuwait	Saudi Arabia	Yugoslavia
Laos	Sierra Leone	Zaire
Lebanon	Singapore	Zambia
Lesotho	Somalia	Zimbabwe
Liberia		

Total: 100 countries and territories

* Most of these countries and territories are known to have carried out executions during the past 10 years. In some of these countries Amnesty International has no record of executions but is unable to ascertain whether or not executions have in fact been carried out.

Appendix 16

Countries which have abolished the death penalty since 1976

1976 *Portugal* abolished the death penalty for all offences.
  Canada abolished the death penalty for ordinary offences.
1978 *Denmark* abolished the death penalty for all offences.
  Spain abolished the death penalty for ordinary offences.
1979 *Luxembourg, Nicaragua* and *Norway* abolished the death penalty for all offences.

Brazil[1], *Fiji* and *Peru* abolished the death penalty for ordinary offences.

1981 *France* abolished the death penalty for all offences.

1982 *The Netherlands* abolished the death penalty for all offences.

1983 *Cyprus* and *El Salvador* abolished the death penalty for ordinary offences.

1984 *Argentina[2]* and *Australia[3]* abolished the death penalty for ordinary offences.

1985 *Australia* abolished the death penalty for all offences.

1987 *The Philippines, Haiti, Liechtenstein* and the *German Democratic Republic* abolished the death penalty for all offences.

1 Brazil had abolished the death penalty in 1882 but reintroduced it in 1969 while under military rule.

2 Argentina had abolished the death penalty for all offences in 1921 and again in 1972 but reintroduced it in 1976 following a military coup.

3 In 1984 the death penalty was abolished in Western Australia, the last Australian state to retain the death penalty for ordinary offences. In 1985 it was abolished entirely in Australia when the state of New South Wales abolished it for piracy, treason and arson at military and naval establishments – the only remaining capital offences.

Appendix 17

Table 1: Distribution of executions among countries, 1985 - mid-1988
(Source: country descriptions)

No. of executions per country	No. of countries	Percentage of total No. of countries	No. of executions	Percentage of total No. of executions
1 – 5	24	38	56	2
6 – 10	9	14	73	2
11 – 20	9	14	122	4
21 – 50	11	18	343	10
51 – 100	3	5	181	5
101 – 200	3	5	405	12
over 200	4	6	2,219	65
Totals	63	100	3,399	100

Note: Countries carrying out over 50 executions between 1985 and mid-1988, with the number of executions recorded shown in parenthesis, were China (500+), Iran (743+), Malaysia (52+), Nigeria (439+), Pakistan (115+), Saudi Arabia (140), Somalia (150+), South Africa (537+), USSR (63+), USA (66). These 10 countries accounted for 83 per cent of all executions recorded. Hundreds of executions are reported from Iraq each year, but Amnesty International does not know the precise figures and is not always able to ascertain whether those executed were tried and convicted of offences punishable by death or were executed extra-judicially.

Table 2: Countries with an age limit of 18 or over, below which people are exempted from the death penalty
(Source: country descriptions, except where indicated)

Country	Minimum age limit	Country	Minimum age limit
Albania	18	Liberia	18
Algeria	18	Libya	18
Angola	18	Madagascar	18
Anguilla	18	Malawi	18
Antigua and Barbuda	18	Mali	18
Argentina	18[1]	Mauritius	18
Bahamas	18	Mongolia	18
Bahrain	18	Montserrat	18
Belgium	18[1]	Namibia	18
Belize	18[2]	New Zealand	18[6]
Bolivia	18[1/3]	Niger	18
Botswana	18	Paraguay	22
British Virgin Islands	18	Poland	18
Brunei Darussalam	18[2]	Qatar	18
Bulgaria	18/20[4]	Romania	18
Burundi	18	Rwanda	18
Cameroon	18	St Christopher and Nevis	18
Canada	18[2]	St Lucia	18
Cayman Islands	18	St Vincent and the Grenadines	18
Central African Republic	18[1]		
Côte d'Ivoire	18	Saudi Arabia	18
Cuba	20	Senegal	18[1]
Czechoslovakia	18	Sierra Leone	18
Dominica	18	South Africa	18[7]
Egypt	18	Sri Lanka	18[1]
Ethiopia	18	Sudan	18
Gabon	18[1]	Suriname	18
Greece	21[2]	Swaziland	18
Grenada	18	Syria	18
Guatemala	18[3]	Tanzania	18
Guinea	18	Togo	18[1]
Guinea-Bissau	18	Trinidad and Tobago	18
Guyana	18[1]	Tunisia	18
Hungary	20	Turkey	18
Iran	18[5]	Turks and Caicos Islands	18
Iraq	18	USSR	18
Jamaica	18	United Arab Emirates	18
Japan	18	United Kingdom	18
Jordan	18	Western Samoa	18
Kenya	18	Yemen (People's Democratic Republic)	18
Korea (Democratic People's Republic)	18[1]		
Kuwait	18	Yugoslavia	18
Lesotho	18	Zambia	18

1 Presumed by virtue of adherence to the International Covenant on Civil and Political Rights (ICCPR) without reservation to the relevant provision in Article 6(5). Several countries have age limits lower than 18 in their legislation but have taken on an obligation under international law not to use the death penalty against offenders under 18 by virtue of their having acceded to the ICCPR without reservation to Article 6(5).

2 *Capital punishment; report of the secretary-general*, UN document number

E/1985/43, 26 April 1985, page 47 and addendum, UN document number
E/1985/43/Add. 1, 8 January 1986, pages 16-17.

3 Presumed by virtue of adherence to the American Convention on Human Rights
without reservation to the relevant provision in Article 4(5).

4 20 for civilians, 18 for soldiers and in wartime.

5 By law, people under 18 at the time of the offence may not be executed for murder.
However, children under 18 were among those executed in the early 1980s, and
occasional reports of the executions of minors continue to reach Amnesty
International.

6 *Capital punishment; report of the secretary-general*, addendum, UN document
number E/1980/9/Add. 1, 18 March 1980, page 5.

7 People under 18 are exempted from the death penalty for murder.

Table 3: Methods of execution provided in law
(Source: country descriptions)

Country	Hanging	Shooting	Beheading	Stoning	Electro-cution	Gas	Lethal injection
Afghanistan		X					
Albania	X	X					
Algeria		X					
Angola		X					
Anguilla	X						
Antigua and Barbuda	X						
Argentina		X					
Bahamas	X						
Bahrain		X					
Bangladesh	X	X					
Barbados	X						
Belgium		X	X				
Belize	X						
Benin		X					
Bermuda	X						
Bolivia		X					
Botswana	X						
Brazil		X					
British Virgin Islands	X						
Brunei Darussalam	X						
Bulgaria		X					
Burkina Faso		X					
Burma	X						
Burundi	X	X					
Cameroon	X	X					
Canada		X					
Cayman Islands	X						
Central African Republic		X					
Chad		X					
Chile		X					
China		X					
Comoros		X					

Country	Hanging	Shooting	Beheading	Stoning	Electro-cution	Gas	Lethal injection
Congo		X	X				
Côte d'Ivoire		X					
Cuba		X					
Cyprus	X						
Czechoslo-vakia	X	X					
Djibouti		X					
Dominica	X						
Egypt	X	X					
El Salvador		X					
Equatorial Guinea	X	X					
Ethiopia	X	X					
Fiji	X						
Gabon		X					
Gambia	X						
Ghana		X					
Greece		X					
Grenada	X						
Guatemala		X					
Guinea		X					
Guinea-Bissau		X					
Guyana	X						
Hong Kong	X						
Hungary	X	X					
India	X	X					
Indonesia		X					
Iran	X	X		X			
Iraq	X	X					
Ireland	X						
Israel	X						
Italy		X					
Jamaica	X						
Japan	X						
Jordan	X	X					
Kampuchea		X					
Kenya	X						
Korea (Democratic People's Republic)		X					
Korea (Republic)	X	X					
Kuwait	X	X					
Lebanon	X	X					
Lesotho	X						
Liberia	X	X					
Libya	X	X					
Madagascar		X					
Malawi	X						
Malaysia	X						
Mali		X					
Mauritania		X	X	X			
Mauritius	X						
Mexico		X					
Montserrat	X						
Morocco		X					

Country	Hanging	Shooting	Beheading	Stoning	Electro-cution	Gas	Lethal injection
Mozambique		X					
Namibia	X						
Nepal	X	X					
New Zealand	X						
Niger		X					
Nigeria	X	X					
Pakistan	X			X			
Papua New Guinea	X						
Paraguay		X					
Peru		X					
Poland	X	X					
Qatar	X	X	X				
Romania		X					
Rwanda		X					
St Christopher and Nevis	X						
St Lucia	X						
St Vincent and the Grenadines	X						
Saudi Arabia			X	X			
Senegal		X					
Sierra Leone	X	X					
Singapore	X						
Somalia		X					
South Africa	X						
Spain		X					
Sri Lanka	X						
Sudan	X	X		X			
Suriname		X					
Swaziland	X						
Switzerland		X					
Syria	X	X					
Taiwan		X					
Tanzania	X						
Thailand		X					
Togo		X					
Tonga	X						
Trinidad and Tobago	X						
Tunisia	X	X					
Turkey	X						
Turks and Caicos Islands	X						
Uganda	X	X					
USSR	X	X					
United Arab Emirates		X	X	X			
United Kingdom	X						
USA	X	X			X	X	X
Viet Nam		X					
Western Samoa		X					
Yemen (Arab Republic)		X	X	X			

Country	Hanging	Shooting	Beheading	Stoning	Electro-cution	Gas	Lethal injection
Yemen (People's Democratic Republic)		X					
Yugoslavia		X					
Zaire	X	X					
Zambia	X						
Zimbabwe	X						
Total No. of countries	78	86	7	7	1	1	1

For more information on Amnesty International's work, particularly in the U.S. and Canadian sections, or a complete listing of AI's publications with dollar prices, write to:

USA: Amnesty International USA
National Office, Publications Dept.
322 Eighth Avenue,
New York, NY 10001

CANADA: Amnesty International
Canadian Section
(English Speaking)
130 Slater Street
Suite 800
Ottawa, Ontario K1P 6E6

Amnistie Internationale
Section Canadienne
(Francophone)
3516 ave du Parc
Montreal, Quebec H2X 2H7

flies *on the* butter

denise hildreth

THOMAS NELSON
Since 1798

NASHVILLE   DALLAS   MEXICO CITY   RIO DE JANEIRO   BEIJING

Published in Nashville, Tennessee by Thomas Nelson. Thomas Nelson is
a registered trademark of Thomas Nelson, Inc.

Thomas Nelson, Inc. titles may be purchased in bulk for educational,
business, fund-raising, or sales promotional use. For information,
please e-mail SpecialMarkets@ThomasNelson.com.

Publisher's Note: This novel is a work of fiction. Names, characters,
places, and incidents are either products of the author's imagination or
used fictitiously. All characters are fictional, and any similarity to people
living or dead is purely coincidental.

Library of Congress Cataloging-in-Publication Data

Hildreth, Denise, 1969-
  Flies on the butter / Denise Hildreth.
    p. cm.
  ISBN: 978-1-59554-208-3 (pbk.)
  ISBN: 978-1-59554-370-7 (mass market)
  1. South Carolina—Fiction. I. Title.
  PS3608.I424F55 2007
  813'.6—dc22
  2006031511

Printed in the United States of America
08 09 10 11 12 QW 5 4 3 2 1